LITERATURE
AND SPIRITUALITY

LITERATURE
AND SPIRITUALITY

Yaw Adu-Gyamfi
Liberty University, Lynchburg, VA

Mark Ray Schmidt
Liberty University, Lynchburg, VA

Longman

Boston   Columbus   Indianapolis   New York   San Francisco
Upper Saddle River   Amsterdam   Cape Town   Dubai   London   Madrid
Milan   Munich   Paris   Montreal   Toronto   Delhi   Mexico City   Sao Paulo
Sydney   Hong Kong   Seoul   Singapore   Taipei   Tokyo

Senior Acquisition Editor: Vivian Garcia
Editorial Assistant: Heather Vomero
Marketing Manager: Joyce Nilsen
Production Manager: Meghan DeMaio
Creative Director: Jayne Conte
Cover Designer: Bruce Kenselaar
Cover Illustration/Photo: © Charles Harton/Fotolia
Manufacturing Manager: Meghan DeMaio
Project Coordination, Text Design, and Electronic Page Makeup: Niraj Bhatt/Aptara®, Inc.
Printer/Binder/Cover Printer: R. R. Donnelley & Sons

For permission to use copyrighted material, we are grateful to all the copyright holders.

Library of Congress Cataloging-in-Publication Data

Literature and spirituality / [edited by] Yaw Adu-Gyamfi, Mark Ray Schmidt.
    p. cm.
    Includes index.
    An anthology.
    Summary: Includes a diverse selection of spiritually-themed works, organized around five general themes. Each section has a general introduction, headnotes for each author, and study questoins.
    ISBN-13: 978-0-205-74488-6
    ISBN-10: 0-205-74488-5
    1. College readers.   2. Readers—Spirituality.   3. Readers—Spiritual life.   4. Spirituality—Literary collections.   5. Spiritual life—Literary collections.   I. Adu-Gyamfi, Yaw, 1963-
II. Schmidt, Mark Ray, 1953-
    PE1127.S75L58 2011
    808'.0427—dc22

                                                                    2010043270

10 9 8 7 6 5 4   —XXX—13 12

Longman
is an imprint of

www.pearsonhighered.com

ISBN-10:   0-205-74488-5
ISBN-13: 978-0-205-74488-6

CONTENTS

GENRE APPROACH TO SPIRITUALITY

NARRATIVE

POETRY

DRAMA

CINEMA

AMERICAN LITERATURE FROM THEISM TO POSTMODERNISM: A HISTORIOGRAPHY OF SPIRITUALITY

SPIRITUALITY IN THE CONTEXT OF THE JUDEO-CHRISTIAN TRADITION

SPIRITUALITY IN NON-WESTERN, NON-JUDEO-CHRISTIAN CONTEXTS

ACKNOWLEDGMENTS

We would like to thank the following professors who offered their insightful feedback throughout the various stages of producing this book: David N. Cremean, Black Hills State University; Nate Gordon, Kishwaukee College; Abigail Keegan, Oklahoma City University; Pam Fox Kuhlken, San Diego State University; Bernadette Flynn Low, Community College of Baltimore County at Dundalk; Carolyn Jones Medine, University of Georgia; Stephanie Pedas, University of Pittsburgh at Bradford; Sanford Schwartz, Pennsylvania State University; John Struloeff, Pepperdine University; Jeanne Urie, Tulsa Community College; Christopher Wheatley, The Catholic University of America. We also want to thank Vivian Garcia and Heather Vomero and others on the Pearson-Longman staff for their hard work on this project. Clearly, this has been a team endeavor.

LITERATURE
AND SPIRITUALITY

Introduction

Art is the daughter of the divine.

—RUDOLF STEINER

What is art, and what is the divine? Is there a relationship between the two? There are many ways to define art, but in very simple terms, art is the expression of human creativity. A work of art is the end result of one or more humans making unique connections—connections within the self of the artist and connections with the external world of persons and things. On most occasions, the artist feels an expansion of his or her self as these new connections are made. Furthermore, the audience, reader, or viewer of the work of art also feels an expansion of his or her self as new connections are discovered in the presence of the work of art. This expansion is similar to the joys of learning a new skill, like learning a new computer software program or learning to ride a bike. We delight in learning and feeling our inner selves growing.

This artistic expansion of our selves through new connections can come in many forms: empathizing with the emotions of characters in an ancient drama, a sense of awe when viewing a landscape painting, or a sense of fear when a short-story character walks into a dark, mysterious room. Art enriches our lives with all sorts of new connections.

But what is the relationship between art and the spiritual? Before we can answer that question, we need to ask, what is the spiritual? The term *spiritual* is often associated with "the beyond"; it is associated with truths

1

and experiences that transcend our immediate experiences. When we are aware of the spiritual, we are discovering unique connections, just as art helps us discover new connections.

The term *the beyond* is helpful in thinking about the spiritual, but a better term might be *the ultimate*. When people define the spiritual as "the beyond," the conclusion is easily made that the spiritual features of life are attachments or extensions of "normal life." And for some people, religion and spiritual concerns are minor additions to "real life." However, for many other people around the world, the spiritual issues of life are the central or essential qualities of life. It is the spiritual that gives meaning, order, and unity to everything—from the universe as a whole to our private selves. From this perspective, "the beyond" is really "the ultimate," and it needs to be carefully studied and considered as the most important feature of life.

Once again, both art and the spiritual draw us into new connections with the world and with ourselves. They help us move from our immediate experiences with the physical world to a new awareness of a deeper reality. With the intangible, creative energy of our minds and hearts, we make pieces of art that are very physical. Yet, those physical things (e.g., novels, poems, paintings) often point us toward the ultimate—the spiritual. In the same way, our spiritual longings, questions, and experiences lead us to write religious textbooks and perform religious rites that are very physical. Yet, those physical books and religious actions point to the spiritual. In both art and religion, an intangible dimension of life becomes physical, yet that physical thing points us back to the intangible again. Put another way, the spiritual and creative energy within humans produces concrete things (e.g., a sculpture or a cathedral), but those things are not the goal of art or religion. The objects of art and religion lead people to intangible experiences and truths.

When we stretch ourselves and go beyond the immediate, physical world, we begin to move into either the realm of the creative or the realm of the spiritual. When we are creative, we are stepping out of the world as it currently exists, and we are looking for new possibilities or at least new connections among things that already exist. When we seek the spiritual, we are stepping out of the immediate, physical world of daily experience, and we are seeking to know and experience God and our souls.

Thus, Steiner, from a certain perspective, is right: "Art is the daughter of the divine." To add another step, religion is also the daughter of the divine. When we creatively explore and experience things beyond the immediate physical world, a metaphorical child is born. Sometimes that child is religion, and sometimes it is a work of art. In either case, we are building and delighting in new connections. And, in either case, our inner selves are expanding.

This anthology of literary works gives a taste of some of the ways that writers have explored, shared, dismissed, or argued about the ultimate, spiritual questions of life. The first goal of this book is to give a range of works that shows authors can take us beyond our immediate, daily experience. The mere exposure to these works is intellectually enriching, emotionally expanding, and suggestive of new ways that the reader can consider the connection between the spiritual and literature.

The second, more subtle goal of this work is that readers will seek to find health in their spiritual lives. Today's culture is filled with distractions and amusements that draw our attention to the immediate and not to "the beyond." Furthermore, today's electronic culture of instant communication and short bits of data does not encourage us to explore our long-term needs—such as inner rest, peace with God, and calm love for each other. In spite of radical differences, the religions of the world share a common concern: humanity is searching for a spiritual peace that can give the individual an anchor with which to survive the storms of life. As the editors of this anthology, we have our firm conclusions about how people can find peace with God. We invite you to also explore this issue for yourself. We hope that these selections will challenge you to seek personal peace and spiritual health.

Yaw Adu-Gyamfi and Mark Ray Schmidt

Chapter 1

Spirituality as Quest

BUDDHA

Siddhartha Gautama, known as the **Buddha,** or the Enlightened One, is the founder of the Buddhist religion. Buddha lived in India about twenty-five hundred years ago. There are many legends about his life, but it is his teachings that are most important and most interesting. Among the records of Buddha's teaching is *Dhammapada,* which is a collection of 423 verses organized into 26 topics (or chapters). *Dhammapada* refers to the path to virtue or the path of correct living. This collection gives a general sense of Buddhism, but there is much more to this tradition.

The first step in Buddhism is to accept the "Four Noble Truths." These four truths are (a) our immediate experiences of life draw us into constant struggle and suffering; (b) this suffering is caused by our desires or our clinging to our dreams of "this-worldly" happiness; (c) if we stop desiring or clinging to our illusions about life and happiness, then we can be enlightened; and (d) to be enlightened, we need to follow the "eightfold path" of right view, right intention, right speech, right discipline, right livelihood, right effort, right mindfulness, and right concentration.

FROM DHAMMAPADA

Chapter XII.
SELF.

157. If a man hold himself dear, let him watch himself carefully; during one at least out of the three watches a wise man should be watchful.

158. Let each man direct himself first to what is proper, then let him teach others; thus a wise man will not suffer.

159. If a man make himself as he teaches others to be, then, being himself well subdued, he may subdue (others); for one's own self is difficult to subdue.

160. Self is the lord of self, who else could be the lord? With self well subdued, a man finds a lord such as few can find.

161. The evil done by oneself, self-begotten, self-bred, crushes the foolish, as a diamond breaks even a precious stone.

162. He whose wickedness is very great brings himself down to that state where his enemy wishes him to be, as a creeper does with the tree which it surrounds.

163. Bad deeds, and deeds hurtful to ourselves, are easy to do; what is beneficial and good, that is very difficult to do.

164. The foolish man who scorns the rule of the venerable (Arahat) of the elect (Ariya), of the virtuous, and follows a false doctrine, he bears fruit to his own destruction, like the fruits of the Ka*tth*aka reed.

165. By oneself the evil is done, by oneself one suffers; by oneself evil is left undone, by oneself one is purified. The pure and the impure (stand and fall) by themselves, no one can purify another.

166. Let no one forget his own duty for the sake of another's, however great; let a man, after he has discerned his own duty, be always attentive to his duty.

Chapter XIII.

The World.

167. Do not follow the evil law! Do not live on in thoughtlessness! Do not follow false doctrine! Be not a friend of the world.

168. Rouse thyself! do not be idle! Follow the law of virtue! The virtuous rests in bliss in this world and in the next.

169. Follow the law of virtue; do not follow that of sin. The virtuous rests in bliss in this world and in the next.

170. Look upon the world as you would on a bubble, look upon it as you would on a mirage: the king of death does not see him who thus looks down upon the world.

171. Come, look at this world, glittering like a royal chariot; the foolish are immersed in it, but the wise do not touch it.

172. He who formerly was reckless and afterwards became sober, brightens up this world, like the moon when freed from clouds.

173. He whose evil deeds are covered by good deeds, brightens up this world, like the moon when freed from clouds.

174. This world is dark, few only can see here; a few only go to heaven, like birds escaped from the net.

175. The swans go on the path of the sun, they go miraculously through the ether; the wise are led out of this world, when they have conquered Mâra and his train.

176. If a man has transgressed the one law, and speaks lies, and scoffs at another world, there is no evil he will not do.

177. The uncharitable do not go to the world of the gods; fools only do not praise liberality; a wise man rejoices in liberality, and through it becomes blessed in the other world.

178. Better than sovereignty over the earth, better than going to heaven, better than lordship over all worlds, is the reward of Sotâpatti, the first step in holiness.

Chapter XVI.

Pleasure.

209. He who gives himself to vanity, and does not give himself to meditation, forgetting the real aim (of life) and grasping at pleasure, will in time envy him who has exerted himself in meditation.

210. Let no man ever cling to what is pleasant, or to what is unpleasant. Not to see what is pleasant is pain, and it is pain to see what is unpleasant.

211. Let, therefore, no man love anything; loss of the beloved is evil. Those who love nothing, and hate nothing, have no fetters.

212. From pleasure comes grief, from pleasure comes fear; he who is free from pleasure knows neither grief nor fear.

213. From affection comes grief, from affection comes fear; he who is free from affection knows neither grief nor fear.

214. From lust comes grief, from lust comes fear; he who is free from lust knows neither grief nor fear.

215. From love comes grief, from love comes fear; he who is free from love knows neither grief nor fear.

216. From greed comes grief, from greed comes fear; he who is free from greed knows neither grief nor fear.

217. He who possesses virtue and intelligence, who is just, speaks the truth, and does what is his own business, him the world will hold dear.

218. He in whom a desire for the Ineffable (Nirvâ*na*) has sprung up, who in his mind is satisfied, and whose thoughts are not bewildered by love, he is called ûrdhva*m*srotas (carried upwards by the stream).

219. Kinsmen, friends, and lovers salute a man who has been long away, and returns safe from afar.

220. In like manner his good works receive him who has done good, and has gone from this world to the other;—as kinsmen receive a friend on his return.

Questions

1. People often associate selfishness with narrow-mindedness and self-serving behaviors. In Chapter XII, Buddha invites people to focus on themselves because that is the path to virtue and maturity. When is it bad to focus on one's self, and when is it good? Why?

2. In Chapter XIII, Buddha gives this warning: "Come, look at this world, glittering like a royal chariot; the foolish are immersed in it, but the wise do not touch it." From this sentence and its context, what seems to be Buddha's understanding of "the world" and how one should relate to it?

3. In Chapter XVI, Buddha discusses pleasure. As Buddha looks at the world, he concludes that there are various kinds of pleasure—some are worthless and some are worthwhile. Compare your understanding of pleasure with Buddha's statements.

4. In what ways do these passages by Buddha enhance one's understanding of spirituality and virtue? In what ways are these passages in agreement or disagreement with other religious traditions?

Lao-Tzu

The *Tao Te Ching* is a collection of poems attributed to a Chinese sage named **Lao-Tzu** (or Laozi). Many myths and legends surround this book and author, but it is clear that this book is the foundation of Taoism (or Daoism). Reaching back to perhaps the seventh century BC, this long tradition teaches one to accept the deeper nature of reality, which is beyond words and comprehension. Taoism does not give its followers a god or any specific ethical and social commands as found in the Hebrew, Christian, or Islamic scriptures. The concern of Taoism is to give people a sense of peace by accepting the underlying unity behind the confusing experiences of life. The Tao, or the "way," is beyond words, but it is allegedly the most real and the most important presence in the universe. The Tao is like a great river flowing along, and humans are like specks in the flow. Rather than fight against the movement of the river (the flow of ultimate reality), one needs to accept it and find peace with everything. Taoism also teaches its followers not to strive to understand the Tao, but to be content with ignorance of it.

from Tâo Teh King

Chapter 1

1. The Tâo that can be trodden is not the enduring and unchanging Tâo. The name that can be named is not the enduring and unchanging name.

2. (Conceived of as) having no name, it is the Originator of heaven and earth; (conceived of as) having a name, it is the Mother of all things.

3. Always without desire we must be found,

If its deep mystery we would sound;

But if desire always within us be,

Its outer fringe is all that we shall see.

4. Under these two aspects, it is really the same; but as development takes place, it receives the different names. Together we call them the Mystery. Where the Mystery is the deepest is the gate of all that is subtle and wonderful.

Chapter 15

1. The skilful masters (of the Tâo) in old times, with a subtle and exquisite penetration, comprehended its mysteries, and were deep (also) so as to elude

men's knowledge. As they were thus beyond men's knowledge, I will make an effort to describe of what sort they appeared to be.

2. Shrinking looked they like those who wade through a stream in winter; irresolute like those who are afraid of all around them; grave like a guest (in awe of his host); evanescent like ice that is melting away; unpretentious like wood that has not been fashioned into anything; vacant like a valley, and dull like muddy water.

3. Who can (make) the muddy water (clear)? Let it be still, and it will gradually become clear. Who can secure the condition of rest? Let movement go on, and the condition of rest will gradually arise.

4. They who preserve this method of the Tâo do not wish to be full (of themselves). It is through their not being full of themselves that they can afford to seem worn and not appear new and complete.

Chapter 47

1. Without going outside his door, one understands (all that takes place) under the sky; without looking out from his window, one sees the Tâo of Heaven. The farther that one goes out (from himself), the less he knows:

2. Therefore the sages got their knowledge without travelling; gave their (right) names to things without seeing them; and accomplished their ends without any purpose of doing so.

Questions

1. Below are four lines from Chapter 1. To better understand them, one needs to remember that *to sound* means to test the depth of a body of water (such as when sailors let down a rope with a weight to measure the depth of a river or harbor). What do these lines mean?

   > *Always without desire we must be found,*
   > *If its deep mystery we would sound;*
   > *But if desire always within us be,*
   > *Its outer fringe is all that we shall see.*

2. In Chapter 15 we read: "Who can (make) the muddy water (clear)? / Let it be still, and it will gradually become clear." What does this mean? Can one force the dirt in water to settle to the bottom? How does this apply to one's everyday life?

3. In Chapter 47, the author explains that true understanding is found within one's self, not in striving to understand the world outside of the individual. Paraphrase the meaning of this poem.

4. Imagine a friend who wants to understand Taoism. Explain the strengths and weaknesses of this tradition. How would it help or hinder a person's daily life?

HERMANN HESSE

Hermann Hesse (1877–1962) grew up in a German home that was very committed to Christianity. However, he left those roots and looked for other ways to understand the nature of spirituality. He often turned to the religious traditions of India for inspiration. In addition to his spiritual struggles, his life was filled with many personal, psychological, and marital problems.

In 1922, Hesse published his novel, *Siddhartha*. This novel should not be read as a historical account. Rather it is a representation of the ideal spiritual quest found in Hinduism and Buddhism. The main character, Siddhartha, is very much like the Buddha, the founder of Buddhism. Both Hesse's character, Siddhartha, and the Buddha live in India from about 500 BC to about 400 BC. Both were born into luxury, but both leave to wander the country for spiritual enlightenment. Both are married and have a son, and both Siddhartha and Buddha leave their families for the higher good of a spiritual journey. Hesse made the parallels even stronger, if one knows that the historical Buddha was originally named Siddhartha Gautama. Yet, Hesse's main character is not Buddha. They are simply very similar to each other. In the novel, the main character (Siddhartha) is a student of the historical Buddha for a short time. Also, in the novel, the Buddha (also called Gotama or Gautama) is mentioned as being very old and near death.

Early in *Siddhartha,* the main character leaves his home to find spiritual enlightenment. He tries the harsh ascetic life of self-disciplined starvation and finds some help, but he moves on. He marries Kamala, has a son, and has material security, but he decides to move on again. Eventually, Siddhartha comes to the river where a ferryman takes people from one side of the river to the other. Here, at the river, Siddhartha finally finds peace and enlightenment. As Hesse describes this state of contentment, one can begin to understand the central themes found in Buddhism and other Eastern religions: (a) Humans need to accept reality and life as it comes. (b) Humans need to free themselves from the daily desires of life. Such desires are only a form of torment. (c) Humans need to accept the cycle of life and stop trying to clearly separate the experiences of life into such categories as past, present, future, life, death, pain, pleasure, reason, and irrationality. In this selection, Siddhartha's peace and enlightenment are tested when he is reunited with his wife for a brief moment before she dies.

FROM SIDDHARTHA

The Ferryman

I will remain by this river, thought Siddhartha. It is the same river which I crossed on my way to the town. A friendly ferryman took me across. I will go to him. My path once led from his hut to a new life which is now old and dead. May my present path, my new life, start from there!

He looked lovingly into the flowing water, into the transparent green, into the crystal lines of its wonderful design. He saw bright pearls rise from the depths, bubbles swimming on the mirror, sky blue reflected in them. The river looked at him with a thousand eyes—green, white, crystal, sky blue. How he loved this river, how it enchanted him, how grateful he was to it! In his heart he heard the newly awakened voice speak, and it said to him: "Love this river, stay by it, learn from it." Yes, he wanted to learn from it, he wanted to listen to it. It seemed to him that whoever understood this river and its secrets, would understand much more, many secrets, all secrets.

But today he only saw one of the river's secrets, one that gripped his soul. He saw that the water continually flowed and flowed and yet it was always there; it was always the same and yet every moment it was new. Who could understand, conceive this? He did not understand it; he was only aware of a dim suspicion, a faint memory, divine voices.

Siddhartha rose, the pangs of hunger were becoming unbearable. He wandered painfully along the river bank, listened to the rippling of the water, listened to the gnawing hunger in his body.

When he reached the ferry, the boat was already there and the ferryman who had once taken the young Samana across, stood in the boat. Siddhartha recognized him. He had also aged very much.

"Will you take me across?" he asked.

The ferryman, astonished to see such a distinguished-looking man alone and on foot, took him into the boat and set off.

"You have chosen a splendid life," said Siddhartha. "It must be fine to live near this river and sail on it every day."

The rower smiled, swaying gently.

"It is fine, sir, as you say, but is not every life, every work fine?"

"Maybe, but I envy you yours."

"Oh, you would soon lose your taste for it. It is not for people in fine clothes."

Siddhartha laughed. "I have already been judged by my clothes today and regarded with suspicion. Will you accept these clothes from me, which I find a nuisance? For I must tell you that I have no money to pay you for taking me across the river."

"The gentleman is joking," laughed the ferryman.

"I am not joking, my friend. You once previously took me across this river without payment, so please do it today also and take my clothes instead."

"And will the gentleman continue without clothes?"

"I should prefer not to go further. I should prefer it if you would give me some old clothes and keep me here as your assistant, or rather your apprentice, for I must learn how to handle the boat."

The ferryman looked keenly at the stranger for a long time.

"I recognize you," he said finally. "You once slept in my hut. It is a long time ago, maybe more than twenty years ago. I took you across the river and we parted good friends. Were you not a Samana? I cannot remember your name."

"My name is Siddhartha and I was Samana when you last saw me."

"You are welcome, Siddhartha. My name is Vasudeva. I hope you will be my guest today and also sleep in my hut, and tell me where you have come from and why you are so tired of your fine clothes."

They had reached the middle of the river and Vasudeva rowed more strongly because of the current. He rowed calmly, with strong arms, watching the end of the boat. Siddhartha sat and watched him and remembered how once, in those last Samana days, he had felt affection for this man. He gratefully accepted Vasudeva's invitation. When they reached the river bank, he helped him to secure the boat. Then Vasudeva led him into the hut, offered him bread and water, which Siddhartha ate with enjoyment, as well as the mango fruit which Vasudeva offered him.

Later, when the sun was beginning to set, they sat on a tree trunk by the river and Siddhartha told him about his origin and his life and how he had seen him today after that hour of despair. The story lasted late into the night.

Vasudeva listened with great attention; he heard all about his origin and childhood, about his studies, his seekings, his pleasures and needs. It was one of the ferryman's greatest virtues that, like few people, he knew how to listen. Without his saying a word, the speaker felt that Vasudeva took in every word, quietly, expectantly, that he missed nothing. He did not await anything with impatience and gave neither praise nor blame—he only listened. Siddhartha felt how wonderful it was to have such a listener who could be absorbed in another person's life, his strivings, his sorrows.

However, towards the end of Siddhartha's story, when he told him about the tree by the river and his deep despair, about the holy Om, and how after his sleep he felt such a love for the river, the ferryman listened with doubled attention, completely absorbed, his eyes closed.

When Siddhartha had finished and there was a long pause, Vasudeva said: "It is as I thought; the river has spoken to you. It is friendly towards you, too; it speaks to you. That is good, very good. Stay with me, Siddhartha, my friend. I once had a wife, her bed was at the side of mine, but she died long ago. I have lived alone for a long time. Come and live with me; there is room and food for both of us."

"I thank you," said Siddhartha, "I thank you and accept. I also thank you, Vasudeva, for listening so well. There are few people who know how to listen and I have not met anybody who can do so like you. I will also learn from you in this respect."

"You will learn it," said Vasudeva, "but not from me. The river has taught me to listen; you will learn from it, too. The river knows everything; one can learn everything from it. You have already learned from the river that it is good to strive downwards, to sink, to seek the depths. The rich and distinguished Siddhartha will become a rower; Siddhartha the learned Brahmin will become a ferryman. You have also learned this from the river. You will learn the other thing, too."

After a long pause, Siddhartha said: "What other thing, Vasudeva?"

Vasudeva rose. "It has grown late," he said, "let us go to bed. I cannot tell you what the other thing is, my friend. You will find out, perhaps you already know. I am not a learned man; I do not know how to talk or think. I only know how to listen and be devout; otherwise I have learned nothing. If I could talk and teach, I would perhaps be a teacher, but as it is I am only a ferryman and it is my task to take people across this river. I have taken thousands of people across and to all of them my river has been nothing but a hindrance on their journey. They have travelled for money and business, to weddings and on pilgrimages; the river has been in their way and the ferryman was there to take them quickly across the obstacle. However, amongst the thousands there have been a few, four or five, to whom the river was not an obstacle. They have heard its voice and listened to it, and the river has become holy to them, as it has to me. Let us now go to bed, Siddhartha."

Siddhartha stayed with the ferryman and learned how to look after the boat, and when there was nothing to do at the ferry, he worked in the rice field with Vasudeva, gathered wood, and picked fruit from the banana trees. He learned how to make oars, how to improve the boat and to make baskets. He was pleased with everything that he did and learned and the days and months passed quickly. But he learned more from the river than Vasudeva could teach him. He leaned from it continually. Above all, he learned from it how to listen, to listen with a still heart, with a waiting, open soul, without passion, without desire, without judgment, without opinions.

He lived happily with Vasudeva and occasionally they exchanged words, few and long-considered words. Vasudeva was no friend of words. Siddhartha was rarely successful in moving him to speak.

He once asked him, "Have you also learned that secret from the river; that there is no such thing as time?"

A bright smile spread over Vasudeva's face.

"Yes, Siddhartha," he said. "Is this what you mean? That the river is everywhere at the same time, at the source and at the mouth, at the waterfall, at the ferry, at the current, in the ocean and in the mountains, everywhere, and that the present only exists for it, not the shadow of the past, nor the shadow of the future?"

"That is it," said Siddhartha, "and when I learned that, I reviewed my life and it was also a river, and Siddhartha the boy, Siddhartha the mature man and Siddhartha the old man, were only separated by shadows, not through reality. Siddhartha's previous lives were also not in the past, and his death and his return to Brahma are not in the future. Nothing was, nothing will be, everything has reality and presence."

Siddhartha spoke with delight. This discovery had made him very happy. Was then not all sorrow in time, all self-torment and fear in time? Were not all difficulties and evil in the world conquered as soon as one conquered time, as soon as one dispelled time? He had spoken with delight, but Vasudeva just smiled radiantly at him and nodded his agreement. He stroked Siddhartha's shoulder and returned to his work.

And once again when the river swelled during the rainy season and roared loudly, Siddhartha said: "Is it not true, my friend, that the river has very many voices? Has it not the voice of a king, of a warrior, of a bull, of a night bird, of a pregnant woman and a sighing man, and a thousand other voices?"

"It is so," nodded Vasudeva, "the voices of all living creatures are in its voice."

"And do you know," continued Siddhartha, "what word it pronounces when one is successful in hearing all its ten thousand voices at the same time?"

Vasudeva laughed joyously; he bent towards Siddhartha and whispered the holy Om in his ear. And this was just what Siddhartha had heard.

As time went on his smile began to resemble the ferryman's, was almost equally radiant, almost equally full of happiness, equally lighting up through a thousand little wrinkles, equally childish, equally senile. Many travellers, when seeing both ferrymen together, took them for brothers. Often they sat together in the evening on the tree trunk by the river. They both listened silently to the water, which to them was not just water, but the voice of life, the voice of Being, of perpetual Becoming. And it sometimes happened that while listening to the river, they both thought the same thoughts, perhaps of a conversation of the previous day, or about one of the travellers whose fate and circumstances occupied their minds, or death, or their childhood; and when the river told them something good at the same moment, they looked at each other, both thinking the same thought, both happy at the same answer to the same question.

Something emanated from the ferry and from both ferrymen that many of the travellers felt. It sometimes happened that a traveller, after looking at the face of one of the ferrymen, began to talk about his life and troubles, confessed sins, asked for comfort and advice. It sometimes happened that someone would ask permission to spend an evening with them in order to listen to the river. It also happened that curious people came along, who had been told that two wise men, magicians or holy men lived at the ferry. The curious ones asked many questions but they received no replies, and they found neither magicians nor wise men. They only found two friendly old men, who appeared to be mute, rather odd and stupid. And the curious ones laughed and said how foolish and credible people were to spread such wild rumors.

The years passed and nobody counted them. Then one day, some monks came along, followers of Gotama, the Buddha, and asked to be taken across the river. The ferrymen learned from them that they were returning to their great teacher as quickly as possible, for the news had spread that the Illustrious One was seriously ill and would soon suffer his last mortal death and attain salvation. Not long afterwards another party of monks arrived and then another, and the monks as well as most of the other travellers talked of nothing but Gotama and his approaching death. And as people come from all sides to a military expedition or to the crowning of a king, so did they gather together like swarms of bees, drawn together by a magnet, to go where the great Buddha was lying on his deathbed, where this great event was taking place and where the savior of an age was passing into eternity.

Siddhartha thought a great deal at this time about the dying sage whose voice had stirred thousands, whose voice he had also once heard, whose holy countenance he had also once looked at with awe. He thought lovingly of him, remembered his path to salvation, and smiling, remembered the words he had once uttered as a young man to the Illustrious One. It seemed to him that they had been arrogant and precocious words. For a long time he knew that he was not separated from Gotama, although he could not accept his teachings. No, a true seeker could not accept any teachings, not if he sincerely wished to find something. But he who had found, could give his approval to every path, every goal; nothing separated him from all the other thousands who lived in eternity, who breathed the Divine.

One day, when very many people were making a pilgrimage to the dying Buddha, Kamala, once the most beautiful of courtesans, was also on her way. She had long retired from her previous way of life, had presented her garden to Gotama's monks, taking refuge in his teachings, and belonged to the women and benefactresses attached to the pilgrims. On hearing of Gotama's approaching death, she had set off on foot, wearing simple clothes, together with her son. They had reached the river on her way, but the boy soon became tired; he wanted to go home, he wanted to rest, he wanted to eat. He was often sulky and tearful. Kamala frequently had to rest with him. He was used to matching his will against hers. She had to feed him, comfort him, and scold him. He could not understand why his mother had to make this weary, miserable pilgrimage to an unknown place, to a strange man who was holy and was dying. Let him die—what did it matter to the boy?

The pilgrims were not far from Vasudeva's ferry, when little Siddhartha told his mother he wanted to rest. Kamala herself was tired, and while the boy ate a banana, she crouched down on the ground, half-closed her eyes and rested. Suddenly, however, she uttered a cry of pain. The boy, startled, looked at her and saw her face white with horror. From under her clothes a small black snake, which had bitten Kamala, crawled away.

They both ran on quickly in order to reach some people. When they were near the ferry, Kamala collapsed and could not go any further. The boy cried out for help, meantime kissing and embracing his mother. She also joined in his loud cries, until the sounds reached Vasudeva, who was standing by the ferry. He came quickly, took the woman in his arms and carried her to the boat. The boy joined him and they soon arrived at the hut, where Siddhartha was standing and was just lighting the fire. He looked up and first saw the boy's face, which strangely reminded him of something. Then he saw Kamala, whom he recognized immediately, although she lay unconscious in the ferryman's arms. Then he knew that it was his own son whose face had so reminded him of something, and his heart beat quickly.

Kamala's wound was washed, but it was already black and her body had swelled. She was given a restorative and her consciousness returned. She was lying on Siddhartha's bed in his hut and Siddhartha, whom she had once loved so much, was bending over her. She thought she was dreaming, and smiling, she looked into her lover's face. Gradually, she realized her condition, remembered the bite and called anxiously for her son.

"Do not worry," said Siddhartha, "he is here."

Kamala looked into his eyes. She found it difficult to speak with the poison in her system. "You have grown old, my dear," she said, "you have become gray, but you are like the young Samana who once came to me in my garden, without clothes and with dusty feet. You are much more like him than when you left Kamaswami and me. Your eyes are like his, Siddhartha. Ah, I have also grown old, old—did you recognize me?"

Siddhartha smiled. "I recognized you immediately, Kamala, my dear."

Kamala indicated her son and said: "Did you recognize him, too? He is your son."

Her eyes wandered and closed. The boy began to cry. Siddhartha put him on his knee, let him weep and stroked his hair. Looking at the child's face, he remembered a Brahmin prayer which he had once learned when he himself was a small child. Slowly and in a singing voice he began to recite it; the words came back to him out of the past and his childhood. The child became quiet as he recited, still sobbed a little and then fell asleep. Siddhartha put him on Vasudeva's bed. Vasudeva stood by the hearth cooking rice. Siddhartha looked at Vasudeva and smiled at him.

"She is dying," said Siddhartha softly.

Vasudeva nodded. The firelight from the hearth was reflected in his kind face.

Kamala again regained consciousness. There was pain in her face; Siddhartha read the pain on her mouth, in her pallid face. He read it quietly, attentively, waiting, sharing her pain. Kamala was aware of this; her glance sought his.

Looking at him she said: "Now I see that your eyes have also changed. They have become quite different. How do I recognize that you are still Siddhartha? You are Siddhartha and yet you are not like him."

Siddhartha did not speak; silently he looked into her eyes.

"Have you attained it?" she asked. "Have you found peace?"

He smiled and placed his hand on hers.

"Yes," she said, "I see it. I also will find peace."

"You have found it," whispered Siddhartha.

Kamala looked at him steadily. It had been her intention to make a pilgrimage to Gotama, to see the face of the Illustrious One, to obtain some of his peace, and instead she had only found Siddhartha, and it was good, just as good as if she had seen the other. She wanted to tell him that, but her tongue no longer obeyed her will. Silently she looked at him and he saw the life fade from her eyes. When the last pain had filled and passed from her eyes, when the last shudder had passed through her body, his fingers closed her eyelids.

He sat there a long time looking at her dead face. For a long time he looked at her mouth, her old tired mouth and her shrunken lips, and remembered how once, in the spring of his life, he had compared her lips with a freshly cut fig. For a long time he looked intently at the pale face, at the tired wrinkles and saw his own face like that, just as white, also dead, and at the same time he saw his face and hers, young, with red lips, with ardent eyes and he was overwhelmed with a feeling of the present and contemporary existence. In this hour he felt more acutely the indestructibleness of every life, the eternity of every moment.

When he rose, Vasudeva had prepared some rice for him but Siddhartha did not eat. In the stable, where the goat was, the two old men straightened some straw and Vasudeva lay down. But Siddhartha went outside and sat in front of the hut all night, listening to the river, sunk in the past, simultaneously affected and encompassed by all the periods of his life. From time to time, however, he rose, walked to the door of the hut and listened to hear if the boy were sleeping.

Early in the morning, before the sun was yet visible, Vasudeva came out of the stable and walked up to his friend.

"You have not slept," he said.

"No, Vasudeva, I sat here and listened to the river. It has told me a great deal, it has filled me with many great thoughts, with thoughts of unity."

"You have suffered, Siddhartha, yet I see that sadness has not entered your heart."

"No, my dear friend. Why should I be sad? I who was rich and happy have become still richer and happier. My son has been given to me."

"I also welcome your son. But now, Siddhartha, let us go to work, there is much to be done. Kamala died on the same bed where my wife died. We shall also build Kamala's funeral pyre on the same hill where I once built my wife's funeral pyre."

While the boy still slept, they built the funeral pyre.

Questions

1. Why did Hesse bring together so many connections in this chapter? For example, Siddhartha comes to the river and remembers that he once crossed it before with the help of the same ferryman. Why did Hesse have Kamala come to the same river? Why does Siddhartha see himself in his son's face?

2. Research the significance of rivers in Hinduism and Buddhism. How does that research help you to better understand the significance of this location for Siddhartha's enlightenment?

3. Notice how often people in this chapter come to recognize someone or something. What is the significance of this theme of realization or recognition?

4. Why is the boy included in this chapter? He seems to be a nuisance to his mother and later to Siddhartha. The boy does not seem to fit into the theme of peace and enlightenment that is developing in Siddhartha's life. What is Hesse doing by introducing this character?

ST. LUKE

St. Luke is known as "the beloved physician," who accompanied the Apostle Paul on his missionary travels. In addition to writing the Acts of the Apostles (or Acts), Luke also wrote the third Gospel account in the Bible—the Gospel according to Luke. Both biblical books seem to be written for predominantly Gentile (non-Jewish) audiences. The latter provides a narrative of Christ's life and teachings, while the former gives an account of the activities of the apostles after the resurrection of Jesus. Little is known about the life of Luke; perhaps he was from Antioch, a major city in ancient Syria. Luke wrote in his introduction to Acts and his introduction to the Gospel according to Luke that he was very careful to accurately record the details about Jesus and the apostles.

The famous parable of the prodigal son is actually the climax of three parables presented by Jesus. In Luke 15:1–2, the religious authorities complain about Jesus' kind and welcoming attitude toward immoral people and social outcasts (e.g., the tax collectors). In response, Jesus tells three stories in order to confront and to correct the religious authorities. Rather than being annoyed with the outcasts, Jesus says that there is excitement in heaven when a sinful, lost person is found. By implication, Jesus is thus explaining why he is currently welcoming and loving sinful, lost people. Jesus is merely doing what is done in heaven. In the first two parables, Jesus tells about a lost sheep and a lost coin to illustrate his point. Then, Jesus gives the very detailed parable of the lost son. In this third parable, Jesus expands and shifts the pattern established in the first two parables. The parable of the prodigal son is much more detailed and it includes a new element—the proud, resistant second son.

THREE PARABLES ABOUT LOSING AND FINDING (INCLUDING THE PRODIGAL SON)

LUKE 15 (BIBLE: NEW INTERNATIONAL VERSION)

1. Now the tax collectors and "sinners" were all gathering around to hear him.
2. But the Pharisees and the teachers of the law muttered, "This man welcomes sinners and eats with them."
3. Then Jesus told them this parable:
4. "Suppose one of you has a hundred sheep and loses one of them. Does he not leave the ninety-nine in the open country and go after the lost sheep until he finds it?
5. And when he finds it, he joyfully puts it on his shoulders
6. and goes home. Then he calls his friends and neighbors together and says, 'Rejoice with me; I have found my lost sheep.'
7. I tell you that in the same way there will be more rejoicing in heaven over one sinner who repents than over ninety-nine righteous persons who do not need to repent.
8. "Or suppose a woman has ten silver coins and loses one. Does she not light a lamp, sweep the house and search carefully until she finds it?
9. And when she finds it, she calls her friends and neighbors together and says, 'Rejoice with me; I have found my lost coin.'
10. In the same way, I tell you, there is rejoicing in the presence of the angels of God over one sinner who repents."
11. Jesus continued: "There was a man who had two sons.
12. The younger one said to his father, 'Father, give me my share of the estate.' So he divided his property between them.
13. "Not long after that, the younger son got together all he had, set off for a distant country and there squandered his wealth in wild living.
14. After he had spent everything, there was a severe famine in that whole country, and he began to be in need.
15. So he went and hired himself out to a citizen of that country, who sent him to his fields to feed pigs.
16. He longed to fill his stomach with the pods that the pigs were eating, but no one gave him anything.
17. "When he came to his senses, he said, 'How many of my father's hired men have food to spare, and here I am starving to death!
18. will set out and go back to my father and say to him: Father, I have sinned against heaven and against you.

19. I am no longer worthy to be called your son; make me like one of your hired men.'
20. So he got up and went to his father.
    "But while he was still a long way off, his father saw him and was filled with compassion for him; he ran to his son, threw his arms around him and kissed him.
21. "The son said to him, 'Father, I have sinned against heaven and against you. I am no longer worthy to be called your son.'
22. "But the father said to his servants, 'Quick! Bring the best robe and put it on him. Put a ring on his finger and sandals on his feet.
23. Bring the fattened calf and kill it. Let's have a feast and celebrate.
24. For this son of mine was dead and is alive again; he was lost and is found.' So they began to celebrate.
25. "Meanwhile, the older son was in the field. When he came near the house, he heard music and dancing.
26. So he called one of the servants and asked him what was going on.
27. 'Your brother has come,' he replied, 'and your father has killed the fattened calf because he has him back safe and sound.'
28. "The older brother became angry and refused to go in. So his father went out and pleaded with him.
29. But he answered his father, 'Look! All these years I've been slaving for you and never disobeyed your orders. Yet you never gave me even a young goat so I could celebrate with my friends.
30. But when this son of yours who has squandered your property with prostitutes comes home, you kill the fattened calf for him!'
31. "'My son,' the father said, 'you are always with me, and everything I have is yours.
32. But we had to celebrate and be glad, because this brother of yours was dead and is alive again; he was lost and is found.'"

Questions

1. At the beginning of Luke 15, the religious leaders are annoyed. Why would Jesus give three, similar parables in response to this simple situation? Why doesn't Jesus give a direct answer to the religious leaders?
2. In the first two parables, the single sheep and the lost coin are passive. However, in the third parable, the prodigal son is very active as he seeks a new life away from his family and his roots. Is there any significance to the qualities attributed to the son?
3. The third parable is much more complex than the first two parables. In the third parable, a second son is introduced. Is he a distraction, or is there a purpose behind his actions and words? If there is a purpose behind the introduction of the second son, what is it?
4. In the third parable, the character of the father is much more developed than the shepherd or the woman in the two earlier stories. What qualities are found in the father? How do these qualities serve Jesus' goals?

AUGUSTINE

Augustine (354–430) lived during the decline of the Roman Empire. His pagan father ensured that Augustine received an excellent education. Beyond this fact, his father's influence on Augustine seems to have been marginal. However, his mother's influence was very powerful. She was a Christian who over the years became very strong in her faith. Perhaps her spiritual growth can be linked to her prayerful struggles with God over the destiny of her rebellious and confused son. Born and educated in northern Africa, Augustine eventually taught rhetoric (effective speaking and critical thinking) in Rome and Milan, Italy. After his conversion to Christianity, he returned to North Africa and served as an influential bishop and a defender of orthodox Christian doctrines.

Augustine's *Confessions* was written later in his life, and in it he looks back at his rebellious youth and his conversion. This work is famous in the history of Western literature because it is considered the first autobiography and it is the first book-length description of the author's life. An autobiography normally focuses on, and often glorifies, an author's accomplishments. Paradoxically, Augustine's constant focus is God. The theme of the book is God's blessings on and God's guidance of Augustine's entire life—beginning with his birth, continuing through his years of willful rebellion against God, and culminating in Augustine's submission to God's overwhelming love, mercy, and grace.

Throughout the book, Augustine speaks directly to God and secondarily to his readers. Constantly God is praised, and constantly Augustine examines his foolish, confused, and sinful life without God. For hundreds of pages, Augustine is able to talk about himself without any self-glorification. This great work of Western literature is often summarized with the phrase, "Our heart is restless until it rests in you" (Book I, Chapter 1).

Confessions is filled with allusions to the Bible. For example, the prophet Isaiah asks in Isaiah 66:1–2, How can we build a home or temple for the God who created everything and controls everything? Then, he answers that God honors and respects the person who is "humble and contrite" in heart. Augustine asked the same question and came to the same conclusion throughout *Confessions* (in particular, see Book I, Chapter 5).

FROM CONFESSIONS

Book I Childhood

Chapter 1 God and the Soul

(1) You are great, O Lord, and greatly to be praised: great is your power and to your wisdom there is no limit. And man, who is a part of your creation, wishes to praise you, man who bears about within himself his mortality, who bears about within himself testimony to his sin and testimony that you resist the

proud. Yet man, this part of your creation, wishes to praise you. You arouse him to take joy in praising you, for you have made us for yourself, and our heart is restless until it rests in you. Lord, grant me to know and understand which is first, to call upon you or to praise you, and also which is first, to know you or to call upon you? But how does one who does not know you call upon you? For one who does not know you might call upon another instead of you. Or must you rather be called upon so that you may be known? Yet "how shall they call upon him in whom they have not believed? Or how shall they believe without a preacher?" "And they shall praise the Lord that seek him," for they that seek him find him, and finding him they shall praise him. Lord, let me seek you by calling upon you, and let me call upon you by believing in you, for you have been preached to us. Lord, my faith calls upon you, that faith which you have given to me, which you have breathed into me by the incarnation of your Son and through the ministry of your preacher.

Chapter 5 *Augustine's Prayer*

(5) Who will give me help, so that I may rest in you? Who will help me, so that you will come into my heart and inebriate it, to the end that I may forget my evils and embrace you, my one good? What are you to me? Have pity on me, so that I may speak! What am I myself to you, that you command me to love you, and grow angry and threaten me with mighty woes unless I do? Is it but a small affliction if I do not love you? Unhappy man that I am, in your mercy, O Lord my God, tell me what you are to me. "Say to my soul: I am your salvation." Say this, so that I may hear you. Behold, my heart's ears are turned to you, O Lord: open them, and "say to my soul: I am your salvation." I will run after that voice, and I will catch hold of you. Do not hide your face from me. Lest I die, let me die, so that I may see it.

(6) Too narrow is the house of my soul for you to enter into it: let it be enlarged by you. It lies in ruins; build it up again. I confess and I know that it contains things that offend your eyes. Yet who will cleanse it? Or upon what other than you shall I call? "From my secret sins cleanse me, O Lord, and from those of others spare your servant." I believe, and therefore I speak out. Lord, all this you know. Have I not accused myself to you, my God, of my sins, and have you not forgiven the iniquity of my heart? I do not contend in judgment with you who are truth itself. I do not deceive myself, lest my iniquity lie to itself. Therefore, I do not contend in judgment with you, for "if you, O Lord, will mark iniquities: Lord, who shall stand it?"

Chapter 6 *The Infant Augustine*

(7) Yet grant me to plead before your mercy, grant me who am dust and ashes to speak, for behold, it is not a man who makes mock of me but your mercy that I address. Perhaps even you deride me, but when you have turned towards me, you will have mercy on me. What do I want to say, Lord, except that I do not know whence I came into what I may call a mortal life or a living death. Whence I know not. Your consolation and your mercies have raised me up, as I have heard from the parents of my flesh, for by one and in

the other you fashioned me in time. I myself do not remember this. Therefore, the comfort of human milk nourished me, but neither my mother nor my nurses filled their own breasts. Rather, through them you gave me an infant's food in accordance with your law and out of the riches that you have distributed even down to the lowest level of things. You gave me to want no more than you gave, and you gave to those who nursed me the will to give what you gave to them. By an orderly affection they willingly gave me what they possessed so abundantly from you. It was good for them that my good should come from them; yet it was not from them but through them. For from you, O God, come all good things, and from you, my God, comes all my salvation. This I afterwards observed when you cried out to me by means of those things which you bestow both inwardly and outwardly. For at that time I knew how to seek the breast, to be satisfied with pleasant things, and to cry at my bodily hurts, but nothing more.

(8) Later on, I began to laugh, at first when asleep and then when awake. This has been told to me concerning myself, and I believe it, since we see other infants acting thus, although I do not remember such acts of my own. Then little by little I perceived where I was, and I wished to make my wants known to those who could satisfy them. Yet I could not do so, because the wants were within me, while those outside could by no sensible means penetrate into my soul. So I tossed my limbs about and uttered sounds, thus making such few signs similar to my wishes as I could, and in such fashion as I could, although they were not like the truth. When they would not obey me, either because they did not understand or because it would be harmful, I grew angry at older ones who were not subject to me and at children for not waiting on me, and took it out on them by crying. That infants are of this sort I have since learned from those whom I have been able to observe. That I was such a one they have unwittingly taught me better than my nurses who knew me.

(9) But see, my infancy is dead long ago, and I still live. Lord, you who live forever and in whom nothing dies—since before the beginning of the ages, and before anything that can even be called "before," you are, and you are God and Lord of all that you have created, and with you stand the causes of all impermanent things and. with you abide the unchanging sources of all changing things, and in you live the sempiternal reasons of all unreasoning and temporal things—tell to me, your suppliant, O God, in your mercy, tell to me, your wretched servant, whether my infancy followed another age of mine that was already dead. Or was it that time which I passed within my mother's womb? Of that time something has been told to me, and I have seen pregnant women. What was there even before this, my joy, my God? Was I anywhere, or anyone? I have no one to tell me this, neither father nor mother could do so, nor the experience of others, nor my own memory. Do you laugh at me for questioning you of such things? Do you command me to praise you and confess to you only for what I know?

(10) I confess to you, O Lord of heaven and earth, and I utter praise to you for my first being and my infancy, which I do not remember. You have endowed man so that he can gather these things concerning himself from others, and even on the words of weak women believe much about himself. For even

then I had being and lived, and already at the close of my infancy I looked for signs by which I could make known my meaning to others. Where except from you, O Lord, could come such a living being? Who has the art and power to make himself? Is there any channel, through which being and life flow into us, that comes from any source but you, Lord, who made us? In you being and life are not different things, because supreme being and supreme life are one and the same. You are supreme and you are not changed. Nor is this present day spent in you—and yet it is spent in you, for in you are all these times. Unless you contained them, they would have no way of passing on. And because your years do not fail, your years are this every day. No matter how many have already been our days and the days of our fathers, they have all passed through this single present day of yours, and from it they have taken their measures and their manner of being. And others still shall also pass away and receive their measures and their manner of being. "But you are the Selfsame," and all things of tomorrow and all beyond, and all things of yesterday and all things before, you shall make into today, and you have already made them into today. . . .

Chapter 13 *Studies in Greek and Latin*

(20) Why I detested the Greek language when I was taught it as a little boy I have not yet fully discovered. I liked Latin very much, not the parts given by our first teachers but what the men called grammarians teach us. The first stages of our education, when we learn reading, writing, and arithmetic, I considered no less a burden and punishment than all the Greek courses. Since I was but "flesh, and a wind that goes and does not return," where could this come from except from sin and vanity of life? Better indeed, because more certain, were those first studies by which there was formed and is formed in me what I still possess, the ability to read what I find written down and to write what I want to, than the later studies wherein I was required to learn by heart I know not how many of Aeneas's wanderings, although forgetful of my own, and to weep over Dido's death, because she killed herself for love, when all the while amid such things, dying to you, O God my life, I most wretchedly bore myself about with dry eyes.

(21) Who can be more wretched than the wretched one who takes no pity on himself, who weeps over Dido's death, which she brought to pass by love for Aeneas, and who does not weep over his own death, brought to pass by not loving you, O God, light of my heart, bread for the inner mouth of my soul, power wedding together my mind and the bosom of my thoughts? I did not love you, and I committed fornication against you, and amid my fornications from all sides there sounded the words, "Well done! Well done!" Love of this world is fornication against you, but "Well done! Well done!" is said, so that it will be shameful for a man to be otherwise. I did not weep over these facts, but I wept over the dead Dido "who sought her end by the sword." I forsook you, and I followed after your lowest creatures, I who was earth, turning to earth. If I had been forbidden to read those tales, I would have grieved because I could not read what would cause me to grieve. Such folly is deemed a higher and more profitable study than that by which I learned to read and write. . . .

Book II Augustine's Sixteenth Year

Chapter 1 The Depths of Vice

(1) I wish to bring back to mind my past foulness and the carnal corruptions of my soul. This is not because I love them, but that I may love you, my God. Out of love for your love I do this. In the bitterness of my remembrance, I tread again my most evil ways, so that you may grow sweet to me, O sweetness that never fails, O sweetness happy and enduring, which gathers me together again from that disordered state in which I lay in shattered pieces, wherein, turned away from you, the one, I spent myself upon the many. For in my youth, I burned to get my fill of hellish things. I dared to run wild in different darksome ways of love. My comeliness wasted away. I stank in your eyes, but I was pleasing to myself and I desired to be pleasing to the eyes of men.

Chapter 2 Love and Lust

(2) What was there to bring me delight except to love and be loved? But that due measure between soul and soul, wherein lie the bright boundaries of friendship, was not kept. Clouds arose from the slimy desires of the flesh and from youth's seething spring. They clouded over and darkened my soul, so that I could not distinguish the calm light of chaste love from the fog of lust. Both kinds of affection burned confusedly within me and swept my feeble youth over the crags of desire and plunged me into a whirlpool of shameful deeds. Your wrath was raised above me, but I knew it not. I had been deafened by the clanking chains of my mortality, the penalty of my pride of soul. I wandered farther away from you, and you let me go. I was tossed about and spilt out in my fornications; I flowed out and boiled over in them, but you kept silent. Ah, my late-found joy! you kept silent at that time, and farther and farther I went from you, into more and more fruitless seedings of sorrow, with a proud dejection and a weariness without rest. . . .

(4) But I, poor wretch, foamed over: I followed after the sweeping tide of passions and I departed from you. I broke all your laws, but I did not escape your scourges. For what mortal man can do that? You were always present to aid me, merciful in your anger, and charging with the greatest bitterness and disgust all my unlawful pleasures, so that I might seek after pleasure that was free from disgust, to the end that, when I could find it, it would be in, none but you, Lord, in none but you. For you fashion sorrow into a lesson to us. You smite so that you may heal. You slay us, so that we may not die apart from you.

Where was I in that sixteenth year of my body's age, and how long was I exiled from the joys of your house? Then it was that the madness of lust, licensed by human shamelessness but forbidden by your laws, took me completely under its scepter, and I clutched it with both hands. My parents took no care to save me by marriage from plunging into ruin. Their only care was that I should learn to make the finest orations and become a persuasive speaker.

Chapter 4 The Stolen Fruit

(9) Surely, Lord, your law punishes theft, as does that law written on the hearts of men, which not even iniquity itself blots out. What thief puts up with another

thief with a calm mind? Not even a rich thief will pardon one who steals from him because of want. But I willed to commit theft, and I did so, not because I was driven to it by any need, unless it were by poverty of justice, and dislike of it, and by a glut of evil-doing. For I stole a thing of which I had plenty of my own and of much better quality. Nor did I wish to enjoy that thing which I desired to gain by theft, but rather to enjoy the actual theft and the sin of theft.

In a garden nearby to our vineyard there was a pear tree, loaded with fruit that was desirable neither in appearance nor in taste. Late one night to which hour, according to our pestilential custom, we had kept up our street games, a group of very bad youngsters set out to shake down and rob this tree. We took great loads of fruit from it, not for our own eating, but rather to throw it to the pigs; even if we did eat a little of it, we did this to do what pleased us for the reason that it was forbidden.

Behold my heart, O Lord, behold my heart upon which you had mercy in the depths of the pit. Behold, now let my heart tell you what it looked for there, that I should be evil without purpose and that there should be no cause for my evil but evil itself. Foul was the evil, and I loved it. I loved to go down to death. I loved my fault, not that for which I did the fault, but I loved my fault itself. Base in soul was I, and I leaped down from your firm clasp even towards complete destruction, and I sought nothing from the shameful deed but shame itself!

Chapter 6 *The Anatomy of Evil*

(12) What was it that I, a wretch, loved in you, my act of theft, my deed of crime done by night, done in the sixteenth year of my age? You were not beautiful, for you were but an act of thievery. In truth, are you anything at all, that I may speak to you? The fruit we stole, was beautiful, for it was your creation, O most beautiful of all beings, creator of all things, God the good, God the supreme good and my true good. Beautiful was the fruit, but it was not what my unhappy soul desired. I had an abundance of better pears, but those pears I gathered solely that I might steal. The fruit I gathered I threw away, devouring in it only iniquity, and that I rejoiced to enjoy. For if I put any of that fruit into my mouth, my sin was its seasoning. But now, O Lord my God, I seek out what was in that theft to give me delight and lo, there is no loveliness in it. I do not say such loveliness as there is in justice and prudence, or in man's mind, and memory, and senses, and vigorous life, nor that with which the stars are beautiful and glorious in their courses, or the land and the sea filled with their living kinds, which by new births replace those that die, nor even that flawed and shadowy beauty found in the vices that deceive us. . . .

(14) Thus the soul commits fornication when it is turned away from you and, apart from you, seeks such pure, clean things as it does not find except when it returns to you. In a perverse way, all men imitate you who put themselves far from you, and rise up in rebellion against you. Even by such imitation of you they prove that you are the creator of all nature, and that therefore there is no place where they can depart entirely from you.

What, therefore, did I love in that theft of mine, in what manner did I perversely or viciously imitate my Lord? Did it please me to go against your law, at least by trickery, for I could not do so with might? Did it please me that as a captive I should imitate a deformed liberty, by doing with impunity things illicit bearing a shadowy likeness of your omnipotence? Behold, your servant flees from his Lord and follows after a shadow! O rottenness! O monstrous life and deepest death! Could a thing give pleasure which could not be done lawfully, and which was done for no other reason but because it was unlawful?

Chapter 7 Grace That Keeps and Heals

(15) "What shall I render to the Lord," for he recalls these things to my memory, but my soul is not made fearful by them? Lord, I will love you, and give thanks to you, and confess to your name, since you have forgiven me so many evils and so many impious works. To your grace and to your mercy I ascribe it that you have dissolved my sins as if they were ice. To your grace I ascribe also whatsoever evils I have not done. For what evil is there that I, who even loved the crime for its own sake, might not have done? I confess that you have forgiven me all my sins, both those which I have done by my own choice and those which, under your guidance, I have not committed. . . .

Book VIII The Grace of Faith

Chapter 5 The Inner Conflict

(11) Thus I understood from my own experience what I had read, how "the flesh lusts against the spirit, and the spirit against the flesh." I was in both camps, but I was more in that which I approved within myself than in that other which I disapproved within me. For now, in the latter, it was not so much myself, since in large part I suffered it against my will rather than did it voluntarily. Yet it was by me that this habit had been made so warlike against me, since I had come willingly to this point where I now willed not. Who can rightly argue against it, when just punishment comes upon the sinner? Nor did I any longer have that former excuse, in which I used to look upon myself as unable to despise the world and to serve you, because knowledge of the truth was still uncertain to me. Now indeed it was certain to me. Yet I was still bound to the earth, and I refused to become your soldier. I was afraid to be lightened of all my heavy burden, even as I should have feared to be encumbered by it.

Chapter 8 In the Garden

(19) Then, during that great struggle in my inner house, which I had violently raised up against my own soul in our chamber, in my heart, troubled both in mind and in countenance, I turn upon Alypius and cry out to him: "What is the trouble with us? What is this? What did you hear? The unlearned rise up and take heaven by storm, and we, with all our erudition but empty of heart, see how we wallow in flesh and blood! Are we ashamed to follow, because they have gone on ahead of us? Is it no shame to us not even to follow them?" I said some such words, and my anguish of mind tore me from him, while astounded he looked at me and kept silent. I did not speak in my usual way. My brow, cheeks, eyes, color, and tone of voice spoke of my state of mind more than the words that I uttered.

Attached to our lodging there was a little garden; we had the use of it, as of the whole house, for our host, the owner of the house, did not live in it. The tumult within my breast hurried me out into it, where no one would stop the raging combat that I had entered into against myself, until it would come to such an end as you knew of, but as I knew not. I suffered from a madness that was to bring health, and I was in a death agony that was to bring life: for I knew what a thing of evil I was, but I did not know the good that I would be after but a little while I rushed, then, into the garden, and Alypius followed in my steps. Even when he was present, I was not less alone-and how could he desert me when I was reduced to such a state? We sat down as far as we could from the house. Suffering from a most fearful wound, I quaked in spirit, angered by a most turbulent anger, because I did not enter into your will and into a covenant with you, my God. For all my bones cried out to me to enter into that covenant, and by their praises they lifted me up to the skies. Not by ships, or in chariots, or on foot do we enter therein; we need not go even so far as I had gone from the house to the place where we were sitting. For not only to go, but even to go in thither was naught else but the will to go, to will firmly and finally, and not to turn and toss, now here, now there, a struggling, half-maimed will, with one part rising upwards and another falling down. . . .

Chapter 11 The Voice of Continence

(25) Thus I was sick and tormented, and I upbraided myself much more bitterly than ever before. I twisted and turned in my chain, until it might be completely broken, although now I was scarcely held by it, but still held by it I was. Within the hidden depths of my soul, O Lord, you urged me on. By an austere mercy you redoubled the scourges of fear and shame, lest I should give in again, and lest that thin little remaining strand should not be broken through but should grow strong again and bind me yet more firmly.

Within myself I said: "Behold, let it be done now, now let it be done," and by those words I was already moving on to a decision. By then I had almost made it, and yet I did not make it. Still, I did not slip back into my former ways, but close by I stood my ground and regained my breath. Again I tried, and I was but a little away from my goal, just a little away from it, and I all but reached it and laid hold of it. Yet I was not quite there, and I did not reach it, and I did not catch hold of it. I still hesitated to die to death and to live to life, for the ingrown worse had more power over me than the untried better. The nearer came that moment in time when I was to become something different, the greater terror did it strike into me. Yet it did not strike me back, nor did it turn me away, but it held me in suspense.

(26) My lovers of old, trifles of trifles and vanities of vanities, held me back. They plucked at my fleshy garment, and they, whispered softly: "Do you cast us off?" and "From that moment we shall no more be with you forever and ever!" and again, "From that moment no longer will this thing and that be allowed to you, forever and ever!" What did they suggest by what I have called "this thing and that," what, O my God, did they suggest? May your mercy turn away all the from your servant's soul! What filth did they suggest! What deeds of shame! But now by far less than half did I hear them. For now it was not as if they were openly

contradicting me, face to face, but as if they were muttering behind my back, and as if they were furtively picking at me as I left them, to make me look back again. Yet they did delay me, for I hesitated to tear myself away, and shake myself free of them, and leap over to that place where I was called to be. For an overpowering habit kept saying to me, "Do you think that you can live without them?" . . .

Chapter 12 *The Voice as of a Child*

(28) But when deep reflection had dredged out of the secret recesses of my soul all my misery and heaped it up in full view of my heart, there arose a mighty storm, bringing with it a mighty downpour of tears. That I might pour it all forth with its own proper sounds, I arose from Alypius's side-to be alone seemed more proper to this ordeal of weeping-and went farther apart, so that not even his presence would be a hindrance to me. Such was I at that moment, and he sensed it, for I suppose that I had said something in which the sound of my voice already appeared to be choked with weeping. So I had arisen, while he, in deep wonder, remained there where we were sitting. I flung myself down, how I do not know, under a certain fig tree, and gave free rein to my tears. The floods burst from my eyes, an acceptable sacrifice to you. Not indeed in these very words but to this effect I spoke many things to you: "And you, O Lord, how long? How long, O Lord, will you be angry forever? Remember not our past iniquities." For I felt that I was held by them, and I gasped forth these mournful words, "How long, how long? Tomorrow and tomorrow? Why not now? Why not in this very hour an end to my uncleanness?"

(29) Such words I spoke, and with most bitter contrition I wept within my heart. And lo, I heard from a nearby house, a voice like that of a boy or a girl, I know not which, chanting and repeating over and over, "Take up and read. Take up and read." Instantly, with altered countenance, I began to think most intently whether children made use of any such chant in some kind of game, but I could not recall hearing it anywhere. I checked the flow of my tears and got up, for I interpreted this solely as a command given to me by God to open the book and read the first chapter I should come upon. For I had heard how Anthony had been admonished by a reading from the Gospel at which he chanced to be present, as if the words read were addressed to him: "Go, sell what you have, and give to the poor, and you shall have treasure in heaven, and come, follow me," and that by such a portent he was immediately converted to you.

So I hurried back to the spot where Alypius was sitting, for I had put there the volume of the apostle when I got up and left him. I snatched it up, opened it, and read in silence the chapter on which my eyes first fell: "Not in rioting and drunkenness, not in chambering and impurities, not in strife and envying; but put you on the Lord Jesus Christ; and make not provision for the flesh in its concupiscences." No further wished; I to read, nor was there need to do so. Instantly, in truth, at the end of this sentence, as if before a peaceful light streaming into my heart, all the dark shadows of doubt fled away.

(30) Then, having inserted my finger, or with some other mark, I closed the book, and, with a countenance now calm, I told it all to Alypius. What had taken place in him, which I did not know about, he then made known to me.

He asked to see what I had read: I showed it to him, and he looked also at what came after what I had read for I did not know what followed. It was this that followed: "Now him that is weak in the faith take unto you," which he applied to himself and disclosed to me. By this admonition he was strengthened, and by a good resolution and purpose, which were entirely in keeping with his character, wherein both for a long time and for the better he had greatly differed from me, he joined me without any painful hesitation.

Thereupon we went in to my mother; we told her the story, and she rejoiced. We related just how it happened. She was filled with exultation and triumph, and she blessed you, "who are able to do above that which we ask or think." She saw that through me you had given her far more than she had long begged for by her piteous tears and groans. For you had converted me to yourself, so that I would seek neither wife nor ambition in this world, for I would stand on that rule of faith where, so many years before, you had showed me to her. You turned her mourning into a joy far richer than that she had desired, far dearer and purer than that she had sought in grandchildren born of my flesh.

Book IX The New Catholic

Chapter 1 A Soul Set Free

(1) "O Lord, I am your servant; I am your servant and the son of your handmaid. You have broken my bonds: I will sacrifice to you the sacrifice of praise." Grant that my heart and my tongue may praise you. Grant that all my bones may say, "Lord who is like unto you?" Grant that they may speak, and deign to answer me and "say to my soul: I am your salvation."

Who am I, and what am I? Is there any evil that is not found in my acts, or if not in my acts, in my words, or if not in my words, in my will? But you, O Lord, are good and merciful, and your right hand has had regard for the depth of my death, and from the very bottom of my heart it has emptied out an abyss of corruption. This was the sum of it: not to will what I willed and to will what you willed.

But throughout these long years where was my free will? Out of what deep and hidden pit was it called forth in a single moment, wherein to bend my neck to your mild yoke and my shoulders to your light burden, O Christ Jesus, "my helper and my redeemer?" How sweet did it suddenly become to me to be free of the sweets of folly: things that I once feared to lose it was now joy to put away. You cast them forth from me, you the true and highest sweetness, you cast them forth, and in their stead you entered in, sweeter than every pleasure, but not to flesh and blood, brighter than every light, but deeper within me than any secret retreat, higher than every honor, but not to those who exalt" themselves. Now was my mind free from the gnawing cares of favor-seeking, of striving for gain, of wallowing in the mire, and of scratching lust's itchy sore. I spoke like a child to you, my light, my wealth, my salvation, my Lord God.

Questions

1. In Book I, Chapter 6, why did Augustine mix his philosophical discussion of God's nature with his personal discussion of how he was nursed as an infant?

2. In Book I, Chapter 13, Augustine compares the limited value of literature and the great value of learning to read and write. Why is Augustine so negative about literature? What is Augustine focusing on, and what is he overlooking?

3. In Book II, Chapters 4 and 6, Augustine focuses on a single moment when he steals some fruit at the age of sixteen. Why is this event important?

4. In Book IX, Chapter 1, Augustine writes, "But throughout these long years where was my free will?" What does he mean by "free will" in this context?

PETRARCH

Known as **"Petrarch,"** Francesco Petrarca (1304–1374) lived in what is now Italy and southern France. He was a self-styled man of the early Renaissance; in other words, he consciously cultivated an image of himself to present to the world. An important part of that image was his constant examination of his inner experiences. Common themes in this self-exposure were (a) his self condemnation, (b) his obsessive love for a mysterious woman named Laura, and (c) his longing for fame and greatness—particularly as a writer. In a sense, his presentation of himself to the public is similar to the ways in which some of today's pop stars and athletes cultivate an image for the public. Petrarch was also a great "Man of Letters." He produced hundreds of carefully worked poems, hundreds of published letters, and many books dealing with wide-ranging topics.

Petrarch's letter, "The Ascent of Mount Ventoux," gives a taste of his style, his public image of himself, and his spiritual concerns. Petrarch wrote what looks like a simple letter to a friend and religious confessor. (The references to "my father" are religious, not biological. His biological father died when Petrarch was a young man.)

The letter gives a simple description of Petrarch's climb up a mountain in the Alps in southern France. Yet, the letter is so much more. Petrarch, who was not a nobleman, compared himself to a Greek king. This was a very presumptuous way to introduce himself to readers who revered kings. Yet, he also made himself look foolish in comparison to his brother, who confidently and directly climbs up the mountain. At the top, Petrarch randomly opens his pocket-copy of Augustine's *Confessions* and begins to read a passage that particularly touches his heart. This is not the only connection that Petrarch has with Augustine. Later, Petrarch wrote a book, *Secretum,* which is an imagined dialogue between the two men. In that book, and in this letter, Petrarch is concerned and frustrated by the large gap between his spiritual ideals and his daily life. This gap between spiritual ideals and daily life has plagued humans throughout history. Earlier, Jesus taunted the religious leaders of his day with this gap, and this gap would soon lead to the Reformation across Europe.

To further understand Petrarch, you are encouraged to read some of his poetry to and about Laura. In these poems, he seems to enjoy glorifying himself while also deprecating himself. He simultaneously presents himself as a fool and as extremely insightful, and as simultaneously religious and irreligious.

THE ASCENT OF MOUNT VENTOUX

Today I climbed the highest mountain in this region, which is not improperly called Ventosum (Windy). The only motive for my ascent was the wish to see what so great a height had to offer. I had had the project in mind for many years, for, as you know, I have lived in these parts from childhood on, having been cast there by the fate which determines human affairs. And so the mountain, which is visible from a great distance, was always before my eyes, and for a long time I planned on doing what I have finally done today. The impulse to make the climb actually took hold of me while I was reading Livy's History of Rome yesterday, and I happened upon the place where Philip of Macedon, the one who waged the war against the Romans, climbed Mount Haemus in Thessaly. From its summit, it was reported that he was able to see two seas, the Adriatic and the Euxine. Whether this is true or false I do not know, for the mountain is too far away, and there is disagreement among the commentators. Pomponius Mela, the cosmographer—not to mention the many others who have talked about this occurrence—accepts the truth of this statement without hesitation while Livy, on the other hand, thinks it false. I, certainly, would not have left the question long in doubt if that mountain had been as easy to explore as this one. But let us drop the matter and return to my mountain here: I thought it proper for a young man in private life to attempt what no one would criticize in an aged king.

When I thought about looking for a companion for the ascent I realized, strangely enough, that hardly any of my friends were suitable—so rarely does one find, even among those most dear to one, the perfect combination of character and purpose. One was too phlegmatic, another too anxious; one too slow, another too hasty; one too sad, another too happy; one too simple, another more sagacious than I would like. I was frightened by the fact that one never spoke while another talked too much; the heavy deliberation of some repelled me as much as the lean incapacity of others. I rejected some for their cold lack of interest and others for their excessive enthusiasm. Such defects as these, however grave, are tolerable enough at home (for charity suffers all things, and friendship rejects no burden), but it is another matter on a journey, where such weaknesses become more serious. So, with only my own pleasure in mind, with great care I looked about weighing the various characteristics of my friends against one another without committing any breach of friendship and silently condemning any trait which might prove to be disagreeable on my journey. And would you believe it? I finally turned to my own family for help and proposed the ascent to my younger brother, the only one I have, and whom you know well. He was delighted beyond measure and gratified by the thought of acting at the same time as a friend as well as a brother.

On the appointed day we left the house and by evening reached Malaucène which lies at the foot of the mountain on the north side. We rested there a day and finally this morning made the ascent with no one except two servants. And it is a most difficult task indeed, for the mountain is a very steep and almost inaccessible mass of rocky terrain. But, as a poet once put it well: 'Remorseless labour conquers all.' The day was long and the air invigorating, our spirits were high and our agile bodies strong, and everything else necessary for such an undertaking helped us on our way. The only difficulty we had to face was the nature of the place itself. We found an old shepherd among the mountain's ridges who tried at great length to discourage us from the ascent, saying that some fifty years before he had, in the same ardour of youth, climbed to the summit and had got nothing from it except fatigue and repentance and torn clothes and scratches from the rocks and briars. Never, according to what he or his friends knew, had anyone ever tried the ascent before or after him. But his counsels merely increased our eagerness to go on, as a young man's mind is usually suspicious of warnings. So the old man, finding his efforts were useless, went along with us a little way and pointed out a steep path among the rocks, continuing to cry out admonitions even after we had left him behind. Having left him with those garments and anything else we thought might prove burdensome to us, we made ready for the ascent and started to climb at a good pace. But, as often happens, fatigue soon followed upon our strenuous effort, and before long we had to rest on some rock. Then we started on again, but more slowly, I especially taking the rocky path at a more modest pace. My brother chose the steepest course straight up the ridge, while I weakly took an easier one which turned along the slopes. And when he called me back showing me the shorter way, I replied that I hoped to find an easier way up on the other side, and that I did not mind taking a longer course if it were not so steep. But this was merely an excuse for my laziness; and when the others had already reached a considerable height I was still wandering in the hollows, and having failed to find an easier means of ascent, I had only lengthened the journey and increased the difficulty of the ascent. Finally I became disgusted with the tedious way I had chosen, and decided to climb straight up. By the time I reached my brother, who had managed to have a good rest while waiting for me, I was tired and irritated. We walked along together for a while, but hardly had we left that rise when I forgot all about the circuitous route I had just taken and again tended to take a lower one. Thus, once again I found myself taking the easy way, the roundabout path of winding hollows, only to find myself soon back in my old difficulty. I was simply putting off the trouble of climbing; but no man's wit can alter the nature of things, and there is no way to reach the heights by going downward. In short, I tell you that I made this same mistake three or more times within a few hours, much to my brother's amusement and my anger.

After being misled in this way a number of times, I finally sat down in a hollow and my thoughts quickly turned from material things to the spiritual, and I said to myself more or less what follows: 'What you have experienced so often today in the ascent of this mountain, certainly happens to you as it does to many others in their journey toward the blessèd life. But this is not so easily perceived by men, for the movements of the body are out in the open while those of the soul are invisible and hidden. The life we call blessèd is to be sought on a high level, and straight is the way that leads to it. Many, also, are the hills that stand in the way that leads to it, and we must ascend from virtue to virtue up glorious steps. At the summit is both the end of our struggles and the goal of our journey's climb. Everyone wishes to reach this goal, but, as Ovid says: "To wish is not enough; you must yearn with ardent eagerness to gain your end." And you certainly both wish and ardently yearn, unless you are deceiving yourself in this matter, as you so often do. What, then, is holding you back? Nothing, surely, except that you take a path which seems at first sight easier leading through low and worldly pleasures. Nevertheless in the end, after long wanderings, you will either have to climb up the steeper path under the burden of labours long deferred to its blessed culmination, or lie down in the valley of your sins; and—I shudder to think of it!—if the shadow of death finds you there, you will spend an eternal night in constant torment.' These thoughts stimulated my body and mind to a remarkable degree and made me face up to the difficulties which still remained. Oh, that my soul might follow that other road for which I long day and night, even as today I conquered material obstacles by bodily force! And why should it not be far easier: after all, the agile, immortal soul can reach its goal in the twinkling of an eye without intermediate space, while progress today had to be slow because my feeble body was burdened by its heavy members.

One mountain peak, the highest of all, the country people call Filiolus ('Sonny'); why, I do not know, unless by antiphrasis, as is sometimes the case, for the peak in question seems to be the father of all the surrounding ones. At its top is a little level place, and it was there that we could, at last, rest our weary bodies.

My good father, since you have listened to the troubles mounting in the heart of a man who ascends, listen now to the rest of the story, and devote one hour, I pray you, to reviewing the events of my day. At first, because I was not accustomed to the quality of the air and the effect of the wide expanse of view spread out before me, I stood there like a dazed person. I could see the clouds under our feet, and the tales I had read of Athos and Olympus seemed less incredible as I myself was witnessing the very same things from a less famous mountain. I turned my eyes toward Italy, the place to which my heart was most inclined. The great and snow-capped Alps seemed to rise close by, though they were far away—those same Alps through which that fierce enemy of the Roman name once made his way, splitting the rocks, if we can believe the story, by means of vinegar. I sighed, I must admit, for Italian skies which I beheld more with my thought than with my eyes, and an inexpressible longing came over me to see once more my friend and my country, though at the same time I reproached myself for this double weakness which came from a soul not yet up to manly resistance—and yet there were excuses for both my desires, and several excellent authorities could be cited to support me.

Then a new idea came to me, and I started thinking in terms of time rather than space. I thought: 'Today marks ten years since you completed your youthful studies and left Bologna. Oh, eternal God! Oh, immutable wisdom! Think of all the changes in your character these intervening years have seen! I suppress a great deal, for I have not yet reached a safe harbour where I can calmly recall past storms. The time, perhaps, will come when I can review all the experiences of the past in their order saying with the words of your St Augustine: "I wish to recall my foul past and the carnal corruption of my soul, not that I love them, but that I may the more love you, O my God." Much that is dubious and evil still clings to me, but what I once loved, I love no longer. Come now, what am I saying? I still love it, but more moderately. No, not so, but with more shame, with more heaviness of heart. Now, at last, I have told the truth. The fact is I love, but I love what I long not to love, what I would like to hate. Though I hate to do so, though constrained, though sad and sorrowing, I love none the less, and I feel in my miserable self the meaning of the well-known words: "I will hate if I can; if not, I will love against my will!" Not three years have passed since that perverse and wicked desire which had me in tight hold and held undisputed sway in my heart began to discover a rebellious opponent who was no longer willing to yield in obedience. These two adversaries have joined in close combat for supremacy, and for a long time now a gruelling war, the outcome of which is still doubtful, has been waging in the field of my mind.'

Thus my thoughts turned back over the last ten years, and then with concentrated thought on the future, I asked myself: 'If you should, by chance, prolong this uncertain life of yours for another ten years, advancing toward virtue in proportion to the distance from which you departed from your original infatuation during the past two years since the new longing first encountered the old, could you not face death on reaching forty years of age, if not with complete assurance at least with hopefulness, calmly dismissing from your thoughts the residuum of life that fades into old age?'

Such thoughts as these, father, occurred to me. I rejoiced in my progress, mourned for my weaknesses, and took pity on universal inconstancy of human conduct. I had by this time forgotten where I was and why we had come; then, dismissing my anxieties to a more appropriate occasion, I decided to look about me and see what we had come to see. The sun was sinking and the shadows of the mountain were already lengthening below, warning us that the time for us to go was near at hand. As if suddenly roused from sleep, I turned to gaze at the west. I could not see the tops of the Pyrenees, which form the barrier between France and Spain, not because of any intervening obstacle that I know of but simply because of the inadequacy of mortal vision. But off to the right I could see most clearly the mountains of the region around Lyons and to the left the bay of Marseilles and the sea that beats against the shores of Aigues-Mortes, though all these places were at a distance requiring a journey of several days to reach them. The Rhône was flowing under our very eyes.

While my thoughts were divided thus, now turning my attention to thoughts of some worldly object before me, now uplifting my soul, as I had done my body, to higher planes, it occurred to me to look at Augustine's *Confessions,* a gift of your love that I always keep with me in memory of the author and the giver. I opened the little volume, small in size but infinitely sweet, with the intention of reading whatever came to hand, for what else could I happen upon if not edifying and devout words. Now I happened by chance to open it to the tenth book. My brother stood attentively waiting to hear what St Augustine would say from my lips. As God is my witness and my brother too, the first words my eyes fell upon were: 'And men go about admiring the high mountains and the mighty waves of the sea and the wide sweep of rivers and the sound of the ocean and the movement of the stars, but they themselves they abandon.' I was ashamed, and asking my brother, who was anxious to hear more, not to bother me, I closed the book, angry with myself for continuing to admire the things of this world when I should have learned a long time ago from the pagan philosophers themselves that nothing is admirable but the soul beside whose greatness nothing can be as great. Then, having seen enough of the mountain I turned an inward eye upon myself, and from that moment on not a syllable passed my lips until we reached the bottom. The words I had read had given me enough food for thought and I could not believe that I happened to turn to them by mere chance. I believed that what I had read there was written for me and no one else, and I remembered that St Augustine had once thought the same thing in his own case, as he himself tells us when opening the book of the Apostle, the first words he saw were: 'Not in rioting and drunkenness, not in chambering and wantonness, not in strife and envy, but put ye on the Lord Jesus Christ, and make not provision for the flesh in its concupiscences.' The same thing happened earlier to St Anthony, as he listened to the Gospel where it is written, 'If thou wilt be perfect, go and sell what thou hast, and give to the poor, and thou shalt have treasure in heaven; and come follow me.' He believed this scripture to have been spoken specifically for him, and by means of it he guided himself to the Kingdom of Heaven, as the biographer Athanasius tells us. And as Anthony on hearing these words asked for nothing more, and as Augustine after reading the Apostle's admonition sought no farther, so did I conclude my reading after the few words which I have recorded. I thought in silence of the vanity in us mortals who neglect what is noblest in ourselves in a vain show only because we look around ourselves for what can be found only within us. I wondered at the natural nobility of that human soul which unless degenerate has deserted its original state and turned to dishonour what God has given it for its honour. How many times I turned back that day to look at the mountain top which seemed scarcely more than a cubit high compared with the height of human contemplation, unless it is immersed in the foulness of earth? As I descended I asked myself: 'If we are willing to endure so much sweat and labour in order to raise our bodies a little closer to heaven, how can a soul struggling toward God, up the steeps of human pride and mortal destiny, fear any cross or prison or sting of fortune?' How few, I thought, are they who are not diverted from this path for fear of hardship or the love of ease! And how happy those few, if any such there be! It is they, I feel, the poet had in mind when he wrote:

> *Blessèd the man who is skilled to understand*
> *The hidden cause of things; who beneath his feet*
> *All fear casts, and death's relentless doom,*
> *And the howlings of greedy Acheron.*

How earnestly should we strive to trample beneath our feet not mountain–tops but the appetites which spring from earthly impulses!

In the middle of the night, unaware of the difficulties of the way back and amid the preoccupations which I have so frankly revealed, we came by the friendly light of a full moon to the little inn which we had left that morning before day-break. Then, while the servants were busy preparing our supper, I spent my time in a secluded part of the house, hurriedly and extemporane-ously writing all this down, fearing that if I were to put off the task, my mood would change on leaving the place, and I would lose interest in writing to you.

You see, dearest father, that I wish to conceal nothing of myself from you. I describe to you not only the course of my life but even my individual thoughts. And I ask for your prayers that these vague and wandering thoughts of mine may some day become coherent and, having been so vainly cast in all directions, that they may direct themselves at last to the one, true, certain, and never-ending good.

Questions

1. Petrarch listed at least two motives for climbing the mountain. How are the two motives connected?
2. Given the shortness of this letter, why did Petrarch give so much space to a comparison of how he climbed the mountain with how his brother climbed the mountain?
3. How would you compare Petrarch's inner struggles with the struggles of Augustine? How would you compare Petrarch's spiritual state with the state of peace that Augustine achieves in *Confessions?*
4. How does Petrarch's view of God and Christianity compare with your views?

JEAN-JACQUES ROUSSEAU

Jean-Jacques Rousseau (1712–1778) was born in the French-speaking city of Geneva, Switzerland. He lived, studied, tutored, and wrote in various European locations, including Geneva, London, Paris, and other cities in Switzerland, France, and Italy. He was born a Calvinist (because of his Genevan citizenship). He later converted to Roman Catholicism while in France, but reverted to Calvinism in order to reclaim his Genevan citizenship. During his life, Rousseau associated with some of the brightest minds of the Enlightenment, such as David Hume and Denis Diderot. Yet, Rousseau helped to push European thought out of the Enlightenment and toward Romanticism's emphasis on exploring one's pas-sions and inner experiences. Rousseau influenced (and continues to influence) the fields of philosophy, educational theory, music, and literature.

The title of Rousseau's autobiography, *Confessions,* alludes to Augustine's autobiography. Both works begin with the birth of the author and review the daily struggles of youth. Both works recount the authors' formal education, youthful mischief, serious moral failures, career moves, philosophical struggles, and personal relationships. Both men were very intelligent and very successful. In spite of this skeletal outline of similarities, the works are radically different. Augustine's *Confessions* is a book-length prayer of confession to a powerful, pursuing, and loving God. In Augustine's work, the reader is flooded with references to God's character and to Augustine's relationship with that God. In contrast, God, religion, and spiritual issues play an extremely minor role in Rousseau's *Confessions*. Rousseau might have regretted a particular action or briefly felt a pang of guilt, but his work lacks Augustine's lengthy discussions of moral guilt, spiritual sorrow, and heartfelt "brokenness." The mind of Augustine was filled with the constant interaction between himself and God, whereas Rousseau's mind, in *Confessions,* was constantly focused on his social relationships—particularly his encounters with women—and on his relationship with himself. Thus, Petrarch and Rousseau, who both admired Augustine, did not share the values or spiritual commitments of Augustine. Spirituality at least was a distant hope for Petrarch, but spirituality did not even seem to appear on Rousseau's horizon.

FROM CONFESSIONS

[Rousseau's mother died after his birth.] I was almost born dead, and they had little hope of saving me. I brought with me the seed of a disorder which has grown stronger with the years, and now gives me only occasional intervals of relief in which to suffer more painfully in some other way. But one of my father's sisters, a nice sensible woman, bestowed such care on me that I survived; and now, as I write this, she is still alive at the age of eighty, nursing a husband rather younger than herself but ruined by drink. My dear aunt, I pardon you for causing me to live, and I deeply regret that I cannot repay you in the evening of your days all the care and affection you lavished on me at the dawn of mine. My nurse Jacqueline is still alive too, and healthy and strong. Indeed the fingers that opened my eyes at birth may well close them at my death.

I suffered before I began to think: which is the common fate of man, though crueller in my case than in another's. I know nothing of myself till I was five or six. I do not know how I learnt to read. I only remember my first books and their effect upon me; it is from my earliest reading that I date the unbroken consciousness of my own existence. My mother had possessed some novels, and my father and I began to read them after our supper. At first it was only to give me some practice in reading. But soon my interest in this entertaining literature became so strong that we read by turns continuously, and spent whole nights so engaged. For we could never leave off till the end of the book. Sometimes my father would say with shame as we heard the morning larks: 'Come, let us go to bed. I am more of a child than you are.'

In a short time I acquired by this dangerous method, not only an extreme facility in reading and expressing myself, but a singular insight for my age into the passions. I had no idea of the facts, but I was already familiar with every feeling. I had grasped nothing; I had sensed everything. These confused emotions which I experienced one after another, did not warp my reasoning powers in any way, for as yet I had none. But they shaped them after a special pattern, giving me the strangest and most romantic notions about human life, which neither experience nor reflection has ever succeeded in curing me of.

The novels gave out in the summer of 1719, and that winter we changed
our reading. Having exhausted my mother's library, we turned to that portion of
her father's which had fallen to us. Fortunately it contained some good books,
as it could hardly fail to do, for the collection had been formed by a minister,
who deserved the title, a man of learning, after the fashion of his day, but of
taste and good sense as well. Lesueur's *History of Church and Empire,* Bossuet's
Discourse upon Universal History, Plutarch's *Lives,* Nani's *History of Venice,*
Ovid's: *Metamorphoses,* La Bruyère, Fontenelle's *Worlds* and his *Dialogues with
the Dead,* and some volumes of Molière were transported to my father's workshop, where I read them to him every day while he worked.

Thus I acquired a sound taste, which was perhaps unique for my years.
Plutarch, of them all, was my especial favourite, and the pleasure I took in reading and re-reading him did something to cure me of my passion for novels.
Soon indeed I came to prefer Agesilaus, Brutus, and Aristides to Orondates,
Artamenes, and Juba. It was this enthralling reading, and the discussions it gave
rise to between my father and myself, that created in me that proud and in-
tractable spirit, that impatience with the yoke of servitude, which has afflicted
me throughout my life, in those situations least fitted to afford it scope.
Continuously preoccupied with Rome and Athens, living as one might say with
their great men, myself born the citizen of a republic and the son of a father
whose patriotism was his strongest passion, I took fire by his example and pictured myself as a Greek or a Roman. I became indeed that character whose life
I was reading; the recital of his constancy or his daring deeds so carrying me
away that my eyes sparkled and my voice rang. [. . .]

[Rousseau rans away from his apprenticeship and goes to France. There
he meets a priest who promises to help him.] Far from thinking of sending me
home, he took such advantage of my desire to run away as to make it impossible for me to go back even if I had wanted to. There was every probability that
he was sending me to perish of hunger or to become a vagabond. He did not
care about that. What he saw was a soul to be plucked from heresy and reconciled to the Church. Honest man or vagabond, what did that matter so long as I
went to Mass? It must not be supposed, however, that this way of thinking is
confined to Catholics. It is common to every dogmatic religion which makes
faith the essential, not deeds.

'God is calling you,' said M. de Pontverre. 'Go to Annecy. There you will find
a good and charitable lady, whom the King, of his bounty, has empowered to save
other souls from the error under which she once laboured herself.' He was speaking of Mme de Warens, a recent convert, who was more or less compelled by the
priests to share a pension of two thousand francs allowed her by the King of
Sardinia, with any riff-raff that came to trade their religion for money. I felt greatly
humiliated at standing in need of a good and charitable woman. What I wanted
was to be given my bare necessities, but not to receive alms, and the idea of a
pious lady did not much attract me. But urged on by M. de Pontverre, hard
pressed by hunger, and glad too to be setting out on a journey with an end in
view, I made up my mind, though with some difficulty, and departed for Annecy.
I could easily have got there in one day, but I did not hurry; I took three.

I did not see a castle on the left or the right without setting off to seek the adventure which I was sure awaited me there. I neither dared to enter nor yet to knock, for I was exceedingly timid. But I sang under what looked the likeliest window, and was very surprised after singing my loudest for a considerable time to see no ladies or maidens appear, attracted by the beauty of my voice or by the wit of my songs. For I knew some good songs, which I had learnt from my comrades and which I sang extremely well.

Finally I arrived and saw Mme de Warens. This stage in my life has been decisive in the formation of my character, and I cannot make up my mind to pass lightly over it. I was half way through my sixteenth year and, without being what is called a handsome youth, I was well-made for my modest size, had a pretty foot, a fine leg, an independent air, lively features, a small mouth, black eyebrows and hair, and small, rather sunken eyes which sparkled with the fire that burnt in my veins. Unfortunately I knew nothing of all this. For all my life I have never thought of my appearance until the moment has passed for turning it to account. So the timidity natural to my years was heightened by my very affectionate nature, which was always troubled by the fear of displeasing. Moreover, whilst I had a fairly cultivated mind, never having seen the world, I was quite innocent of good manners; and my education, far from remedying this defect, merely increased my nervousness by making me conscious of my shortcomings.

Fearing therefore that my appearance did not speak in my favour, I sought my advantage in other ways. I wrote a fine letter in a rhetorical style, mingling phrases from books with the language of an apprentice, thus endeavouring with all my eloquence to win Mme de Warens's favour. With this letter I enclosed M. de Pontverre's and set out to make the dreaded call. I did not find Mme de Warens in, but was told that she had just left to go to church. It was Palm Sunday in the year 1728. I ran after her, saw her, caught her up, and spoke to her. Indeed I ought to remember the place, for often since I have bathed it with my tears and smothered it with kisses. I should like to surround that happy spot with railings of gold, and make it an object of universal veneration. Whoever delights to honour the memorials of man's salvation should approach it only on his knees.

It was a passage behind her house, with a stream on the right dividing it from her garden, and a yard wall on the left. It led by a private door into the Franciscan church. As she was about to enter that door I called. Mme de Warens turned back. How the sight of her affected me! I had expected M. de Pontverre's 'good lady' to be a disagreeable and pious old woman; to my mind, she could not be otherwise. But what I saw was a face full of charm, large and lovely blue eyes beaming with kindness, a dazzling complexion and the outline of an enchanting neck. Nothing escaped the rapid glance of the young proselyte. For in a moment I was hers, and certain that a faith preached by such missionaries would not fail to lead to paradise. She smiled as she took the letter that I held out to her with a trembling hand. She opened it, glanced over M. de Pontverre's enclosure, came to mine, and read it all through. Indeed she would have read it through again if her footman had not warned that it was time to go into church. 'Well, my child,' she said to me in a voice that made me start, 'you're very young to go wandering about the country. It's a shame, really it is.' Then without waiting for my reply, she added, 'Go to my house and wait for me there. Tell them to give you some breakfast. After mass I'll come and talk to you. [. . .]

She had been at Annecy six years* when I arrived, and she was then twenty-eight, having been born with the century. Her beauty was of a kind that endures, lying more in the expression than in the features; and so it was still at its height. Her manner was tender and caressing, her gaze was very mild, her smile angelic, her mouth small like mine, her hair, which was ash blond and extraordinarily plentiful, she wore with an affected negligence that increased her attraction. She was small in stature, almost short, and rather, stout, though not in an ungainly way; but a lovelier head, a lovelier throat, lovelier hands, and lovelier arms it would have been impossible to find. [. . .]

From the first day the sweetest intimacy was established between us, and it continued to prevail during the rest of her life. 'Little one' was my name, hers was 'Mamma', and we always remained 'Little one' and 'Mamma', even when the passage of the years had almost effaced the difference between our ages. The two names, I find, admirably express the tone of our behaviour, the simplicity of our habits and, what is more, the relation between our hearts. To me she was the most tender of mothers, who never thought of her own pleasure but always of my good. And if there was a sensual side of my attachment to her, that did not alter its character, but only made it more enchanting. I was intoxicated with delight at having a young and pretty mamma whom I loved to caress. I use *caress* in the strict sense of the word, for she never thought of grudging me kisses or the tender caresses of a mother, and it never entered my thoughts to abuse them. It will be objected that we had in the end a relationship of a different character. I agree. But wait, I cannot tell everything at the same time.

The sudden moment of our first meeting was the only truly passionate one she ever made me feel. But that moment was the product of surprise. My glances never went wandering indiscreetly beneath her kerchief, though an ill-concealed plumpness in that region might well have attracted them. I felt neither emotions nor desires in her presence; my stare was one of blissful calm, in which I enjoyed I knew not what. I could have spent my life like that and eternity as well, without a moment's boredom. She is the only person with whom I never suffered from that inability to find words that makes the maintenance of conversation such a penance to me. Our time together was spent less in conversation than in one interminable gossip, which required an interruption to bring it to an end. I needed no compulsion to talk; it almost needed compulsion to silence me. As she often thought over her plans, she often fell into reveries. I let her dream on. I gazed on her in silence and was the happiest of men. I had another singular habit. I never claimed the favour of being alone with her, but I ceaselessly sought opportunities for private interviews, which I enjoyed with a passion that turned to fury whenever troublesome visitors came to disturb us. As soon as anyone arrived—whether man or woman, it did not matter which— I went out grumbling, for I could never bear to remain with a third party. Then I would stay in her ante-chamber, counting the minutes and continually cursing her eternal visitors, quite unable to conceive how they could have so much to say since I had so much more.

I only felt the full strength of my attachment to her when she was out of my sight. When I could see her I was merely happy. But my disquiet when she was away became almost painful. My inability to live without her caused me outbreaks of tenderness which often concluded with tears. I shall always remember how, on a Saint's day, while she was at vespers, I went for a walk outside the town, with my heart fill of the thought of her and with a burning desire to spend my days beside her. I had sense enough to see that for the present this was impossible, that a happiness so deeply enjoyed must needs be short. This gave my thoughts a sad tinge, but not a gloomy one. For it was tempered by a flattering hope. The sound of the bells, which has always singularly moved me, the song of the birds, the beauty of the day, the calm of the countryside, the scattered country dwellings, one of which I fancifully pictured as our common home—all these produced so vivid an impression upon me, raised in me so tender, sad, and touching a mood, that I saw myself ecstatically transported into that happy time and place in which my heart would possess everything it could desire, and in which I should enjoy it all with indescribable rapture, yet without so much as a thought of sensual pleasure. I do not remember ever having leapt into the future with greater force and illusion than I did then. And what has struck me most about my memory of this dream, now that it has been realized, is that eventually I found things exactly as I imagined them. If ever a waking man's dream seemed like a prophetic vision, that reverie of mine did. I was only deceived in my dream's seeming duration. For in it days and years and a whole life passed in changeless tranquillity, whilst in reality the whole experience was only a momentary one. Alas, my most lasting happiness was in a dream. Its fruition was almost immediately succeeded by my awakening.

I should never finish were I to describe in detail all the follies which the memory of my dear Mamma caused me to commit when I was out of her sight. How often have I kissed my bed because she had slept in it; my curtains, all the furniture of my room, since they belonged to her and her fair hand had touched them; even the floor on to which I threw myself, calling to mind how she had walked there! Sometimes even in her presence I fell into extravagances that seemed as if they could only have been inspired by the most violent love. One day at table, just as she had put some food into her mouth, I cried out that I had seen a hair in it. She spat the morsel back on her plate, whereupon I seized it greedily and swallowed it. In a word, there was but one difference between myself and the most passionate of lovers. But that difference was an essential one, and sufficient to render my whole condition inexplicable in the light of reason. [. . .]

I had returned from Italy a different person from the one who had gone there. Perhaps no one of my age had ever come back in as strange a state as I. I had preserved my physical but not my moral virginity. The progress of the years had told upon me, and my restless temperament had at last made itself felt. Its first quite involuntary outbreak indeed had caused me some alarm about my health, a fact which illustrates better than anything else the innocence in which I had lived till then. Soon I was reassured, however, and learned that dangerous means of cheating nature, which leads in young men of my temperament to various kinds of excesses, that eventually imperil their health, their strength, and sometimes their lives. This vice, which shame and timidity find so convenient, has a particular attraction for lively imaginations. It allows them to dispose, so to speak, of the whole female sex at their will, and to make any beauty who tempts them serve their pleasure without the need of first obtaining her consent. Seduced by this fatal advantage, I set about destroying the sturdy constitution which Nature had restored to me, and which I had allowed sufficient time to ripen. Added to my temptations, too, were the circumstances in which I lived, in the house of a pretty woman, fondling her image in my secret heart, seeing her continually throughout the day, and surrounded at night by objects to remind me of her, lying in a bed where I knew she had lain. How much to stimulate me! Let the reader imagine my condition, and he will think of me as already half-dead! But I was far from it. What might have been my undoing was in fact my salvation, at least for a time. Intoxicated with the pleasure of living beside her, and burning with desire to spend my life with her, I saw in her always, whether she were absent or present, a tender mother, a beloved sister, a delightful friend, and nothing more. I saw her always in that way, as always the same, and never any other woman. Her picture was always present in my heart and left room for no one else. For me she was the only woman in the whole world; and the utter sweetness of the feelings she inspired in me, leaving my senses no time to be roused by others, safeguarded me against her and all her sex. In a word, I was chaste because I loved her. I cannot easily describe her effect upon me. But from its results any reader can judge the nature of my affection for her. All that I can say is that, extraordinary though this state of things may seem, in the sequel it will appear even more so. [. . .]

[Believing that a sickness would lead to death, Rousseau re-evaluates his life.] This accident, which might have killed me altogether, only extinguished my passions; and I thank Heaven every day for this beneficial effect which it had on my soul, I can well say that I did not begin to live until I looked on myself as a dead man. Estimating the things I was about to leave behind me at their true value, I began to concern myself with nobler preoccupations, as if in anticipation of the duties I should soon have to fulfil and which I had seriously neglected till then. I had frequently made fun of religion in my own way, but I had never been totally without it. So it was less difficult for me to revert to a subject which many people find so melancholy, but which is sweet to anyone who finds in it a source of hope and consolation. Mamma was more helpful to me in this respect than all the theologians in the world could have been.

Since she always reduced things to a system, she had not failed to treat religion in this way, and her system was made up of the most ill-assorted ideas, some of them extremely sensible, and others most foolish, of feelings that were the product of her character and of prejudices derived from her education. Believers in general create God in their own image; the good make Him good, the evil, evil; fanatics, being full of hatred and bile, can see only Hell, because they wish to damn the whole world, while gentle, loving souls hardly believe in such a place. I can scarcely get over my astonishment at finding the good

Fénelon speak of it in his *Telemachus* as if he really believed in it. But I hope that he was lying at the time; for after all, however truthful a man may be, he must lie sometimes if he is a bishop. Mamma did not lie to me. Being a creature free from gall, she could not imagine a vindictive and ever-wrathful deity; where fanatics see justice and punishment she saw only mercy and pity. Often she would say that there would be no justice in God if he were to be strictly just towards us. For since he has not made us such as to be good he would then be requiring of us more than he has given. The queer thing was that though she did not believe in Hell she believed in purgatory. This arose from the fact that she did not know what to do about the souls of the wicked, being equally incapable of damning them and of putting them with the good until they become so themselves; and it must be admitted that the wicked are always a considerable embarrassment, in this world and in the next.

Another queer thing. Her system clearly destroyed the whole doctrine of original sin and redemption, and shook the complete basis or common Christianity, so that Catholicism, at any rate, could not subsist with it. Yet Mamma was a good Catholic, or claimed to be, and it is clear that her claim was made in very good faith. In her opinion the Scriptures were too literally and too severely interpreted. All that is written there about eternal torments was in her opinion to be interpreted as a warning, or in a figurative sense. The death of Jesus Christ seemed to her an example of truly divine charity, to teach men to love God and to love one another. In brief, she was true to the faith she had embraced, and sincerely accepted its whole creed; but when it came to the discussion of each separate article, it turned out that her belief was quite different from the Church's, though she always submitted to its authority. In such matters she displayed a simplicity of heart and a candour which were more eloquent than any arguments and which frequently embarrassed even her confessor, from whom she kept nothing, 'I am a good Catholic,' she would say to him, 'and wish always to be one. I accept the decisions of our Holy Mother Church with all the strength of my heart. I am not mistress of my faith, but I am mistress of my will, which I unreservedly submit. I endeavour to believe everything. What more can you ask of me?'

If Christian morality had not existed, I think that she would have followed its principles, so completely did it coincide with her character. She did all that was prescribed; but she would have done it all the same if it had not been prescribed. In unimportant matters she loved to obey; and if she had not been allowed, or even required, to eat meat on fast days, she would have fasted in private and to please God, without paying the least regard to considerations of prudence. But her whole morality was subordinated to M. de Tavel's principles; or rather she claimed to find nothing contradictory to it in them. She could have slept with twenty men every day with a clear conscience, and with no more scruple about it than desire. I know that plenty of religious people are no more scrupulous on this point, but the difference is that they are led away by their passions, and she only by her sophistry. During the most moving–I could even say the most edifying–conversation she could allude to this subject without any change in her voice or manner, or any thought of being self-contradictory. She could even interrupt her talk, if need be, for the act itself, and then resume it with the same serenity as before: so absolute was her conviction that the whole question was no more than one of social convention which every intelligent person was at liberty to interpret, apply, or reject, without reference to anything else and without the least danger of offending God. Although I was certainly not of her opinion on this point, I confess that I had not the courage to dispute it, out of shame for the ungallant role I should have had to assume in order to do so. I might have tried to establish a rule for others, whilst trying to secure exemption for myself. But not only was her temperament a sufficient protection against the abuse of her principles, I knew also that she was not a woman to be deceived, and that to obtain an exemption for myself was to establish one for any man who might please her. I merely mention this is passing, along with the rest of her inconsistencies, although it had very little effect on her conduct—at that time none at all; but I have promised to give a faithful account of her principles, and I wish to keep my word. I will return now to myself.

Finding in her all the principles I needed to fortify my soul against the terror of death and its aftermath, I drew with security on this source of confidence. I became more closely attached to her than ever before; and would gladly have handed my whole life over to her, now that I felt it about to leave me. From this redoubled attachment to her, from the conviction that I had not long to live and from my profound confidence in my future fate, arose an habitual state of tranquillity, of sensual enjoyment even, which in allaying all those passions that banish our hopes and fears to a distance, left me to the untroubled, unapprehensive enjoyment of the few days that remained to me.

Questions

1. Rousseau's *Confessions* opens with these remarks: "I have begun on a work which is without precedent, whose accomplishment will have no imitator. I propose to set before my fellow-mortals a man in all the truth of nature; and this man shall be myself." Why did Rousseau begin with this statement? In what way is this work "without precedent" and with "no imitator"?

2. Often authors imagine that they are building a relationship with their future readers—their audience. As Rousseau was writing, what kind of relationship did he hope to build with his readers? How was this relationship similar to or different from Augustine's attempts to build a relationship with his audience?

3. The term *confession* can mean many things, depending on the context. What shades of meaning does Rousseau's work give to this term? What shades of meaning does Augustine give to the term?

4. Mdm. de Warens (called "Mamma") played a complex role in Rousseau's life. She was a friend, a protector, a mother figure, and a sexual partner. In this selection from *Confessions*, she was also presented as a spiritual savior. How was she a savior, and how would you explain the dynamics of Rousseau's relationship with her?

EMMA LAZARUS

Emma Lazarus (1849–1887) was the Jewish-American poet who wrote "The New Colossus," the poem inscribed on the base of the Statue of Liberty. She was born in New York City to affluent Jewish parents. She received a rich education in literature and languages, and she began her literary career at the age of eleven. She published *Songs of a Semite* in 1882, "The New Colossus" in 1883, and *Poems and Translations* in 1886, works that made her popular during the 1880s. During her life, Lazarus received critical acclaim and support from eminent writers such as Ralph Waldo Emerson. The general public also enjoyed her work. During this time of popularity, she also campaigned against the persecution of Jews in Russia and Eastern Europe, engaged in relief work for new immigrants, and spoke out in favor of the establishment of a Jewish homeland.

"The New Colossus" was popular for many reasons. It expressed many ideas and values that were present in the American imagination. First, this poem expresses a sense of calling, which the early settlers in Massachusetts felt; they viewed themselves and America as a special "City upon a Hill" that welcomes all who seek freedom and a new life. Next, this poem also evokes many biblical passages that are part of the American consciousness: "Come unto me, all ye that labour and are heavy laden, and I will give you rest" (Matthew 11:28 KJV), "But Jesus called them unto him, and said, Suffer little children to come unto me, and forbid them not: for of such is the kingdom of God" (Luke 18:16 KJV), and so forth. Such images of welcoming the poor and needy have been a normal part of the American mind-set from the early Pilgrims and Puritans to the present day; these images culminated in a multicultural viewpoint in the American psyche. Lazarus is representative of those who took such established Judeo-Christian values and widened the scope of who should be welcomed. She embraced the first settlers' perception of America as a "New Jerusalem," a place of God's providence, and spoke of it as a "Mother to Exiles" who offers a "world-wide welcome" to the "tired," "poor," "wretched refuse," "homeless," "tempest-tost," and "huddled masses yearning to breathe free." These ideas and images are still part of the public and spiritual discourse of the majority of Americans.

THE NEW COLOSSUS

Not like the brazen giant of Greek fame,
With conquering limbs astride from land to land;
Here at our sea-washed, sunset gates shall stand
A mighty woman with a torch, whose flame
5   *Is the imprisoned lightning, and her name*
Mother of Exiles. From her beacon-hand
Glows world-wide welcome; her mild eyes command
The air-bridged harbor that twin cities frame.
"Keep, ancient lands, your storied pomp!" cries she
10   *With silent lips. "Give me your tired, your poor,*

Your huddled masses yearning to breathe free,
The wretched refuse of your teeming shore.
Send these, the homeless, tempest-tost to me,
I lift my lamp beside the golden door!"

Questions

1. "The New Colossus" was very popular in the nineteenth century and enjoyed critical acclaim. That popularity, however, has diminished. What literary merits and cultural factors contributed to its popularity? What factors do you think account for its current diminished reputation?
2. Research and discuss the religious and spiritual allusions in the poem.
3. "The New Colossus" assumes that the reader knows about the first Colossus, a great statue in another famous harbor. One statue is male, and the other is female. One expresses power and victory, and the other expresses freedom and new beginnings. Research and compare both statues; make a chart to help you compare the two statues.
4. Pilgrimage is often an important part of religious experiences: Medieval Christians would travel to holy sites (see Geoffrey Chaucer's *The Canterbury Tales*), the Jews traveled from Egypt to "the Promised Land," Muslims travel to Mecca, Hindus and Buddhists take part in spiritual travels, and so forth. How does this poem fit into this long tradition of seeking and traveling?

T. S. Eliot

T. S. Eliot (1888–1965) was born in St. Louis, Missouri, and received a very good education in the United States. In 1914, he made Great Britain his new home. Eventually, he became a British citizen and a member of the Anglican Church. Eliot wrote both poems and plays that present the reader with unsettling feelings and penetrating questions. Often, he viewed life through the lens of alienation and struggle. Eliot published a relatively small number of poems. It seems that his goal was to give the world only those poems that he had carefully crafted and that would have a powerful effect on his readers. Eliot won the Nobel Prize in Literature in 1948.

"The Waste Land" was published in 1922. It gives a very disjointed collage of images and voices. The poem leaves the reader both intrigued and frustrated. This poem seems to echo the thoughts of all of humanity as Eliot used phrases, quotations, and allusions from representative authors from both the Western and Eastern cultural traditions. He also included phrases written in Greek, Latin, German, French, and Sanskrit to give the impression that the entire world is speaking in this poem. The reader hears voices, but there is no unity or harmony.

Eliot wrote "The Journey of the Magi" after becoming a Christian and joining the Church of England. The narrator of the poem reflects back on a journey he had taken many years ago and ponders its meaning. This journey is mentioned in Matthew 2:1–12.

THE WASTE LAND

"Nam Sibyllam quidem Cumis ego ipse oculis meis vidi in ampulla pendere, et cum illi pueri dicerent: Σίβυλλα τί θέλεισ; respondebat illa: αποθανείν θέλω."

For Ezra Pound
il miglior fabbro.

I. The Burial of the Dead

    April is the cruellest month, breeding
    Lilacs out of the dead land, mixing
    Memory and desire, stirring
    Dull roots with spring rain.
5   *Winter kept us warm, covering*
    Earth in forgetful snow, feeding
    A little life with dried tubers.
    Summer surprised us, coming over the Starnbergersee
    With a shower of rain; we stopped in the colonnade,
10   *And went on in sunlight, into the Hofgarten,*
    And drank coffee, and talked for an hour.
    Bin gar keine Russin, stamm' aus Litauen, echt deutsch.
    And when we were children, staying at the archduke's,
    My cousin's, he took me out on a sled,
15   *And I was frightened. He said, Marie,*
    Marie, hold on tight. And down we went.
    In the mountains, there you feel free.
    I read, much of the night, and go south in the winter.

    What are the roots that clutch, what branches grow
20   *Out of this stony rubbish? Son of man,*
    You cannot say, or guess, for you know only
    A heap of broken images, where the sun beats,
    And the dead tree gives no shelter, the cricket no relief,
    And the dry stone no sound of water. Only
25   *There is shadow under this red rock,*
    (Come in under the shadow of this red rock),
    And I will show you something different from either
    Your shadow at morning striding behind you
    Or your shadow at evening rising, to meet you;
30   *I will show you fear in a handful of dust.*
        Frisch weht der Wind.
        Der Heimat zu
        Mein Irisch Kind,
        Wo weilest du?
35   *"You gave me hyacinths first a year ago;*
    "They called me the hyacinth girl."

—Yet when we came back, late, from the Hyacinth garden,
Your arms full, and your hair wet, I could not
Speak, and my eyes failed, I was neither
Living nor dead, and I knew nothing,   40
Looking into the heart of light, the silence.
Oed' und leer das Meer.

Madame Sosostris, famous clairvoyante,
Had a bad cold, nevertheless
Is known to be the wisest woman in Europe,   45
With a wicked pack of cards. Here, said she,
Is your card, the drowned Phoenician Sailor,
(Those are pearls that were his eyes. Look!)
Here is Belladonna, the Lady of the Rocks,
The lady of situations.   50
Here is the man with three staves, and here the Wheel,
And here is the one-eyed merchant, and this card,
Which is blank, is something he carries on his back,
Which I am forbidden to see. I do not find
The Hanged Man. Fear death by water.   55
I see crowds of people, walking round in a ring.
Thank you. If you see dear Mrs. Equitone,
Tell her I bring the horoscope myself:
One must be so careful these days.

Unreal City,   60
Under the brown fog of a winter dawn,
A crowd flowed over London Bridge, so many,
I had not thought death had undone so many.
Sighs, short and infrequent, were exhaled,
And each man fixed his eyes before his feet.   65
Flowed up the hill and down King William Street,
To where Saint Mary Woolnoth kept the hours
With a dead sound on the final stroke of nine.
There I saw one I knew, and stopped him, crying: "Stetson!
"You who were with me in the ships at Mylae!   70
"That corpse you planted last year in your garden,
"Has it begun to sprout? Will it bloom this year?
"Or has the sudden frost disturbed its bed?
"Oh keep the Dog far hence, that's friend to men,
"Or with his nails he'll dig it up again!
"You! hypocrite lecteur!—mon semblable,—mon frère!"

II. A Game of Chess

The Chair she sat in, like a burnished throne,
Glowed on the marble, where the glass
Held up by standards wrought with fruited vines

80   *From which a golden Cupidon peeped out*
      (Another hid his eyes behind his wing)
      Doubled the flames of sevenbranched candelabra
      Reflecting light upon the table as
      The glitter of her jewels rose to meet it,
85   *From satin cases poured in rich profusion.*
      In vials of ivory and coloured glass
      Unstoppered, lurked her strange synthetic perfumes,
      Unguent, powdered, or liquid—troubled, confused
      And drowned the sense in odours; stirred by the air
90   *That freshened from the window, these ascended*
      In fattening the prolonged candle-flames,
      Flung their smoke into the laquearia,
      Stirring the pattern on the coffered ceiling.
      Huge sea-wood fed with copper
95   *Burned green and orange, framed by the coloured stone,*
      In which sad light a carvéd dolphin swam.
      Above the antique mantel was displayed
      As though a window gave upon the sylvan scene
      The change of Philomel, by the barbarous king
100   *So rudely forced; yet there the nightingale*
      Filled all the desert with inviolable voice
      And still she cried, and still the world pursues,
      "Jug Jug" to dirty ears.
      And other withered stumps of time
105   *Were told upon the walls; staring forms*
      Leaned out, leaning, hushing the room enclosed.
      Footsteps shuffled on the stair.
      Under the firelight, under the brush, her hair
      Spread out in fiery points
110   *Glowed into words, then would be savagely still.*

      "My nerves are bad to-night. Yes, bad. Stay with me.
      Speak to me. Why do you never speak. Speak.
      What are you thinking of? What thinking? What?
      I never know What you are thinking. Think."

115   *I think we are in rats' alley*
      Where the dead men lost their bones.

      "What is that noise?"
      The wind under the door.
      "What is that noise now? What is the wind doing?"
120   *Nothing again nothing.*
      "Do
      "You know nothing? Do you see nothing? Do you remember
      "Nothing?"

I remember
Those are pearls that were his eyes.   125
"Are you alive, or not? Is there nothing in your head?"
But
O O O O that Shakespeherian Rag—
It's so elegant
So intelligent   130
"What shall I do now? What shall I do?"
"I shall rush out as I am, and walk the street
"With my hair down, so. What shall we do to-morrow?
"What shall we ever do?"
The hot water at ten.   135

JOURNEY OF THE MAGI

"A cold coming we had of it,
Just the worst time of the year
For a journey, and such a long journey:
The ways deep and the weather sharp,
The very dead of winter."   5
And the camels galled, sore-footed, refractory,
Lying down in the melting snow.
There were times we regretted
The summer palaces on slopes, the terraces,
And the silken girls bringing sherbet.   10
Then the camel men cursing and grumbling

And running away, and wanting their liquor and women,
And the night-fires going out, and the lack of shelters,
And the cities hostile and the towns unfriendly
And the villages dirty and charging high prices: 15
A hard time we had of it.
At the end we preferred to travel all night,
Sleeping in snatches,
With the voices singing in our ears, saying
That this was all folly.   20

Then at dawn we came down to a temperate valley,
Wet, below the snow line, smelling of vegetation;
With a running stream and a water-mill beating the darkness,
And three trees on the low sky,
And an old white horse galloped away in the meadow.   25
Then we came to a tavern with vine-leaves over the lintel,
Six hands at an open door dicing for pieces of silver,
And feet kicking the empty wine-skins.
But there was no information, and so we continued

30   *And arrived at evening, not a moment too soon*
      Finding the place; it was (you may say) satisfactory.

      All this was a long time ago, I remember,
      And I would do it again, but set down
      This set down
35   *This: were we led all that way for*
      Birth or Death? There was a Birth, certainly,
      We had evidence and no doubt. I had seen birth and death,
      But had thought they were different; this Birth was
      Hard and bitter agony for us, like Death, our death.
40   *We returned to our places, these Kingdoms,*
      But no longer at ease here, in the old dispensation,
      With an alien people clutching their gods.
      I should be glad of another death.

Questions

1. What feelings did you find within yourself as you read "The Waste Land"? When we read a work of literature, we come with expectations. How did Eliot satisfy or not satisfy your expectations as you read "The Waste Land"? Given that Eliot carefully crafted this poem, why would he intentionally meet some of your expectations and not satisfy others?
2. What section of "The Waste Land" is the most intriguing? Why?
3. In "The Journey of the Magi," why did Eliot build such a strong connection between birth and death? For example, toward the end of the poem, Eliot wrote, "this Birth was / Hard and bitter agony for us, like / Death, our death." How can this birth be a death for the narrator? Do you recall other links between birth and death in Christianity?
4. Later in "The Journey of the Magi," Eliot wrote, "We returned to our places, these Kingdoms, / But no longer at ease here, [. . .] / With an alien people clutching their gods. / I should be glad of another death." What does this passage mean?

NAGUIB MAHFOUZ

Naguib Mahfouz (1911–2006) was the first Egyptian and the first Arabic-language writer to win the prestigious Nobel Prize in Literature. During his long, productive life, Mahfouz published thirty-three novels and sixteen collections of short stories. Many of his novels and stories have become movies. His works usually deal with the modernization of Egypt, which Mahfouz witnessed. For example, he witnessed the nationalistic spirit that guided Egypt after its independence from Great Britain, and he witnessed the secularism and religious extremism that continuously pushed at each other during his life. His works have been very popular in Arabic-speaking countries and across the world. He was also hated by Islamic extremists, some of whom stabbed Mahfouz outside of his home when he was eighty-two years old. He survived the attack, but was physically weakened by it.

The story below chronicles a sick man's search for Zaabalawi, a holy man, who is said to have healing powers. As the main character travels, the reader is introduced to various religious traditions in Egypt and to the effects of contemporary materialism on traditional lifestyles. It is interesting to remember that throughout history and across many religions, the spiritual journey or the spiritual quest has been a recurring theme in literature. Is the search for Zaabalawi a symbolic quest for religion in a society that has forgotten its religious past and lost touch with the faith that anchored its ancestors?

ZAABALAWI

Finally, I became convinced that I had to find Sheikh Zaabalawi.

The first time I had heard of his name had been in a song:

Oh what's become of the world, Zaabalawi?
They've turned it upside down and taken away its taste.

It had been a popular song in my childhood, and one day it had occurred to me to demand of my father, in the way children have of asking endless questions:

"Who is Zaabalawi?"

He had looked at me hesitantly as though doubting my ability to understand the answer. However, he had replied, "May his blessing descend upon you, he's a true saint of God, a remover of worries and troubles. Were it not for him I would have died miserably—"

In the years that followed, I heard my father many a time sing the praises of this good saint and speak of the miracles he performed. The days passed and brought with them many illnesses, for each one of which I was able, without too much trouble and at a cost I could afford, to find a cure, until I became afflicted with that illness for which no one possesses a remedy. When I had tried everything in vain and was overcome by despair, I remembered by chance what I had heard in my childhood: Why, I asked myself, should I not seek out Sheikh Zaabalawi? I recollected my father saying that he had made his acquaintance in Khan Gaafar at the house of Sheikh Qamar, one of those sheikhs who practiced law in the religious courts, and so I took myself off to his house. Wishing to make sure that he was still living there, I made inquiries of a vendor of beans whom I found in the lower part of the house.

"Sheikh Qamar!" he said, looking at me in amazement. "He left the quarter ages ago. They say he's now living in Garden City and has his office in al-Azhar Square."

I looked up the office address in the telephone book and immediately set off to the Chamber of Commerce Building, where it was located. On asking to see Sheikh Qamar, I was ushered into a room just as a beautiful woman with a most intoxicating perfume was leaving it. The man received me with a smile and motioned me toward a fine leather-upholstered chair. Despite the thick soles of my shoes, my feet were conscious of the lushness of the costly carpet. The man wore a lounge suit and was smoking a cigar; his manner of sitting was that of someone well satisfied both with himself and with his worldly possessions. The look of warm welcome he gave me left no doubt in my mind that he thought me a prospective client, and I felt acutely embarrassed at encroaching upon his valuable time.

"Welcome!" he said, prompting me to speak.

"I am the son of your old friend Sheikh Ali al-Tatawi," I answered so as to put an end to my equivocal position.

A certain languor was apparent in the glance he cast at me; the languor was not total in that he had not as yet lost all hope in me.

"God rest his soul," he said. "He was a fine man."

The very pain that had driven me to go there now prevailed upon me to stay.

"He told me," I continued, "of a devout saint named Zaabalawi whom he met at Your Honor's. I am in need of him, sir, if he be still in the land of the living."

The languor became firmly entrenched in his eyes, and it would have come as no surprise if he had shown the door to both me and my father's memory.

"That," he said in the tone of one who has made up his mind to terminate the conversation, "was a very long time ago and I scarcely recall him now."

Rising to my feet so as to put his mind at rest regarding my intention of going, I asked, "Was he really a saint?"

"We used to regard him as a man of miracles."

"And where could I find him today?" I asked, making another move toward the door.

"To the best of my knowledge he was living in the Birgawi Residence in al-Azhar," and he applied himself to some papers on his desk with a resolute movement that indicated he would not open his mouth again. I bowed my head, in thanks, apologized several times for disturbing him, and left the office, my head so buzzing with embarrassment that I was oblivious to all sounds around me.

I went to the Birgawi Residence, which was situated in a thickly populated quarter. I found that time had so eaten at the building that nothing was left of it save an antiquated façade and a courtyard that, despite being supposedly in the charge of a caretaker, was being used as a rubbish dump. A small, insignificant fellow, a mere prologue to a man, was using the covered entrance as a place for the sale of old books on theology and mysticism.

When I asked him about Zaabalawi, he peered at me through narrow, inflamed eyes and said in amazement, "Zaabalawi! Good heavens, what a time ago that was! Certainly he used to live in this house when it was habitable. Many were the times he would sit with me talking of bygone days, and I would be blessed by his holy presence. Where, though, is Zaabalawi today?"

He shrugged his shoulders sorrowfully and soon left me, to attend to an approaching customer. I proceeded to make inquiries of many shopkeepers in the district. While I found that a large number of them had never even heard of Zaabalawi, some, though recalling nostalgically the pleasant times they had spent with him, were ignorant of his present whereabouts, while others openly made fun of him, labeled him a charlatan, and advised me to put myself in the hands of a doctor—as though I had not already done so. I therefore had no alternative but to return disconsolately home.

With the passing of days like motes in the air, my pains grew so severe that I was sure I would not be able to hold out much longer. Once again I fell to wondering about Zaabalawi and clutching at the hope his venerable name stirred within me. Then it occurred to me to seek the help of the local sheikh of the district; in fact, I was surprised I had not thought of this to begin with. His office was in the nature of a small shop, except that it contained a desk and a telephone, and I found him sitting at his desk, wearing a jacket over his striped galabeya. As he did not interrupt his conversation with a man sitting beside him, I stood waiting till the man had gone. The sheikh then looked up at me coldly. I told myself that I should win him over by the usual methods, and it was not long before I had him cheerfully inviting me to sit down.

"I'm in need of Sheikh Zaabalawi," I answered his inquiry as to the purpose of my visit.

He gazed at me with the same astonishment as that shown by those I had previously encountered.

"At least," he said, giving me a smile that revealed his gold teeth, "he is still alive. The devil of it is, though, he has no fixed abode. You might well bump into him as you go out of here, on the other hand you might spend days and months in fruitless searching."

"Even you can't find him!"

"Even I! He's a baffling man, but I thank the Lord that he's still alive!"

He gazed at me intently, and murmured, "It seems your condition is serious."

"Very."

"May God come to your aid! But why don't you go about it systematically?" He spread out a sheet of paper on the desk and drew on it with unexpected speed and skill until he had made a full plan of the district, showing all the various quarters, lanes, alleyways, and squares. He looked at it admiringly and said, "These are dwelling-houses, here is the Quarter of the Perfumers, here the Quarter of the Coppersmiths, the Mouski, the police and fire stations. The drawing is your best guide. Look carefully in the cafés, the places where the dervishes perform their rites, the mosques and prayer-rooms, and the Green Gate, for he may well be concealed among the beggars and be indistinguishable from them. Actually, I myself haven't seen him for years, having been somewhat preoccupied with the cares of the world, and was only brought back by your inquiry to those most exquisite times of my youth."

I gazed at the map in bewilderment. The telephone rang, and he took up the receiver.

"Take it," he told me, generously. "We're at your service."

Folding up the map, I left and wandered off through the quarter, from square to street to alleyway, making inquiries of everyone I felt was familiar with the place. At last the owner of a small establishment for ironing clothes told me, "Go to the calligrapher Hassanein in Umm al-Ghulam—they were friends."

I went to Umm al-Ghulam, where I found old Hassanein working in a deep, narrow shop full of signboards and jars of color. A strange smell, a mixture of glue and perfume, permeated its every corner. Old Hassanein was squatting on a sheepskin rug in front of a board propped against the wall; in the middle of it he had inscribed the word "Allah" in silver lettering. He was engrossed in embellishing the letters with prodigious care. I stood behind him, fearful of disturbing him or breaking the inspiration that flowed to his masterly hand. When my concern at not interrupting him had lasted some time, he suddenly inquired with unaffected gentleness, "Yes?"

Realizing that he was aware of my presence, I introduced myself. "I've been told that Sheikh Zaabalawi is your friend; I'm looking for him," I said.

His hand came to a stop. He scrutinized me in astonishment. "Zaabalawi! God be praised!" he said with a sigh.

"He *is* a friend of yours, isn't he?" I asked eagerly.

"He was, once upon a time. A real man of mystery: he'd visit you so often that people would imagine he was your nearest and dearest, then would disappear as though he'd never existed. Yet saints are not to be blamed."

The spark of hope went out with the suddenness of a lamp snuffed by a power-cut.

"He was so constantly with me," said the man, "that I felt him to be a part of everything I drew. But where is he today?"

"Perhaps he is still alive?"

"He's alive, without a doubt. . . . He had impeccable taste, and it was due to him that I made my most beautiful drawings."

"God knows," I said, in a voice almost stifled by the dead ashes of hope, "how dire my need for him is, and no one knows better than you of the ailments in respect of which he is sought."

"Yes, yes. May God restore you to health. He is, in truth, as is said of him, a man, and more. . . ."

Smiling broadly, he added, "And his face possesses an unforgettable beauty. But where is he?"

Reluctantly I rose to my feet, shook hands, and left. I continued wandering eastward and westward through the quarter, inquiring about Zaabalawi from everyone who, by reason of age or experience, I felt might be likely to help me. Eventually I was informed by a vendor of lupine that he had met him a short while ago at the house of Sheikh Gad, the well-known composer. I went to the musician's house in Tabakshiyya, where I found him in a room tastefully furnished in the old style, its walls redolent with history. He was seated on a divan, his famous lute beside him, concealing within itself the most beautiful melodies of our age, while somewhere from within the house came the sound of pestle and mortar and the clamor of children. I immediately greeted him and introduced myself, and was put at my ease by the unaffected way in which he received me. He did not ask, either in words or gesture, what had brought me, and I did not feel that he even harbored any such curiosity. Amazed at his understanding and kindness, which boded well, I said, "O Sheikh Gad, I am an admirer of yours, having long been enchanted by the renderings of your songs."

"Thank you," he said with a smile.

"Please excuse my disturbing you," I continued timidly, "but I was told that Zaabalawi was your friend, and I am in urgent need of him."

"Zaabalawi!" he said, frowning in concentration. "You need him? God be with you, for who knows, O Zaabalawi, where you are."

"Doesn't he visit you?" I asked eagerly.

"He visited me some time ago. He might well come right now; on the other hand I mightn't see him till death!"

I gave an audible sigh and asked, "What made him like that?"

The musician took up his lute. "Such are saints or they would not be saints," he said, laughing.

"Do those who need him suffer as I do?"

"Such suffering is part of the cure!"

He took up the plectrum and began plucking soft strains from the strings. Lost in thought, I followed his movements. Then, as though addressing myself, I said, "So my visit has been in vain."

He smiled, laying his cheek against the side of the lute. "God forgive you," he said, "for saying such a thing of a visit that has caused me to know you and you me!"

I was much embarrassed and said apologetically, "Please forgive me; my feelings of defeat made me forget my manners."

"Do not give in to defeat. This extraordinary man brings fatigue to all who seek him. It was easy enough with him in the old days when his place of abode was known. Today, though, the world has changed, and after having enjoyed a position attained only by potentates, he is now pursued by the police on a charge of false pretenses. It is therefore no longer an easy matter to reach him, but have patience and be sure that you will do so."

He raised his head from the lute and skillfully fingered the opening bars of a melody. Then he sang:

I make lavish mention, even though I blame myself, of those I love,
For the stories of the beloved are my wine.

With a heart that was weary and listless, I followed the beauty of the melody and the singing.

"I composed the music to this poem in a single night," he told me when he had finished. "I remember that it was the eve of the Lesser Bairam. Zaabalawi was my guest for the whole of that night, and the poem was of his choosing. He would sit for a while just where you are, then would get up and

play with my children as though he were one of them. Whenever I was overcome by weariness or my inspiration failed me, he would punch me playfully
in the chest and joke with me, and I would bubble over with melodies, and
thus I continued working till I finished the most beautiful piece I have ever
composed."

"Does he know anything about music?"

"He is the epitome of things musical. He has an extremely beautiful
speaking voice, and you have only to hear him to want to burst into song and
to be inspired to creativity. . . ."

"How was it that he cured those diseases before which men are powerless?"

"That is his secret. Maybe you will learn it when you meet him."

But when would that meeting occur? We relapsed into silence, and the
hubbub of children once more filled the room.

Again the sheikh began to sing. He went on repeating the words "and I
have a memory of her" in different and beautiful variations until the very walls
danced in ecstasy. I expressed my wholehearted admiration, and he gave me a
smile of thanks. I then got up and asked permission to leave, and he accompanied
me to the front door. As I shook him by the hand, he said, "I hear that nowadays
he frequents the house of Hagg Wanas al-Damanhouri. Do you know him?"

I shook my head, though a modicum of renewed hope crept into my heart.

"He is a man of private means," the sheikh told me, "who from time to
time visits Cairo, putting up at some hotel or other. Every evening, though, he
spends at the Negma Bar in Alfi Street."

I waited for nightfall and went to the Negma Bar. I asked a waiter about
Hagg Wanas, and he pointed to a corner that was semisecluded because of its
position behind a large pillar with mirrors on all four sides. There I saw a man
seated alone at a table with two bottles in front of him, one empty, the other
two-thirds empty. There were no snacks or food to be seen, and I was sure that
I was in the presence of a hardened drinker. He was wearing a loosely flowing
silk galabeya and a carefully wound turban; his legs were stretched out toward
the base of the pillar, and as he gazed into the mirror in rapt contentment, the
sides of his face, rounded and handsome despite the fact that he was approaching old age, were flushed with wine. I approached quietly till I stood but a few
feet away from him. He did not turn toward me or give any indication that he
was aware of my presence.

"Good evening, Mr. Wanas," I greeted him cordially.

He turned toward me abruptly, as though my voice had roused him from
slumber, and glared at me in disapproval. I was about to explain what had
brought me to him when he interrupted in an almost imperative tone of voice
that was none the less not devoid of an extraordinary gentleness, "First, please
sit down, and, second, please get drunk!"

I opened my mouth to make my excuses but, stopping up his ears with
his fingers, he said, "Not a word till you do what I say."

I realized I was in the presence of a capricious drunkard and told myself
that I should at least humor him a bit. "Would you permit me to ask one question?" I said with a smile, sitting down.

Without removing his hands from his ears he indicated the bottle. "When engaged in a drinking bout like this, I do not allow any conversation between myself and another unless, like me, he is drunk, otherwise all propriety is lost and mutual comprehension is rendered impossible."

I made a sign indicating that I did not drink.

"That's your lookout," he said offhandedly. "And that's my condition!"

He filled me a glass, which I meekly took and drank. No sooner had the wine settled in my stomach than it seemed to ignite. I waited patiently till I had grown used to its ferocity, and said, "It's very strong, and I think the time has come for me to ask you about—"

Once again, however, he put his fingers in his ears. "I shan't listen to you until you're drunk!"

He filled up my glass for the second time. I glanced at it in trepidation; then, overcoming my inherent objection, I drank it down at a gulp. No sooner had the wine come to rest inside me than I lost all willpower. With the third glass, I lost my memory, and with the fourth the future vanished. The world turned round about me and I forgot why I had gone there. The man leaned toward me attentively, but I saw him—saw everything—as a mere meaningless series of colored planes. I don't know how long it was before my head sank down onto the arm of the chair, and I plunged into deep sleep. During it, I had a beautiful dream the like of which I had never experienced. I dreamed that I was in an immense garden surrounded on all sides by luxuriant trees, and the sky was nothing but stars seen between the entwined branches, all enfolded in an atmosphere like that of sunset or a sky overcast with cloud. I was lying on a small hummock of jasmine petals, more of which fell upon me like rain, while the lucent spray of a fountain unceasingly sprinkled the crown of my head and my temples. I was in a state of deep contentedness; of ecstatic serenity. An orchestra of warbling and cooing played in my ear. There was an extraordinary sense of harmony between me and my inner self, and between the two of us and the world, everything being in its rightful place, without discord or distortion. In the whole world there was no single reason for speech or movement, for the universe moved in a rapture of ecstasy. This lasted but a short while. When I opened my eyes, consciousness struck at me like a policeman's fist and I saw Wanas al-Damanhouri regarding me with concern. Only a few drowsy customers were left in the bar.

"You have slept deeply," said my companion. "You were obviously hungry for sleep."

I rested my heavy head in the palms of my hands. When I took them away in astonishment and looked down at them, I found that they glistened with drops of water.

"My head's wet," I protested.

"Yes, my friend tried to rouse you," he answered quietly.

"Somebody saw me in this state?"

"Don't worry, he is a good man. Have you not heard of Sheikh Zaabalawi?"

"Zaabalawi!" I exclaimed, jumping to my feet.

"Yes," he answered in surprise. "What's wrong?"

"Where is he?"

"I don't know where he is now. He was here and then he left."

I was about to run off in pursuit but found I was more exhausted than I had imagined. Collapsed over the table, I cried out in despair, "My sole reason for coming to you was to meet him! Help me to catch up with him or send someone after him."

The man called a vendor of prawns and asked him to seek out the sheikh and bring him back. Then he turned to me. "I didn't realize you were afflicted. I'm very sorry. . . ."

"You wouldn't let me speak," I said irritably.

"What a pity! He was sitting on this chair beside you the whole time. He was playing with a string of jasmine petals he had around his neck, a gift from one of his admirers, then, taking pity on you, he began to sprinkle some water on your head to bring you around."

"Does he meet you here every night?" I asked, my eyes not leaving the doorway through which the vendor of prawns had left.

"He was with me tonight, last night and the night before that, but before that I hadn't seen him for a month."

"Perhaps he will come tomorrow," I answered with a sigh.

"Perhaps."

"I am willing to give him any money he wants."

Wanas answered sympathetically, "The strange thing is that he is not open to such temptations, yet he will cure you if you meet him."

"Without charge?"

"Merely on sensing that you love him."

The vendor of prawns returned, having failed in his mission.

I recovered some of my energy and left the bar, albeit unsteadily. At every street corner I called out "Zaabalawi!" in the vague hope that I would be rewarded with an answering shout. The street boys turned contemptuous eyes on me till I sought refuge in the first available taxi.

The following evening I stayed up with Wanas al-Damanhouri till dawn, but the sheikh did not put in an appearance. Wanas informed me that he would be going away to the country and would not be returning to Cairo until he had sold the cotton crop.

I must wait, I told myself; I must train myself to be patient. Let me content myself with having made certain of the existence of Zaabalawi, and even of his affection for me, which encourages me to think that he will be prepared to cure me if a meeting takes place between us.

Sometimes, however, the long delay wearied me. I would become beset by despair and would try to persuade myself to dismiss him from my mind completely. How many weary people in this life know him not or regard him as a mere myth! Why, then, should I torture myself about him in this way?

No sooner, however, did my pains force themselves upon me than I would again begin to think about him, asking myself when I would be fortunate enough to meet him. The fact that I ceased to have any news of Wanas and was told he had gone to live abroad did not deflect me from my purpose;

the truth of the matter was that I had become fully convinced that I had to find Zaabalawi.

Yes, I have to find Zaabalawi.

Questions

1. Can "Zaabalawi" be read as social criticism? Why or why not?
2. Can "Zaabalawi" be read as religious allegory? Why or why not?
3. How did Mahfouz use time, setting, and character to communicate the themes of change and spiritual poverty? Did the author set a tone in the story when he wrote that the nameless narrator has a disease that resists modern medical science? What did he mean when he wrote that the home of Birgawi is "eaten" by time?
4. Consider the tensions in the story. Zaabalawi, the Muslim holy man, is found in a bar. And, the narrator must first get intoxicated in order to meet Zaabalawi. (Alcohol, in general, and intoxication, in particular, are prohibited under Islamic law.) What other tensions do you see in the story?

MOVIE GUIDE FOR *THE FIDDLER ON THE ROOF* (1971)

Directed by Norman Jewison

Screenplay by Sholem Aleichem and Joseph Stein

History as the Context

This award-winning picture explores a community of poor Jews in Russia at the beginning of the twentieth century. The story takes place before the Russian communists seized power in 1917. During this time, the Czar is the distant, authoritarian ruler of the sweeping, but backward Russian empire. The official religion is Russian Orthodoxy. Although fictional, the village of Anatevka in *The Fiddler on the Roof* represents hundreds of communities in Russia and Eastern Europe where Jews struggled to follow their traditions. It also represents hundreds of communities where, from time to time, mobs and governmental authorities harassed, looted, killed, and evicted Jews. (For more historical background, do a study of pogroms against the Jews in Russia and other areas.)

The 1960s as the Context

In addition to this historical context is another, more contemporary context. This movie is based on the original Broadway play, which was produced in the late 1960s. The 1960s were a period of cultural revolution in the United States and in other Western societies. Traditional standards of sexual morality, gender roles, racial relationships, and economic relationships were suddenly questioned by college students, black activists, war protesters, hippies, and others. Although the cultural revolution of the 1960s seems light-years removed from the story of poor Jews in *The Fiddler on the Roof,* the two situations are actually very similar. Knowingly or unknowingly, the producers of *The Fiddler on the Roof* were helping their audience explore their own social dilemmas. When should traditions be broken, and when should they be preserved? What values should guide such decisions? Both the contemporary audiences of the movie and the Jewish characters portrayed in the movie are torn between the security of their traditions and the excitement of expanding freedoms. They are wondering whether or not their traditions are based on fixed moral truths or mere social habits.

The Focus of Attention

This film has two gravitational centers. One is Tevye, the charming dairyman with five daughters. The other center is the community of Jews in Anatevka. Our twenty-first century sensibilities lead us to focus on individuals, rather than communities. As a result, our minds constantly follow Tevye. (And the techniques used by the filmmakers also focus on Tevye a great deal.) Yet, the community of Jews is equally important—perhaps it is more important in truly understanding the story.

To establish the importance of community, the movie begins by showing how tradition guides each person to contribute to the group. Some persons are fathers, some are mothers, and some are sons and daughters. There is a rabbi; there is a beggar; there are rich and poor members of the community; and there is a matchmaker who helps arrange marriages. Tradition guides each person's thoughts and actions. Early in the movie, Tevye asks, "How did this tradition get started?" Then he answers himself, "I don't know." Throughout the story, Tevye values knowledge and wants to learn, yet his ignorance is not a major problem. He and the other members of the community are satisfied with the security that tradition provides. Yet, those traditions are continually under attack in this story.

Internal and External Tensions

The central drama of the film is the tension between the traditions and the internal and external forces that are attacking them. One external force is the Russian government. Other external forces include the young Jewish scholar/socialist who visits the family, the friendly Gentile who befriends and romances one of Tevye's daughters, and a railway train that takes one daughter away. Forces within the characters are also working against the traditions. An example of such an internal force is the belief that romantic love is an overwhelming power that must be obeyed. In the minds of Tevye and his wife, romantic love is not essential (listen to the song, "Do You Love Me?"). However, the daughters of Tevye are convinced that romantic love must be followed and obeyed regardless of where it might lead a person. Slowly through the movie, Tevye and his wife begin to allow their daughters' inner commitment to romantic love to erode the family's obedience to and confidence in tradition. Yet, Tevye is never comfortable with the slow erosion of his roots.

Tevye

In the middle of this battle for and against tradition is Tevye's relationship with God. In one sense, the traditions are very closely linked to God and the Jewish faith, yet Tevye is able to separate the traditions from his understanding of God. Thus, Tevye is able to discuss with God whether or not a tradition should be obeyed.

This leads to one of the most intriguing features of the film: Tevye's dialogues with God. Tevye is constantly looking up toward heaven and talking to God in the most honest ways. Although Tevye is extremely ignorant about the Hebrew Bible (various characters are constantly correcting his misuse of Scripture), Tevye's relationship with God lacks pretense or formality. It is not "traditional" in the sense of being a mindless ritual. His lack of biblical understanding does not hinder Tevye from having clarity in his voice and in his mind as he relates every thought and feeling to his God.

Fascinating characters are often very complex personalities, and Tevye is no exception. Early in the movie, we hear Tevye express regret that he has five daughters; thus, he devalues his children because they are females. Yet, throughout the movie, he cherishes, respects, values, and honors his daughters (except when the third daughter, Chava, marries a Gentile). Although Tevye enjoys his simple life and although he knows that there is nothing wrong with being poor, he still longs to be a rich man. He associates riches with social respect, ease, and knowledge. Yet, if he would only step back and look at himself, Tevye would discover that he already has a great deal of social respect and ease—and even if he does not have a great deal of knowledge, he has at least enough wisdom to make his way through life. Another tension within Tevye is his repeated attempts to show his authority and to put on an air of harshness when he is really very tender toward his animals, the town beggar, his daughters, his wife, and others.

The Community

Returning to the community, it is important to notice that when Tevye's family is celebrating the Sabbath in their home, the camera sweeps across the faces and the homes of the other Jews in the village. The candles and the prayers of the Sabbath unite the people into a single unit, even though they inhabit many buildings. In the same way, the closing scenes of the film encourage us to visualize how the Hebrew race has maintained their faith and traditions in spite of thousands of years of persecution. As the movie ends and the unity of the Jewish community in Anatevka is destroyed, the audience imagines the Jewish people throughout history who have continued to have deep roots in something larger than a particular piece of land, a national government, or even a language. A spiritual presence is with the Jews. They might be battling large, evil forces, yet there is a stronger and better presence that is guiding the Jews. Thus, the movie ends on a positive note. Evil has been faced. Pain has been experienced. But a more powerful Good is present and is real.

Tips for Watching This Movie

A good movie deserves to be watched more than once. A little research can make the second viewing even richer. Here are some topics to consider when watching *The Fiddler on the Roof* for a second time:

1. Study the role that tradition has played in the community. Then list the many situations, characters, and forces that are working against tradition. Also consider the values and worldviews that are working against the community's traditions.
2. Study the culture, politics, and economics of Russia between 1900 and 1917. Then, watch the movie with this deeper understanding of Russia.
3. Study the changes in American culture in the late 1960s and early 1970s so that you can better understand the experiences of the original audiences of this film. Make a chart that lists the changes faced by the Jews in this movie and the changes faced by the original American audiences of the film.

Key Characters and Their Relationships

Tevye, a poor dairyman, who is the father of five daughters

Golde, Tevye's wife

Yente, the village matchmaker

Lazar Wolf, the wealthy butcher, who wants to marry the first daughter, Tzeitel

Tzeitel, the first daughter of Tevye and Golde

Motel (pronounced "mottle"), the tailor, who eventually marries Tzeitel

Hodel, the second daughter of Tevye and Golde, who loves Perchik

Perchik, the visiting scholar, socialist, and revolutionary who loves Hodel

Chava, the third daughter of Tevye and Golde, who loves Fyedka

Fyedka, the young Gentile, who loves books and Chava

The Constable, the Gentile friend of Tevye, who also represents Russian power in the village

Questions

1. What does the fiddler represent in the movie? Repeatedly, he mysteriously appears, plays his tune, and beckons Tevye. What is he communicating? What role does he play in the overall story?
2. What characters did you personally enjoy the most in this movie? Why? What traditions in this film are most attractive to you? Why?
3. What traditions guide our lives today? Often they are so ordinary that they are not noticed. For example, many people in the United States take for granted an extreme individualism. This individualism is expressed by husbands and wives each having his or her own career, his or her own bank account, and his or her own "personal space." It is also seen when each child in a family has his or her own TV, computer, phone, and, later, a car.

Should we accept the traditions guiding us today? What values should guide us in either accepting or rejecting today's traditions?

4. In many ways, today's culture is anti-traditional. We automatically question and reject traditions whether or not they are good. For example, many persons today are dismissing marriage as a worn-out tradition, in spite of the fact that marriage (in one form or another) is found in essentially every culture throughout history. Is this constant rejection of traditions good, bad, or indifferent?

Chapter 2

Spirituality in the Context of Pride, Rebellion, and Submission

C. S. LEWIS

C. S. Lewis (1898–1963) was a respected scholar of Medieval and Renaissance literature at Oxford and Cambridge universities. Yet, he also wrote very popular children's novels (e.g., *The Lion, the Witch and the Wardrobe; The Horse and His Boy*). He wrote popular fiction, science fiction, poetry, and essays. He saw himself as a simple layman in the Church of England, but his books and essays are cherished by Christians around the world.

In Belfast, Ireland, Lewis began writing stories and poetry as a boy. His education in England was interrupted by his service in the British Army during World War I. As a youth, Lewis gave up any belief in God and lived for many years as an atheist. Over time, he returned to a belief in a god; eventually, he became a passionate Christian.

During World War II, Lewis gave radio talks on Christianity that were later organized into the extremely popular *Mere Christianity*. Lewis filled this and his other works with many simple illustrations. Yet, his style of writing for "the common man" is deceptive. *Mere Christianity* discusses some of the most profound philosophical and theological issues.

The Screwtape Letters is a book-length collection of short and humorous letters from an experienced demon to his nephew demon, who is just now taking up the trade of tempting humans. Lewis used these letters as a vehicle for thoughtfully exploring many spiritual issues: (a) the relationship that can exist between the Creator God and the lone individual, (b) the issue of good and evil in a world created by a totally good God, (c) the relationship between the physical and spiritual dimensions of human life, and so forth. In *The Screwtape Letters*, the world has been turned upside down. Satan is called "Our Father" or "Our Father Below." God is called "the Enemy." "The patient" is the human victim of the demon's attacks. World War II is mentioned in the letters in order to root them in the day-to-day experiences of Lewis's readers.

In *The Lion, the Witch, and the Wardrobe*, four children stumble into another world called Narnia, where the White Witch has cruelly ruled a kingdom of talking animals. Some of the animals submit and willingly follow the witch, but some are secretly hoping that Aslan, the true authority of Narnia, will return to the land and overthrow the witch. There are prophecies that Aslan (a great lion) and four humans will come to Narnia to "set things right." In the prophecies, four humans will someday sit upon the four thrones in Cair Paravel and bring peace to the kingdom.

In the early chapters of *The Lion, the Witch, and the Wardrobe*, Edmund, one of the children, is constantly shown to be selfish and deceitful. Once in Narnia, Edmund becomes a traitor and helps the evil White Witch. Eventually, Edmund realizes his mistake, but there are consequences for Edmund's treachery. Edmund becomes a prisoner of the witch. According to the magical laws of Narnia, the witch has the right to sacrifice all traitors on "The Stone Table." In an odd twist, Aslan gives himself to be sacrificed in Edmund's place. Thus, the Christian theme of "substitutionary atonement" is enacted. Lewis's story also parallels the Christian theme of Christ's resurrection, which validates his atoning work for humanity.

FROM MERE CHRISTIANITY

Book I, Chapter 5. We Have Cause To Be Uneasy

I ended my last chapter with the idea that in the Moral Law somebody or something from beyond the material universe was actually getting at us. And I expect when I reached that point some of you felt a certain annoyance. You may even have thought that I had played a trick on you—that I had been carefully wrapping up to look like philosophy what turns out to be one more "religious jaw." You may have felt you were ready to listen to me as long as you thought I had anything new to say; but if it turns out to be only religion, well, the world has tried that and you cannot put the clock back. If anyone is feeling that way I should like to say three things to him.

First, as to putting the clock back. Would you think I was joking if I said that you can put a clock back, and that if the clock is wrong it is often a very sensible thing to do? But I would rather get away from that whole idea of clocks. We all want progress. But progress means getting nearer to the place where you want to be. And if you have taken a wrong turning, then to go forward does not get you any nearer. If you are on the wrong road, progress means doing an about-turn and walking back to the right road; and in that case the man who turns back soonest is the most progressive man. We have all seen this when doing arithmetic. When I have started a sum the wrong way, the sooner I admit this and go back and start over again, the faster I shall get on. There is nothing progressive about being pigheaded and refusing to admit a mistake. And I think if you look at the present state of the world, it is pretty plain that humanity has been making some big mistake. We are on the wrong road. And if that is so, we must go back. Going back is the quickest way on.

Then, secondly, this has not yet turned exactly into a "religious jaw." We have not yet got as far as the God of any actual religion, still less the God of that particular religion called Christianity. We have only got as far as a Somebody or

Something behind the Moral Law. We are not taking anything from the Bible or the Churches, we are trying to see what we can find out about this Somebody on our own steam. And I want to make it quite clear that what we find out on our own steam is something that gives us a shock. We have two bits of evidence about the Somebody. One is the universe He has made. If we used that as our only clue, then I think we should have to conclude that He was a great artist (for the universe is a very beautiful place), but also that He is quite merciless and no friend to man (for the universe is a very dangerous and terrifying place). The other bit of evidence is that Moral Law which He has put into our minds. And this is a better bit of evidence than the other, because it is inside information. You find out more about God from the Moral Law than from the universe in general just as you find out more about a man by listening to his conversation than by looking at a house he has built. Now, from this second bit of evidence we conclude that the Being behind the universe is intensely interested in right conduct—in fair play, unselfishness, courage, good faith, honesty and truthfulness. In that sense we should agree with the account given by Christianity and some other religions, that God is "good." But do not let us go too fast here. The Moral Law does not give us any grounds for thinking that God is "good" in the sense of being indulgent, or soft, or sympathetic. There is nothing indulgent about the Moral Law. It is as hard as nails. It tells you to do the straight thing and it does not seem to care how painful, or dangerous, or difficult it is to do. If God is like the Moral Law, then He is not soft. It is no use, at this stage, saying that what you mean by a "good" God is a God who can forgive. You are going too quickly. Only a Person can forgive. And we have not yet got as far as a personal God—only as far as a power, behind the Moral Law, and more like a mind than it is like anything else. But it may still be very unlike a Person. If it is pure impersonal mind, there may be no sense in asking it to make allowances for you or let you off, just as there is no sense in asking the multiplication table to let you off when you do your sums wrong. You are bound to get the wrong answer. And it is no use either saying that if there is a God of that sort—an impersonal absolute goodness—then you do not like Him and are not going to bother about Him. For the trouble is that one part of you is on His side and really agrees with His disapproval of human greed and trickery and exploitation. You may want Him to make an exception in your own case, to let you off this one time; but you know at bottom that unless the power behind the world really and unalterably detests that sort of behaviour, then He cannot be good. On the other hand, we know that if there does exist an absolute goodness it must hate most of what we do. That is the terrible fix we are in. If the universe is not governed by an absolute goodness, then all our efforts are in the long run hopeless. But if it is, then we are making ourselves enemies to that goodness every day, and are not in the least likely to do any better tomorrow, and so our case is hopeless again. We cannot do without it, and we cannot do with it. God is the only comfort, He is also the supreme terror: the thing we most need and the thing we most want to hide from. He is our only possible ally, and we have made ourselves His enemies. Some people talk as if meeting the gaze of absolute goodness would be fun. They need to think again.

They are still only playing with religion. Goodness is either the great safety or the great danger—according to the way you react to it. And we have reacted the wrong way.

Now my third point. When I chose to get to my real subject in this roundabout way, I was not trying to play any kind of trick on you. I had a different reason. My reason was that Christianity simply does not make sense until you have faced the sort of facts I have been describing. Christianity tells people to repent and promises them forgiveness. It therefore has nothing (as far as I know) to say to people who do not know they have done anything to repent of and who do not feel that they need any forgiveness. It is after you have realised that there is a real Moral Law, and a Power behind the law, and that you have broken that law and put yourself wrong with that Power—it is after all this, and not a moment sooner, that Christianity begins to talk. When you know you are sick, you will listen to the doctor. When you have realised that our position is nearly desperate you will begin to understand what the Christians are talking about. They offer an explanation of how we got into our present state of both hating goodness and loving it. They offer an explanation of how God can be this impersonal mind at the back of the Moral Law and yet also a Person. They tell you how the demands of this law, which you and I cannot meet, have been met on our behalf, how God Himself becomes a man to save man from the disapproval of God. It is an old story and if you want to go into it you will no doubt consult people who have more authority to talk about it than I have. All I am doing is to ask people to face the facts—to understand the questions which Christianity claims to answer. And they are very terrifying facts. I wish it was possible to say something more agreeable. But I must say what I think true. Of course, I quite agree that the Christian religion is, in the long run, a thing of unspeakable comfort. But it does not begin in comfort; it begins in the dismay I have been describing, and it is no use at all trying to go on to that comfort without first going through that dismay. In religion, as in war and everything else, comfort is the one thing you cannot get by looking for it. If you look for truth, you may find comfort in the end; if you look for comfort you will not get either comfort or truth—only soft soap and wishful thinking to begin with and, in the end, despair. Most of us have got over the pre-war wishful thinking about international politics. It is time we did the same about religion.

Book II, Chapter 2. The Invasion

Very well then, atheism is too simple. And I will tell you another view that is also too simple. It is the view I call Christianity-and-water, the view which simply says there is a good God in Heaven and everything is all right—leaving out all the difficult and terrible doctrines about sin and hell and the devil, and the redemption. Both these are boys' philosophies.

It is no good asking for a simple religion. After all, real things are not simple. They look simple, but they are not. The table I am sitting at looks simple: but ask a scientist to tell you what it is really made of—all about the atoms and how the light waves rebound from them and hit my eye and what they do to the optic nerve and what it does to my brain—and, of course, you find that what we call "seeing a table" lands you in mysteries and complications which you can hardly get to the end of. A child saying a child's prayer looks simple. And if you are content to stop there, well and good. But if you are not—and the modern world usually is not—if you want to go on and ask what is really happening—then you must be prepared for something difficult. If we ask for something more than simplicity, it is silly then to complain that the something more is not simple.

Very often, however, this silly procedure is adopted by people who are not silly, but who, consciously or unconsciously, want to destroy Christianity. Such people put up a version of Christianity suitable for a child of six and make that the object of their attack. When you try to explain the Christian doctrine as it is really held by an instructed adult, they then complain that you are making their heads turn round and that it is all too complicated and that if there really were a God they are sure He would have made "religion" simple, because simplicity is so beautiful, etc. You must be on your guard against these people for they will change their ground every minute and only waste your time. Notice, too, their idea of God "making religion simple": as if "religion" were something God invented, and not His statement to us of certain quite unalterable facts about His own nature.

Besides being complicated, reality, in my experience, is usually odd. It is not neat, not obvious, not what you expect. For instance, when you have grasped that the earth and the other planets all go round the sun, you would naturally expect that all the planets were made to match—all at equal distances from each other, say, or distances that regularly increased, or all the same size, or else getting bigger or smaller as you go farther from the sun. In fact, you find no rhyme or reason (that we can see) about either the sizes or the distances; and some of them have one moon, one has four, one has two, some have none, and one has a ring.

Reality, in fact, is usually something you could not have guessed. That is one of the reasons I believe Christianity. It is a religion you could not have guessed. If it offered us just the kind of universe we had always expected, I should feel we were making it up. But, in fact, it is not the sort of thing anyone would have made up. It has just that queer twist about it that real things have. So let us leave behind all these boys' philosophies—these over-simple answers. The problem is not simple and the answer is not going to be simpler either.

What is the problem? A universe that contains much that is obviously bad and apparently meaningless, but containing creatures like ourselves who know that it is bad and meaningless. There are only two views that face all the facts. One is the Christian view that this is a good world that has gone wrong, but still retains the memory of what it ought to have been. The other is the view called Dualism. Dualism means the belief that there are two equal and independent powers at the back of everything, one of them good and the other bad, and that this universe is the battlefield in which they fight out an endless war. I personally think that next to Christianity Dualism is the manliest and most sensible creed on the market. But it has a catch in it.

The two powers, or spirits, or gods—the good one and the bad one—are supposed to be quite independent. They both existed from all eternity. Neither of them made the other, neither of them has any more right than the other to call itself God. Each presumably thinks it is good and thinks the other bad. One of them likes hatred and cruelty, the other likes love and mercy, and each backs its own view. Now what do we mean when we call one of them the Good Power and the other the Bad Power? Either we are merely saying that we happen to prefer the one to the other—like preferring beer to cider—or else we are saying that, whatever the two powers think about it, and whichever we humans, at the moment, happen to like, one of them is actually wrong, actually mistaken, in regarding itself as good. Now if we mean merely that we happen to prefer the first, then we must give up talking about good and evil at all. For good means what you ought to prefer quite regardless of what you happen to like at any given moment. If "being good" meant simply joining the side you happened to fancy, for no real reason, then good would not deserve to be called good. So we must mean that one of the two powers is actually wrong and the other actually right.

But the moment you say that, you are putting into the universe a third thing in addition to the two Powers: some law or standard or rule of good which one of the powers conforms to and the other fails to conform to. But since the two powers are judged by this standard, then this standard, or the Being who made this standard, is farther back and higher up than either of them, and He will be the real God. In fact, what we meant by calling them good and bad turns out to be that one of them is in a right relation to the real ultimate God and the other in a wrong relation to Him.

The same point can be made in a different way. If Dualism is true, then the bad Power must be a being who likes badness for its own sake. But in reality we have no experience of anyone liking badness just because it is bad. The nearest we can get to it is in cruelty. But in real life people are cruel for one of two reasons—either because they are sadists, that is, because they have a sexual perversion which makes cruelty a cause of sensual pleasure to them, or else for the sake of something they are going to get out of it—money, or power, or safety. But pleasure, money, power, and safety are all, as far as they go, good things. The badness consists in pursuing them by the wrong method, or in the wrong way, or too much. I do not mean, of course, that the people who do this are not desperately wicked. I do mean that wickedness, when you examine it, turns out to be the pursuit of some good in the wrong way. You can be good for the mere sake of goodness: you cannot be bad for the mere sake of badness. You can do a kind action when you are not feeling kind and when it gives you no pleasure, simply because kindness is right; but no one ever did a cruel action simply because cruelty is wrong—only because cruelty was pleasant or useful to him. In other words badness cannot succeed even in being bad in the same way in which goodness is good. Goodness is, so to speak, itself: badness is only spoiled goodness. And there must be something good first before it can be spoiled. We called sadism a sexual perversion; but you must first have the idea of a normal sexuality before you can talk of its being perverted; and you can see which is the perversion, because you can explain the perverted from the normal, and cannot explain the normal from the perverted. It follows that this Bad Power, who is supposed to be on an equal footing with the Good Power, and to love badness in the same way as the Good Power loves goodness, is a mere bogy. In order to be bad he must have good things to want and then to pursue in the wrong way: he must have impulses which were originally good in order to be able to pervert them. But if he is bad he cannot supply himself either with good things to desire or with good impulses to pervert. He must be getting both from the Good Power. And if so, then he is not independent. He is part of the Good Power's world: he was made either by the Good Power or by some power above them both.

Put it more simply still. To be bad, he must exist and have intelligence and will. But existence, intelligence and will are in themselves good. Therefore he must be getting them from the Good Power: even to be bad he must borrow or steal from his opponent. And do you now begin to see why Christianity has always said that the devil is a fallen angel? That is not a mere story for the children. It is a real recognition of the fact that evil is a parasite, not an original thing. The powers which enable evil to carry on are powers given it by goodness. All the things which enable a bad man to be effectively bad are in themselves good things—resolution, cleverness, good looks, existence itself. That is why Dualism, in a strict sense, will not work.

But I freely admit that real Christianity (as distinct from Christianity-and-water) goes much nearer to Dualism than people think. One of the things that surprised me when I first read the New Testament seriously was that it talked so much about a Dark Power in the universe—a mighty evil spirit who was held to be the Power behind death and disease, and sin. The difference is that Christianity thinks this Dark Power was created by God, and was good when he was created, and went wrong. Christianity agrees with Dualism that this universe is at war. But it does not think this is a war between independent powers. It thinks it is a civil war, a rebellion, and that we are living in a part of the universe occupied by the rebel.

Enemy-occupied territory—that is what this world is. Christianity is the story of how the rightful king has landed, you might say landed in disguise, and is calling us all to take part in a great campaign of sabotage. When you go to church you are really listening-in to the secret wireless from our friends: that is why the enemy is so anxious to prevent us from going. He does it by playing on our conceit and laziness and intellectual snobbery. I know someone will ask me, "Do you really mean, at this time of day, to re-introduce our old friend the devil—hoofs and horns and all?" Well, what the time of day has to do with it I do not know. And I am not particular about the hoofs and horns. But in other respects my answer is "Yes, I do." I do not claim to know anything about his personal appearance. If anybody really wants to know him better I would say to that person, "Don't worry. If you really want to, you will. Whether you'll like it when you do is another question."

Questions

1. The term *culture* refers to the fact that humans often pass their knowledge from one generation to the next. Each generation does not need to reinvent the wheel or the airplane or fire-making. Culture allows each generation

to begin where the earlier generation stopped learning. As a result, humanity can make progress in science, technology, and other areas. However, after observing the wars and genocides of the twentieth century, Lewis concluded that humans are not making progress morally or spiritually. What do you think? Is humanity making progress in the areas of morality and religion?

2. Lewis was a soldier in World War I, and he observed the long struggle of Europe and England in fighting against Hitler's Germany in World War II. In *Mere Christianity* and in other works, Lewis used warfare as a metaphor to explain the spiritual situation of humanity. The warfare metaphor is also found throughout the Bible. How important is this metaphor for understanding Christianity? This metaphor seems to separate Christianity from Hinduism, Buddhism, and other traditions. Why does this occur?

3. Many people have compared Jesus to Socrates, to Buddha, and to other great moral teachers. Why did Lewis state without hesitation that Jesus is not another great moral teacher?

FROM THE SCREWTAPE LETTERS

1

My dear Wormwood,

I note what you say about guiding your patient's reading and taking care that he sees a good deal of his materialist friend. But are you not being a trifle *naïve?* It sounds as if you supposed that *argument* was the way to keep him out of the Enemy's clutches. That might have been so if he had lived a few centuries earlier. At that time the humans still knew pretty well when a thing was proved and when it was not; and if it was proved they really believed it. They still connected thinking with doing and were prepared to alter their way of life as the result of a chain of reasoning. But what with the weekly press and other such weapons we have largely altered that. Your man has been accustomed, ever since he was a boy, to have a dozen incompatible philosophies dancing about together inside his head. He doesn't think of doctrines as primarily 'true' or 'false', but as 'academic' or 'practical', 'outworn' or 'contemporary', 'conventional' or 'ruthless'. Jargon, not argument, is your best ally in keeping him from the Church. Don't waste time trying to make him think that materialism is *true!* Make him think it is strong, or stark, or courageous—that it is the philosophy of the future. That's the sort of thing he cares about.

The trouble about argument is that it moves the whole struggle on to the Enemy's own ground. He can argue too; whereas in really practical propaganda of the kind I am suggesting He has been shown for centuries to be greatly the inferior of Our Father Below. By the very act of arguing, you awake the patient's reason; and once it is awake, who can foresee the result? Even if a particular train of thought can be twisted so as to end in our favour, you will find that you have been strengthening in your patient the fatal habit of attending to universal issues and withdrawing his attention from the stream of immediate sense experiences. Your business is to fix his attention on the stream. Teach him to call it 'real life' and don't let him ask what he means by 'real'.

Remember, he is not, like you, a pure spirit. Never having been a human (oh that abominable advantage of the Enemy's!) you don't realise how enslaved they are to the pressure of the ordinary. I once had a patient, a sound atheist, who used to read in the British Museum. One day, as he sat reading, I saw a train of thought in his mind beginning to go the wrong way. The Enemy, of course, was at his elbow in a moment. Before I knew where I was I saw my twenty years' work beginning to totter. If I had lost my head and begun to attempt a defence by argument. I should have been undone. But I was not such a fool. I struck instantly at the part of the man which I had best under my control and suggested that it was just about time he had some lunch. The Enemy presumably made the counter-suggestion (you know how one can never *quite* overhear what He says to them?) that this was more important than lunch. At least I think that must have been His line for when I said 'Quite. In fact much *too* important to tackle at the end of a morning,' the patient brightened up considerably; and by the time I had added 'Much better come back after lunch and go into it with a fresh mind,' he was already half way to the door. Once he was in the street the battle was won. I showed him a newsboy shouting the midday paper, and a No. 73 bus going past, and before he reached the bottom of the steps I had got into him an unalterable conviction that, whatever odd ideas might come into a man's head when he was shut up alone with his books, a healthy dose of 'real life' (by which he meant the bus and the newsboy) was enough to show him that all 'that sort of thing' just couldn't be true. He knew he'd had a narrow escape and in later years was fond of talking about 'that inarticulate sense for actuality which is our ultimate safeguard against the aberrations of mere logic'. He is now safe in Our Father's house.

You begin to see the point? Thanks to processes which we set at work in them centuries ago, they find it all but impossible to believe in the unfamiliar while the familiar is before their eyes. Keep pressing home on him the *ordinariness* of things. Above all, do not attempt to use science (I mean, the real sciences) as a

defence against Christianity. They will positively encourage him to
think about realities he can't touch and see. There have been sad
cases among the modern physicists. If he must dabble in science,
keep him on economics and sociology; don't let him get away from
that invaluable 'real life'. But the best of all is to let him read no
science but to give him a grand general idea that he knows it all
and that everything he happens to have picked up in casual talk
and reading is 'the results of modern investigation'. Do remember
you are there to fuddle him. From the way some of you young
fiends talk, anyone would suppose it was our job to *teach!*

Your affectionate uncle

SCREWTAPE

8

My dear Wormwood,

So you 'have great hopes that the patient's religious phase is dying
away', have you? I always thought the Training College had gone to
pieces since they put old Slubgob at the head of it, and now I am
sure. Has no one ever told you about the law of Undulation?

Humans are amphibians—half spirit and half animal. (The
Enemy's determination to produce such a revolting hybrid was one
of the things that determined Our Father to withdraw his support
from Him.) As spirits they belong to the eternal world, but as
animals they inhabit time. This means that while their spirit can be
directed to an eternal object, their bodies, passions, and
imaginations are in continual change, for to be in time means to
change. Their nearest approach to constancy, therefore, is
undulation—the repeated return to a level from which they
repeatedly fall back, a series of troughs and peaks. If you had
watched your patient carefully you would have seen this
undulation in every department of his life—his interest in his work,
his affection for his friends, his physical appetites, all go up and
down. As long as he lives on earth periods of emotional and bodily
richness and liveliness will alternate with periods of numbness and
poverty. The dryness and dullness through which your patient is
now going are not, as you fondly suppose, your workmanship;
they are merely a natural phenomenon which will do us no good
unless you make a good use of it.

To decide what the best use of it is, you must ask what use the
Enemy wants to make of it, and then do the opposite. Now it may
surprise you to learn that in His efforts to get permanent possession

of a soul, He relies on the troughs even more than on the peaks; some of His special favourites have gone through longer and deeper troughs than anyone else. The reason is this. To us a human is primarily food; our aim is the absorption of its will into ours, the increase of our own area of selfhood at its expense. But the obedience which the Enemy demands of men is quite a different thing. One must face the fact that all the talk about His love for men, and His service being perfect freedom, is not (as one would gladly believe) mere propaganda, but an appalling truth. He really *does* want to fill the universe with a lot of loathsome little replicas of Himself—creatures whose life, on its miniature scale, will be qualitatively like His own, not because He has absorbed them but because their wills freely conform to His. We want cattle who can finally become food; He wants servants who can finally become sons. "We want to suck in, He wants to give out. We are empty and would be filled; He is full and flows over. Our war aim is a world in which Our Father Below has drawn all other beings into himself: the Enemy wants a world full of beings united to Him but still distinct.

And that is where the troughs come in. You must have often wondered why the Enemy does not make more use of His power to be sensibly present to human souls in any degree He chooses and at any moment. But you now see that the Irresistible and the Indisputable are the two weapons which the very nature of His scheme forbids Him to use. Merely to override a human will (as His felt presence in any but the faintest and most mitigated degree would certainly do) would be for Him useless. He cannot ravish. He can only woo. For His ignoble idea is to eat the cake and have it; the creatures are to be one with Him, but yet themselves; merely to cancel them, or assimilate them, will not serve. He is prepared to do a little overriding at the beginning. He will set them off with communications of His presence which, though faint, seem great to them, with emotional sweetness, and easy conquest over temptation. But He never allows this state of affairs to last long. Sooner or later He withdraws, if not in fact, at least from their conscious experience, all those supports and incentives. He leaves the creature to stand up on its own legs—to carry out from the will alone duties which have lost all relish. It is during such trough periods, much more than during the peak periods, that it is growing into the sort of creature He wants it to be. Hence the prayers offered in the state of dryness are those which please Him best. We can drag our patients along by continual tempting, because we design them only for the table, and the more their will is interfered with the better. He cannot 'tempt' to virtue as we do to vice. He wants them to learn to walk and must therefore take away His hand; and if only the will to walk is really there He is pleased even with their stumbles. Do not be deceived, Wormwood. Our cause is never more in danger than when a human, no longer desiring, but still intending, to do our Enemy's will, looks round upon a universe from which every trace of Him seems to have vanished, and asks why he has been forsaken, and still obeys.

But of course the troughs afford opportunities to our side also. Next week I will give you some hints on how to exploit them,

Your affectionate uncle

SCREWTAPE

Questions

1. In the first letter, Screwtape warns Wormwood not to encourage "in your patient the fatal habit of attending to universal issues." Furthermore, Wormwood is told that it is good for the patient to keep his attention on "the stream of immediate sense experiences." What does Screwtape mean by this passage? What was Lewis's underlying message?

2. In the first letter, Screwtape separates real science from something else. What exactly is that "something else"? At first glance, it looks as if Lewis was against sociology, economics, and other scientific studies. What was Lewis's real concern?

3. The eighth letter introduces many fruitful ideas about the individual's relationship with God. Rather than forcing people to love Him, God woos people into loving Him. Furthermore, Screwtape explains that God sometimes pulls back and allows the humans to struggle in their spiritual growth. Do you agree with this description of the spiritual experience? Does God sometimes seem to pull away from us?

FROM THE LION, THE WITCH AND THE WARDROBE

THE TRIUMPH OF THE WITCH

AS SOON AS THE WITCH HAD GONE ASLAN said, "We must move from this place at once, it will be wanted for other purposes. We shall encamp tonight at the Fords of Beruna."

Of course everyone was dying to ask him how he had arranged matters with the witch; but his face was stern and everyone's ears were still ringing with the sound of his roar and so nobody dared.

After a meal, which was taken in the open air on the hill-top (for the sun had got strong by now and dried the grass), they were busy for a while taking the pavilion down and packing things up. Before two o'clock they were on the march and set off in a Northeasterly direction, walking at an easy pace for they had not far to go.

During the first part of the journey Aslan explained to Peter his plan of campaign. "As soon as she has finished her business in these parts," he said, "the Witch and her crew will almost certainly fall back to her house and prepare for a siege. You may or may not be able to cut her off and prevent her from reaching it." He then went on to outline two plans of battle—one for fighting the Witch and her people in the wood and another for assaulting her castle. And all the time he was advising Peter how to conduct the operations, saying things like, "You must put your Centaurs in such and such a place" or "You must post scouts to see that she doesn't do so-and-so," till at last Peter said,

"But you will be there yourself, Aslan."

"I can give you no promise of that," answered the Lion. And he continued giving Peter his instructions.

For the last part of the journey it was Susan and Lucy who saw most of him. He did not talk very much and seemed to them to be sad.

It was still afternoon when they came down to a place where the river valley had widened out and the river was broad and shallow. This was the Fords of Beruna and Aslan gave orders to halt on this side of the water. But Peter said,

"Wouldn't it be better to camp on the far side—for fear she should try a night attack or anything?"

Aslan, who seemed to have been thinking about something else, roused himself with a shake of his magnificent mane and said, "Eh? What's that?" Peter said it all over again.

"No," said Aslan in a dull voice, as if it didn't matter. "No. She will not make an attack tonight." And then he sighed deeply. But presently he added, "All the same it was well thought of. That is how a soldier ought to think. But it doesn't really matter." So they proceeded to pitch their camp.

Aslan's mood affected everyone that evening. Peter was feeling uncomfortable too at the idea of fighting the battle on his own; the news that Aslan might not be there had come as a great shock to him. Supper that evening was a quiet meal. Everyone felt how different it had been last night or even that morning. It was as if the good times, having just begun, were already drawing to their end.

This feeling affected Susan so much that she couldn't get to sleep when she went to bed. And after she had lain counting sheep and turning over and over she heard Lucy give a long sigh and turn over just beside her in the darkness.

"Can't you get to sleep either?" said Susan.

"No," said Lucy. "I thought you were asleep. I say, Susan!"

"What?"

"I've a most horrible feeling—as if something were hanging over us."

"Have you? Because, as a matter of fact, so have I."

"Something about Aslan," said Lucy. 'Either some dreadful thing is going to happen to him, or something dreadful that he's going to do."

"There's been something wrong with him all afternoon," said Susan. "Lucy! What was that he said about not being with us at the battle? You don't think he could be stealing away and leaving us tonight, do you?"

"Where is he now?" said Lucy. "Is he here in the pavilion?"

"I don't think so."

"Susan! let's go outside and have a look round. We might see him."

"All right. Let's," said Susan; "we might just as well be doing that as lying awake here."

Very quietly the two girls groped their way among the other sleepers and crept out of the tent. The moonlight was bright and everything was quite still except for the noise of the river chattering over the stones. Then Susan suddenly caught Lucy's arm and said, "Look!" On the far side of the camping ground, just where the trees began, they saw the Lion slowly walking away from them into the wood. Without a word they both followed him.

He led them up the steep slope out of the river valley and then slightly to the right—apparently by the very same route which they had used that afternoon in coming from the Hill of the Stone Table. On and on he led them, into dark shadows and out into pale moonlight, getting their feet wet with the heavy dew. He looked somehow different from the Aslan they knew. His tail and his head hung low and he walked slowly as if he were very, very tired. Then, when they were crossing a wide open place where there were no shadows for them to hide in, he stopped and looked round. It was no good trying to run away so they came toward him. When they were closer he said,

"Oh, children, children, why are you following me?"

"We couldn't sleep," said Lucy—and then felt sure that she need say no more and that Aslan knew all they had been thinking.

"Please, may we come with you—wherever you're going?" asked Susan.

"Well—" said Aslan, and seemed to be thinking. Then he said, "I should be glad of company tonight. Yes, you may come, if you will promise to stop when I tell you, and after that leave me to go on alone."

"Oh, thank you, thank you. And we will," said the two girls.

Forward they went again and one of the girls walked on each side of the Lion. But how slowly he walked! And his great, royal head drooped so that his nose nearly touched the grass. Presently he stumbled and gave a low moan.

"Aslan! Dear Aslan!" said Lucy, "what is wrong? Can't you tell us?"

"Are you ill, dear Aslan?" asked Susan.

"No," said Aslan. "I am sad and lonely. Lay your hands on my mane so that I can feel you are there and let us walk like that."

And so the girls did what they would never have dared to do without his permission, but what they had longed to do ever since they first saw him—buried their cold hands in the beautiful sea of fur and stroked it and, so doing, walked with him. And presently they saw that they were going with him up the slope of the hill on which the Stone Table stood. They went up at the side where the trees came furthest up, and when they got to the last tree (it was one that had some bushes about it) Aslan stopped and said,

"Oh, children, children. Here you must stop. And whatever happens, do not let yourselves be seen. Farewell."

And both the girls cried bitterly (though they hardly knew why) and clung to the Lion and kissed his mane and his nose and his paws and his great, sad eyes. Then he turned from them and walked out on to the top of the hill. And Lucy and Susan, crouching in the bushes, looked after him and this is what they saw.

A great crowd of people were standing all round the Stone Table and though the moon was shining many of them carried torches which burned with evil-looking red flames and black smoke. But such people! Ogres with monstrous teeth, and wolves, and bull-headed men; spirits of evil trees and poisonous plants; and other creatures whom I won't describe because if I did the grown-ups would probably not let you read this book—Cruels and Hags and Incubuses, Wraiths, Horrors, Efreets, Sprites, Orknies, Wooses, and Ettins. In fact here were all those who were on the Witch's side and whom the Wolf had summoned at her command. And right in the middle, standing by the Table, was the Witch herself.

A howl and a gibber of dismay went up from the creatures when they first saw the great Lion pacing toward them, and for a moment even the Witch herself seemed to be struck with fear. Then she recovered herself and gave a wild, fierce laugh.

"The fool!" she cried. "The fool has come. Bind him fast."

Lucy and Susan held their breaths waiting for Aslan's roar and his spring upon his enemies. But it never came. Four Hags, grinning and leering, yet also (at first) hanging back and half afraid of what they had to do, had approached him. "Bind him, I say!" repeated the White Witch. The Hags made a dart at him and shrieked with triumph when they found that he made no resistance at all. Then others—evil dwarfs and apes—rushed in to help them, and between them they rolled the huge Lion over on his back and tied all his four paws together, shouting and cheering as if they had done something brave, though, had the Lion chosen, one of those paws could have been the death of them all. But he made no noise, even when the enemies, straining and tugging, pulled the cords so tight that they cut into his flesh. Then they began to drag him toward the Stone Table.

"Stop!" said the Witch. "Let him first be shaved."

Another roar of mean laughter went up from her followers as an ogre with a pair of shears came forward and squatted down by Aslan's head. Snip-snip-snip went the shears and masses of curling gold began to fall to the ground. Then the ogre stood back and the children, watching from their hiding-place, could see the face of Aslan looking all small and different without its mane. The enemies also saw the difference.

"Why, he's only a great cat after all!" cried one.

"Is *that* what we were afraid of?" said another.

And they surged round Aslan, jeering at him, saying things like "Puss, Puss! Poor Pussy," and "How many mice have you caught today, Cat?" and "Would you like a saucer of milk, Pussums?"

"Oh, how *can* they?" said Lucy, tears streaming down her cheeks. "The brutes, the brutes!" for now that the first shock was over the shorn face of Aslan looked to her braver, and more beautiful, and more patient than ever.

"Muzzle him!" said the Witch. And even now, as they worked about his face putting on the muzzle, one bite from his jaws would have cost two or three of them their hands. But he never moved. And this seemed to enrage all that rabble. Everyone was at him now. Those who had been afraid to come near him even after he was bound began to find their courage, and for a few minutes the two girls could not even see him—so thickly was he surrounded by the whole crowd of creatures kicking him, hitting him, spitting on him, jeering at him.

At last the rabble had had enough of this. They began to drag the bound and muzzled Lion to the Stone Table, some pulling and some pushing. He was so huge that even when they got him there it took all their efforts to hoist him onto the surface of it. Then there was more tying and tightening of cords.

"The cowards! The cowards!" sobbed Susan. "Are they *still* afraid of him, even now?"

When once Aslan had been tied (and tied so that he was really a mass of cords) on the flat stone, a hush fell on the crowd. Four Hags, holding four torches, stood at the corners of the Table. The Witch bared her arms as she had bared them the previous night when it had been Edmund instead of Aslan. Then she began to whet her knife. It looked to the children, when the gleam of the torchlight fell on it, as if the knife were made of stone, not of steel, and it was of a strange and evil shape.

At last she drew near. She stood by Aslan's head. Her face was working and twitching with passion, but his looked up at the sky, still quiet, neither angry nor afraid, but a little sad. Then, just before she gave the blow, she stooped down and said in a quivering voice,

"And now, who has won? Fool, did you think that by all this you would save the human traitor? Now I will kill you instead of him as our pact was and so the Deep Magic will be appeased. But when you are dead what will prevent me from killing him as well? And who will take him out of my hand *then?* Understand that you have given me Narnia forever, you have lost your own life and you have not saved his. In that knowledge, despair and die."

The children did not see the actual moment of the killing. They couldn't bear to look and had covered their eyes.

DEEPER MAGIC FROM BEFORE THE DAWN OF TIME

WHILE THE TWO GIRLS STILL CROUCHED in the bushes with their hands over their faces, they heard the voice of the Witch calling out,

"Now! Follow me all and we will set about what remains of this war! It will not take us long to crush the human vermin and the traitors now that the great Fool, the great Cat, lies dead."

At this moment the children were for a few seconds in very great danger. For with wild cries and a noise of skirling pipes and shrill horns blowing, the whole of that vile rabble came sweeping off the hilltop and down the slope right past their hiding-place. They felt the Specters go by them like a cold wind and they felt the ground shake beneath them under the galloping feet of the Mino-taurs; and overhead there went a flurry of foul wings and a blackness of vultures and giant bats. At any other time they would have trembled with fear; but now the sadness and shame and horror of Aslan's death so filled their minds that they hardly thought of it.

As soon as the wood was silent again Susan and Lucy crept out onto the open hilltop. The moon was getting low and thin clouds were passing across her, but still they could see the shape of the Lion lying dead in his bonds. And down they both knelt in the wet grass and kissed his cold face and stroked his beautiful fur—what was left of it—and cried till they could cry no more. And then they looked at each other and held each other's hands for mere loneliness and cried again; and then again were silent. At last Lucy said,

"I can't bear to look at that horrible muzzle. I wonder could we take it off?"

So they tried. And after a lot of working at it (for their fingers were cold and it was now the darkest part of the night) they succeeded. And when they saw his face without it they burst out crying again and kissed it and fondled it and wiped away the blood and the foam as well as they could. And it was all more lonely and hopeless and horrid than I know how to describe.

"I wonder could we untie him as well?" said Susan presently. But the enemies, out of pure spitefulness, had drawn the cords so tight that the girls could make nothing of the knots.

I hope no one who reads this book has been quite as miserable as Susan and Lucy were that night; but if you have been—if you've been up all night and cried till you have no more tears left in you—you will know that there comes in the end a sort of quietness. You feel as if nothing was ever going to happen again. At any rate that was how it felt to these two. Hours and hours seemed to go by in this dead calm, and they hardly noticed that they were getting colder and colder. But at last Lucy noticed two other things. One was that the sky on the east side of the hill was a little less dark than it had been an hour ago. The other was some tiny movement going on in the grass at her feet. At first she took no interest in this. What did it matter? Nothing mattered now! But at last she saw that whatever-it-was had begun to move up the upright stones of the Stone Table. And now whatever-they-were were moving about on Aslan's body. She peered closer. They were little gray things.

"Ugh!" said Susan from the other side of the Table. "How beastly! There are horrid little mice crawling over him. Go away, you little beasts." And she raised her hand to frighten them away.

"Wait!" said Lucy, who had been looking at them more closely still. "Can you see what they're doing?"

Both girls bent down and stared.

"I do believe—" said Susan. "But how queer! They're nibbling away at the cords!"

"That's what I thought," said Lucy. "I think they're friendly mice. Poor little things—they don't realize he's dead. They think it'll do some good untying him."

It was quite definitely lighter by now. Each of the girls noticed for the first time the white face of the other. They could see the mice nibbling away; dozens and dozens, even hundreds, of little field mice. And at last, one by one, the ropes were all gnawed through.

The sky in the East was whitish by now and the stars were getting fainter—all except one very big one low down on the Eastern horizon. They felt colder than they had been all night. The mice crept away again.

The girls cleared away the remains of the gnawed ropes. Aslan looked more like himself without them. Every moment his dead face looked nobler, as the light grew and they could see it better.

In the wood behind them a bird gave a chuckling sound. It had been so still for hours and hours that it startled them. Then another bird answered it. Soon there were birds singing all over the place.

It was quite definitely early morning now, not late night.

"I'm so cold," said Lucy.

"So am I," said Susan. "Let's walk about a bit."

They walked to the Eastern edge of the hill and looked down. The one big star had almost disappeared. The country all looked dark gray, but beyond, at the very end of the world, the sea showed pale. The sky began to turn red. They walked to and fro more times than they could count between the dead Aslan and the Eastern ridge, trying to keep warm; and oh, how tired their legs felt. Then at last, as they stood for a moment looking out toward the sea and Cair Paravel (which they could now just make out) the red turned to gold along the line where the sea and the sky met and very slowly up came the edge of the sun. At that moment they heard from behind them a loud noise—a great cracking, deafening noise as if a giant had broken a giant's plate.

"What's that?" said Lucy, clutching Susan's arm.

"I—I feel afraid to turn round," said Susan; "something awful is happening."

"They're doing something worse to *Him*" said Lucy. "Come on!" And she turned, pulling Susan round with her.

The rising of the sun had made everything look so different—all colors and shadows were changed—that for a moment they didn't see the important thing. Then they did. The Stone Table was broken into two pieces by a great crack that ran down it from end to end; and there was no Aslan.

"Oh, oh, oh!" cried the two girls, rushing back to the Table.

"Oh, it's *too* bad," sobbed Lucy; "they might have left the body alone."

"Who's done it?" cried Susan. "What does it mean? Is it more magic?"

"Yes!" said a great voice behind their backs. "It is more magic." They looked round. There, shining in the sunrise, larger than they had seen him before, shaking his mane (for it had apparently grown again) stood Aslan himself.

"Oh, Aslan!" cried both the children, staring up at him, almost as much frightened as they were glad.

"Aren't you dead then, dear Aslan?" said Lucy.

"Not now," said Aslan.

"You're not—not a—?" asked Susan in a shaky voice. She couldn't bring herself to say the word *ghost* Aslan stooped his golden head and licked her forehead. The warmth of his breath and a rich sort of smell that seemed to hang about his hair came all over her.

"Do I look it?" he said.

"Oh, you're real, you're real! Oh, Aslan!" cried Lucy, and both girls flung themselves upon him and covered him with kisses.

"But what does it all mean?" asked Susan when they were somewhat calmer.

"It means," said Aslan, "that though the Witch knew the Deep Magic, there is a magic deeper still which she did not know. Her knowledge goes back only to the dawn of time. But if she could have looked a little further back, into the stillness and the darkness before Time dawned, she would have read there a different incantation. She would have known . that when a willing victim who had committed no treachery was killed in a traitor's stead, the Table would crack and Death itself would start working backward. And now—"

"Oh yes. Now?" said Lucy, jumping up and clapping her hands.

"Oh, children," said the Lion, "I feel my strength coming back to me. Oh, children, catch me if you can!" He stood for a second, his eyes very bright, his limbs quivering, lashing himself with his tail. Then he made a leap high over their heads and landed on the other side of the Table. Laughing, though she didn't know why, Lucy scrambled over it to reach him. Aslan leaped again. A mad chase began. Round and round the hilltop he led them, now hopelessly out of their reach, now letting them almost catch his tail, now diving between them, now tossing them in the air with his huge and beautifully velveted paws and catching them again, and now stopping unexpectedly so that all three of them rolled over together in a happy laughing heap of fur and arms and legs. It was such a romp as no one has ever had except in Narnia; and whether it was more like playing with a thunderstorm or playing with a kitten Lucy could never make up her mind. And the funny thing was that when all three finally lay together panting in the sun the girls no longer felt in the least tired or hungry or thirsty.

"And now," said Aslan presently, "to business. I feel I am going to roar. You had better put your fingers in your ears."

And they did. And Aslan stood up and when he opened his mouth to roar his face became so terrible that they did not dare to look at it. And they saw all the trees in front of him bend before the blast of his roaring as grass bends in a meadow before the wind. Then he said,

"We have a long journey to go. You must ride on me." And he crouched down and the children climbed onto his warm, golden back, and Susan sat first, holding on tightly to his mane and Lucy sat behind holding on tightly to Susan. And with a great heave he rose underneath them and then shot off, faster than any horse could go, down hill and into the thick of the forest.

That ride was perhaps the most wonderful thing that happened to them in Narnia. Have you ever had a gallop on a horse? Think of that; and then take away the heavy noise of the hoofs and the jingle of the bits and imagine instead the almost noiseless padding of the great paws. Then imagine instead of the black or gray or chestnut back of the horse the soft roughness of golden fur, and the mane flying back in the wind. And then imagine you are going about twice as fast as the fastest racehorse. But this is a mount that doesn't need to be guided and never grows tired. He rushes on and on, never missing his footing, never hesitating, threading his way with perfect skill between tree trunks, jumping over bush and briar and the smaller streams, wading the larger, swimming the largest of all. And you are riding not on a road nor in a park nor even on the downs, but right across Narnia, in spring, down solemn avenues of beech and across sunny glades of oak, through wild orchards of snow-white cherry trees, past roaring waterfalls and mossy rocks and echoing caverns, up windy slopes alight with gorse bushes, and across the shoulders of heathery mountains and along giddy ridges and down, down, down again into wild valleys and out into acres of blue flowers.

It was nearly midday when they found themselves looking down a steep hillside at a castle—a little toy castle it looked from where they stood—which seemed to be all pointed towers. But the Lion was rushing down at such a speed that it grew larger every moment and before they had time even to ask themselves what it was they were already on a level with it. And now it no longer looked like a toy castle but rose frowning in front of them. No face looked over the battlements and the gates were fast shut. And Aslan, not at all slacking his pace, rushed straight as a bullet toward it.

"The Witch's home!" he cried. "Now, children, hold tight."

Next moment the whole world seemed to turn upside down, and the children felt as if they had left their insides behind them; for the Lion had gathered himself together for a greater leap than any he had yet made and jumped—or you may call it flying rather than jumping—right over the castle wall. The two girls, breathless but unhurt, found themselves tumbling off his back in the middle of a wide stone courtyard full of statues.

Questions

1. The theme of battle is constant throughout this novel. Why would Lewis use this theme in a children's novel?
2. In the description of the resurrection of Aslan, note the confusion in the girls' minds. They wonder if Aslan really died, and they wonder if Aslan is really alive. Both questions are affirmed. What is the significance of these issues?
3. Why did Lewis present Aslan and the girls as laughing and tumbling, and later flying through the air? What emotional responses are drawn out of the reader in this section of the novel? Is there a relationship between these responses and Lewis's view of Christianity?

ALEXANDER SOLZHENITSYN

Alexander Solzhenitsyn (1918–2008) is known around the world for his novels and short stories about Soviet Russia. He was a creative, honest, and skillful writer. He was also a historian of the Communist political system, which attempted to dominate the lives, the hearts, and the minds of the Russian people. As a young man, Solzhenitsyn was a faithful Russian who served his country in World War II. However, toward the end of the war, he was put on trial for writing a few negative comments about the Soviet dictator, Joseph Stalin, in a private letter to a friend. As a result, he was imprisoned in a Siberian work camp. Eventually, he was freed from prison, but his movement within Russia was restricted by the government.

In his writings, Solzhenitsyn was a harsh critic of the soulless materialism of Communism. Yet, Solzhenitsyn maintained a constant love and respect for the common people of Russia. Later, while living in exile in the United States, he was also a critic of the equally soulless materialism of Western consumerism and Western pop culture.

During a brief period when some freedom of speech was allowed, Solzhenitsyn's first novel, *One Day in the Life of Ivan Denisovich,* was published for Russian readers. As a result, he was instantly respected around the world for his literary skills and insight. In this novel, the reader follows one day in the life of a simple peasant living in a Siberian work camp. Toward the end of the day (and the end of the novel), Ivan Denisovich Shukhov and the other prisoners have a few moments of freedom as they prepare to go to sleep after laboring in the cold Siberian winter. In this passage, it is mentioned that the prisoners are allowed to get parcels from home. Shukhov's family is too poor to send him anything, but Tsezar (a member of Shukhov's squad, or gang) receives a package of food. (Throughout the novel, food is a dominant theme in the minds of the prisoners.)

This passage also includes Alyoshka, a "Baptist" who is in the squad. In Russian culture, the term *Baptist* is a general term that refers to anyone who is a non-Russian Orthodox Christian and who has a commitment to a personal relationship with Jesus Christ. Although he was personally supportive of the Russian Orthodox Church in many ways; in this novel, Solzhenitsyn presented Alyoshka as an example of those Christians who have a more real and personal religious life. Alyoshka is a minor character in the novel, but he surfaces from time to time to give a contrasting and spiritual perspective to the other characters' constant cravings for food and warmth. His "Testament" is a hand-copied portion of the Bible, which Alyoshka keeps hidden near his bunk.

Among the other characters in this passage is "the Captain" (Buynovsky), who is a former naval officer who has been falsely charged with being an enemy of the state. At the end of the day, the Captain is sent to a punishment cell. During an earlier search by the guards, he was found to be wearing an extra piece of clothing in order to stay warm. His penalty is ten days in a cell.

When reading this selection, it is helpful to know that *skilly* is a thin stew and that the prisoners are called *lags* or *zeks*. It is also helpful to know that the prisoners have numbers painted on their clothes; thus, "YU-81" is a member of another squad. Shukhov does not know his name, but his number is clearly visible on this clothing. The squads also have numbers. Shukhov's squad is "the 104th."

FROM ONE DAY IN THE LIFE OF IVAN DENISOVICH

Shukhov finished off his skilly, not taking much notice of those around him—it didn't much matter, he was content with his lawful portion and had no hankering after anything more. All the same, he did notice the tall old man, Yu-81, sit down opposite him when the place became free. Shukhov knew that he belonged to Gang 64, and standing in line in the parcel room he'd heard that 64 had been sent to Sotsgorodok in place of 104, and spent the whole day stringing up barbed wire—making themselves a compound—with nowhere to get warm.

He'd heard that this old man had been in prison time out of mind—in fact, as long as the Soviet state had existed; that all the amnesties had passed him by, and that as soon as he finished one tenner they'd pinned another on him.

This was Shukhov's chance to take a close look at him. With hunched-over lags all round, he was as straight-backed as could be. He sat tall, as though he'd put something on the bench under him. That head hadn't needed a barber for ages: the life of luxury had caused all his hair to fall out. The old man's eyes didn't dart around to take in whatever was going on in the mess, but stared blindly at something over Shukhov's head. He was steadily eating his thin skilly, but instead of almost dipping his head in the bowl like the rest of them, he carried his battered wooden spoon up high. He had no teeth left, upper or lower, but his bony gums chewed his bread just as well without them. His face was worn thin, but it wasn't the weak face of a burnt-out invalid, it was like dark chiseled stone. You could tell from his big chapped and blackened hands that in all his years inside he'd never had a soft job as a trusty. But he refused to knuckle under: he didn't put his three hundred grams [of bread] on the dirty table, splashed all over, like the others, he put it on a rag he washed regularly.

No time to go on studying him, though. Shukhov licked his spoon and tucked it inside his boot, crammed his cap on his head, rose, picked up the bread—his own ration and Tsezar's—and left. You went out by the back porch, past two orderlies with nothing to do other than lift the catch, let you out, and lower the catch again.

Shukhov left with a well-filled belly, at peace with himself, and decided to pop over to the Latvian even though it was nearly lights-out. He strode briskly toward Hut 7, without stopping to leave the bread at No. 9.

The moon was as high as it would ever be, it looked like a hole cut in the sky. The sky was cloudless. With here and there the brightest stars you ever saw. But Shukhov had less time still for studying the sky. All he knew was that the frost wasn't easing up. Somebody had heard from the free workers—it had been on the radio—that they were expecting thirty degrees below at night and forty by morning.

You could hear things a long way off. A tractor roaring in the settlement. The grating noise of an excavator over toward the highroad. The crunch of every pair of felt boots walking or running across the camp.

There was no wind now.

He was going to buy homegrown tobacco at the same price as before—a ruble for a tumblerful. Outside the camp, it cost three rubles, or more, depending on the quality. But prices in the camps weren't like those anywhere else. You weren't allowed to hang on to money, so what little you had bought more. This camp paid no money wage. (In Ust-Izhma, Shukhov had earned thirty rubles a month—better than nothing.) If a man's family sent him money, it wasn't passed on to him but credited to his personal account. This credit gave him the right to buy toilet soap, moldy gingerbread, and Prima cigarettes once a month in the camp shop. Whether you liked them or not, you had to buy the goods once you'd ordered them through the commandant. If you didn't buy, the money was written off and you'd seen the last of it.

Money came Shukhov's way only from the private jobs he did: two rubles for making slippers from rags supplied by the customer, an agreed price for patching a jerkin.

Hut 7 wasn't divided into two large sections like No. 9. In Hut 7, ten doors opened onto a large corridor. Seven double-decker bunks were wedged into every room, and occupied by a single gang. There was also a cubicle below the night-tub storeroom, and another for the hut monitor. The artists had a cubicle as well.

Shukhov went into the room where his Latvian was. He was lying on the lower bed space with his feet up on the brace, gabbling away to his neighbor in Latvian.

Shukhov sat down by him, and mumbled some sort of greeting. The other man answered without lowering his feet. It was a small room, and they were all curious to know who this was and why he had come. Both of them realized this, so Shukhov sat there talking about nothing. How're you getting along, then? Not too bad. Cold today. Yes, it is.

He waited for the others to start talking again—they were arguing about the Korean War: would there be a world war now that the Chinese had joined in?—then bent his head toward the Latvian: "Any homegrown?"

"Yes."

"Let's have a look."

The Latvian swung his feet down from the angle brace, lowered them to the gangway, and rose. A skinflint, this Latvian—frightened to death he might stuff one smoke too many into the tumbler.

He showed Shukhov the pouch and snapped open the clasp.

Shukhov took a pinch on his palm and saw that it was the same as last time—same cut, and dark brown. He raised it to his nose and sniffed—yes, it was the same. But what he said to the Latvian was "Doesn't seem the same, somehow."

"It is! It is the same!" the Latvian said angrily. "I never have any other sort, it's always the same."

"All right, all right," Shukhov said agreeably. "Give me a good tumblerful and I'll try a puff. Maybe I'll take two lots."

He said, Give me a good tumblerful, because the Latvian always packed the tobacco loosely.

The Latvian took another pouch fatter than the first from under his pillow and got a beaker from his locker. A plastic one, but Shukhov had measured it and knew it held the same as a glass tumbler.

The Latvian shook tobacco into it.

"Come on, press it down a bit," Shukhov said, pushing his own finger into the beaker.

"I don't need your help." The Latvian snatched the beaker away angrily and pressed the tobacco down himself, but less firmly. He shook in some more.

In the meantime, Shukhov unbuttoned his jerkin and groped in the quilted lining for the bit of paper which only his fingers could feel. He used both hands to ease it gradually through the padding toward a little hole in quite a different part of the lining, loosely drawn together with two little stitches. When he had worked it as far as the hole, he pulled the stitches out with his fingernails, folded the piece of paper lengthwise yet again (it was already folded into a long, narrow strip), and drew it out. A two-ruble note. A well-worn one that didn't crackle.

Somebody in the room was bellowing: "Old Man Whiskers [Stalin] won't ever let you go! He wouldn't trust his own brother, let alone a bunch of cretins like you!"

The good thing about hard-labor camps is that you have all the freedom in the world to sound off. In Ust-Izhma you'd only have to whisper that people couldn't buy matches outside and they'd clap another ten on you. Here you could shout anything you liked from a top bunk and the stoolies wouldn't report it, because the security officer couldn't care less.

But Shukhov couldn't afford to hang around talking.

"It's still pretty loose," he complained.

"Here, then!" the other man said, adding an extra pinch.

Shukhov took his pouch from his inside pocket and tipped the home-grown into it from the beaker.

"Right," he said. He didn't want to rush off with his first sweet cigarette on the go. "Fill me another."

He haggled a bit more while the beaker was filled again, then handed his two rubles over, nodded to the Latvian, and went on his way.

Once outside, he was in a great hurry to reach his own hut. He didn't want to miss Tsezar when he got back with the parcel.

But Tsezar was there already, sitting on his lower bunk, feasting his eyes. He had arranged what he had brought on the bunk and on the nightstand. Both were screened from the lamp overhead by Shukhov's upper bunk, and it was pretty dark down there.

Shukhov bent over, inserted himself between Tsezar's bed space and the captain's, and held his hand out.

"Your bread, Tsezar Markovich."

He didn't say, "You got it, then"—that would have been a hint that he was entitled to a share for keeping Tsezar's place in the line. He knew his rights, of course. But even after eight years on general duties he was no scrounger, and as time went by, he was more and more determined not to be.

He couldn't control his eyes, though—the hawk eyes of an old camp hand. They skimmed over the contents of Tsezar's parcel laid out on the bed and the nightstand. The wrappings had not all been removed, and some bags had not been opened at all, but a quick glance and a sniff to make sure told Shukhov that Tsezar had been sent sausage, condensed milk, a big smoked fish, some fatback, biscuits with a nice smell, cake with a different nice smell, at least two kilos of lump sugar, and maybe some butter, as well as cigarettes, pipe tobacco, and quite a few other things.

He learned all this in the time it took to say: "Your bread, Tsezar Markovich."

Tsezar's eyes were wild and his hair all tousled. He was drunk with excitement. (People who received parcels of groceries always got into that state.) He waved the bread away: "Keep it, Ivan Denisovich."

The skilly, and two hundred grams of bread as well—that was a full supper, worth quite as much as Shukhov's share of Tsezar's parcel.

He immediately stopped expecting anything from the goodies on display. No good letting your belly get excited when there's nothing to come.

He'd got four hundred grams of bread, and another two hundred, and at least two hundred in his mattress. That was plenty. He could wolf down two hundred now, gobble up five hundred and fifty in the morning, and still have four hundred to take to work. He was really living it up! The bread in the mattress could stay there a bit. Good job he'd stitched the hole up in time. Somebody in Gang 75 had had things pinched from his nightstand. (Ask the Supreme Soviet to look into it!)

Some people take the view that a man with a parcel is always a tightwad, you have to gouge what you can out of him. But when you think of it—it's easy come, easy go. Even those lucky people are sometimes glad to earn an extra bowl of gruel between parcels. Or scrounge a [cigarette] butt. A bit for the warder, a bit for the team foreman, and you can't leave out the trusty in the parcel room. If you do, he'll mislay your parcel next time around and it'll be there a week before it gets on the list. Then there's the clerk in the storeroom, where all the groceries have to be handed in—Tsezar will be taking a bagful there before work parade next morning to be kept safe from thieves, and hut searches, and because the commandant has so ordered—if you don't make the clerk a handsome gift, he'll pinch a bit here and a bit there . . . He sits there all day behind a locked door with other men's groceries, the rat, and there's no way of checking up on him. Then there's payment for services rendered (by Shukhov to Tsezar, for instance). Then there'll be a little something for the bathhouse man, so he'll pick you out a decent set of clean underwear. Then there's the barber, who shaves you "with paper"— wiping the razor on a scrap of paper, not your bare knee—it may not amount to much, but you have to give him three or four cigarettes. Then there'll be somebody in the CES—to make sure your letters are put aside separately and not lost. Then supposing you want to wangle a day off and rest up in the compound—you need to fix the doctor. You're bound to give something to your neighbor who eats from the same nightstand, like the captain does with Tsezar. And counts every bite you take. The most shameless zek can't hold out against that.

So those who always think the other man's radish is plumper than their own might feel envy, but Shukhov knew what was what and didn't let his belly rumble for other people's goodies.

By now he'd pulled his boots off, climbed up on his bunk, taken the fragment of steel out of his mitten, examined it, and made up his mind to look for a good stone next day and hone himself a cobbler's knife—work at it a bit morning and evening and in four days he'd have a great little knife with a sharp, curved blade.

For the time being, the steel had to be hidden, even at night. He could wedge it between his bedboards and one of the crossbars. While the captain wasn't there for the dust to fall in his face, Shukhov turned back his heavy mattress (stuffed with sawdust, not shavings) at the pillow end, and set about hiding the blade.

His neighbors up top—Alyoshka the Baptist and the two Estonian brothers on the next bunk across the gangway—could see him, but Shukhov knew he was safe with them.

Fetyukov passed down the hut, sobbing. He was bent double. His lips were smeared with blood. He must have been beaten up again for licking out bowls. He walked past the whole team without looking at anybody, not trying to hide his tears, climbed onto his bunk, and buried his face in his mattress.

You felt sorry for him, really. He wouldn't see his time out. He didn't know how to look after himself.

At that point the captain appeared, looking happy, carrying specially brewed tea in a mess tin. There were two buckets of tea in the hut, if you could call it tea. Warm and tea-colored, all right, but like dishwater. And the bucket made it smell of moldy wood pulp. Tea for the common working man, that was. Buynovsky must have gotten a handful of real tea from Tsezar, popped it in the mess tin, and fetched hot water from the boiler. He settled down at his nightstand, mighty pleased with himself.

"Nearly scalded my fingers under the tap," he said, showing off.

Down below there, Tsezar unfolded a sheet of paper and laid things out on it. Shukhov put his mattress back in place, so he wouldn't see and get upset. But yet again they couldn't manage without him. Tsezar rose to his full height in the gangway, so that his eyes were on a level with Shukhov's, and winked: "Denisovich! Lend us your ten-day gadget."

The little folding knife, he meant. Shukhov had one hidden in his bed. Smaller than your finger crooked at the middle knuckle, but the devil would cut fatback five fingers thick. Shukhov had made a beautiful job of that knife and kept it well honed.

He felt for the knife, drew it out, and handed it over. Tsezar gave him a nod and vanished again.

The knife was another earner. Because you could land in the hole (ten days!) for keeping it. Only somebody with no conscience at all would say lend us your knife so we can cut our sausage, and don't think you're getting any.

Tsezar had put himself in debt to Shukhov again.

Now that he'd dealt with the bread and the knives, Shukhov fished out his pouch. He took from it a pinch exactly as big as that he had borrowed and held it out across the gangway to the Estonian, with a thank-you.

The Estonian's lips straightened into a smile of sorts, he muttered something to his brother, and they rolled a separate cigarette to sample Shukhov's tobacco.

Go ahead and try it, it's no worse than yours! Shukhov would have tried it himself, but the clock in his guts said it was very close to roll call. Just the time for the warders to come prowling round the huts. If he wanted a smoke he'd have to go out in the corridor quick, and he fancied it was a bit warmer up on his top bunk. It wasn't at all warm in the hut, and the ceiling was still patterned with hoarfrost. You'd get pretty chilly at night, but for the time being, it was just about bearable.

All his little jobs done, Shukhov began breaking bits from his two hundred grams. He couldn't help listening to the captain and Tsezar drinking tea and talking down below.

"Help yourself, Captain, don't be shy! Have some of this smoked fish. Have some sausage."

"Thank you, I will."

"Butter yourself a piece of this loaf! It's a real Moscow baton!"

"Dear-oh-dear-oh-dear, I just can't believe that somewhere or other batons are still being baked. This sudden abundance reminds me of something that once happened to me. It was at Sevastopol, before the Yalta Conference. The town was absolutely starving and we had to show an American admiral around. So they set up a shop specially, chockful of foodstuff, but it wasn't to be opened until they saw us half a block away, so that the locals wouldn't have time to crowd the place out. Even so, the shop was half full one minute after it opened. And you couldn't ask for the wrong thing. 'Look, butter!' people were shouting, 'Real butter! And white bread!'"

Two hundred harsh voices were raising a din in their half of the hut, but Shukhov still thought he could make out the clanging on the rail. Nobody else heard, though. Shukhov also noticed that the warder they called Snub Nose—a short, red-faced young man—had appeared in the hut. He was holding a piece of paper, and this and his whole manner showed that he hadn't come to catch people smoking or drive them outside for roll call, but was looking for somebody in particular.

Snub Nose consulted his piece of paper and asked: "Where's 104?"

"Here," they answered. The Estonians concealed their cigarettes and waved the smoke away.

"Where's the foreman?"

"What do you want?" Tyurin spoke from his bed, swinging his legs over the edge so that his feet barely touched the floor.

"Have the men who were told to submit written explanations got them ready?"

"They're doing it," Tyurin said confidently.

"They should have been in by now."

"Some of my men are more or less illiterate, it's hard work for them." (Tsezar and the captain, he was talking about. He was sharp, Tyurin. Never stuck for an answer.) "We've got no pens, or ink."

"Well, you should have."

"They keep confiscating it."

"Watch it, foreman, just mind what you're saying, or I'll have you in the cell block," Snub Nose promised, mildly. "The explanatory notes will be in the warders' barracks before work parade in the morning! And you will report that all prohibited articles have been handed in to the personal-property store. Understood?"

"Understood."

("The captain's in the clear!" Shukhov thought. The captain himself was purring over his sausage and didn't hear a thing.)

"Now, then," said the warder. "Shcha-301—is he in your gang?"

"I'll have to look at the list," the foreman said, pretending ignorance. "How can anybody be expected to remember these blasted numbers?" (If he could drag it out till roll call, he might save Buynovsky at least for the night.)

"Buynovsky—is he here?"

"Eh? That's me!" the captain piped up from his hiding place under Shukhov's top bunk.

The quick louse is always first on the comb.

"You, is it? Right then, Shcha-301. Get ready."

"To go where?"

"You know where."

The captain only sighed and groaned. Taking a squadron of torpedo boats out into a stormy sea in the pitch dark must have been easier for him than leaving his friends' company for the icy cell block.

"How many days?" he asked in a faint voice.

"Ten. Come along now, hurry it up!"

Just then the orderlies began yelling, "Roll call! Everybody out for roll call!"

The warder sent to call the roll must be in the hut already.

The captain looked back, wondering whether to take his overcoat. If he did, though, they'd whip it off him and leave him just his jerkin. So better go as he was. The captain had hoped for a while that Volkovoy would forget—but Volkovoy never forgot or forgave—and had made no preparations, hadn't even hidden himself a bit of tobacco in his jerkin. No good holding it in his hand—they'd take it off him the moment they frisked him.

All the same, Tsezar slipped him a couple of cigarettes while he was putting his cap on.

"Well, so long, chums," the captain said with a miserable look, nodding to his teammates, and followed the warder out of the hut.

Several voices called after him, "Keep smiling," "Don't let them get you down"—but there was nothing much you could say. Gang 104 had built the punishment block themselves and knew all about it: the walls were stone, the floor cement, there were no windows at all, the stove was kept just warm enough for the ice on the wall to melt and form puddles on the floor. You slept on bare boards, got three hundred grams of bread a day, skilly only every third day.

Ten days! Ten days in that cell block, if they were strict about it and made you sit out the whole stint, meant your health was ruined for life. It meant tuberculosis and the rest of your days in the hospital.

Fifteen days in there and you'd be six feet under.

Thank heaven for your cozy hut, and keep your nose clean.

"Outside, I said—I'll count to three," the hut orderly shouted. "If anybody's not outside when I get to three, I'll take down his number and report him to the warder."

The hut orderly's another arch-bastard. Imagine—they lock him in with us for the whole night and he isn't afraid of anybody, because he's got the camp brass behind him. It's the other way around—everybody's afraid of him. He'll either betray you to the warders or punch you in the kisser. Disabled, supposed to be, because he lost a finger in a brawl, but he looks like a hood. And that's just what he is—convicted as a common criminal, but they pinned a charge under Article 58, subsection 14 on him as well, which is why he landed in this camp.

There was nothing to stop him jotting your name down, handing it to the warder, and it was two days in the hole, normal working hours. Men had been drifting toward the door, but now they all crowded out, those on the top bunks flopping down like bears to join the milling crowd, trying to push their way through the narrow opening.

Shukhov sprang down nimbly, holding the cigarette he'd just rolled and had been wanting so long, thrust his feet into his boots and was ready to go—but he took pity on Tsezar. Not that he wanted to earn a bit more from Tsezar, he just pitied the man with all his heart: Tsezar might think a lot of himself, but he didn't know the first thing about the facts of life. When you got a parcel, you didn't sit gloating over it, you rushed it off to the storeroom before roll call. Eating could wait. But what could Tsezar do with his parcel now? If he turned out for roll call carrying that great big bag, what a laugh that would be—five hundred men would be roaring with laughter. If he left the stuff where it was, it would very likely be pinched by the first man back from roll call. (In Ust-Izhma the system was even tougher: the crooks would always be home from work first, and by the time the others got in, their nightstands would be cleaned out.)

Shukhov saw that Tsezar was in a panic—but he should have thought about it sooner. He was shoving the fatback and sausage under his shirt—if nothing else, he might be able to take them out to roll call and save them.

Shukhov took pity on him and told him how it was done:

"Sit tight, Tsezar Markovich—lie low, out of the light, and go out last. Don't stir till the warder and the orderlies come around the beds looking in every nook and cranny—then you can go out. Tell 'em you aren't well! And I'll go out first and hop back in first. That's the way to do it."

And off he dashed.

He had to be pretty rough to start with, shoving his way through the crowd (taking good care, though, of the cigarette in his clenched hand). But there was no more shoving in the corridor shared by both halves of the hut and near the outer door. The crafty lot stuck like flies to the walls, leaving free passage for one at a time between the ranks: go out in the cold if you're stupid enough, we'll hang on here a bit! We've been freezing outside all day as it is, why freeze for an extra ten minutes now? We aren't that stupid, you know. You croak today—I'll wait till tomorrow!

Any other time, Shukhov would have propped himself up against the wall with the rest. But now he strode by, sneering.

"What are you afraid of, never seen a Siberian frost before? The wolves are out sunbathing—come and try it! Give us a light, old man!"

He lit up just inside the door and went out on the porch. "Wolf's sunshine" was what they jokingly called the moonlight where Shukhov came from.

The moon had risen very high. As far again and it would be at its highest. Sky white with a greenish tinge, stars bright but far between. Snow sparkling white, barracks walls also white. Camp lights might as well not be there.

A crowd of black jackets was growing thicker outside the next hut. They were coming out to line up. And outside that other one. From hut to hut the buzz of conversation was almost drowned out by the crunch of snow under boots.

Five men went down the steps and lined up facing the door. Three others followed them. Shukhov took his place in the second rank with those three. After a munch of bread and with a cig in his mouth, it wasn't too bad standing there. The Latvian hadn't cheated him—it was really good tobacco, heady and sweet-smelling.

Men gradually trickled through the door, and by now there were two or three more ranks of five behind Shukhov. Those already out were in a foul temper. What did the lousy bastards think they were doing, hanging around in the corridor instead of coming outside? Leaving us to freeze.

No zek ever lays eyes on a clock or watch. What good would it do him, anyway? All a zek needs to know is—how soon is reveille? How long till work parade? Till dinnertime? Till lights-out?

Anyway, evening roll call is supposed to be at nine. But that's not the end of it, because they can make you go through the whole rigmarole twice or three times over. You can't get to sleep before ten. And reveille, they figure, is at five. Small wonder that the Moldavian fell asleep just now before quitting time. If a zek manages to get warm, he's asleep right away. By the end of the week there's so much lost sleep to make up for that if you aren't bundled out to work on Sunday the hut is one great heap of sleeping bodies.

Aha—zeks were pouring down from the porch now—the warder and the hut orderly were kicking their behinds. Give it to them, the swine!

"What the hell are you playing at up there?" the front ranks yelled at them. "Skimming the cream from dung? If you'd come out sooner, they'd have finished counting long ago."

The whole hut came tumbling out. Four hundred men—eighty ranks of five. They lined up—neat fives to begin with, then higgledy-piggledy.

"Sort yourselves out at the back there!" the hut orderly roared from the steps.

They don't do it, the bastards.

Tsezar came out hunched up, acting the invalid, followed by two orderlies from the other half of the hut, two from Shukhov's, and another man with a limp. These five became the front rank, so that Shukhov was now in the third. Tsezar was packed off to the rear.

After this, the warder came out onto the porch. "Form up in fives," he shouted at the rear ranks. He had a good pair of tonsils.

"Form up in fives," the hut orderly bellowed. His tonsils were even healthier.

Still they don't move, damn their eyes.

The hut orderly shot down the steps, hurled himself at them, cursing and thumping backs.

He took care which backs he thumped, though. Only the meek were lambasted.

They finally lined up properly. He went back to his place, and shouted with the warder: "First five! Second! Third!"

Each five shot off into the hut as its number was called. Finished for the day.

Unless there's a second roll call, that is. Any herdsman can count better than those good-for-nothings. He may not be able to read, but the whole time he's driving his herd he knows whether all his calves are there or not. This lot are supposed to be trained, but it's done them no good.

The winter before, there'd been no drying rooms in the camp and everybody kept his boots in the barracks overnight—so they'd chased everybody out for a second, a third, or even a fourth count. The men didn't even dress, but rolled out wrapped in their blankets. Since then, drying rooms had been built—not for every hut, but each gang got a chance to dry its boots every third day. So now they'd started doing second counts inside the huts: driving the men from one half to the other.

Shukhov wasn't first in, but he ran without taking his eyes off the one man in front. He hurried to Tsezar's bed, sat on it, and tugged his boots off. Then he climbed up onto a handy bunk and stood his boots on the stove to dry. You just had to get in first. Then back to Tsezar's bed. He sat with his legs tucked under him, one eye watching to see that Tsezar's sack wasn't swiped from under his pillow, the other on the lookout for anybody storming the stove and knocking his boots off their perch.

He had to shout at one man. "Hey! You there, Ginger! Want a boot in your ugly mug? Put your own boots up, but don't touch other people's!"

Zeks were pouring into the hut now. In Gang 20 there were shouts of "Hand over your boots!"

The men taking the boots to the drying room would be let out and the door locked behind them. They'd come running back, shouting: "Citizen warder! Let us in!"

Meanwhile, the warders would gather in the HQ hut with their boards to check their bookkeeping and see whether anyone had escaped.

None of that mattered to Shukhov at present. Ah—here comes Tsezar, diving between the bunks on his way home.

"Thanks, Ivan Denisovich."

Shukhov nodded and scrambled up top like a squirrel. He could finish eating his two hundred grams, he could smoke a second cigarette, or he could just go to sleep.

Only, he was in such high spirits after such a good day he didn't really feel much like sleeping.

Making his bed wasn't much of a job: he just whisked off his blackish blanket, lay down on the mattress (he couldn't have slept on a sheet since he'd left home in '41—in fact, he couldn't for the life of him see why women bothered with sheets, it just made extra washing), laid his head on the pillow stuffed with shavings, shoved his feet into his jerkin, spread his jacket over his blanket, and—

"Thank God, another day over!"

He was thankful that he wasn't sleeping in the punishment cell. Here it was just about bearable.

Shukhov lay with his head toward the window, Alyoshka on the other half of the bunk with his head at the other end, where light from the bulb would reach him. He was reading his Testament again.

The lamp wasn't all that far away. They could read or even sew.

Alyoshka heard Shukhov thank God out loud, and looked around.

"There you are, Ivan Denisovich, your soul is asking to be allowed to pray to God. Why not let it have its way, eh?"

Shukhov shot a glance at him: the light in his eyes was like candle flame. Shukhov sighed.

"Because, Alyoshka, prayers are like petitions—either they don't get through at all, or else it's 'complaint rejected.'"

Four sealed boxes stood in front of the staff hut, and were emptied once a month by someone delegated for that purpose. Many prisoners dropped petitions into those boxes, then waited, counting the days, expecting an answer in two months, one month . . .

There would be no answer. Or else—"complaint rejected."

"That's because you never prayed long enough or fervently enough, that's why your prayers weren't answered. Prayer must be persistent. And if you have faith and say to a mountain, 'Make way,' it will make way."

Shukhov grinned, rolled himself another cigarette, and got a light from the Estonian.

"Don't talk rot, Alyoshka. I never saw mountains going anywhere. Come to think of it I've never seen any mountains. But when you and your whole Baptist club did all that praying in the Caucasus, did one single mountain ever move over?"

Poor devils. What harm does their praying do anybody? Collected twenty-five years all around. That's how things are nowadays: twenty-five is the only kind of sentence they hand out.

"We didn't pray for anything like that, Denisych," Alyoshka said earnestly. He moved around with his Testament until he was almost face to face with Shukhov. "The Lord's behest was that we should pray for no earthly or transient thing except our daily bread. 'Give us this day our daily bread.'"

"Our ration, you mean?" Shukhov asked.

Alyoshka went on undeterred, exhorting Shukhov with his eyes more than his words, patting and stroking his hand.

"Ivan Denisovich! We shouldn't pray for somebody to send us a parcel, or for an extra portion of skilly. What people prize highly is vile in the sight of God! We must pray for spiritual things, asking God to remove the scum of evil from our hearts."

"No, you listen to me. There's a priest at our church in Polomnya . . ."

"Don't tell me about your priest!" Alyoshka begged, his brow creased with pain.

"No, you just listen." Shukhov raised himself on his elbow. "In our parish, Polomnya, nobody was better off than the priest. If we got a roofing job, say, we charged other people thirty-five a day but we charged him a hundred. And there was never a peep out of him. He was paying alimony to three women in three different towns and living with his fourth family. The local bishop was under his thumb, our priest greased his palm well. If they sent any other priest along, ours would make his life hell, he wasn't going to share with anybody."

"Why are you telling me about this priest? The Orthodox Church has turned its back on the Gospels—*they* don't get put inside, or else they get off with five years because their faith is not firm."

Shukhov calmly observed Alyoshka's agitation, puffing on his cigarette.

"Look, Alyoshka"—smoke got into the Baptist's eyes as Shukhov pushed his outstretched hand aside—"I'm not against God, see. I'm quite ready to believe in God. But I just don't believe in heaven and hell. Why do you think everybody deserves either heaven or hell? What sort of idiots do you take us for? That's what I don't like."

Shukhov lay back again, after carefully dropping his ash into the space behind his head, between the bunk and the window, so as not to burn the captain's belongings. Lost in thought, he no longer heard Alyoshka's muttering.

"Anyway," he concluded, "pray as much as you like, but they won't knock anything off your sentence. You'll serve your time from bell to bell whatever happens."

Alyoshka was horrified. "That's just the sort of thing you shouldn't pray for! What good is freedom to you? If you're free, your faith will soon be choked by thorns! Be glad you're in prison. Here you have time to think about your soul. Remember what the Apostle Paul says, 'What are you doing, weeping and breaking my heart? For I am ready not only to be imprisoned but even to die in Jerusalem for the name of the Lord Jesus.'"

Shukhov stared at the ceiling and said nothing. He no longer knew whether he wanted to be free or not. To begin with, he'd wanted it very much, and counted up every evening how many days he still had to serve. Then he'd got fed up with it. And still later it had gradually dawned on him that people like himself were not allowed to go home but were packed off into exile. And there was no knowing where the living was easier—here or there.

The one thing he might want to ask God for was to let him go home.

But *they* wouldn't let him go home.

Alyoshka wasn't lying, though. You could tell from his voice and his eyes that he was glad to be in prison.

"Look, Alyoshka," Shukhov explained, "it's worked out pretty well for you. Christ told you to go to jail, and you did it, for Christ. But what am I here for? Because they weren't ready for the war in '41—is that the reason? Was that my fault?"

"No second roll call, by the look of it," Kildigs growled from his bed. He yawned.

"Wonders never cease," Shukhov said. "Maybe we can get some sleep."

At that very minute, just as the hut was growing quiet, they heard the rattle of a bolt at the outer door of the hut. The two men who'd taken the boots to be dried dashed into the hut shouting, "Second roll call!"

A warder followed them, shouting, "Out into the other half!"

Some of them were already sleeping! They all began stirring, grumbling and groaning as they drew their boots on (very few of them were in their underpants—they mostly slept as they were, in their padded trousers—without them, your feet would be frozen stiff even under a blanket).

Shukhov swore loudly. "Damn them to hell!" But he wasn't all that angry, because he hadn't fallen asleep yet.

Tsezar's hand reached up to place two biscuits, two lumps of sugar, and one round chunk of sausage on Shukhov's bed.

"Thank you, Tsezar Markovich," Shukhov said, lowering his head into the gangway between bunks. "Better give me your bag to put under my pillow for safety." (A passing zek's thieving hands wouldn't find it so quickly up there—and anyway, who would expect Shukhov to have anything?)

Tsezar passed his tightly tied white bag up to Shukhov. Shukhov tucked it under his mattress and was going to wait a bit until more men had been herded out so that he wouldn't have to stand barefoot on the corridor floor so long. But the warder snarled at him: "You over there! In the corner!"

So Shukhov sprang to the floor, landing lightly on his bare feet (his boots and foot rags were so cozy up there on the stove it would be a pity to move them). He had cobbled so many pairs of slippers—but always for others, never for himself. Still, he was used to it, and it wouldn't be for long.

Slippers were confiscated if found in the daytime.

The gangs who'd handed in their boots for drying were all right now if they had slippers, but some had only foot rags tied around their feet, and others were barefoot.

"Get on with it! Get on with it!" the warder roared.

The hut orderly joined in: "Want a bit of the stick, you scum?"

Most of them were crammed into the other half of the hut, with the last few crowding into the corridor. Shukhov stood against the partition wall by the night bucket. The floor was damp to his feet, and an icy draft blew along it from the lobby.

Everybody was out now, but the warder and the hut orderly went to look yet again to see whether anybody was hiding, or curled up asleep in a dark spot. Too few or too many at the count meant trouble—yet another recheck. The two of them went around and around, then came back to the door.

One by one, but quickly now, they were allowed back in. Shukhov squeezed in eighteenth, dashed to his bunk, hoisted his foot onto a bracket, and—heave-ho!—up he went.

Great. Feet into his jerkin sleeve again, blanket on top, jacket over that, and we're asleep! All the zeks in the other half of the barracks would now be herded into our half—but that was their bad luck.

Tsezar came back. Shukhov lowered the bag to him.

Now Alyoshka was back. He had no sense at all, Alyoshka, never earned a thing, but did favors for everybody.

"Here you are, Alyoshka!" Shukhov handed him one biscuit.

Alyoshka was all smiles. "Thank you! You won't have any for yourself!"

"Eat it!"

If we're without, we can always earn something.

He himself took the lump of sausage—and popped it into his mouth. Get the teeth to it. Chew, chew, chew! Lovely meaty smell! Meat juice, the real thing. Down it went, into his belly.

End of sausage.

The other stuff he planned to eat before work parade.

He covered his head with the skimpy, grubby blanket and stopped listening to the zeks from the other half crowding in between the bunks to be counted.

Shukhov felt pleased with life as he went to sleep. A lot of good things had happened that day. He hadn't been thrown in the hole. The gang hadn't been dragged off to Sotsgorodok. He'd swiped the extra gruel at dinnertime. The foreman had got a good rate for the job. He'd enjoyed working on the wall. He hadn't been caught with the blade at the search point. He'd earned a bit from Tsezar that evening. He'd bought his tobacco. And he hadn't taken sick, had got over it.

The end of an unclouded day. Almost a happy one.

Just one of the 3,653 days of his sentence, from bell to bell. The extra three were for leap years.

Questions

1. There is tension in many of Shukhov's relationships. He will think positive thoughts about various persons around him, yet he will be very negative in his actions and comments as he actually relates to those same characters. Why does he do this?

2. When discussing religion, why does Shukhov start talking about the priest in his hometown?

3. Solzhenitsyn presented Shukhov as a practical, hardworking, and self-motivated man. Alyoshka was presented as being less practical, but as a man of patience and inner peace. Both men have admirable qualities, but they are very different. What can we learn from their similarities and differences?

4. An underlying plot in Solzhenitsyn's novel is the attempt of the government to control the lives, the thoughts, and the hearts of the people. Do you think that there is something within each human that enables us to resist such a government? Many authors in the twentieth century strived to understand and describe an elusive inner strength that would help people resist (for example, see Aldous Huxley's *Brave New World* and George Orwell's *1984*). If there is an inner strength, what is it? And where does it come from?

JOHN MILTON

John Milton (1608–1674) is one of the most well-known poets in the history of English literature. His most famous work is the lengthy poem *Paradise Lost*. He was also active in the political and religious debates of his day. He served in various governmental positions and wrote tracts promoting various political and social goals. In 1651, he became blind, which forced him into retirement and into full-time writing. The poem, "On His Blindness," focuses on this key event in Milton's life.

Note the multiple meanings that Milton created in the minds of his readers. For example, in the first line, the phrase "my light" sounds like "my life." In the second line, "this dark world and wide" suggests both Milton's personal experience with blindness and the theological view that this world is corrupted by sin and that the people of this world are blinded because of Satan's influence. Later, Milton wonders about the usefulness of his life as a blind man; he wrote that his only "talent" is to uselessly avoid death. Yet, Milton longed to be useful to God and to have an eternal impact on this world.

ON HIS BLINDNESS (WHEN I CONSIDER HOW MY LIGHT IS SPENT)

> When I consider how my light is spent
>   Ere half my days, in this dark world and wide,
>   And that one talent which is death to hide,
>   Lodged with me useless, though my soul more bent
> To serve therewith my Maker, and present   5
>   My true account, lest he returning chide;
>   "Doth God exact day-labor, light denied?"
>   I fondly ask; but Patience to prevent
> That murmur soon replies, "God doth not need
>   Either man's work or his own gifts; who best   10
>   Bear his mild yoke, they serve him best. His state
> Is kingly. Thousands at his bidding speed
>   And post o'er land and ocean without rest;
>   They also serve who only stand and wait."

Questions

1. What is Milton describing when he wrote that his soul is "bent / To serve therewith my Maker, and present / My true account"?
2. What did Milton mean by ". . . his state / Is kingly: thousands at his bidding speed, / And post o'er land and ocean without rest; / They also serve who only stand and waite." ?
3. What tension is present at the beginning of the poem and what resolution seems to be developing in the mind of Milton as he concludes the poem?
4. What is the overall message of this poem? Do you think that he was right or wrong?

JOHN DONNE

John Donne (1572–1631) was born into a financially secure Roman Catholic family in England. At that time, Roman Catholics were not given full rights as citizens of England, thus his career was hindered in many ways. For example, he completed his studies at both Cambridge and Oxford universities, but he did not get degrees because of his faith. Yet, later, he was able to study law and practice it. His life was marked by many swings. He was in deep poverty at times, but he enjoyed affluence at other times. He spent time in prison, but he was also in leadership positions in the government. Later in his life, he switched from being a faithful Roman Catholic to being an active priest in the Church of England.

Donne was a passionate man throughout his life, and this passion comes through in his poetry. In "Batter My Heart," Donne compares his heart to a town that has been conquered by enemy forces. Like the conquered town, he hopes that he can submit his heart to its rightful owner (God), but he is not free. His heart (like the town) has been overwhelmed by an enemy army. Then, Donne shifted to the image of a woman who is engaged to be married to the wrong person. Just as the woman needs her true lover to come and save her, Donne concluded that only the passionate love of God will set him free.

When reading this selection, it is helpful to know that a viceroy is a representative of a king, who should act so that the king's will is done.

HOLY SONNET 14: BATTER MY HEART, THREE-PERSONED GOD

> Batter my heart, three-personed God; for You
> As yet but knock, breathe, shine, and seek to mend;
> That I may rise and stand, o'erthrow me, and bend
> Your force to break, blow, burn and make me new.
> 5   I, like an usurped town; to another due,
> Labor to admit You, but Oh, to no end;
> Reason, Your viceroy in me, me should defend,
> But is captived, and proves weak or untrue.
> Yet dearly I love You, and would be loved fain,
> 10   But am betrothed unto Your enemy.
> Divorce me, untie or break that knot again;
> Take me to You, imprison me, for I,
> Except You enthrall me, never shall be free,
> Nor ever chaste, except You ravish me.

Questions

1. What does Donne mean by the first two lines: "Batter my heart, three per-soned God; for you / As yet but knock, breathe, shine, and seek to mend"? If you look carefully, the sentence is inverted. Donne is saying, ". . . for you / As yet but knock, breathe, shine, and seek to mend," but please start battering "my heart, three-personed God." Why is there this fervent plea for God to *batter Donne's heart?*

2. What does Donne mean by these lines: "Reason, your viceroy in me, me should defend, / But is captivated and proves weak or untrue"?

3. As the poem was being written, what relationship existed between the poet and God? What sort of relationship did the poet seek?

4. Donne was torn by his feelings and commitments. Have you ever felt torn in similar ways? How did you deal with or resolve your situation?

GEORGE HERBERT

George Herbert (1593–1633) taught at Cambridge University and served in the British Parliament under King James I, and later became a priest in the Church of England. Throughout his life, he was known for his intelligence and for his skillful, careful use of English and Latin. During the final years of his life, he was known for his dedicated service to his small congregation.

He wrote many poems, including a collection of poems called *The Temple*. "The Collar" is found in this collection. Like some of the psalms, this poem is an honest presentation of the individual's struggle to submit to God and to find God's gift of inner peace. For example, in Psalm 32, we find David in a similar struggle with God:

> *How long, O LORD? Will you forget me forever?*
> *How long will you hide your face from me?*
> *How long must I wrestle with my thoughts*
> *   and every day have sorrow in my heart?*
> *How long will my enemy triumph over me? (Psalm 13:1–2 New*
> *   International Version)*

In "The Collar," we hear two voices in Herbert's heart as he considers his relationship with God. A key phrase in this debate is when the poet speaks to himself: "Not so, my heart: but there is fruit." The ending of the poem also helps to give clarity to the poem's setting and to Herbert's inner conflict: "But as I raved and grew more fierce and wild / At every word, / Methoughts I heard one calling 'Child!' / And I replied 'My Lord'."

THE COLLAR

> *I struck the board, and cry'd, "No more;*
> *   I will abroad!*
> *What? shall I ever sigh and pine?*
> *My lines and life are free; free as the road,*
> *   Loose as the wind, as large as store,*   5
> *   Shall I be still in suit?*
> *Have I no harvest but a thorn*
> *To let me blood, and not restore*
> *What I have lost with cordial fruit?*
> *   Sure there was wine*   10
> *Before my sighs did dry it: there was corn*
> *   Before my tears did drown it.*
> *Is the year only lost to me?*
> *   Have I no bays to crown it?*
> *No flowers, no garlands gay? all blasted?*   15
> *   All wasted?*
> *Not so, my heart: but there is fruit,*

> *And thou hast hands.*
> *Recover all thy sight-blown age*
20 | *On double pleasures: leave thy cold dispute*
> *Of what is fit, and not; forsake thy cage;*
> *Thy rope of sands,*
> *Which petty thoughts have made, and made to thee*
> *Good cable, to enforce and draw,*
25 | *And be thy law,*
> *14 bays: laurel crowns to signify victory and honor.*
> *While thou didst wink and wouldst not see.*
> *Away; take heed:*
> *I will abroad.*
30 | *Call in thy death's head there: tie up thy fears.*
> *He that forbears*
> *To suit and serve his need,*
> *Deserves his load."*
> *But as I rav'd and grew more fierce and wild*
35 | *At every word,*
> *Me thought I heard one calling, "Child:"*
> *And I replied, "My Lord."*

Questions

1. At one point, Herbert wrote, "Shall I be still in suit?" The word *suit* means many things in English. It can refer to clothing, a preference, a match between a desire and a satisfaction, or a legal action that demands the correction of a wrong that was done. Does an examination of this word's meaning help you to understand this poem?
2. Why is the poem separated into a short introduction, a long section that is surrounded by quotation marks, and a short conclusion?
3. Why do you think that this poem is entitled, "The Collar"? The word *collar* has more than one meaning.
4. What is the overall message of this poem? Do you agree with the message?

THE ANVIL—GOD'S WORD

"The Anvil—God's Word" is written by an unnamed poet, thus it is impossible to give a personal context for the writing of the poem. However, we can know something about the cultural context of this poem. The image of the blacksmith shop seems to have its roots in the nineteenth century, perhaps in American culture. At that time, the blacksmith shop was common in most communities; it was a place where metal was heated, beaten, and shaped into tools or other objects. On a more symbolic level, the blacksmith shop was a place where humans molded the hard reality of iron into their wishes. Yet, according to this poem, one thing is not submitting to the beating power of the human desires. One thing is not being changed and shaped.

There is also a connection between this poem and many of the verbal exchanges that Jesus had in the Gospels of the New Testament. Often, Jesus surprised people with his comments; he would overturn their expectations. For example, Jesus surprised his audiences by saying that the rich people are not automatically blessed by God (see Matthew 19:23–26), that the religious leaders might be excluded from God's kingdom (see Matthew 23:1–27), and that "the meek shall inherit the earth" (see Matthew 5:5). In this poem, the speaker, who visits the blacksmith's shop, assumes that all of the noise from the shop represents a continuing struggle between many anvils and many hammers. But this expectation is overturned; the blacksmith explains that only one singing anvil has worn out the many noisy hammers.

THE ANVIL—GOD'S WORD

LAST EVE I passed beside a blacksmith's door,
  And heard the anvil ring the vesper chime;
Then, looking in, I saw upon the floor
  Old hammers, worn with beating years of time.

"How many anvils have you had," said I,
  "To wear and batter all these hammers so?"
"Just one," said he, and then, with twinkling eye,
  "The anvil wears the hammers out, you know."

And so, thought I, the anvil of God's Word,
  For ages skeptic blows have beat upon;
Yet, though the noise of falling blows was heard,
  The anvil is unharmed—the hammers gone.

Questions

1. What is the significance of the narrator walking past the blacksmith's shop in the evening and hearing the anvil ring "the vesper chime"?
2. The blacksmith's "twinkling eye" is mentioned in the poem. What are some possible meanings that could be attached to the phrase *twinkling eye?*
3. In Christianity, what meanings are associated with the term *God's Word?*
4. If the anvil is God's Word, what are the many hammers on the floor? From your imagination and from your knowledge of history, what might be some examples of hammers that have worn themselves out beating against God's Word?

CHINUA ACHEBE

Chinua Achebe (b. 1930) is known around the world for his novels, stories, and poems. Most of his life has been spent in Nigeria, but he has also lived in Great Britain and the United States. His first and most widely read novel is *Things Fall*

Apart (1958). In Achebe's works, the reader is given a taste of the tensions felt by Africans in the late twentieth century and the early twenty-first century. In many ways, European civilization, technology, languages, and religion are attractive to Africans. However, Achebe also shows the alienation felt by Africans as their cultural roots, local languages, and traditional religions are lost. Should people embrace the beliefs and lifestyles of Europeans, or should they resist those pressures and fight for their heritage? In many ways, Africans are not given a choice—their heritages are simply slipping away. This is the context of Achebe's works.

The story, "Dead Man's Path," introduces the reader to these tensions. All of the characters are Africans, but their lives are guided by various social and religious influences. Beneath the cultural tensions, Achebe also exposed bits and pieces of the common human heart. Michael Obi, the new headmaster, is a person of energy, intelligence, pride, and insensitivity. In one sense, Obi is a product of the cultural tensions found in Africa. In another sense, Obi is simply an example of the pride and insensitivity that often corrupt human relationships. The personal dimensions of Obi's spiritual life were not discussed in the story. Yet, his lack of love suggests a gap between the true nature of Christianity and some of the colonial missionary projects experienced by Africans.

DEAD MEN'S PATH

Michael Obi's hopes were fulfilled much earlier than he had expected. He had was appointed headmaster of Ndume Central School in January 1949. It had always been an unprogressive school, so the Mission authorities decided to send a young and energetic man to run it. Obi accepted this responsibility with enthusiasm. He had many wonderful ideas and this was an opportunity to put them into practice. He had had sound secondary school education which designated him a "pivotal teacher" in the official records and set him apart from the other headmasters in the mission field. He was outspoken in his condemnation of the narrow views of these older and often less-educated ones.

"We shall make a good job of it, shan't we?" he asked his young wife when they first heard the joyful news of his promotion.

"We shall do our best," she replied. "We shall have such beautiful gardens and everything will be just *modern* and delightful. . . ." In their two years of married life she had become completely infected by his passion for "modern methods" and his denigration of "these old and superannuated people in the teaching field who would be better employed as traders in the Onitsha market." She began to see herself already as the admired wife of the young headmaster, the queen of the school.

The wives of the other teachers would envy her position. She would set the fashion in everything. . . Then, suddenly, it occurred to her that there might not be other wives. Wavering between hope and fear, she asked her husband, looking anxiously at him.

"All our colleagues are young and unmarried," he said with enthusiasm which for once she did not share. "Which is a good thing," he continued.

"Why?"

"Why? They will give all their time and energy to the school."

Nancy was downcast. For a few minutes she became skeptical about the new school; but it was only for a few minutes. Her little personal misfortune could not blind her to her husband's happy prospects. She looked at him as he sat folded up in a chair. He was stoop-shouldered and looked frail. But he sometimes surprised people with sudden bursts of physical energy. In his present posture, however, all his bodily strength seemed to have retired behind his deep-set eyes, giving them an extraordinary power of penetration. He was only twenty-six, but looked thirty or more. On the whole, he was not unhandsome.

"A penny for your thoughts, Mike," said Nancy after a while, imitating the woman's magazine she read.

"I was thinking what a grand opportunity we've got at last to show these people how a school should be run."

Ndume School was backward in every sense of the word. Mr. Obi put his whole life into the work, and his wife hers too. He had two aims. A high standard of teaching was insisted upon, and the school compound was to be turned into a place of beauty. Nancy's dream-gardens came to life with the coming of the rains, and blossomed. Beautiful hibiscus and allamanda hedges in brilliant red and yellow marked out the carefully tended school compound from the rank neighborhood bushes.

One evening as Obi was admiring his work he was scandalized to see an old woman from the village hobble right across the compound, through a marigold flower-bed and the hedges. On going up there he found faint signs of an almost disused path from the village across the school compound to the bush on the other side.

"It amazes me," said Obi to one of his teachers who had been three years in the school, "that you people allowed the villagers to make use of this footpath. It is simply incredible." He shook his head.

"The path," said the teacher apologetically, "appears to be very important to them. Although it is hardly used, it connects the village shrine with their place of burial."

"And what has that got to do with the school?" asked the headmaster.

"Well, I don't know," replied the other with a shrug of the shoulders. "But I remember there was a big row some time ago when we attempted to close it."

"That was some time ago. But it will not be used now," said Obi as he walked away. "What will the Government Education Officer think of this when he comes to inspect the school next week? The villagers might, for all I know, decide to use the schoolroom for a pagan ritual during the inspection."

Heavy sticks were planted closely across the path at the two places where it entered and left the school premises. These were further strengthened with barbed wire.

Three days later the village priest of *Ani* called on the headmaster. He was an old man and walked with a slight stoop. He carried a stout walking-stick which he usually tapped on the floor, by way of emphasis, each time he made a new point in his argument.

"I have heard," he said after the usual exchange of cordialities, "that our ancestral footpath has recently been closed. . ."

"Yes," replied Mr. Obi. "We cannot allow people to make a highway of our school compound."

"Look here, my son," said the priest bringing down his walking-stick, "this path was here before you were born and before your father was born. The whole life of this village depends on it. Our dead relatives depart by it and our ancestors visit us by it. But most important, it is the path of children coming in to be born. . ."

Mr. Obi listened with a satisfied smile on his face.

"The whole purpose of our school," he said finally, "is to eradicate just such beliefs as that. Dead men do not require footpaths. The whole idea is just fantastic. Our duty is to teach your children to laugh at such ideas."

"What you say may be true," replied the priest, "but we follow the practices of our fathers. If you reopen the path we shall have nothing to quarrel about. What I always say is: let the hawk perch and let the eagle perch." He rose to go.

"I am sorry," said the young headmaster. "But the school compound cannot be a thoroughfare. It is against our regulations. I would suggest your constructing another path, skirting our premises. We can even get our boys to help in building it. I don't suppose the ancestors will find the little detour too burdensome."

"I have no more words to say," said the old priest, already outside.

Two days later a young woman in the village died in childbed. A diviner was immediately consulted and he prescribed heavy sacrifices to propitiate ancestors insulted by the fence.

Obi woke up next morning among the ruins of his work. The beautiful hedges were torn up not just near the path but right round the school, the flowers trampled to death and one of the school buildings pulled down. . . That day, the white Supervisor came to inspect the school and wrote a nasty report on the state of the premises but more seriously about the "tribal-war situation developing between the school and the village, arising in part from the misguided zeal of the new headmaster."

Questions

1. What intercultural issues and problems does this story demonstrate? More specifically, how does this story help us understand "missionary work"?
2. What is unique about Michael Obi, and what qualities found in Obi are also found in people around the world?
3. If we assume that improving the school would ultimately be good for the people in the area, how should the next headmaster approach his or her job?
4. Why do people both embrace and fear innovation? What factors assist humans in dealing with innovation? When should people resist innovation?

MOVIE GUIDE FOR *CHARIOTS OF FIRE* (1981)

Directed by Hugh Hudson

Screenplay by Colin Welland

Two Stories and Two Personalities

Chariots of Fire is a fairly accurate, fact-based account of two runners who are preparing for the 1924 Olympics in Paris. One is a committed Christian from Scotland and one is a secular Jew from England—both are running for Great Britain in the Olympics. As the men train, their commitments and relationships expose their worldviews.

This British film is neither a simplistic TV sitcom nor an exciting but shallow Hollywood moneymaker. This fast-moving story gives the audience much to consider. *Chariots of Fire* won four Academy Awards, including Best Picture, and was nominated for three others. When released, this movie was very successful with critics and in making money. But the filmmakers did more than make money. They told the stories of two powerful personalities.

The Jewish runner is Harold Abrahams. The key tension in Abrahams' life is his need for acceptance and respect. Because his father was a Jew from Lithuania, Abrahams feels very alienated. There is a quiet, but real prejudice against Jews in England, and Abrahams is hypersensitive to that prejudice. He is driven to confront that narrow-mindedness and prove his worth in his alien environment.

The Christian runner is Eric Liddell. He grew up in China because his parents were missionaries there. But his family's roots were in Scotland. His parents are briefly introduced in the movie as "Mr. L" and "Mrs. L." The young lady who repeatedly confronts Eric about his constant running is not his sweetheart; she is his sister. The entire family is deeply committed to sharing their Christian faith with others. The first tension in Eric Liddell's life is how to balance his running with his commitment to missionary work. Later, Liddell will be forced to choose between his convictions about Christian living and his commitment to running in the Olympics. Liddell's understanding of Christian living includes keeping the Sabbath (Sunday) as a day of rest.

The Historical Context of the Movie

Early in the movie, the First World War (1914–1918) is mentioned several times as a recent event. That war began when the French, Germans, English, Austrians, and others naïvely thought that a war would invigorate their individual cultures and prove their superiority. However, much of the war was fought with men hiding for months in trenches as artillery shells randomly dropped down on them. Only occasionally would an army break out of the relative safety of the trenches and surge forward. Such advances of short distances often cost tens of thousands of lives. For example, on July 1, 1916, the British began the Somme Offensive against German forces. On that single day, 19,000 British soldiers were killed and 57,000 were wounded. New technology—such as machine guns, barbed wire, airplanes, and mustard gas—and old tactics led to about ten million soldiers being killed in battles, about six million civilian deaths, and twenty million wounded soldiers. After four years of fighting and very little movement in the battle lines, the war ended in November 1918 without any clear resolution.

This context is helpful in understanding many details. For example, the disfigured men at the railway station are veterans who a few years before gloriously marched off to war for the good of Great Britain. Now, they watch handsome, young men of great privilege march off to a prestigious university. At the freshman dinner, a speech is given that challenges the new students to fill the empty places of students who once attended Cambridge University. Those empty places were caused by the war. On the wall is a long list of students who recently attended the school, but are now dead because of the war.

The Structure of the Movie

The bulk of the movie takes place in the early 1920s as the runners prepare for the Olympics in 1924. To give a contemporary framework, the movie begins and ends with a funeral in London. The funeral provides "bookends" that hold the rest of the story together. Interestingly, the funeral for Abrahams takes place in a church. This could mean that Abrahams, who was a Jew throughout his youth (as shown in the movie), had at some point converted to Christianity.

The letter writing of Aubrey Montague (one of the other runners) also gives structure to the movie. The letter writing operates like a narrator's voice and gives a vantage point from which to understand the flashbacks and the movement of time as the story unfolds.

Tips for Watching This Movie

Just as we study poems, short stories, and plays, we can also learn to study movies. Rather than passively watching films, we need to study the values, personalities, and messages presented on screen. *Chariots of Fire* also needs to be carefully studied because it uses British accents and multiple flashbacks, which are sometimes difficult to follow. Yet, the rewards of such study are great. Below are tools or tips for getting more out of this movie:

1. Remember to watch the movie several times. During the first viewing, just sit back and enjoy the movie. During the second or third viewing, study the details. Look at the characters' values, relationships, and worldviews. Watching the movie with a group of friends or family members can be enriching because you can pool your insights.
2. Some research will give deeper understanding of individual scenes or elements in the movie that are unclear during the first viewing. Below are some topics to explore:
   A. Notice how people view the Olympics. At this time, the athletes in the Olympics were supposed to be amateurs, not professionals. It was believed that people should be naturally good at their sport, not artifi-

cially trained. (Notice how the American team is viewed as artificial and mechanical in their training.)

B. Research the long history of prejudice against Jews in Great Britain and Europe.

C. Although England and Scotland are part of the United Kingdom in the movie, there is a long history of differences and tensions between the two regions.

D. Christianity plays an important role in this movie, but what exactly do Christians believe? The teachings of Christianity are left very vague. Why is that?

Key Characters and Their Relationships

Harold Abrahams, Jewish runner from England, who attends Cambridge University (his father is from Lithuania)

Eric Liddell, Christian runner from Scotland, who grew up in China; because he is a poor missionary, he does not go to a university

Sybil Gordon, the actress, who becomes Abrahams' sweetheart

Sam Mussabini, the professional running coach hired by Abrahams

Jennie Liddel, sister of Eric Liddel

"Mr. L" and "Mrs. L", the father and mother of Eric Liddel, missionaries to China

Aubrey Montague, the Cambridge runner who writes letters home about his athletic training and his college experiences

Lord Birkenhead, head of the British Olympic Committee

Prince of Wales, the future King of Great Britain

Questions

1. What is significant about Abrahams and his coach drinking at the bar after his Olympic win? What spiritual issues lie behind their thoughts and feelings?
2. In the movie, what training methods are used by the various athletes? What do these methods say about the values and worldviews of the athletes?
3. What does this movie say about social pressures and ways of dealing with such pressures?
4. Everyone has a perspective on life—a worldview, an emotional center, and/or a spiritual vision. How would you compare the spiritual vision of Abrahams with the spiritual vision of Liddell?

Chapter 3

Products of Spirituality: Belief, Prayers, Worship, and Morality

There are major similarities and major differences between the biblical story and the Koran's story of **Joseph.** The basic outline of Joseph's life is easily seen in the two narratives. In both accounts, a single, monotheistic God oversees and guides the life of a young man named Joseph. In both accounts, Joseph has a dream (or dreams), which causes jealousy and hatred in his brothers. As a result of these tensions, Joseph ends up in Egypt as a slave. In both stories, Joseph is accused of sexual misconduct with his master's wife, is sent to prison, interprets dreams, and ends up serving an Egyptian king by overseeing the distribution of food during a famine.

Yet, the personality and character of Joseph are different in the two stories. In the Bible, Joseph is hardworking, innocent, continually blessed by God, humble, forgiving, emotional, and committed to his family's welfare. In the Koran, Joseph longs for the master's wife, but he shifts the blame onto her; he wants to vindicate himself; and he seems presumptuous when he asks the king for the authority to oversee the granaries.

The qualities of Jacob, Joseph's father, are also different. In the Bible, Jacob is emotional, foolish in his favoritism, unthinking when he sends Joseph to check on the jealous brothers, self-focused, and irrational when dealing with the brothers during the famine. In the Koran, Jacob is worried about Joseph's safety when he allows Joseph to accompany the brothers; he is more "preachy" or "pushy" about his faith; he seems unusually easygoing about his missing son; and he lacks the emotions found in the biblical account.

The biblical story of Joseph demonstrates the Bible's emphasis on giving dates, place names, genealogies, and other details to root the narratives in real history. The Koran's version of Joseph illustrates its tendency to omit names and details; it seems to assume that the reader is familiar with the details that are given in the biblical account. While the Koran omits many details, it tends to focus on clearly stating what the reader should learn. On the other hand, the biblical story of Joseph demonstrates the Bible's general tendency of not giving

110

a concluding moral to the story; the reader is responsible for interpreting the narrative in light of moral principles given in other sections of the Bible.

JOSEPH IN THE BIBLE

(BIBLE: NEW INTERNATIONAL VERSION)

Genesis 37—Joseph's Dreams

1. Jacob lived in the land where his father had stayed, the land of Canaan.
2. This is the account of Jacob.

   Joseph, a young man of seventeen, was tending the flocks with his brothers, the sons of Bilhah and the sons of Zilpah, his father's wives, and he brought their father a bad report about them.

3. Now Israel loved Joseph more than any of his other sons, because he had been born to him in his old age; and he made a richly ornamented robe for him.
4. When his brothers saw that their father loved him more than any of them, they hated him and could not speak a kind word to him.
5. Joseph had a dream, and when he told it to his brothers, they hated him all the more.
6. He said to them, "Listen to this dream I had:
7. We were binding sheaves of grain out in the field when suddenly my sheaf rose and stood upright, while your sheaves gathered around mine and bowed down to it."
8. His brothers said to him, "Do you intend to reign over us? Will you actually rule us?" And they hated him all the more because of his dream and what he had said.
9. Then he had another dream, and he told it to his brothers. "Listen," he said, "I had another dream, and this time the sun and moon and eleven stars were bowing down to me."
10. When he told his father as well as his brothers, his father rebuked him and said, "What is this dream you had? Will your mother and I and your brothers actually come and bow down to the ground before you?"
11. His brothers were jealous of him, but his father kept the matter in mind.

Joseph Sold by His Brothers

12. Now his brothers had gone to graze their father's flocks near Shechem,
13. and Israel said to Joseph, "As you know, your brothers are grazing the flocks near Shechem. Come, I am going to send you to them."

    "Very well," he replied.

14. So he said to him, "Go and see if all is well with your brothers and with the flocks, and bring word back to me." Then he sent him off from the Valley of Hebron.

When Joseph arrived at Shechem,

15. a man found him wandering around in the fields and asked him, "What are you looking for?"

16. He replied, "I'm looking for my brothers. Can you tell me where they are grazing their flocks?"

17. "They have moved on from here," the man answered. "I heard them say, 'Let's go to Dothan.'"

So Joseph went after his brothers and found them near Dothan.

18. But they saw him in the distance, and before he reached them, they plotted to kill him.

19. "Here comes that dreamer!" they said to each other.

20. "Come now, let's kill him and throw him into one of these cisterns and say that a ferocious animal devoured him. Then we'll see what comes of his dreams."

21. When Reuben heard this, he tried to rescue him from their hands. "Let's not take his life," he said.

22. "Don't shed any blood. Throw him into this cistern here in the desert, but don't lay a hand on him." Reuben said this to rescue him from them and take him back to his father.

23. So when Joseph came to his brothers, they stripped him of his robe—the richly ornamented robe he was wearing—

24. and they took him and threw him into the cistern. Now the cistern was empty; there was no water in it.

25. As they sat down to eat their meal, they looked up and saw a caravan of Ishmaelites coming from Gilead. Their camels were loaded with spices, balm and myrrh, and they were on their way to take them down to Egypt.

26. Judah said to his brothers, "What will we gain if we kill our brother and cover up his blood?

27. Come, let's sell him to the Ishmaelites and not lay our hands on him; after all, he is our brother, our own flesh and blood." His brothers agreed.

28. So when the Midianite merchants came by, his brothers pulled Joseph up out of the cistern and sold him for twenty shekels of silver to the Ishmaelites, who took him to Egypt.

29. When Reuben returned to the cistern and saw that Joseph was not there, he tore his clothes.

30. He went back to his brothers and said, "The boy isn't there! Where can I turn now?"

31. Then they got Joseph's robe, slaughtered a goat and dipped the robe in the blood.

32. They took the ornamented robe back to their father and said, "We found this. Examine it to see whether it is your son's robe."

33. He recognized it and said, "It is my son's robe! Some ferocious animal has devoured him. Joseph has surely been torn to pieces."

34. Then Jacob tore his clothes, put on sackcloth and mourned for his son many days.

35. All his sons and daughters came to comfort him, but he refused to be comforted. "No," he said, "in mourning will I go down to the grave to my son." So his father wept for him.
36. Meanwhile, the Midianites sold Joseph in Egypt to Potiphar, one of Pharaoh's officials, the captain of the guard. [. . .]

Genesis 39—Joseph and Potiphar's Wife

1. Now Joseph had been taken down to Egypt. Potiphar, an Egyptian who was one of Pharaoh's officials, the captain of the guard, bought him from the Ishmaelites who had taken him there.
2. The LORD was with Joseph and he prospered, and he lived in the house of his Egyptian master.
3. When his master saw that the LORD was with him and that the LORD gave him success in everything he did,
4. Joseph found favor in his eyes and became his attendant. Potiphar put him in charge of his household, and he entrusted to his care everything he owned.
5. From the time he put him in charge of his household and of all that he owned, the LORD blessed the household of the Egyptian because of Joseph. The blessing of the LORD was on everything Potiphar had, both in the house and in the field.
6. So he left in Joseph's care everything he had; with Joseph in charge, he did not concern himself with anything except the food he ate.

Now Joseph was well-built and handsome,

7. and after a while his master's wife took notice of Joseph and said, "Come to bed with me!"
8. But he refused. "With me in charge," he told her, "my master does not concern himself with anything in the house; everything he owns he has entrusted to my care.
9. No one is greater in this house than I am. My master has withheld nothing from me except you, because you are his wife. How then could I do such a wicked thing and sin against God?"
10. And though she spoke to Joseph day after day, he refused to go to bed with her or even be with her.
11. One day he went into the house to attend to his duties, and none of the household servants was inside.
12. She caught him by his cloak and said, "Come to bed with me!" But he left his cloak in her hand and ran out of the house.
13. When she saw that he had left his cloak in her hand and had run out of the house,
14. she called her household servants. "Look," she said to them, "this Hebrew has been brought to us to make sport of us! He came in here to sleep with me, but I screamed.
15. When he heard me scream for help, he left his cloak beside me and ran out of the house."

16. She kept his cloak beside her until his master came home.
17. Then she told him this story: "That Hebrew slave you brought us came to me to make sport of me.
18. But as soon as I screamed for help, he left his cloak beside me and ran out of the house."
19. When his master heard the story his wife told him, saying, "This is how your slave treated me," he burned with anger.
20. Joseph's master took him and put him in prison, the place where the king's prisoners were confined.

But while Joseph was there in the prison,

21. the LORD was with him; he showed him kindness and granted him favor in the eyes of the prison warden.
22. So the warden put Joseph in charge of all those held in the prison, and he was made responsible for all that was done there.
23. The warden paid no attention to anything under Joseph's care, because the LORD was with Joseph and gave him success in whatever he did.

Genesis 40—The Cupbearer and the Baker

1. Some time later, the cupbearer and the baker of the king of Egypt offended their master, the king of Egypt.
2. Pharaoh was angry with his two officials, the chief cupbearer and the chief baker,
3. and put them in custody in the house of the captain of the guard, in the same prison where Joseph was confined.
4. The captain of the guard assigned them to Joseph, and he attended them. After they had been in custody for some time,
5. each of the two men—the cupbearer and the baker of the king of Egypt, who were being held in prison—had a dream the same night, and each dream had a meaning of its own.
6. When Joseph came to them the next morning, he saw that they were dejected.
7. So he asked Pharaoh's officials who were in custody with him in his master's house, "Why are your faces so sad today?"
8. "We both had dreams," they answered, "but there is no one to interpret them."

Then Joseph said to them, "Do not interpretations belong to God? Tell me your dreams."

9. So the chief cupbearer told Joseph his dream. He said to him, "In my dream I saw a vine in front of me,
10. and on the vine were three branches. As soon as it budded, it blossomed, and its clusters ripened into grapes.
11. Pharaoh's cup was in my hand, and I took the grapes, squeezed them into Pharaoh's cup and put the cup in his hand."

12. "This is what it means," Joseph said to him. "The three branches are three days.

13. Within three days Pharaoh will lift up your head and restore you to your position, and you will put Pharaoh's cup in his hand, just as you used to do when you were his cupbearer.

14. But when all goes well with you, remember me and show me kindness; mention me to Pharaoh and get me out of this prison.

15. For I was forcibly carried off from the land of the Hebrews, and even here I have done nothing to deserve being put in a dungeon."

16. When the chief baker saw that Joseph had given a favorable interpretation, he said to Joseph, "I too had a dream: On my head were three baskets of bread.

17. In the top basket were all kinds of baked goods for Pharaoh, but the birds were eating them out of the basket on my head."

18. "This is what it means," Joseph said. "The three baskets are three days.

19. Within three days Pharaoh will lift off your head and hang you on a tree. And the birds will eat away your flesh."

20. Now the third day was Pharaoh's birthday, and he gave a feast for all his officials. He lifted up the heads of the chief cupbearer and the chief baker in the presence of his officials:

21. He restored the chief cupbearer to his position, so that he once again put the cup into Pharaoh's hand,

22. but he hanged the chief baker, just as Joseph had said to them in his interpretation.

23. The chief cupbearer, however, did not remember Joseph; he forgot him.

Genesis 41—Pharaoh's Dreams

1. When two full years had passed, Pharaoh had a dream: He was standing by the Nile,

2. when out of the river there came up seven cows, sleek and fat, and they grazed among the reeds.

3. After them, seven other cows, ugly and gaunt, came up out of the Nile and stood beside those on the riverbank.

4. And the cows that were ugly and gaunt ate up the seven sleek, fat cows. Then Pharaoh woke up.

5. He fell asleep again and had a second dream: Seven heads of grain, healthy and good, were growing on a single stalk.

6. After them, seven other heads of grain sprouted—thin and scorched by the east wind.

7. The thin heads of grain swallowed up the seven healthy, full heads. Then Pharaoh woke up; it had been a dream.

8. In the morning his mind was troubled, so he sent for all the magicians and wise men of Egypt. Pharaoh told them his dreams, but no one could interpret them for him.

9. Then the chief cupbearer said to Pharaoh, "Today I am reminded of my shortcomings.

10. Pharaoh was once angry with his servants, and he imprisoned me and the chief baker in the house of the captain of the guard.
11. Each of us had a dream the same night, and each dream had a meaning of its own.
12. Now a young Hebrew was there with us, a servant of the captain of the guard. We told him our dreams, and he interpreted them for us, giving each man the interpretation of his dream.
13. And things turned out exactly as he interpreted them to us: I was restored to my position, and the other man was hanged."
14. So Pharaoh sent for Joseph, and he was quickly brought from the dungeon. When he had shaved and changed his clothes, he came before Pharaoh.
15. Pharaoh said to Joseph, "I had a dream, and no one can interpret it. But I have heard it said of you that when you hear a dream you can interpret it."
16. "I cannot do it," Joseph replied to Pharaoh, "but God will give Pharaoh the answer he desires."
17. Then Pharaoh said to Joseph, "In my dream I was standing on the bank of the Nile,
18. when out of the river there came up seven cows, fat and sleek, and they grazed among the reeds.
19. After them, seven other cows came up—scrawny and very ugly and lean. I had never seen such ugly cows in all the land of Egypt.
20. The lean, ugly cows ate up the seven fat cows that came up first.
21. But even after they ate them, no one could tell that they had done so; they looked just as ugly as before. Then I woke up.
22. "In my dreams I also saw seven heads of grain, full and good, growing on a single stalk.
23. After them, seven other heads sprouted—withered and thin and scorched by the east wind.
24. The thin heads of grain swallowed up the seven good heads. I told this to the magicians, but none could explain it to me."
25. Then Joseph said to Pharaoh, "The dreams of Pharaoh are one and the same. God has revealed to Pharaoh what he is about to do.
26. The seven good cows are seven years, and the seven good heads of grain are seven years; it is one and the same dream.
27. The seven lean, ugly cows that came up afterward are seven years, and so are the seven worthless heads of grain scorched by the east wind: They are seven years of famine.
28. "It is just as I said to Pharaoh: God has shown Pharaoh what he is about to do.
29. Seven years of great abundance are coming throughout the land of Egypt,
30. but seven years of famine will follow them. Then all the abundance in Egypt will be forgotten, and the famine will ravage the land.
31. The abundance in the land will not be remembered, because the famine that follows it will be so severe.
32. The reason the dream was given to Pharaoh in two forms is that the matter has been firmly decided by God, and God will do it soon.

33. "And now let Pharaoh look for a discerning and wise man and put him in charge of the land of Egypt.

34. Let Pharaoh appoint commissioners over the land to take a fifth of the harvest of Egypt during the seven years of abundance.

35. They should collect all the food of these good years that are coming and store up the grain under the authority of Pharaoh, to be kept in the cities for food.

36. This food should be held in reserve for the country, to be used during the seven years of famine that will come upon Egypt, so that the country may not be ruined by the famine."

37. The plan seemed good to Pharaoh and to all his officials.

38. So Pharaoh asked them, "Can we find anyone like this man, one in whom is the spirit of God ?"

39. Then Pharaoh said to Joseph, "Since God has made all this known to you, there is no one so discerning and wise as you.

40. You shall be in charge of my palace, and all my people are to submit to your orders. Only with respect to the throne will I be greater than you."

Joseph in Charge of Egypt

41. So Pharaoh said to Joseph, "I hereby put you in charge of the whole land of Egypt."

42. Then Pharaoh took his signet ring from his finger and put it on Joseph's finger. He dressed him in robes of fine linen and put a gold chain around his neck.

43. He had him ride in a chariot as his second-in-command, and men shouted before him, "Make way !" Thus he put him in charge of the whole land of Egypt.

44. Then Pharaoh said to Joseph, "I am Pharaoh, but without your word no one will lift hand or foot in all Egypt."

45. Pharaoh gave Joseph the name Zaphenath-Paneah and gave him Asenath daughter of Potiphera, priest of On, to be his wife. And Joseph went throughout the land of Egypt.

46. Joseph was thirty years old when he entered the service of Pharaoh king of Egypt. And Joseph went out from Pharaoh's presence and traveled throughout Egypt.

47. During the seven years of abundance the land produced plentifully.

48. Joseph collected all the food produced in those seven years of abundance in Egypt and stored it in the cities. In each city he put the food grown in the fields surrounding it.

49. Joseph stored up huge quantities of grain, like the sand of the sea; it was so much that he stopped keeping records because it was beyond measure.

50. Before the years of famine came, two sons were born to Joseph by Asenath daughter of Potiphera, priest of On.

51. Joseph named his firstborn Manasseh and said, "It is because God has made me forget all my trouble and all my father's household."

52. The second son he named Ephraim and said, "It is because God has made me fruitful in the land of my suffering."

53. The seven years of abundance in Egypt came to an end,

54. and the seven years of famine began, just as Joseph had said. There was famine in all the other lands, but in the whole land of Egypt there was food.

55. When all Egypt began to feel the famine, the people cried to Pharaoh for food. Then Pharaoh told all the Egyptians, "Go to Joseph and do what he tells you."

56. When the famine had spread over the whole country, Joseph opened the storehouses and sold grain to the Egyptians, for the famine was severe throughout Egypt.

57. And all the countries came to Egypt to buy grain from Joseph, because the famine was severe in all the world.

Genesis 42—Joseph's Brothers Go to Egypt

1. When Jacob learned that there was grain in Egypt, he said to his sons, "Why do you just keep looking at each other?"

2. He continued, "I have heard that there is grain in Egypt. Go down there and buy some for us, so that we may live and not die."

3. Then ten of Joseph's brothers went down to buy grain from Egypt.

4. But Jacob did not send Benjamin, Joseph's brother, with the others, because he was afraid that harm might come to him.

5. So Israel's sons were among those who went to buy grain, for the famine was in the land of Canaan also.

6. Now Joseph was the governor of the land, the one who sold grain to all its people. So when Joseph's brothers arrived, they bowed down to him with their faces to the ground.

7. As soon as Joseph saw his brothers, he recognized them, but he pretended to be a stranger and spoke harshly to them. "Where do you come from?" he asked.

"From the land of Canaan," they replied, "to buy food."

8. Although Joseph recognized his brothers, they did not recognize him.

9. Then he remembered his dreams about them and said to them, "You are spies! You have come to see where our land is unprotected."

10. "No, my lord," they answered. "Your servants have come to buy food.

11. We are all the sons of one man. Your servants are honest men, not spies."

12. "No!" he said to them. "You have come to see where our land is unprotected."

13. But they replied, "Your servants were twelve brothers, the sons of one man, who lives in the land of Canaan. The youngest is now with our father, and one is no more."

14. Joseph said to them, "It is just as I told you: You are spies!

15. And this is how you will be tested: As surely as Pharaoh lives, you will not leave this place unless your youngest brother comes here.

16. Send one of your number to get your brother; the rest of you will be kept in prison, so that your words may be tested to see if you are telling the truth. If you are not, then as surely as Pharaoh lives, you are spies!"

17. And he put them all in custody for three days.

18. On the third day, Joseph said to them, "Do this and you will live, for I fear God:

19. If you are honest men, let one of your brothers stay here in prison, while the rest of you go and take grain back for your starving households.

20. But you must bring your youngest brother to me, so that your words may be verified and that you may not die." This they proceeded to do.

21. They said to one another, "Surely we are being punished because of our brother. We saw how distressed he was when he pleaded with us for his life, but we would not listen; that's why this distress has come upon us."

22. Reuben replied, "Didn't I tell you not to sin against the boy? But you wouldn't listen! Now we must give an accounting for his blood."

23. They did not realize that Joseph could understand them, since he was using an interpreter.

24. He turned away from them and began to weep, but then turned back and spoke to them again. He had Simeon taken from them and bound before their eyes.

25. Joseph gave orders to fill their bags with grain, to put each man's silver back in his sack, and to give them provisions for their journey. After this was done for them,

26. they loaded their grain on their donkeys and left.

27. At the place where they stopped for the night one of them opened his sack to get feed for his donkey, and he saw his silver in the mouth of his sack.

28. "My silver has been returned," he said to his brothers. "Here it is in my sack."

Their hearts sank and they turned to each other trembling and said, "What is this that God has done to us?"

29. When they came to their father Jacob in the land of Canaan, they told him all that had happened to them. They said,

30. "The man who is lord over the land spoke harshly to us and treated us as though we were spying on the land.

31. But we said to him, 'We are honest men; we are not spies.

32. We were twelve brothers, sons of one father. One is no more, and the youngest is now with our father in Canaan.'

33. "Then the man who is lord over the land said to us, 'This is how I will know whether you are honest men: Leave one of your brothers here with me, and take food for your starving households and go.

34. But bring your youngest brother to me so I will know that you are not spies but honest men. Then I will give your brother back to you, and you can trade in the land.'"

35. As they were emptying their sacks, there in each man's sack was his pouch of silver! When they and their father saw the money pouches, they were frightened.

36. Their father Jacob said to them, "You have deprived me of my children. Joseph is no more and Simeon is no more, and now you want to take Benjamin. Everything is against me!"

37. Then Reuben said to his father, "You may put both of my sons to death if I do not bring him back to you. Entrust him to my care, and I will bring him back."

38. But Jacob said, "My son will not go down there with you; his brother is dead and he is the only one left. If harm comes to him on the journey you are taking, you will bring my gray head down to the grave in sorrow."

Genesis 43—The Second Journey to Egypt

1. Now the famine was still severe in the land.

2. So when they had eaten all the grain they had brought from Egypt, their father said to them, "Go back and buy us a little more food."

3. But Judah said to him, "The man warned us solemnly, 'You will not see my face again unless your brother is with you.'

4. If you will send our brother along with us, we will go down and buy food for you.

5. But if you will not send him, we will not go down, because the man said to us, 'You will not see my face again unless your brother is with you.'"

6. Israel asked, "Why did you bring this trouble on me by telling the man you had another brother?"

7. They replied, "The man questioned us closely about ourselves and our family. 'Is your father still living?' he asked us. 'Do you have another brother?' We simply answered his questions. How were we to know he would say, 'Bring your brother down here'?"

8. Then Judah said to Israel his father, "Send the boy along with me and we will go at once, so that we and you and our children may live and not die.

9. I myself will guarantee his safety; you can hold me personally responsible for him. If I do not bring him back to you and set him here before you, I will bear the blame before you all my life.

10. As it is, if we had not delayed, we could have gone and returned twice."

11. Then their father Israel said to them, "If it must be, then do this: Put some of the best products of the land in your bags and take them down to the man as a gift—a little balm and a little honey, some spices and myrrh, some pistachio nuts and almonds.

12. Take double the amount of silver with you, for you must return the silver that was put back into the mouths of your sacks. Perhaps it was a mistake.

13. Take your brother also and go back to the man at once.

14. And may God Almighty grant you mercy before the man so that he will let your other brother and Benjamin come back with you. As for me, if I am bereaved, I am bereaved."

15. So the men took the gifts and double the amount of silver, and Benjamin also. They hurried down to Egypt and presented themselves to Joseph.

16. When Joseph saw Benjamin with them, he said to the steward of his house, "Take these men to my house, slaughter an animal and prepare dinner; they are to eat with me at noon."

17. The man did as Joseph told him and took the men to Joseph's house.

18. Now the men were frightened when they were taken to his house. They thought, "We were brought here because of the silver that was put back into

our sacks the first time. He wants to attack us and overpower us and seize us as slaves and take our donkeys."

19. So they went up to Joseph's steward and spoke to him at the entrance to the house.

20. "Please, sir," they said, "we came down here the first time to buy food.

21. But at the place where we stopped for the night we opened our sacks and each of us found his silver—the exact weight—in the mouth of his sack. So we have brought it back with us.

22. We have also brought additional silver with us to buy food. We don't know who put our silver in our sacks."

23. "It's all right," he said. "Don't be afraid. Your God, the God of your father, has given you treasure in your sacks; I received your silver." Then he brought Simeon out to them.

24. The steward took the men into Joseph's house, gave them water to wash their feet and provided fodder for their donkeys.

25. They prepared their gifts for Joseph's arrival at noon, because they had heard that they were to eat there.

26. When Joseph came home, they presented to him the gifts they had brought into the house, and they bowed down before him to the ground.

27. He asked them how they were, and then he said, "How is your aged father you told me about? Is he still living?"

28. They replied, "Your servant our father is still alive and well." And they bowed low to pay him honor.

29. As he looked about and saw his brother Benjamin, his own mother's son, he asked, "Is this your youngest brother, the one you told me about?" And he said, "God be gracious to you, my son."

30. Deeply moved at the sight of his brother, Joseph hurried out and looked for a place to weep. He went into his private room and wept there.

31. After he had washed his face, he came out and, controlling himself, said, "Serve the food."

32. They served him by himself, the brothers by themselves, and the Egyptians who ate with him by themselves, because Egyptians could not eat with Hebrews, for that is detestable to Egyptians.

33. The men had been seated before him in the order of their ages, from the firstborn to the youngest; and they looked at each other in astonishment.

34. When portions were served to them from Joseph's table, Benjamin's portion was five times as much as anyone else's. So they feasted and drank freely with him.

Genesis 44—A Silver Cup in a Sack

1. Now Joseph gave these instructions to the steward of his house: "Fill the men's sacks with as much food as they can carry, and put each man's silver in the mouth of his sack.

2. Then put my cup, the silver one, in the mouth of the youngest one's sack, along with the silver for his grain." And he did as Joseph said.

3. As morning dawned, the men were sent on their way with their donkeys.

4. They had not gone far from the city when Joseph said to his steward, "Go after those men at once, and when you catch up with them, say to them, 'Why have you repaid good with evil?

5. Isn't this the cup my master drinks from and also uses for divination? This is a wicked thing you have done.'"

6. When he caught up with them, he repeated these words to them.

7. But they said to him, "Why does my lord say such things? Far be it from your servants to do anything like that!

8. We even brought back to you from the land of Canaan the silver we found inside the mouths of our sacks. So why would we steal silver or gold from your master's house?

9. If any of your servants is found to have it, he will die; and the rest of us will become my lord's slaves."

10. "Very well, then," he said, "let it be as you say. Whoever is found to have it will become my slave; the rest of you will be free from blame."

11. Each of them quickly lowered his sack to the ground and opened it.

12. Then the steward proceeded to search, beginning with the oldest and ending with the youngest. And the cup was found in Benjamin's sack.

13. At this, they tore their clothes. Then they all loaded their donkeys and returned to the city.

14. Joseph was still in the house when Judah and his brothers came in, and they threw themselves to the ground before him.

15. Joseph said to them, "What is this you have done? Don't you know that a man like me can find things out by divination?"

16. "What can we say to my lord?" Judah replied. "What can we say? How can we prove our innocence? God has uncovered your servants' guilt. We are now my lord's slaves—we ourselves and the one who was found to have the cup."

17. But Joseph said, "Far be it from me to do such a thing! Only the man who was found to have the cup will become my slave. The rest of you, go back to your father in peace."

18. Then Judah went up to him and said: "Please, my lord, let your servant speak a word to my lord. Do not be angry with your servant, though you are equal to Pharaoh himself.

19. My lord asked his servants, 'Do you have a father or a brother?'

20. And we answered, 'We have an aged father, and there is a young son born to him in his old age. His brother is dead, and he is the only one of his mother's sons left, and his father loves him.'

21. "Then you said to your servants, 'Bring him down to me so I can see him for myself.'

22. And we said to my lord, 'The boy cannot leave his father; if he leaves him, his father will die.'

23. But you told your servants, 'Unless your youngest brother comes down with you, you will not see my face again.'

24. When we went back to your servant my father, we told him what my lord had said.

25. "Then our father said, 'Go back and buy a little more food.'

26. But we said, 'We cannot go down. Only if our youngest brother is with us will we go. We cannot see the man's face unless our youngest brother is with us.'

27. "Your servant my father said to us, 'You know that my wife bore me two sons.

28. One of them went away from me, and I said, "He has surely been torn to pieces." And I have not seen him since.

29. If you take this one from me too and harm comes to him, you will bring my gray head down to the grave in misery.'

30. "So now, if the boy is not with us when I go back to your servant my father and if my father, whose life is closely bound up with the boy's life,

31. sees that the boy isn't there, he will die. Your servants will bring the gray head of our father down to the grave in sorrow.

32. Your servant guaranteed the boy's safety to my father. I said, 'If I do not bring him back to you, I will bear the blame before you, my father, all my life!'

33. "Now then, please let your servant remain here as my lord's slave in place of the boy, and let the boy return with his brothers.

34. How can I go back to my father if the boy is not with me? No! Do not let me see the misery that would come upon my father."

Genesis 45—Joseph Makes Himself Known

1. Then Joseph could no longer control himself before all his attendants, and he cried out, "Have everyone leave my presence!" So there was no one with Joseph when he made himself known to his brothers.

2. And he wept so loudly that the Egyptians heard him, and Pharaoh's household heard about it.

3. Joseph said to his brothers, "I am Joseph! Is my father still living?" But his brothers were not able to answer him, because they were terrified at his presence.

4. Then Joseph said to his brothers, "Come close to me." When they had done so, he said, "I am your brother Joseph, the one you sold into Egypt!

5. And now, do not be distressed and do not be angry with yourselves for selling me here, because it was to save lives that God sent me ahead of you.

6. For two years now there has been famine in the land, and for the next five years there will not be plowing and reaping.

7. But God sent me ahead of you to preserve for you a remnant on earth and to save your lives by a great deliverance.

8. "So then, it was not you who sent me here, but God. He made me father to Pharaoh, lord of his entire household and ruler of all Egypt.

9. Now hurry back to my father and say to him, 'This is what your son Joseph says: God has made me lord of all Egypt. Come down to me; don't delay.

10. You shall live in the region of Goshen and be near me—you, your children and grandchildren, your flocks and herds, and all you have.

11. I will provide for you there, because five years of famine are still to come. Otherwise you and your household and all who belong to you will become destitute.'

12. "You can see for yourselves, and so can my brother Benjamin, that it is really I who am speaking to you.

13. Tell my father about all the honor accorded me in Egypt and about everything you have seen. And bring my father down here quickly."

14. Then he threw his arms around his brother Benjamin and wept, and Benjamin embraced him, weeping.

15. And he kissed all his brothers and wept over them. Afterward his brothers talked with him.

16. When the news reached Pharaoh's palace that Joseph's brothers had come, Pharaoh and all his officials were pleased.

17. Pharaoh said to Joseph, "Tell your brothers, 'Do this: Load your animals and return to the land of Canaan,

18. and bring your father and your families back to me. I will give you the best of the land of Egypt and you can enjoy the fat of the land.'

19. "You are also directed to tell them, 'Do this: Take some carts from Egypt for your children and your wives, and get your father and come.

20. Never mind about your belongings, because the best of all Egypt will be yours.'"

21. So the sons of Israel did this. Joseph gave them carts, as Pharaoh had commanded, and he also gave them provisions for their journey.

22. To each of them he gave new clothing, but to Benjamin he gave three hundred shekels of silver and five sets of clothes.

23. And this is what he sent to his father: ten donkeys loaded with the best things of Egypt, and ten female donkeys loaded with grain and bread and other provisions for his journey.

24. Then he sent his brothers away, and as they were leaving he said to them, "Don't quarrel on the way!"

25. So they went up out of Egypt and came to their father Jacob in the land of Canaan.

26. They told him, "Joseph is still alive! In fact, he is ruler of all. Egypt." Jacob was stunned; he did not believe them.

27. But when they told him everything Joseph had said to them, and when he saw the carts Joseph had sent to carry him back, the spirit of their father Jacob revived.

28. And Israel said, "I'm convinced! My son Joseph is still alive. I will go and see him before I die."

Genesis 46—Jacob Goes to Egypt

1. So Israel set out with all that was his, and when he reached Beersheba, he offered sacrifices to the God of his father Isaac.

2. And God spoke to Israel in a vision at night and said, "Jacob! Jacob!" "Here I am," he replied.

3. "I am God, the God of your father," he said. "Do not be afraid to go down to Egypt, for I will make you into a great nation there.

4. I will go down to Egypt with you, and I will surely bring you back again. And Joseph's own hand will close your eyes."

5. Then Jacob left Beersheba, and Israel's sons took their father Jacob and their children and their wives in the carts that Pharaoh had sent to transport him.

6. They also took with them their livestock and the possessions they had acquired in Canaan, and Jacob and all his offspring went to Egypt.

7. He took with him to Egypt his sons and grandsons and his daughters and granddaughters—all his offspring.

8. These are the names of the sons of Israel (Jacob and his descendants) who went to Egypt: [. . .]

26. All those who went to Egypt with Jacob—those who were his direct descendants, not counting his sons' wives—numbered sixty-six persons.

27. With the two sons who had been born to Joseph in Egypt, the members of Jacob's family, which went to Egypt, were seventy in all.

28. Now Jacob sent Judah ahead of him to Joseph to get directions to Goshen. When they arrived in the region of Goshen,

29. Joseph had his chariot made ready and went to Goshen to meet his father Israel. As soon as Joseph appeared before him, he threw his arms around his father and wept for a long time.

30. Israel said to Joseph, "Now I am ready to die, since I have seen for myself that you are still alive."

31. Then Joseph said to his brothers and to his father's household, "I will go up and speak to Pharaoh and will say to him, 'My brothers and my father's household, who were living in the land of Canaan, have come to me.

32. The men are shepherds; they tend livestock, and they have brought along their flocks and herds and everything they own.'

33. When Pharaoh calls you in and asks, 'What is your occupation?'

34. you should answer, 'Your servants have tended livestock from our boyhood on, just as our fathers did.' Then you will be allowed to settle in the region of Goshen, for all shepherds are detestable to the Egyptians."

Genesis 47

1. Joseph went and told Pharaoh, "My father and brothers, with their flocks and herds and everything they own, have come from the land of Canaan and are now in Goshen."

2. He chose five of his brothers and presented them before Pharaoh.

3. Pharaoh asked the brothers, "What is your occupation?"

"Your servants are shepherds," they replied to Pharaoh, "just as our fathers were."

4. They also said to him, "We have come to live here awhile, because the famine is severe in Canaan and your servants' flocks have no pasture. So now, please let your servants settle in Goshen."

5. Pharaoh said to Joseph, "Your father and your brothers have come to you,

6. and the land of Egypt is before you; settle your father and your brothers in the best part of the land. Let them live in Goshen. And if you know of any among them with special ability, put them in charge of my own livestock."

7. Then Joseph brought his father Jacob in and presented him before Pharaoh. After Jacob blessed Pharaoh,

8. Pharaoh asked him, "How old are you?"

9. And Jacob said to Pharaoh, "The years of my pilgrimage are a hundred and thirty. My years have been few and difficult, and they do not equal the years of the pilgrimage of my fathers."

10. Then Jacob blessed Pharaoh and went out from his presence.

11. So Joseph settled his father and his brothers in Egypt and gave them property in the best part of the land, the district of Rameses, as Pharaoh directed.

12. Joseph also provided his father and his brothers and all his father's household with food, according to the number of their children. [. . .]

33. When Jacob had finished giving instructions to his sons, he drew his feet up into the bed, breathed his last and was gathered to his people.

Genesis 50

1. Joseph threw himself upon his father and wept over him and kissed him.

2. Then Joseph directed the physicians in his service to embalm his father Israel. So the physicians embalmed him,

3. taking a full forty days, for that was the time required for embalming. And the Egyptians mourned for him seventy days.

4. When the days of mourning had passed, Joseph said to Pharaoh's court, "If I have found favor in your eyes, speak to Pharaoh for me. Tell him,

5. 'My father made me swear an oath and said, "I am about to die; bury me in the tomb I dug for myself in the land of Canaan." Now let me go up and bury my father; then I will return.'"

6. Pharaoh said, "Go up and bury your father, as he made you swear to do."

7. So Joseph went up to bury his father. All Pharaoh's officials accompanied him—the dignitaries of his court and all the dignitaries of Egypt—

8. besides all the members of Joseph's household and his brothers and those belonging to his father's household. Only their children and their flocks and herds were left in Goshen.

9. Chariots and horsemen also went up with him. It was a very large company.

10. When they reached the threshing floor of Atad, near the Jordan, they lamented loudly and bitterly; and there Joseph observed a seven-day period of mourning for his father.

11. When the Canaanites who lived there saw the mourning at the threshing floor of Atad, they said, "The Egyptians are holding a solemn ceremony of mourning." That is why that place near the Jordan is called Abel Mizraim.

12. So Jacob's sons did as he had commanded them:

13. They carried him to the land of Canaan and buried him in the cave in the field of Machpelah, near Mamre, which Abraham had bought as a burial place from Ephron the Hittite, along with the field.

14. After burying his father, Joseph returned to Egypt, together with his brothers and all the others who had gone with him to bury his father.

Joseph Reassures His Brothers

15. When Joseph's brothers saw that their father was dead, they said, "What if Joseph holds a grudge against us and pays us back for all the wrongs we did to him?"

16. So they sent word to Joseph, saying, "Your father left these instructions before he died:

17. 'This is what you are to say to Joseph: I ask you to forgive your brothers the sins and the wrongs they committed in treating you so badly.' Now please forgive the sins of the servants of the God of your father." When their message came to him, Joseph wept.

18. His brothers then came and threw themselves down before him. "We are your slaves," they said.

19. But Joseph said to them, "Don't be afraid. Am I in the place of God?

20. You intended to harm me, but God intended it for good to accomplish what is now being done, the saving of many lives.

21. So then, don't be afraid. I will provide for you and your children." And he reassured them and spoke kindly to them.

The Death of Joseph

22. Joseph stayed in Egypt, along with all his father's family. He lived a hundred and ten years

23. and saw the third generation of Ephraim's children. Also the children of Makir son of Manasseh were placed at birth on Joseph's knees.

24. Then Joseph said to his brothers, "I am about to die. But God will surely come to your aid and take you up out of this land to the land he promised on oath to Abraham, Isaac and Jacob."

25. And Joseph made the sons of Israel swear an oath and said, "God will surely come to your aid, and then you must carry my bones up from this place."

26. So Joseph died at the age of a hundred and ten. And after they embalmed him, he was placed in a coffin in Egypt.

JOSEPH IN THE KORAN

SURA XII

In the Name of God, the Compassionate, the Merciful

ELIF. LAM. RA. These are signs of the clear Book.

An Arabic Koran have we sent it down, that ye might understand it.

In revealing to thee this Koran, one of the most beautiful of narratives will we narrate to thee, of which thou hast hitherto been regardless.

When Joseph said to his Father, "O my Father! Verily I beheld eleven stars and the sun and the moon—beheld them make obeisance to me!"

He said, "O my son! tell not thy vision to thy brethren, lest they plot a plot against thee: for Satan is the manifest foe of man.

It is thus that thy Lord shall choose thee and will teach thee the interpretation of dark sayings, and will perfect his favours on thee and on the family of

Jacob, as of old he perfected it on thy fathers Abraham and Isaac; verily thy Lord is Knowing, Wise!"

Now in JOSEPH and his brethren are signs for the enquirers;

When they said, "Surely better loved by our Father, than we, who are more in number, is Joseph and his brother; verily, our father hath clearly erred.

Slay ye Joseph! or drive him to some other land, and on you alone shall your father's face be set! and after this, ye shall live as upright persons."

10   One of them said, "Slay not Joseph, but cast him down to the bottom of the well: if ye do so, some wayfarers will take him up."

They said, "O our Father! why dost thou not entrust us with Joseph? indeed we mean him well.

Send him with us to-morrow that he may enjoy himself and sport: we will surely keep him safely."

He said, "Verily, your taking him away will grieve me; and I fear lest while ye are heedless of him the wolf devour him."

They said, "Surely if the wolf devour him, and we so many, we must in that case be weak indeed."

And when they went away with him they agreed to place him at the bottom of the well. And We revealed to him, "Thou wilt yet tell them of this their deed, when they shall not know thee."

And they came at nightfall to their father weeping.

They said, "O our Father! of a truth, we went to run races, and we left Joseph with our clothes, and the wolf devoured him: but thou wilt not believe us even though we speak the truth."

And they brought his shirt with false blood upon it. He said, "Nay, but yourselves have managed this affair. But patience is seemly: and the help of God is to be implored that I may bear what you tell me."

And wayfarers came and sent their drawer of water, and he let down his bucket. "Good news!" said he, "This is a youth!" And they kept his case secret, to make merchandise of him. But God knew what they did.

20   And they sold him for a paltry price—for some dirhems counted down, and at no high rate did they value him.

And he who bought him—an Egyptian—said to his wife, "Treat him hospitably; haply he may be useful to us, or we may adopt him as a son." Thus did we settle Joseph in the land, and we instructed him in the interpretation of dark sayings, for God is equal to his purpose; but most men know it not.

And when he had reached his age of strength we bestowed on him judgment and knowledge; for thus do we recompense the well doers.

And she in whose house he was conceived a passion for him, and she shut the doors and said, "Come hither." He said, "God keep me! Verily, my lord hath given me a good home: and the injurious shall not prosper."

But she longed for him; and he had longed for her had he not seen a token from his lord. Thus we averted evil and defilement from him, for he was one of our sincere servants.

And they both made for the door, and she rent his shirt behind; and at the door they met her lord. "What," said she, "shall be the recompense of him who would do evil to thy family, but a prison or a sore punishment?"

He said, "She solicited me to evil." And a witness out of her own family witnessed: "If his shirt be rent in front she speaketh truth, and he is a liar:

But if his shirt be rent behind, she lieth and he is true."

And when his lord saw his shirt torn behind, he said, "This is one of your devices! verily your devices are great!"

Joseph! leave this affair. And thou, *O wife,* ask pardon for thy crime, for thou hast sinned."

And in the city, the women said, "The wife of the Prince hath solicited her 30 servant: he hath fired her with his love: but we clearly see her manifest error."

And when she heard of their cabal, she sent to them and got ready a banquet for them, and gave each one of them a knife, and said, "*Joseph* shew thyself to them." And when they saw him they were amazed at him, and cut their hands, and said, "God keep us! This is no man! This is no other than a noble angel!"

She said, "This is he about whom ye blamed me. I wished him to yield to my desires, but he stood firm. But if he obey not my command, he shall surely be cast into prison, and become one of the despised."

He said, "O my Lord! I prefer the prison to compliance with their bidding: but unless thou turn away their snares from me, I shall play the youth with them, and become one of the unwise."

And his Lord heard him and turned aside their snares from him: for he is the Hearer, the Knower.

Yet resolved they, even after they had seen the signs *of his innocence,* to imprison him for a time.

And there came into the prison with him two youths. Said one of them, "Methought in my dream that I was pressing grapes." And the other said, "I dreamed that I was carrying bread on my head, of which the birds did eat. Declare to us the interpretation of this, for we see thou art a virtuous person."

He said, "There shall not come to you *in a dream* any food wherewith ye shall be fed, but I will acquaint you with its interpretation ere it come to pass to you. This is *a part* of that which my Lord hath taught me: for I have abandoned the religion of those who believe not in God and who deny the life to come;

And I follow the religion of my fathers, Abraham and Isaac and Jacob. We may not associate aught with God. This is of God's bounty towards us and towards mankind: but the greater part of mankind are not thankful.

O my two fellow prisoners! are sundry lords best, or God, the One, the Mighty? 40

Ye worship beside him mere names which ye have named, ye and your fathers, for which God hath not sent down any warranty. Judgment belongeth to God alone. He hath bidden you worship none but Him. This is the right faith: but most men know it not.

O my two fellow prisoners! as to one of you, he will serve wine unto his Lord: but as to the other, he will be crucified and the birds shall eat from off his head. The matter is decreed concerning which ye enquire."

And he said unto him who he judged would be set at large, "Remember me with thy lord." But Satan caused him to forget the remembrance of his Lord, so he remained some years in prison.

And the King said, "Verily, I saw *in a dream* seven fat kine which seven lean devoured; and seven green ears and other withered. O nobles, teach me my vision, if a vision yet are able to expound."

They said, "They are confused dreams, nor know we aught of the unravelling of dreams."

And he of the twain who had been set at large, said, "I will tell you the interpretation; let me go for it."

"Joseph, man of truth! teach us of the seven fat kine which seven lean devoured, and of the seven green ears, and other withered, that I may return to the men, and that they may be informed."

He said, "Ye shall sow seven years as is your wont, and the corn which ye reap leave ye in its ear, except a little of which ye shall eat.

Then after that shall come seven grievous years which shall eat what ye have stored for them, except a little which ye shall have kept.

Then shall come after this a year, in which men shall have rain, and in which they shall press the grape."

50   And the King said, "Bring him to me." And when the messenger came to Joseph he said, "Go back to thy lord, and ask him what meant the women who cut their hands, for my lord well knoweth the snare they laid."

Then said the Prince to the women, "What was your purpose when ye solicited Joseph?" They said, "God keep us! we know not any ill of him." The wife of the Prince said, "Now doth the truth appear. It was I who would have led him into unlawful love, and he is one of the truthful."

"By this" (said Joseph) "may my lord know that I did not in his absence play him false, and that God guideth not the machinations of deceivers.

Yet I hold not myself clear, for the heart is prone to evil, save theirs on whom my Lord hath mercy; for gracious is my Lord, Merciful."

And the King said, "Bring him to me: I will take him for my special service." And when he had spoken with him he said, "From this day shalt thou be with us, invested with place and trust."

He said, "Set me over the granaries of the land, I will be their prudent keeper!"

Thus did we stablish Joseph in the land that he might house himself therein at pleasure. We bestow our favours on whom we will, and suffer not the reward of the righteous to perish.

And truly the recompense of the life to come is better, for those who have believed and feared God.

And Joseph's brethren came and went in to him and he knew them, but they recognised him not.

And when he had provided them with their provision, he said, "Bring me your brother from your father. See ye not that I fill the measure, and am the best of hosts?

60   But if ye bring him not to me, then no measure of corn shall there be for you from me, nor shall ye come near me."

They said, "We will ask him of his father, and we will surely do it."

Said he to his servants, "Put their money into their camel-packs, that they may perceive it when they have returned to their family: haply they will come back to us."

And when they returned to their father, they said, "O, our father! corn is withholden from us: send, therefore, our brother with us and we shall have our measure; and all care of him will we take."

He said, "Shall I entrust you with him otherwise than as I before entrusted you with his brother? But God is the best guardian, and of those who shew compassion He is the most compassionate."

And when they opened their goods they found their money had been returned to them. They said, "O, our father, what more can we desire? Here is our money returned to us; we will provide corn for our families, and will take care of our brother, and shall receive a camel's burden more of corn. This is an easy quantity."

He said, "I will not send him with you but on your oath before God that ye will, indeed, bring him back to me, unless hindrances encompass you." And when they had given him their pledge, he said, "God is witness of what we say."

And he said, "O, my sons! Enter not by one gate, but enter by different gates. Yet can I not help you against aught decreed by God: judgment belongeth to God alone. In Him put I my trust, and in Him let the trusting trust."

And when they entered as their father had bidden them, it did not avert from them anything decreed of God; but it only *served to satisfy* a desire in the soul of Jacob which he had charged them to perform; for he was possessed of knowledge which we had taught him; but most men have not that knowledge.

And when they came in to Joseph, he took his brother to him. He said, "Verily, I am thy brother. Be not thou grieved for what they did."

And when he had provided them with their provisions, he placed his 70 drinking cup in his brother's camel-pack. Then a crier cried after them, "O travellers! ye are surely thieves."

They turned back to them and said, "What is that ye miss?"

"We miss," said they, "the prince's cup. For him who shall restore it, a camel's load of corn! I pledge myself for it."

They said, "By God! ye know certainly that we came not to do wrong in the land and we have not been thieves."

"What," said *the Egyptians,* "shall be the recompense of him *who hath stolen it,* if ye be found liars?"

They said, "That he in whose camel-pack it shall be found be given up to you in satisfaction for it. Thus recompense we the unjust."

And Joseph began with their sacks, before the sack of his brother, and then from the sack of his brother he drew it out. This stratagem did we suggest to Joseph. By the King's law he had no power to seize his brother, had not God pleased. We uplift into grades *of wisdom* whom we will. And there is one knowing above every one else endued with knowledge.

They said, "If he steal, a brother of his hath stolen heretofore." But Joseph kept his secret, and did not discover it to them. Said he, *aside,* "Ye are in the worse condition. And God well knoweth what ye state."

They said, "O Prince! Verily he hath a very aged father; in his stead, therefore, take one of us, for we see that thou art a generous person."

He said, "God forbid that we should take but him with whom our property was found, for then should we act unjustly."

80   And when they despaired of Benjamin, they went apart for counsel. The eldest of them said, "Know ye not how that your father hath taken a pledge from you before God, and how formerly ye failed in duty with regard to Joseph? I will not quit the land till my father give me leave, or God decide for me; for of those who decide is He the best.

Return ye to your father and say, 'O our father! Verily, thy son hath stolen: we bear witness only of what we know: we could not guard against the unforeseen.

Enquire for thyself in the city where we have been, and of the caravan with which we have arrived; and we are surely speakers of the truth.'

He said, "Nay, ye have arranged all this among yourselves: But patience is seemly: God, may be, will bring them back to me together; for he is the Knowing, the Wise."

And he turned away from them and said, "Oh! how I am grieved for Joseph!" and his eyes became white with grief, for he bore a silent sorrow.

They said, "By God thou wilt only cease to think of Joseph when thou art at the point of death, or dead."

He said, "I only plead my grief and my sorrow to God: but I know from God what ye know not:

Go, my sons, and seek tidings of Joseph and his brother, and despair not of God's mercy, for none but the unbelieving despair of the mercy of God."

And when they came in to Joseph, they said, "O Prince, distress hath reached us and our family, and little is the money that we have brought. But give us full measure, and bestow it as alms, for God will recompense the almsgivers."

He said, "Know ye what ye did to Joseph and his brother in your ignorance?"

90   They said, "Canst thou indeed be Joseph?" He said, "I am Joseph, and this is my brother. Now hath God been gracious to us. For whoso feareth God and endureth. . . . God verily will not suffer the reward of the righteous to perish!"

They said, "By God! now hath God chosen thee above us, and we have indeed been sinners!"

He said, "No blame be on you this day. God will forgive you, for He is the most merciful of those who shew mercy.

Go ye with this my shirt and throw it on my father's face, and he shall recover his sight: and bring me all your family."

And when the caravan was departed, their father said, "I surely perceive the smell of Joseph: think ye that I dote?"

They said, "By God, it is thy old mistake."

And when the bearer of good tidings came, he cast it on his face, and Jacob's eyesight returned.

·   Then he said, "Did I not tell you that I knew from God what ye knew not?"

They said, "Our father, ask pardon for our crimes for us, for we have indeed been sinners."

He said, "I will ask your pardon of my Lord, for he is Gracious, Merciful."

100   And when they came into Joseph he took his parents to him, and said, "Enter ye Egypt, if God will, secure."

And he raised his parents to the seat of state, and they fell down bowing themselves unto him. Then said he, "O my father, this is the meaning of my dream of old. My Lord hath now made it true, and he hath surely been gracious to me, since he took me forth from the prison, and hath brought you up out of the desert, after that Satan had stirred up strife between me and my brethren; for my Lord is gracious to whom He will; for He is the Knowing, the Wise.

O my Lord, thou hast given me dominion, and hast taught me to expound dark sayings. Maker of the Heavens and of the Earth! My guardian art thou in this world and in the next! Cause thou me to die a Muslim, and join me with the just."

This is one of the secret histories which we reveal unto thee. Thou wast not present with Joseph's brethren when they conceived their design and laid their plot: but the greater part of men, though thou long for it, will not believe.

Thou shalt not ask of them any recompense for this *message*. It is simply an instruction for all mankind.

And many as are the signs in the Heavens and on the Earth, yet they will pass them by, and turn aside from them:

And most of them believe not in God, without also joining other deities with Him.

What! Are they sure that the overwhelming chastisement of God shall not come upon them, or that that Hour shall not come upon them suddenly, while they are unaware?

SAY: This is my way: resting on a clear proof, I call you to God, I and whoso followeth me: and glory be to God! I am not one of those who add other deities to Him.

Never before thee have we sent any but men, chosen out of the people of the cities, to whom we made revelations. Will they not journey through the land, and see what hath been the end of those who were before them? But the mansions of the next life shall be better for those who fear God. Will they not then comprehend?

When at last the Apostles lost all hope, and deemed that they were reck- 110 oned as liars, our aid reached them, and we delivered whom we would; but our vengeance was not averted from the wicked.

Certainly in their histories is an example for men of understanding. This is no new tale of fiction, but a confirmation of previous scriptures, and an explanation of all things, and guidance and mercy to those who believe.

Questions

1. Often when we read two descriptions of a single event, we learn more than when we have only one perspective. What new insights did you gain by reading and comparing the two stories of Joseph?

2. The Koran gives one type of relationship between Joseph and his brothers, and the Bible gives a different type of relationship between Joseph and his brothers. What can we learn by comparing these two versions of Joseph's relationship?

3. Over the years, many people have seen the biblical Joseph as a "type" (a representation or illustration) that foreshadows Jesus Christ. Such an interpretation takes the qualities of Joseph and compares them with qualities found in Jesus. This leads to the following question: Is there a hidden

message to be found in these two accounts of Joseph's life? Are there parallels between Joseph and other people or events? Should we view Joseph as a type or as a representation of truths that go beyond the immediate story?

4. Narratives are evaluated by many factors. At times, we praise a story because it develops rich, believable characters. Sometimes we praise stories because they capture our attention emotionally, and we lose ourselves in the story. We often value narratives that make us think deeply about our personal lives and about the universal human condition. How would you evaluate these two accounts of Joseph's life?

PSALMS

The biblical book Psalms contains 150 poems. Actually, the psalms are lyrics from songs used by the Hebrew people. These songs were used in worship at the Temple in Jerusalem, were sung as people traveled to and from Jerusalem, and were used in daily life to express the many positive and negative emotions of the people. For thousands of years, people have found their very private thoughts and longings already recorded in these ancient poems. Thus, the psalms prove that there are some features of our hearts and lives that are common to all of humanity.

Quite a few psalms were written by David, but many other authors (both identified and unidentified) are found in this collection. Some of the psalms offer continuous praise and thanks to God. Some are psalms of lament; they are sorrowful meditations about personal or social pain and disappointment that are honestly expressed to God. Some are psalms of complaint, in which the author lists the struggles of the community and asks where God is in those struggles. Honesty is a key unifying quality in the psalms. Whether the author is happy, thankful, sad, or angry, the psalmist is honest with God. Another unifying quality in the psalms is the return to faith, confidence, and inner peace at the end of these works. Although life is often filled with pain, betrayal, and temporary defeat, the authors of the psalms conclude that God is in ultimate control and that God is good.

In Psalm 51, we hear the heart of King David of Israel. After David is confronted with his sins of murder and adultery, David repents. (Read 2 Samuel 11:1–12:25.) In this psalm, David writes that he will not bring an animal sacrifice until he first brings to God a "broken and contrite heart." Later, David will bring the animal sacrifice. Thus, David affirms the importance of a person's moral and spiritual attitudes over his or her mere actions. This theme of repentance is also found in Psalm 31.

In Psalm 104, the psalmist praises the power and wisdom of God as seen in creation. A sense of wonder, awe, and delight are brought to the readers' minds as the physical world and the spiritual world are brought into harmony. Although God is beyond the created order of physical things, this psalm leads one to conclude that God is intimately guiding creation. The physical world is not following blind forces. This is a poetic version of today's discussions of intelligent design.

In Psalm 139, David is overwhelmed by the intimacy of God. The Lord knows every detail of David's life and thoughts; in fact, God seems to delight in these simple details. In response to God's love and attention, David comes to hate anyone who would pollute God's creation or who would reject God's love for humanity. Perhaps after realizing that this hatred is too strong of a reaction, David concludes the psalm by asking God to examine his thoughts and correct them.

PSALM 51

For the director of music. A psalm of David. When the prophet Nathan came to him after David had committed adultery with Bathsheba.

Have mercy on me, O God,
*   according to your unfailing love;*
according to your great compassion
*   blot out my transgressions.*
Wash away all my iniquity   5
*   and cleanse me from my sin.*
For I know my transgressions,
*   and my sin is always before me.*
Against you, you only, have I sinned
*   and done what is evil in your sight,*   10
so that you are proved right when you speak
*   and justified when you judge.*
Surely I was sinful at birth,
*   sinful from the time my mother conceived me.*
Surely you desire truth in the inner parts;   15
*   you teach me wisdom in the inmost place.*
Cleanse me with hyssop, and I will be clean;
*   wash me, and I will be whiter than snow.*
Let me hear joy and gladness;
*   let the bones you have crushed rejoice.*   20
Hide your face from my sins
*   and blot out all my iniquity.*
Create in me a pure heart, O God,
*   and renew a steadfast spirit within me.*
Do not cast me from your presence   25
*   or take your Holy Spirit from me.*
Restore to me the joy of your salvation
*   and grant me a willing spirit, to sustain me.*
Then I will teach transgressors your ways,
*   and sinners will turn back to you.*   30
Save me from bloodguilt, O God,
*   the God who saves me,*
*   and my tongue will sing of your righteousness.*
O Lord, open my lips,
*   and my mouth will declare your praise.*   35

You do not delight in sacrifice, or I would bring it;
   you do not take pleasure in burnt offerings.
The sacrifices of God are a broken spirit;
   a broken and contrite heart,
40   *O God, you will not despise.*
In your good pleasure make Zion prosper;
   build up the walls of Jerusalem.
Then there will be righteous sacrifices,
   whole burnt offerings to delight you;
45   *then bulls will be offered on your altar.*

PSALM 104

Praise the LORD, O my soul.
O LORD my God, you are very great;
   you are clothed with splendor and majesty.
He wraps himself in light as with a garment;
5   *he stretches out the heavens like a tent*
   and lays the beams of his upper chambers on their waters.
He makes the clouds his chariot
   and rides on the wings of the wind.
He makes winds his messengers,
10   *flames of fire his servants.*
He set the earth on its foundations;
   it can never be moved.
You covered it with the deep as with a garment;
   the waters stood above the mountains.
15   *But at your rebuke the waters fled,*
   at the sound of your thunder they took to flight;
they flowed over the mountains,
   they went down into the valleys,
   to the place you assigned for them.
20   *You set a boundary they cannot cross;*
   never again will they cover the earth.
He makes springs pour water into the ravines;
   it flows between the mountains.
They give water to all the beasts of the field;
25   *the wild donkeys quench their thirst.*
The birds of the air nest by the waters;
   they sing among the branches.
He waters the mountains from his upper chambers;
   the earth is satisfied by the fruit of his work.
30   *He makes grass grow for the cattle,*
   and plants for man to cultivate—
   bringing forth food from the earth:

wine that gladdens the heart of man,
   oil to make his face shine,
   and bread that sustains his heart.   35
The trees of the LORD are well watered,
   the cedars of Lebanon that he planted.
There the birds make their nests;
   the stork has its home in the pine trees.
The high mountains belong to the wild goats;   40
   the crags are a refuge for the coneys.
The moon marks off the seasons,
   and the sun knows when to go down.
You bring darkness, it becomes night,
   and all the beasts of the forest prowl.   45
The lions roar for their prey
   and seek their food from God.
The sun rises, and they steal away;
   they return and lie down in their dens.
Then man goes out to his work,   50
   to his labor until evening.
How many are your works, O LORD!
   In wisdom you made them all;
   the earth is full of your creatures.
There is the sea, vast and spacious,   55
   teeming with creatures beyond number—
   living things both large and small.
There the ships go to and fro,
   and the leviathan, which you formed to frolic there.
These all look to you   60
   to give them their food at the proper time.
When you give it to them,
   they gather it up;
when you open your hand,
   they are satisfied with good things.   65
When you hide your face,
   they are terrified;
when you take away their breath,
   they die and return to the dust.
When you send your Spirit,   70
   they are created,
   and you renew the face of the earth.
May the glory of the LORD endure forever;
   may the LORD rejoice in his works—
he who looks at the earth, and it trembles,   75
   who touches the mountains, and they smoke.
I will sing to the LORD all my life;
   I will sing praise to my God as long as I live.

May my meditation be pleasing to him,
80   *as I rejoice in the LORD.*
But may sinners vanish from the earth
      and the wicked be no more.
Praise the LORD, O my soul.
Praise the LORD.

PSALM 139

For the director of music. Of David. A psalm.

O LORD, you have searched me
      and you know me.
You know when I sit and when I rise;
      you perceive my thoughts from afar.
5   *You discern my going out and my lying down;*
      you are familiar with all my ways.
Before a word is on my tongue
      you know it completely, O LORD.
You hem me in—behind and before;
10   *you have laid your hand upon me.*
Such knowledge is too wonderful for me,
      too lofty for me to attain.
Where can I go from your Spirit?
      Where can I flee from your presence?
15   *If I go up to the heavens, you are there;*
      if I make my bed in the depths, you are there.
If I rise on the wings of the dawn,
      if I settle on the far side of the sea,
even there your hand will guide me,
20   *your right hand will hold me fast.*
If I say, "Surely the darkness will hide me
      and the light become night around me,"
even the darkness will not be dark to you;
      the night will shine like the day,
25   *for darkness is as light to you.*
For you created my inmost being;
      you knit me together in my mother's womb.
I praise you because I am fearfully and wonderfully made;
      your works are wonderful,
30   *I know that full well.*
My frame was not hidden from you
      when I was made in the secret place.
When I was woven together in the depths of the earth,
      your eyes saw my unformed body.

All the days ordained for me 35
  were written in your book
  before one of them came to be.
How precious to me are your thoughts, O God!
  How vast is the sum of them!
Were I to count them, 40
  they would outnumber the grains of sand.
When I awake,
  I am still with you.
If only you would slay the wicked, O God!
  Away from me, you bloodthirsty men! 45
They speak of you with evil intent;
  your adversaries misuse your name.
Do I not hate those who hate you, O LORD,
  and abhor those who rise up against you?
I have nothing but hatred for them; 50
  I count them my enemies.
Search me, O God, and know my heart;
  test me and know my anxious thoughts.
See if there is any offensive way in me,
  and lead me in the way everlasting. 55

Questions-

1. In Psalm 51, David focuses on his personal relationship with God. Why does David write in verse 13 that he will teach the transgressors? Why does David shift to this public dimension of religion?
2. Psalms 51 and 139 give very different perspectives of the individual's relationship with God. How would you harmonize these two perspectives?
3. In Psalm 139, David feels very close to God; yet, every day we meet people who feel very distant from God in their lives. How would you explain this difference?
4. Why was Psalm 104 written? Why does the author want to review all of the qualities of nature and their relationship to the divine?

BHAGAVAD-GĪTĀ

The **Bhagavad-Gītā** is one of hundreds of sacred texts in Hinduism, the dominant religion in India. The term *Hinduism* is often misleading, because people use it with the implication that the term refers to a single religion. In reality, it is a modern term used to describe the many ancient religions found in India. In a sense, a "Hindu" is a person who follows any religious tradition that has its origins in the subcontinent of India. Some Hindus are pantheists (god is in everything); some are polytheists (there are many gods); and some are monotheists (there is only one God). Thus, Hinduism includes many contradictory beliefs.

However, there are some commonly shared beliefs. (a) Reincarnation is the Hindu belief that the human body is merely a temporary container for a small spark or small bit of the grand eternal soul. The small spark or the individual soul cycles through many physical lives and deaths on earth. (b) Because all creatures have this spark of life, reverence is shown toward humans, cows, insects, and other living creatures. (c) There is also a moral order or structure, called "dharma," that unifies all of life. It is the duty of all humans to live in harmony with dharma. To fight against dharma is to foolishly fight against reality. Included in this moral structure, or dharma, is the social order into which a person is born. Thus, each person should find peace in fulfilling his or her social role. (d) The goal of human life is to find inner peace via an acceptance of dharma. This inner peace is found by looking beyond good and evil, pain and pleasure, wealth and poverty, and life and death. Peace is found by disciplining one's mind and emotions to accept all of reality as it is.

Judaism, Christianity, and Islam have fairly clearly defined collections of religious texts; in contrast, Hinduism has many, many texts and thousands upon thousands of lines of poetry that express many perspectives. The *Bhagavad-Gītā* is the most common text used to illustrate the basic elements of Hindu thought. It contains the story of Prince Arjuna, who is waiting for the start of a great battle in ancient India. Because of complex familial relationships and political alignments, the prince looks across the battlefield and sees that he is about to fight and probably kill his cousins and friends. He drops his bow and does not want to fight, but his charioteer (who is a manifestation of the god Krishna) challenges him to consider the situation (and his obligations) from a higher, more spiritual point of view.

FROM THE BHAGAVAD-GĪTĀ

FROM THE SECOND TEACHING

Philosophy and Spiritual Discipline

LORD KRISHNA:

11   *You grieve for those beyond grief,*
and you speak words of insight;
but learned men do not grieve
for the dead or the living.

12   *Never have I not existed,*
nor you, nor these kings;
and never in the future
shall we cease to exist.

13   *Just as the embodied self*
enters childhood, youth, and old age,
so does it enter another body;
this does not confound a steadfast man.

14   *Contacts with matter make us feel*
heat and cold, pleasure and pain.

Arjuna, you must learn to endure
fleeting things—they come and go!

When these cannot torment a man,
when suffering and joy are equal
for him and he has courage,
he is fit for immortality.

15

Nothing of nonbeing comes to be,
nor does being cease to exist;
the boundary between these two
is seen by men who see reality.

16

Indestructible is the presence
that pervades all this;
no one can destroy
this unchanging reality.

17

Our bodies are known to end,
but the embodied self is enduring,
indestructible, and immeasurable;
therefore, Arjuna, fight the battle!

18

He who thinks this self a killer
and he who thinks it killed,
both fail to understand;
it does not kill, nor is it killed.

19

It is not born,
it does not die;
having been,
it will never not be;
unborn, enduring,
constant, and primordial,
it is not killed
when the body is killed.

20

Arjuna, when a man knows the self
to be indestructible, enduring, unborn,
unchanging, how does he kill
or cause anyone to kill?

21

As a man discards
worn-out clothes
to put on new
and different ones,
so the embodied self
discards
its worn-out bodies
to take on other new ones.

22

23   *Weapons do not cut it,*
     fire does not burn it,
     waters do not wet it,
     wind does not wither it.

24   *It cannot be cut or burned;*
     it cannot be wet or withered;
     it is enduring, all-pervasive,
     fixed, immovable, and timeless.

25   *It is called unmanifest,*
     inconceivable, and immutable;
     since you know that to be so,
     you should not grieve!

26   *If you think of its birth*
     and death as ever-recurring,
     then too, Great Warrior,
     you have no cause to grieve!

27   *Death is certain for anyone born,*
     and birth is certain for the dead;
     since the cycle is inevitable,
     you have no cause to grieve!

28   *Creatures are unmanifest in origin,*
     manifest in the midst of life,
     and unmanifest again in the end.
     Since this is so, why do you lament?

29   *Rarely someone*
     sees it,
     rarely another
     speaks it,
     rarely anyone
     hears it—
     even hearing it,
     no one really knows it.

30   *The self embodied in the body*
     of every being is indestructible;
     you have no cause to grieve
     for all these creatures, Arjuna!

31   *Look to your own duty;*
     do not tremble before it;
     nothing is better for a warrior
     than a battle of sacred duty.

32   *The doors of heaven open*
     for warriors who rejoice

to have a battle like this
thrust on them by chance.

If you fail to wage this war   33
of sacred duty,
you will abandon your own duty
and fame only to gain evil.

People will tell   34
of your undying shame,
and for a man of honor
shame is worse than death.

     * * *

Be intent on action,   47
not on the fruits of action;
avoid attraction to the fruits
and attachment to inaction!

Perform actions, firm in discipline,   48
relinquishing attachment;
be impartial to failure and success—
this equanimity is called discipline.

Arjuna, action is far inferior   49
to the discipline of understanding;
so seek refuge in understanding—pitiful
are men drawn by fruits of action.

Disciplined by understanding,   50
one abandons both good and evil deeds;
so arm yourself for discipline—
discipline is skill in actions.

Wise men disciplined by understanding   51
relinquish the fruit born of action;
freed from these bonds of rebirth,
they reach a place beyond decay.

When your understanding passes beyond   52
the swamp, of delusion,
you will be indifferent to all
that is heard in sacred lore.

When your understanding turns   53
from sacred lore to stand fixed,
immovable in contemplation,
then you will reach discipline.

ARJUNA: 54
Krishna, what defines a man
deep in contemplation whose insight

and thought are sure? How would he speak?
How would he sit? How would he move?

55   LORD KRISHNA:
When he gives up desires in his mind,
is content with the self within himself,
then he is said to be a man
whose insight is sure, Arjuna.

56   *When suffering does not disturb his mind,*
when his craving for pleasures has vanished,
when attraction, fear, and anger are gone,
he is called a sage whose thought is sure.

57   *When he shows no preference*
in fortune or misfortune
and neither exults nor hates,
his insight is sure.

58   *When, like a tortoise retracting*
its limbs, he withdraws his senses
completely from sensuous objects,
his insight is sure.

FROM THE THIRD TEACHING

Discipline of Action

ARJUNA:
1   *If you think understanding*
is more powerful than action,
why, Krishna, do you urge me
to this horrific act?

2   *You confuse my understanding*
with a maze of words;
speak one certain truth
so I may achieve what is good.

LORD KRISHNA:
3   *Earlier I taught the twofold*
basis of good in this world—
for philosophers, disciplined knowledge;
for men of discipline, action.

4   *A man cannot escape the force*
of action by abstaining from actions;
he does not attain success
just by renunciation.

5   *No one exists for even an instant*
without performing action;

however unwilling, every being is forced
to act by the qualities of nature.

When his senses are controlled 6
but he keeps recalling
sense objects with his mind,
he is a self-deluded hypocrite.

When he controls his senses 7
with his mind and engages in the discipline
of action with his faculties of action,
detachment sets him apart.

Perform necessary action; 8
it is more powerful than inaction;
without action you even fail
to sustain your own body.

Action imprisons the world 9
unless it is done as sacrifice;
freed from attachment, Arjuna,
perform action as sacrifice!

* * *

Always perform with detachment 19
any action you must do;
performing action with detachment,
one achieves supreme good.

Janaka and other ancient kings 20
attained perfection by action alone;
seeing the way to preserve
the world, you should act.

Whatever a leader does, 21
the ordinary people also do.
He sets the standard
for the world to follow.

In the three worlds, 22
there is nothing I must do,
nothing unattained to be attained,
yet I engage in action.

What if I did not engage 23
relentlessly in action?
Men retrace my path
at every turn, Arjuna.

These worlds would collapse 24
if I did not perform action;
I would create disorder in society,
living beings would be destroyed.

25   *As the ignorant act with attachment*
        to actions, Arjuna,
        so wise men should act with detachment
        to preserve the world.

FROM THE SIXTH TEACHING

The Man of Discipline

10   *A man of discipline should always*
        discipline himself, remain in seclusion,
        isolated, his thought and self well controlled,
        without possessions or hope.

11   *He should fix for himself*
        a firm seat in a pure place,
        neither too high nor too low,
        covered in cloth, deerskin, or grass.

12   *He should focus his mind and restrain*
        the activity of his thought and senses;
        sitting on that seat, he should practice
        discipline for the purification of the self.

13   *He should keep his body, head,*
        and neck aligned, immobile, steady;
        he should gaze at the tip of his nose
        and not let his glance wander.

14   *The self tranquil, his fear dispelled,*
        firm in his vow of celibacy, his mind restrained,
        let him sit with discipline,
        his thought fixed on me, intent on me.

15   *Disciplining himself,*
        his mind controlled,
        a man of discipline finds peace,
        the pure calm that exists in me.

16   *Gluttons have no discipline,*
        nor the man who starves himself,
        nor he who sleeps excessively
        or suffers wakefulness.

17   *When a man disciplines his diet*
        and diversions, his physical actions,
        his sleeping and waking,
        discipline destroys his sorrow.

18   *When his controlled thought*
        rests within the self alone,

without craving objects of desire,
he is said to be disciplined.

"He does not waver, like a lamp sheltered
from the wind" is the simile recalled
for a man of discipline, restrained in thought
and practicing self-discipline.

When his thought ceases,
checked by the exercise of discipline,
he is content within the self,
seeing the self through himself.

Absolute joy beyond the senses
can only be grasped by understanding;
when one knows it, he abides there
and never wanders from this reality.

Obtaining it, he thinks
there is no greater gain;
abiding there, he is unmoved,
even by deep suffering.

Since he knows that discipline
means unbinding the bonds of suffering,
he should practice discipline resolutely,
without despair dulling his reason.

He should entirely relinquish
desires aroused by willful, intent;
he should entirely control
his senses with his mind.

He should gradually become tranquil,
firmly controlling his understanding;
focusing his mind on the self,
he should think nothing.

Wherever his faltering mind
unsteadily wanders,
he should restrain it
and bring it under self-control.

When his mind is tranquil, perfect joy
comes to the man of discipline;
his passion is calmed, he is without sin,
being one with the infinite spirit.

Constantly disciplining himself,
free from sin, the man of discipline
easily achieves perfect joy
in harmony with the infinite spirit.

19

20

21

22

23

24

25

26

27

28

29   *Arming himself with discipline,*
        seeing everything with an equal eye,
        he sees the self in all creatures
        and all creatures in the self.

30   *He who sees me everywhere*
        and sees everything in me
        will not be lost to me,
        and I will not be lost to him.

31   *I exist in all creatures,*
        so the disciplined man devoted to me
        grasps the oneness of life;
        wherever he is, he is in me.

32   *When he sees identity in everything,*
        whether joy or suffering,
        through analogy with the self,
        he is deemed a man of pure discipline.

FROM THE ELEVENTH TEACHING

The Vision of Krishna's Totality

ARJUNA:

1   *To favor me you revealed*
        the deepest mystery of the self,
        and by your words
        my delusion is dispelled.

2   *I heard from you in detail*
        how creatures come to be and die,
        Krishna, and about the self
        in its immutable greatness.

3   *Just as you have described*
        yourself, I wish to see your form
        in all its majesty,
        Krishna, Supreme among Men.

4   *If you think I can see it,*
        reveal to me

Questions

1. The *Bhagavad-Gītā* challenges its readers to accept reality and find inner peace. In contrast, the Bible challenges its readers to hate and reject part of reality (sin), but accept another part of reality, which is God's love and grace, and then find inner peace. What other similarities and differences exist between the Bible's discussions on finding peace and the *Bhagavad-Gītā's* approach to finding peace?

2. In the *Bhagavad-Gītā*, the reader is encouraged to control, limit, and re- press his or her desires. Yet, one of the most fundamental desires is the

longing to understand. Humans are simply curious. Is it wrong to want to understand? If so, why? Yet, Hinduism and Buddhism often tell a person to suppress all desires and find a mental state of tranquility. How do Christianity and other religions deal with this tension?

3. There is an emphasis on "oneness" near the end of this passage. For example, Krishna says, "He who sees me everywhere / and sees everything in me, / will not be lost to me, / and I will not be lost to him." In what sense is there a similar oneness found in the Bible's description of Christ (see Colossians 1:16–20)? How would you compare the individual's relationship with Christ (as discussed in the Bible) with the individual's relationship with Krishna (as discussed in the *Bhagavad-Gītā*)?

4. The role of self-discipline is very important in the *Bhagavad-Gītā*. How would you explain the relationship between self-discipline and the topics of peace, passion, and the divine? Below is a passage that illustrates the intersection of these topics:

> *When his mind is tranquil, perfect joy*
> *comes to the man of discipline;*
> *his passion is calmed, he is without sin,*
> *being one with the infinite spirit.*

MAHĀDĒVIYAKKA

Mahādēviyakka lived in southern India in the twelfth century and wrote beautiful love poetry to her god, Siva. Although little is known about her life, she is remembered for her complete devotion to Siva. Legend says that she was forced to marry a king, but that she broke off that relationship in order to live a life of spiritual pilgrimage and to worship Siva. Such abandonment of one's family has been a long-standing tradition in Hinduism. It is not uncommon for older men, who have completed the task of raising their families, to leave their homes and to wander the countryside in search of spiritual enlightenment. This tradition is also seen in the travels of Siddhartha in Hesse's novel. Mahādēviyakka is breaking the norm because she is young and she is a woman. A few hundred years after Mahādēviyakka, Hinduism saw a similar devotion expressed in the life and poetry of Mīrābāī. Mīrābāī, another woman, wrote of her overwhelming love for, union with, and devotion to her god, Krishna.

HUSBAND INSIDE

> *Husband inside,*
> *lover outside.*
> *I can't manage them both.*

This world
5   *and that other,*
cannot manage them both.

O lord white as jasmine

I cannot hold in one hand
both the round nut
10 *and the long bow.*

Questions

1. Who is the "Husband inside"? Who is the "lover outside"? What stops the speaker from managing both? What does "This world" denote and connote? What does "that other" world denote and connote? What stops the speaker from managing both?

2. The *Bhagavad-Gītā* is a religious text that codifies a set of guidelines for spiritual, moral, and social practices. It lays down dharma for married couples and members of various castes. How does Mahādēviyakka's poem create an alternative path of religious devotion that rejects the traditional expectations of women? Conduct some historical and cultural research to explore the revolutionary implications of Mahādēviyakka's poem.

3. The conflict that Mahādēviyakka experiences between her family life (both her husband and her marital home) and her religion suggests several moral tensions in her view of reality. Is it necessary to violate one set of moral commitments in order to honor a "higher calling"? Is the dharma at odds with itself?

4. Mahādēviyakka's life and poetry give us one view of a young woman finding her place in the cosmos. How would you compare her struggles and her conclusions with the stories of Ruth and Esther in the Hebrew Bible?

MĪRĀBĀĪ

Mīrābāī (c. 1498–c. 1547) lived among the elite in India, but her religious commitments led her to violate some of the expectations of her class. From an early age, she was extremely devoted to the Hindu god, Krishna. This overwhelming devotion guided her thoughts and feelings for her whole life. As an expression of this devotion, she wrote hundreds of poems of praise to Krishna. The stories about Mīrābāī and her poetry continue to be very popular in India.

A defining moment in her life was when her husband died and she refused to follow the Hindu tradition of *sati* (this tradition dictated that a widow should throw herself on the funeral bier of her husband to be burned alive). The logic behind this violation of tradition was Mīrābāī's union with and devotion to Krishna; that commitment to Krishna was more powerful than her commitments to her husband and society. In this sense, Mīrābāī is like Mahād⁻ ēviyakka, who abandoned her royal husband and family. Both women are revered for their poetry and for their extreme devotion to their god. They illustrate the Bhakti tradition in India—a tradition of devotion to, and intimacy with, a god. These women and other Bhakti poets strive to capture their participation with the divine in their writings.

LET US GO TO A REALM BEYOND GOING

Let us go to a realm beyond going,
Where death is afraid to go,
Where the high-flying birds alight and play,
Afloat in the full lake of love.
There they gather—the good, the true—
To strengthen an inner regimen,
To focus on the dark form of the Lord
And refine their minds like fire.
Garbed in goodness—their ankle bells—
They dance the dance of contentment
And deck themselves with the sixteen signs
Of beauty, and a golden crown—
There where the love of the Dark One comes first
And everything else is last.

Questions

1. Mīrābāī suggested that it is necessary to leave one's daily responsibilities in order to find spiritual enlightenment. Do you think that everyday responsibilities are in conflict with spiritual development? How would you compare Joseph's spiritual development while serving as a slave, a prisoner, and a servant of the pharaoh with Mīrābāī's conclusions?
2. Can Mīrābāī's poem be reduced to a single theme? What would it be?
3. How would you compare Mīrābāī's feelings and thoughts with other works in this anthology? For example, how would you compare Mīrābāī's religious eroticism with that of Mahādēviyakka? How does Mīrābāī's poem relate to the ideas found in the *Bhagavad-Gītā* or in Milton's poem about blindness?
4. How is the "realm beyond going" (the spiritual realm) different from the human, secular, natural world that Mīrābāī lives in? What purpose does this powerful allusion or motif serve for Mīrābāī?

NAVAJO

Navajo poetry and chants are rooted in a culture that has adapted and survived many pressures for hundreds of years in the American Southwest. The Navajos were influenced by neighboring tribes such as the Pueblo people, later by the Spanish, who traded with them, and more recently by the advanced technology and different cultural and religious traditions that came with Anglo settlers. Today, there are about a quarter of a million people who claim membership in the Navajo Nation, many of whom continue to actively use the Navajo language.

HEALING PRAYER FROM THE BEAUTYWAY CHANT

Out of the East, Beauty has come home,
Out of the South, Beauty has come home,
Out of the West, Beauty has come home,
Out of the North, Beauty has come home,
5   *Out of the highest heavens and the lowest lands,*
  Beauty has come home.
  Everywhere around us, Beauty has come home.
As we live each day, everything evil will leave us.
  We will be entirely healed,
10   *Our bodies will exult in the fresh winds,*
  Our steps will be firm.
As we live each day,
  Everything before us will be Beautiful;
  Everything behind us will be Beautiful;
15   *Everything above us will be Beautiful;*
  Everything below us will be Beautiful;
  Everything around us will be Beautiful;
  All our thoughts will be Beautiful;
  All our words will be Beautiful;
20   *All our dreams will be Beautiful.*
We will be forever restored, forever whole.
All things will be Beautiful forever.

Questions

1. How does this poem/chant compare with prayers found in your personal experience or in your culture?
2. How would you compare this poem/chant with one or two of the more traditional Western poems in this anthology?
3. Using the chant as ethnography, write a summary description of the world envisaged "after Beauty has come home" (lines 6–7). Is such a world conceivable? Is it possible? How is such a world different from other views of the world?
4. What is the importance and significance of repetition in this poem/chant? In what ways is repetition important in literature and in life?

ANNE BRADSTREET

Anne Bradstreet (1612–1672) was born in England and came to the fragile, new North American colonies in 1630. She was very well educated and was the first woman in the thirteen British colonies to publish a book— a collection of poems. Both her father and her husband served as governors of the Massachusetts Bay Colony. Bradstreet thus had many privileges, but she also endured many personal struggles as an early colonist. She endured long periods of illness, and her family home, along with her library, once burned. Some view her as an early feminist, but she seemed to be a strong, intelligent woman who was deeply committed to cultivating a healthy and loving home.

Bradstreet's poetry is filled with references to classical literature and to the Bible. Yet, her work is very personal and rooted in her daily experiences in Massachusetts. Most of all, her work is a constant exploration of her relationship with God and of her spiritual beliefs. Her poem, "Contemplations," is a sweeping work that begins with simple observations about trees against the sky and ends with similar observations. Yet, throughout the poem, she considers the glory of God, the beautiful qualities of creation, and the nature of human life and death.

When reading this selection, it is helpful to know that "Phoebus" is a classical reference to the sun and its god-like qualities; "Methuselah" is a reference to the oldest man in the Bible; the "Father of lies" is a reference to Satan; and "Philomel" is a musical instrument, which is similar to a violin.

CONTEMPLATIONS

1

Some time now past in the autumnal tide,
When Phoebus wanted but one hour to bed,
The trees all richly clad, yet void of pride,
Were gilded o'er by his rich golden head.
Their leaves and fruits seemed painted, but was true,   5
Of green, of red, of yellow, mixed hue;
Rapt were my senses at this delectable view.

2

I wist not what to wish, yet sure thought I,
If so much excellence abide below,
How excellent is He that dwells on high,   10
Whose power and beauty by his works we know?
Sure he is goodness, wisdom, glory, light,
That hath this under world so richly dight;
More heaven than earth was here, no winter and no night.

3

15   *Then on a stately oak I cast mine eye,*
      Whose ruffling top the clouds seemed to aspire;
      How long since thou wast in thine infancy?
      Thy strength, and stature, more thy years admire,
20   *Hath hundred winters past since thou wast born?*
      Or thousand since thou breakest thy shell of horn?
      If so, see these as nought, eternity doth scorn.

4

      Then higher on the glistering Sun I gazed,
      Whose beams was shaded by the leavie tree;
      The more I looked, the more I grew amazed,
25   *And softly said, "What glory's like to thee?"*
      Soul of this world, this universe's eye,
      No wonder some made thee a deity;
      Had I not better known, alas, the same had I.

5

      Thou as a bridegroom from thy chamber rushes,
30   *And as a strong man, joys to run a race;*
      The morn doth usher thee with smiles and blushes;
      The Earth reflects her glances in thy face.
      Birds, insects, animals with vegative,
      Thy heat from death and dullness doth revive,
35   *And in the darksome womb of fruitful nature dive.*

6

      Thy swift annual and diurnal course,
      Thy daily straight and yearly oblique path,
      Thy pleasing fervor and thy scorching force,
      All mortals here the feeling knowledge hath.
40   *Thy presence makes it day, thy absence night,*
      Quaternal seasons caused by thy might;
      Hail creature, full of sweetness, beauty, and delight.

7

      Art thou so full of glory that no eye
      Hath strength thy shining rays once to behold?
45   *And is thy splendid throne erect so high,*
      As to approach it, can no earthly mould?
      How full of glory then must thy Creator be,
      Who gave this bright light luster unto thee?
      Admired, adored for ever, be that Majesty.

8

Silent alone, where none or saw, or heard,   50
In pathless paths I led my wand'ring feet,
My humble eyes to lofty skies I reared
To sing some song, my mazed Muse thought meet.
My great Creator I would magnify,
That nature had thus decked liberally;   55
But Ah, and Ah, again, my imbecility!

9

I heard the merry grasshopper then sing.
The black-clad cricket bear a second part;
They kept one tune and played on the same string,
Seeming to glory in their little art.   60
Shall creatures abject thus their voices raise
And in their kind resound their Maker's praise,
Whilst I, as mute, can warble forth no higher lays?

10

When present times look back to ages past,
And men in being fancy those are dead,   65
It makes things gone perpetually to last,
And calls back months and years that long since fled.
It makes a man more aged in conceit
Than was Methuselah, or's grandsire great,
While of their persons and their acts his mind doth treat.   70

11

Sometimes in Eden fair he seems to be,
Sees glorious Adam there made lord of all,
Fancies the apple, dangle on the tree,
That turned his sovereign to a naked thrall.
Who like a miscreant's driven from that place,   75
To get his bread with pain and sweat of face,
A penalty imposed on his backsliding race.

12

Here sits our grandame in retired place,
And in her lap her bloody Cain new-born;
The weeping imp oft looks her in the face,   80
Bewails his unknown hap and fate forlorn;
His mother sighs to think of Paradise,
And how she lost her bliss to be more wise,
Believing him that was, and is, father of lies.

13

85   *Here Cain and Abel come to sacrifice,*
      Fruits of the earth and fatlings each do bring,
      On Abel's gift the fire descends from skies,
      But no such sign on false Cain's offering;
      With sullen hateful looks he goes his ways,
90   *Hath thousand thoughts to end his brother's days,*
      Upon whose blood his future good he hopes to raise.

14

      There Abel keeps his sheep, no ill he thinks;
      His brother comes, then acts his fratricide;
      The virgin Earth of blood her first draught drinks,
95   *But since that time she often hath been cloyed.*
      The wretch with ghastly face and dreadful mind
      Thinks each he sees will serve him in his kind,
      Though none on earth but kindred near then could he find.

15

      Who fancies not his looks now at the bar,
100   *His face like death, his heart with horror fraught,*
      Nor malefactor ever felt like war,
      When deep despair with wish of life hath fought,
      Branded with guilt and crushed with treble woes,
      A vagabond to Land of Nod he goes.
105   *A city builds, that walls might him secure from foes.*

16

      Who thinks not oft upon the fathers' ages,
      Their long descent, how nephews' sons they saw,
      The starry observations of those sages,
      And how their precepts to their sons were law,
110   *How Adam sighed to see his progeny,*
      Clothed all in his black sinful livery,
      Who neither guilt nor yet the punishment could fly.

17

      Our life compare we with their length of days
      Who to the tenth of theirs doth now arrive?
115   *And though thus short, we shorten many ways,*
      Living so little while we are alive;
      In eating, drinking, sleeping, vain delight.
      So unawares comes on perpetual night,
      And puts all pleasures vain into eternal flight.

18

When I behold the heavens as in their prime,   120
And then the earth (though old) still clad in green,
The stones and trees, insensible of time,
Nor age nor wrinkle on their front are seen;
If winter come and greenness then do fade,
A spring returns, and they more youthful made;   125
But man grows old, lies down, remains where once he's laid.

19

By birth more noble than those creatures all,
Yet seems by nature and by custom cursed,
No sooner born, but grief and care makes fall
That state obliterate he had at first: 130
Nor youth, nor strength, nor wisdom spring again,
Nor habitations long their names retain,
But in oblivion to the final day remain.

20

Shall I then praise the heavens, the trees, the earth
Because their beauty and their strength last longer?   135
Shall I wish there, or never to had birth,
Because they're bigger, and their bodies stronger?
Nay, they shall darken, perish, fade and die,
And when unmade, so ever shall they lie,
But man was made for endless immortality.   140

21

Under the cooling shadow of a stately elm
Close sat I by a goodly river's side,
Where gliding streams the rocks did overwhelm,
A lonely place, with pleasures dignified.
I once that loved the shady woods so well,   145
Now thought the rivers did the trees excel,
And if the sun would ever shine, there would I dwell.

22

While on the stealing stream I fixt mine eye,
Which to the longed-for ocean held its course,
I marked, nor crooks, nor rubs that there did lie   150
Could hinder ought, but still augment its force.
"O happy flood," quoth I, "that holds thy race
Till thou arrive at thy beloved place,
Nor is it rocks or shoals that can obstruct thy pace;

23

155   *Nor is't enough, that thou alone mayst slide,*
But hundred brooks in thy clear waves do meet,
So hand in hand along with thee they glide
To Thetis' house, where all embrace and greet.
Thou emblem true of what I count the best,
160   *O could I lead my rivulets to rest,*
So may we press to that vast mansion, ever blest."

24

Ye fish, which in this liquid region 'bide,
That for each season have your habitation,
Now salt, now fresh where you think best to glide
165   *To unknown coasts to give a visitation,*
In lakes and ponds you leave your numerous fry;
So nature taught, and yet you know not why,
You wat'ry folk that know not your felicity.

25

Look how the wantons frisk to taste the air,
170   *Then to the colder bottom straight they dive;*
Eftsoon to Neptune's glassy hall repair
To see what trade they great ones there do drive,
Who forage o'er the spacious sea-green field,
And take the trembling prey before it yield,
175   *Whose armour is their scales, their spreading fins their shield.*

26

While musing thus with contemplation fed,
And thousand fancies buzzing in my brain,
The sweet-tongued Philomel perched o'er my head
And chanted forth a most melodious strain
180   *Which rapt me so with wonder and delight,*
I judged my hearing better than my sight,
And wished me wings with her a while to take my flight.

27

"O merry Bird," said I, "that fears no snares,
That neither toils nor hoards up in thy barn,
185   *Feels no sad thoughts nor cruciating cares*
To gain more good or shun what might thee harm.
Thy clothes ne'er wear, thy meat is everywhere,
Thy bed a bough, thy drink the water clear,
Reminds not what is past, nor what's to come dost fear."

28

"*The dawning morn with songs thou dost prevent,*   190
Sets hundred notes unto thy feathered crew,
So each one tunes his pretty instrument,
And warbling out the old, begin anew,
And thus they pass their youth in summer season,
Then follow thee into a better region,   195
Where winter's never felt by that sweet airy legion."

29

Man at the best a creature frail and vain,
In knowledge ignorant, in strength but weak,
Subject to sorrows, losses, sickness, pain,
Each storm his state, his mind, his body break,   200
From some of these he never finds cessation,
But day or night, within, without, vexation,
Troubles from foes, from friend, from dearest, near'st relation.

30

And yet this sinful creature, frail and vain,
This lump of wretchedness, of sin and sorrow,   205
This weatherbeaten vessel wracked with pain,
Joys not in hope of an eternal morrow;
Nor all his losses, crosses, and vexation,
In weight, in frequency and long duration
Can make him deeply groan in that divine translation.   210

31

The mariner that on smooth waves doth glide
Sings merrily and steers his bark with ease,
As if he had command of wind and tide,
And now become great master of the seas:
But suddenly a storm spoils all the sport,   215
And makes him long for a more quiet port,
Which 'gainst all adverse winds may serve for fort.

32

So he that saileth in this world of pleasure,
Feeding on sweets, that never bit of th' sour,
That's full of friends, of honour, and of treasure,   220
Fond fool, he takes this earth ev'n for heav'n's bower.
But sad affliction comes and makes him see
Here's neither honour, wealth, nor safety;
Only above is found all with security.

33

225 *O Time the fatal wrack of mortal things,*
That draws oblivion's curtains over kings;
Their sumptuous monuments, men know them not,
Their names without a record are forgot,
Their parts, their ports, their pomp's all laid in th' dust,
230 *Nor wit nor gold, nor buildings scape time's rust;*
But he whose name is graved in the white stone
Shall last and shine when all of these are gone.
1664–1665?   *1678*

Questions

1. At one point, Bradstreet wrote, "And though thus short, we shorten many ways, / living so little while we are alive." What did she mean by "living so little while we are alive"? How does this thought fit into the rest of the poem?
2. What did Bradstreet mean later, when she wrote, "In knowledge ignorant, in strength but weak"?
3. At the end of the poem, Bradstreet observed how kings and monuments are forgotten, because of "O Time the fatal wrack of mortal things." Then she wrote, "But he whose name is grav'd in the white stone, / Shall last and shine when all these are gone." What is the difference between the forgotten kings and the person whose name is written in the white stone?
4. What portions of this poem can you relate to your own thoughts and experiences?

THOMAS JEFFERSON

Thomas Jefferson is often called the author of the Declaration of Independence of the United States of America. The ideas in this statement circulated for years in the thirteen British colonies of North America. The war against Great Britain was a year old when the representatives of the colonies gathered and decided to formally declare their independence. At that time, a committee of five representatives from five colonies was chosen to draft the document. Jefferson, one of the committee members, was known to be a gifted writer and a clear thinker, so he was given the task of drafting the document. After many revisions, it was formally approved on July 4, 1776. In one sense, the Declaration of Independence is an expression of Jefferson's style, personality, and beliefs. In another sense, it is an expression of those sociopolitical concerns and spiritual beliefs, such as deism and rationalism, which were popular in the colonies. Otherwise, it would not have been accepted by the colonial representatives and most Americans.

THE DECLARATION OF INDEPENDENCE

IN CONGRESS, July 4, 1776.

The Unanimous Declaration of the Thirteen United States of America

When in the Course of human events, it becomes necessary for one people to dissolve the political bands which have connected them with another, and to assume among the powers of the earth, the separate and equal station to which the Laws of Nature and of Nature's God entitle them, a decent respect to the opinions of mankind requires that they should declare the causes which impel them to the separation.

We hold these truths to be self-evident, that all men are created equal, that they are endowed by their Creator with certain unalienable Rights, that among these are Life, Liberty and the pursuit of Happiness.—That to secure these rights, Governments are instituted among Men, deriving their just powers from the consent of the governed,—That whenever any Form of Government becomes destructive of these ends, it is the Right of the People to alter or to abolish it, and to institute new Government, laying its foundation on such principles and organizing its powers in such form, as to them shall seem most likely to effect their Safety and Happiness. Prudence, indeed, will dictate that Governments long established should not be changed for light and transient causes; and accordingly all experience hath shewn, that mankind are more disposed to suffer, while evils are sufferable, than to right themselves by abolishing the forms to which they are accustomed. But when a long train of abuses and usurpations, pursuing invariably the same Object evinces a design to reduce them under absolute Despotism, it is their right, it is their duty, to throw off such Government, and to provide new Guards for their future security.—Such has been the patient sufferance of these Colonies; and such is now the necessity which constrains them to alter their former Systems of Government. The history of the present King of Great Britain is a history of repeated injuries and usurpations, all having in direct object the establishment of an absolute Tyranny over these States. To prove this, let Facts be submitted to a candid world.

He has refused his Assent to Laws, the most wholesome and necessary for the public good.

He has forbidden his Governors to pass Laws of immediate and pressing importance, unless suspended in their operation till his Assent should be obtained; and when so suspended, he has utterly neglected to attend to them.

He has refused to pass other Laws for the accommodation of large districts of people, unless those people would relinquish the right of Representation in the Legislature, a right inestimable to them and formidable to tyrants only.

He has called together legislative bodies at places unusual, uncomfortable, and distant from the depository of their public Records, for the sole purpose of fatiguing them into compliance with his measures.

He has dissolved Representative Houses repeatedly, for opposing with manly firmness his invasions on the rights of the people.

He has refused for a long time, after such dissolutions, to cause others to be elected; whereby the Legislative powers, incapable of Annihilation, have returned to the People at large for their exercise; the State remaining in the mean time exposed to all the dangers of invasion from without, and convulsions within.

He has endeavoured to prevent the population of these States; for that purpose obstructing the Laws for Naturalization of Foreigners; refusing to pass others to encourage their migrations hither, and raising the conditions of new Appropriations of Lands.

He has obstructed the Administration of Justice, by refusing his Assent to Laws for establishing Judiciary powers.

He has made Judges dependent on his Will alone, for the tenure of their offices, and the amount and payment of their salaries.

He has erected a multitude of New Offices, and sent hither swarms of Officers to harrass our people, and eat out their substance.

He has kept among us, in times of peace, Standing Armies without the Consent of our legislatures.

He has affected to render the Military independent of and superior to the Civil power.

He has combined with others to subject us to a jurisdiction foreign to our constitution, and unacknowledged by our laws; giving his Assent to their Acts of pretended Legislation:

For Quartering large bodies of armed troops among us:

For protecting them, by a mock Trial, from punishment for any Murders which they should commit on the Inhabitants of these States:

For cutting off our Trade with all parts of the world:

For imposing Taxes on us without our Consent:

For depriving us in many cases, of the benefits of Trial by Jury:

For transporting us beyond Seas to be tried for pretended offences

For abolishing the free System of English Laws in a neighbouring Province, establishing therein an Arbitrary government, and enlarging its Boundaries so as to render it at once an example and fit instrument for introducing the same absolute rule into these Colonies:

For taking away our Charters, abolishing our most valuable Laws, and altering fundamentally the Forms of our Governments:

For suspending our own Legislatures, and declaring themselves invested with power to legislate for us in all cases whatsoever.

He has abdicated Government here, by declaring us out of his Protection and waging War against us.

He has plundered our seas, ravaged our Coasts, burnt our towns, and destroyed the lives of our people.

He is at this time transporting large Armies of foreign Mercenaries to compleat the works of death, desolation and tyranny, already begun with circumstances of Cruelty & perfidy scarcely paralleled in the most barbarous ages, and totally unworthy the Head of a civilized nation.

He has constrained our fellow Citizens taken Captive on the high Seas to bear Arms against their Country, to become the executioners of their friends and Brethren, or to fall themselves by their Hands.

He has excited domestic insurrections amongst us, and has endeavoured to bring on the inhabitants of our frontiers, the merciless Indian Savages, whose known rule of warfare, is an undistinguished destruction of all ages, sexes and conditions.

In every stage of these Oppressions We have Petitioned for Redress in the most humble terms: Our repeated Petitions have been answered only by repeated injury. A Prince whose character is thus marked by every act which may define a Tyrant, is unfit to be the ruler of a free people.

Nor have We been wanting in attentions to our Brittish brethren. We have warned them from time to time of attempts by their legislature to extend an unwarrantable jurisdiction over us. We have reminded them of the circumstances of our emigration and settlement here. We have appealed to their native justice and magnanimity, and we have conjured them by the ties of our common kindred to disavow these usurpations, which, would inevitably interrupt our connections and correspondence. They too have been deaf to the voice of justice and of consanguinity. We must, therefore, acquiesce in the necessity, which denounces our Separation, and hold them, as we hold the rest of mankind, Enemies in War, in Peace Friends.

We, therefore, the Representatives of the united States of America, in General Congress, Assembled, appealing to the Supreme Judge of the world for the rectitude of our intentions, do, in the Name, and by Authority of the good People of these Colonies, solemnly publish and declare, That these United Colonies are, and of Right ought to be Free and Independent States; that they are Absolved from all Allegiance to the British Crown, and that all political connection between them and the State of Great Britain, is and ought to be totally dissolved; and that as Free and Independent States, they have full Power to levy War, conclude Peace, contract Alliances, establish Commerce, and to do all other Acts and Things which Independent States may of right do. And for the support of this Declaration, with a firm reliance on the protection of divine Providence, we mutually pledge to each other our Lives, our Fortunes and our sacred Honor.

Questions

1. Research both the Age of Rationalism and the terms *Divine Providence* and *Laws of Nature and of Nature's God*. These terms and the worldview that they represented were popular with Americans in the eighteenth century. At the beginning of the twenty-first century, these terms seem odd. They are not part of our cultural and political discourse. What has changed about how people look at life, society, and political affairs?
2. The most well-known passage in the Declaration of Independence is "We hold these truths to be self-evident, that all men are created equal, that they are endowed by their Creator with certain unalienable Rights, that among these are Life, Liberty and the pursuit of Happiness." What does

endowed mean? Why was it used here? What does *unalienable* mean? Why is it used here? Do you agree with these concepts?

3. Why were three rights, "Life, Liberty, and the pursuit of Happiness," chosen to illustrate the rights of all humans? What meaning would you attach to each of these three rights? Would you give a different list? Why or why not?

4. The Judeo-Christian heritage of the colonists taught them to obey the government and to live as peacemakers. (For biblical examples, see Esther 1:1–10:3, Daniel 1:1–6:28, Romans 13:1–7, and James 3:13–18.) That heritage also has examples of good people who resisted authorities. (For biblical examples, see Exodus 3:1–14:31 and Acts 4:1–22 and 5:17–41.) How does the Declaration of Independence express this heritage of obedient peacemaking, while also expressing a commitment to a higher authority and higher truths that causes one to resist tyranny?

GERARD MANLEY HOPKINS

Gerard Manley Hopkins (1844–1889) was a very innovative poet. He was educated at Oxford University and lived most of his life in England. His final years were spent in Dublin, Ireland. He grew up in the Church of England, but under the influence of John Henry Newman, he joined the Roman Catholic Church and later became a Jesuit priest. He seemed to have been a sensitive person who very carefully examined his thoughts and actions. At one point, he burned all of his poems and dedicated his life to God. Later, he took up writing poetry again, but he only shared his poems with his friends. As part of his service within the Roman Catholic Church, he taught Classical Greek at various church-supported schools.

In "God's Grandeur," Hopkins created, within a very short space, many thought-provoking images of nature, humanity, technology, and God's ultimate authority. He also gave a sense of history and technological change in contrast to the timelessness of God's created order.

GOD'S GRANDEUR

The world is charged with the grandeur of God.
It will flame out, like shining from shook foil;
It gathers to a greatness, like the ooze of oil
Crushed. Why do men then now not reck his rod?
5 *Generations have trod, have trod, have trod;*
And all is seared with trade; bleared, smeared with toil;
And wears man's smudge and shares man's smell: the soil

Is bare now, nor can foot feel, being shod.
And for all this, nature is never spent;
  There lives the dearest freshness deep down things;   10
And though the last lights off the black West went
  Oh, morning, at the brown brink eastward, springs—
Because the Holy Ghost over the bent
  World broods with warm breast and with ah! bright wings.

Questions

1. What did Hopkins mean by the question, "Why do men then now not reck his rod?"
2. At one point, the poet wrote that "the soil / Is bare now, nor can foot feel, being shod." How is this passage connected to the overall themes of the poem?
3. With words and images, Hopkins shifted from negative to positive themes. What seems to be the overall message of this poem?
4. How would you compare Hopkins' viewpoint with current discussions about protecting the environment from the effects of humanity?

RALPH WALDO EMERSON

Ralph Waldo Emerson (1803–1882) of Boston was a poet and writer who greatly influenced nineteenth-century American thought and literature. He worked for the abolition of slavery, and he promoted a philosophical and religious perspective called Transcendentalism. Emerson saw Jesus as a great moral teacher, but not divine. In contrast to those writers who denied the importance of spirituality, Emerson felt that the spiritual dimensions of life are absolutely important. A generation after Rousseau, both men shared a common concern for carefully exploring one's self and for personal independence. Emerson concluded that each person needs to find the spiritual in his or her own way. Established churches and ancient revelations were suspect; Emerson longed for a fresh, new approach to the spiritual.

Paradoxically, this new approach by Emerson and the Transcendentalists, who shared his views, followed many of the conclusions long established in Eastern religions: (a) Introspective meditation is the only means for finding sure truth about God and the self; (b) God is a general, ultimate force in nature (the "Oversoul"), not the personal God of the biblical tradition; and (c) human reason is an unreliable tool for understanding life's problems. More specific to the readings below, Emerson embraced the Eastern idea that all of reality is a unity: good and evil are ultimately one; life and death are an eternal cycle; and the material and spiritual realms are really a unity. In "Uriel," Emerson portrayed a young god (or angel), named Uriel, who upsets the established beliefs of the other gods (or angels). In "Each and All," Emerson reflected on seemingly random objects (i.e., sea shells, Napoleon, songbirds, and romantic love) and found a unity there.

EACH AND ALL

Little thinks, in the field, yon red-cloaked clown,
Of thee, from the hill-top looking down;
And the heifer, that lows in the upland farm,
Far-heard, lows not thine ear to charm;
5   The sexton tolling his bell at noon,
Dreams not that great Napoleon
Stops his horse, and lists with delight,
Whilst his files sweep round yon Alpine height;
Nor knowest thou what argument
10   Thy life to thy neighbor's creed has lent.
All are needed by each one,
Nothing is fair or good alone.

I thought the sparrow's note from heaven,
Singing at dawn on the alder bough;
15   I brought him home, in his nest, at even;—
He sings the song, but it pleases not now;
For I did not bring home the river and sky;
He sang to my ear, they sang to my eye.

The delicate shells lay on the shore;
20   The bubbles of the latest wave
Fresh pearls to their enamel gave;
And the bellowing of the savage sea
Greeted their safe escape to me;
I wiped away the weeds and foam,
25   I fetched my sea-born treasures home;
But the poor, unsightly, noisome things
Had left their beauty on the shore
With the sun, and the sand, and the wild uproar.

The lover watched his graceful maid
30   As 'mid the virgin train she strayed,
Nor knew her beauty's best attire
Was woven still by the snow-white quire.
At last she came to this hermitage,
Like the bird from the woodlands to the cage,—
35   The gay enchantment was undone,
A gentle wife, but fairy none.

Then I said, "I covet Truth;

URIEL

It fell in the ancient periods
Which the brooding soul surveys,
Or ever the wild Time coined itself
Into calendar months and days.

This was the lapse of Uriel,   5
Which in Paradise befell.
Once among the Pleiads walking,
Said overheard the young gods talking,
And the treason too long pent
To his ears was evident.   10
The young deities discussed
Laws of form and metre just,
Orb, quintessence, and sunbeams,
What subsisteth, and what seems.
One, with low tones that decide,   15
And doubt and reverend use defied,
With a look that solved the sphere,
And stirred the devils everywhere,
Gave his sentiment divine
Against the being of a line: 20
"Line in nature is not found,
Unit and universe are round;
In vain produced, all rays return,
Evil will bless, and ice will burn."
As Uriel spoke with piercing eye,   25
A shudder ran around the sky;
The stern old war-gods shook their heads,
The seraphs frowned from myrtle-beds;
Seemed to the holy festival,
The rash word boded ill to all;   30
The balance-beam of Fate was bent;
The bonds of good and ill were rent;
Strong Hades could not keep his own,
But all slid to confusion.
A sad self-knowledge withering fell   35
On the beauty of Uriel.
In heaven once eminent, the god
Withdrew that hour into his cloud,
Whether doomed to long gyration
In the sea of generation,   40
Or by knowledge grown too bright
To hit the nerve of feebler sight.
Straightway a forgetting wind

Stole over the Celestial kind,
45   *And their lips the secret kept,*
If in ashes the fibre-seed slept.
But now and then truth-speaking things
Shamed the angels' veiling wings,
And, shrilling from the solar course,
50   *Or from fruit of chemic force,*
Procession of a soul in matter,
Or the speeding change of water,
Or out of the good of evil born,
Came Uriel's voice of cherub scorn;
55   *And a blush tinged the upper sky,*
And the gods shook, they knew not why.

Questions

1. What does Emerson mean by these lines from "Uriel"?

Line in nature is not found,
Unit and universe are round;
In vain produced, all rays return,
Evil will bless, and ice will burn.

2. Near the end of "Uriel," Emerson wrote, "But now and then truth-speaking things / Shamed the angels' veiling wings." In the biblical tradition, angels bring truth and guidance, but these lines suggest that some angels are veiling (hiding) the truth. Do angels exist? If so, what role do they play in our lives?

3. In the middle of "Each and All," Emerson wrote, "And fetched my sea-born treasures home; / But the poor, unsightly, noisome things / Had left their beauty on the shore." Why did Emerson shift from calling his collection a "treasure" to calling it "unsightly, noisome things"?

4. After introducing many things of beauty, but also many tensions, why did Emerson end "Each and All" with the line "I yielded myself to the perfect whole"? What seemed to be his point? Submission is often a feature of religions, but the object of submission varies widely. To what does Emerson submit?

YOUNG LEE

Young Lee (b. 1957) was born in Indonesia to parents who were recent exiles from Communist China. After suffering political and racial persecution in Indonesia, the family moved to several countries and eventually settled in the United States in 1964. His father was a passionate Christian, who served as a medical doctor, an instructor at a Christian college, an evangelist, and a pastor in Hong Kong and Pennsylvania. Lee's heritage can be seen in his poems. It seems that his gentle, meditative tone is related to his Chinese heritage, his

Christian heritage, and his father's medical training. There is also a simple gracefulness in Lee's work; perhaps this quality is related to the importance of humility and honor in both the Christian and Chinese traditions.

THE GIFT

> To pull the metal splinter from my palm   1
> my father recited a story in a low voice.
> I watched his lovely face and not the blade.
> Before the story ended, he'd removed
> the iron sliver I thought I'd die from.   5
>
> I can't remember the tale,
> but hear his voice still, a well
> of dark water, a prayer.
> And I recall his hands,
> two measures of tenderness   10
> he laid against my face,
> the flames of discipline
> he raised above my head.
> Had you entered that afternoon
> you would have thought you saw a man   15
> planting something in a boy's palm,
> a silver tear, a tiny flame.
> Had you followed that boy
> you would have arrived here,
> where I bend over my wife's right hand.   20
>
> Look how I shave her thumbnail down
> so carefully she feels no pain.
> Watch as I lift the splinter out.
> I was seven when my father
> took my hand like this.   25
>
> and I did not hold that shard
> between my fingers and think,
> Metal that will bury me,
> christen it Little Assassin,
> One Going Deep for My Heart.   30
> And I did not lift up my wound and cry,
> Death visited here!
> I did what a child does
> when he's given something to keep.
> I kissed my father.   35

Questions

1. Do you discover more in this poem, knowing that Lee's father was a medical doctor and a pastor?

2. Why did Lee shift from focusing on his father to focusing on his wife? What thoughts about time and generations are brought to mind because of this shift?

3. In the poem, Lee wrote: "And I recall his hands, / two measures of tenderness / he laid against my face, / the flames of discipline / he raised above my head." What did the poet mean by "the flames of discipline"? Is the discipline positive or negative? What does it mean that the "flames" are "raised above my head"?

4. What passage in this poem was most meaningful to you?

WOLE SOYINKA

Wole Soyinka (originally named Akinwande Oluwole Soyinka) (b. 1934) was the first African to win the Nobel Prize in Literature (1986). He was born and raised in Nigeria. He earned several awards for his writing when he was a young adult. He studied at the Government College in Ibadan, Nigeria, and later at the University of Leeds in England, from which he was graduated with an honors degree in English. During his long, productive life, Soyinka has taught literature at numerous universities and has written widely. His works include novels, poems, essays, and serious and comic plays.

He has also served as a spokesman for justice and democracy in Nigeria and other lands. At one point, he was held as a political prisoner for almost two years. He writes in English and has a very strong background in European literature, yet he also appeals to Yoruba mythology and religion in his works. Soyinka refers to Ogun, the god of iron, farming, and war, as "my god."

As explained in his literary essays, most importantly *Myth, Literature and the African World* (1975), Soyinka uses myth to promote his political messages. His most popular collection of poetry is *Idanre and Other Poems* (1967). "Dawn," the first poem in this collection, is perhaps the most well-known poem by Soyinka.

DAWN

Breaking earth upon
A spring-haired elbow, lone
A palm beyond head-grains, spikes
A guard of prim fronds, piercing
High hairs of the wind
As one who bore the pollen highest

Blood-drops in the air, above
The even belt of tassels, above
Coarse leaf teasing on the waist, steals
The lone intruder, tearing wide

The chaste hide of the sky
O celebration of the rites of dawn
Night-spread in tatters and a god
Received, aflame with kernels.

Questions

1. Along with the farming and warring traditions, Ogun is associated with the blacksmith who makes and shapes iron implements for farming or warfare. How does this paradoxically represent both Ogun and humanity?
2. Did Soyinka use Ogun as a metaphor for the human potential for good and/or evil? Is Ogun a metaphor for the positive and/or negative uses of iron and technology?
3. Consider the ironies of Soyinka's title, "Dawn." How does this metaphor point to a theme of hope and technological advancement and, ironically, to a theme of disaster and death?
4. The color red pervades Soyinka's poem ("blood-drops" and "aflame with kernels"). What is communicated by the use of this color?

AMY TAN

Amy Tan (b. 1952) was born in Oakland, California, to recent immigrants from China. Her father, a Baptist minister and an electrical engineer, moved with his wife to the United States to escape the civil war in China in the late 1940s. Tan was a teenager when her father died, and the central relationship in her young-adult life was with her mother. This relationship, with its many ups and downs, was later explored and developed in some of Tan's writing. Tan has published numerous books and short stories that have been read in many languages around the world. One of her children's books, *The Chinese Siamese Cat*, was adapted by the Public Broadcasting Service (PBS) into a children's television series, *Sagwa, the Chinese Siamese Cat*. Her novel, *The Joy Luck Club*, was also made into a very successful movie.

TWO KINDS

My mother believed you could be anything you wanted to be in America. You could open a restaurant. You could work for the government and get good retirement. You could buy a house with almost no money down. You could become rich. You could become instantly famous.

"Of course you can be prodigy, too," my mother told me when I was nine. "You can be best anything. What does Auntie Lindo know? Her daughter, she is only best tricky."

America was where all my mother's hopes lay. She had come here in 1949 after losing everything in China: her mother and father, her family home, her first husband, and two daughters, twin baby girls. But she never looked back with regret. There were so many ways for things to get better.

We didn't immediately pick the right kind of prodigy. At first my mother thought I could be a Chinese Shirley Temple. We'd watch Shirley's old movies on TV as though they were training films. My mother would poke my arm and say, "*Ni kan*"—You watch. And I would see Shirley tapping her feet, or singing a sailor song, or pursing her lips into a very round O while saying, "Oh my goodness."

5   "*Ni kan*," said my mother as Shirley's eyes flooded with tears. "You already know how. Don't need talent for crying!"

Soon after my mother got this idea about Shirley Temple, she took me to a beauty training school in the Mission district and put me in the hands of a student who could barely hold the scissors without shaking. Instead of getting big fat curls, I emerged with an uneven mass of crinkly black fuzz. My mother dragged me off to the bathroom and tried to wet down my hair.

"You look like Negro Chinese," she lamented, as if I had done this on purpose.

The instructor of the beauty training school had to lop off these soggy clumps to make my hair even again. "Peter Pan is very popular these days," the instructor assured my mother. I now had hair the length of a boy's, with straight-across bangs that hung at a slant two inches above my eyebrows. I liked the haircut and it made me actually look forward to my future fame.

In fact, in the beginning, I was just as excited as my mother, maybe even more so. I pictured this prodigy part of me as many different images, trying each one on for size. I was a dainty ballerina girl standing by the curtains, waiting to hear the right music that would send me floating on my tiptoes. I was like the Christ child lifted out of the straw manger, crying with holy indignity. I was Cinderella stepping from her pumpkin carriage with sparkly cartoon music filling the air.

10   In all of my imaginings, I was filled with a sense that I would soon become *perfect*. My mother and father would adore me. I would be beyond reproach. I would never feel the need to sulk for anything.

But sometimes the prodigy in me became impatient. "If you don't hurry up and get me out of here, I'm disappearing for good," it warned. "And then you'll always be nothing."

Every night after dinner, my mother and I would sit at the Formica kitchen table. She would present new tests, taking her examples from stories of amazing children she had read in *Ripley's Believe It or Not,* or *Good Housekeeping, Reader's Digest,* and a dozen other magazines she kept in a pile in our bathroom. My mother got these magazines from people whose houses she cleaned. And since she cleaned many houses each week, we had a great assortment. She would look through them all, searching for stories about remarkable children.

The first night she brought out a story about a three-year-old boy who knew the capitals of all the states and even most of the European countries. A teacher was quoted as saying the little boy could also pronounce the names of the foreign cities correctly.

"What's the capital of Finland?" my mother asked me, looking at the magazine story.

All I knew was the capital of California, because Sacramento was the 15 name of the street we lived on in Chinatown. "Nairobi!" I guessed, saying the most foreign word I could think of. She checked to see if that was possibly one way to pronounce "Helsinki" before showing me the answer.

The tests got harder—multiplying numbers in my head, finding the queen of hearts in a deck of cards, trying to stand on my head without using my hands, predicting the daily temperatures in Los Angeles, New York, and London.

One night I had to look at a page from the Bible for three minutes and then report everything I could remember. "Now Jehoshaphat had riches and honor in abundance and . . . that's all I remember, Ma," I said.

And after seeing my mother's disappointed face once again, something inside of me began to die. I hated the tests, the raised hopes and failed expectations. Before going to bed that night, I looked in the mirror above the bathroom sink and when I saw only my face staring back—and that it would always be this ordinary face—I began to cry. Such a sad, ugly girl! I made high-pitched noises like a crazed animal, trying to scratch out the face in the mirror.

And then I saw what seemed to be the prodigy side of me—because I had never seen that face before. I looked at my reflection, blinking so I could see more clearly. The girl staring back at me was angry, powerful. This girl and I were the same. I had new thoughts, willful thoughts, or rather thoughts filled with lots of won'ts. I won't let her change me, I promised myself. I won't be what I'm not.

So now on nights when my mother presented her tests, I performed list- 20 lessly, my head propped on one arm. I pretended to be bored. And I was. I got so bored I started counting the bellows of the foghorns out on the bay while my mother drilled me in other areas. The sound was comforting and reminded me of the cow jumping over the moon. And the next day, I played a game with myself, seeing if my mother would give up on me before eight bellows. After a while I usually counted only one, maybe two bellows at most. At last she was beginning to give up hope.

Two or three months had gone by without any mention of my being a prodigy again. And then one day my mother was watching *The Ed Sullivan Show* on TV. The TV was old and the sound kept shorting out. Every time my mother got halfway up from the sofa to adjust the set, the sound would go back on and Ed would be talking. As soon as she sat down, Ed would go silent again. She got up, the TV broke into loud piano music. She sat down. Silence. Up and down, back and forth, quiet and loud. It was like a stiff embraceless dance between her and the TV set. Finally she stood by the set with her hand on the sound dial.

She seemed entranced by the music, a little frenzied piano piece with this mesmerizing quality, sort of quick passages and then teasing lilting ones before it returned to the quick playful parts.

"*Ni kan*," my mother said, calling me over with hurried hand gestures, "Look here."

I could see why my mother was fascinated by the music. It was being pounded out by a little Chinese girl, about nine years old, with a Peter Pan haircut. The girl had the sauciness of a Shirley Temple. She was proudly modest like a proper Chinese child. And she also did this fancy sweep of a curtsy, so that the fluffy skirt of her white dress cascaded slowly to the floor like the petals of a large carnation.

25   In spite of these warning signs, I wasn't worried. Our family had no piano and we couldn't afford to buy one, let alone reams of sheet music and piano lessons. So I could be generous in my comments when my mother bad-mouthed the little girl on TV.

"Play note right, but doesn't sound good! No singing sound," complained my mother.

"What are you picking on her for?" I said carelessly. "She's pretty good. Maybe she's not the best, but she's trying hard." I knew almost immediately I would be sorry I said that.

"Just like you," she said. "Not the best. Because you not trying." She gave a little huff as she let go of the sound dial and sat down on the sofa.

The little Chinese girl sat down also to play an encore of "Anitra's Dance" by Grieg. I remember the song, because later on I had to learn how to play it.

30   Three days after watching *The Ed Sullivan Show,* my mother told me what my schedule would be for piano lessons and piano practice. She had talked to Mr. Chong, who lived on the first floor of our apartment building. Mr. Chong was a retired piano teacher and my mother had traded housecleaning services for weekly lessens and a piano for me to practice on every day, two hours a day, from four until six.

When my mother told me this, I felt as though I had been sent to hell. I whined and then kicked my foot a little when I couldn't stand it anymore.

"Why don't you like me the way I am? I'm *not* a genius! I can't play the piano. And even if I could, I wouldn't go on TV if you paid me a million dollars!" I cried.

My mother slapped me. "Who ask you be genius?" she shouted. "Only ask you be your best. For you sake. You think I want you be genius? Hnnh! What for! Who ask you!"

"So ungrateful," I heard her mutter in Chinese. "If she had as much talent as she has temper, she would be famous now."

35   Mr. Chong, whom I secretly nicknamed Old Chong, was very strange, always tapping his fingers to the silent music of an invisible orchestra. He looked ancient in my eyes. He had lost most of the hair on top of his head and he wore thick glasses and had eyes that always looked tired and sleepy. But he must have been younger than I thought, since he lived with his mother and was not yet married.

I met Old Lady Chong once and that was enough. She had this peculiar smell like a baby that had done something in its pants. And her fingers felt like a dead person's, like an old peach I once found in the back of the refrigerator; the skin just slid off the meat when I picked it up.

I soon found out why Old Chong had retired from teaching piano. He was deaf. "Like Beethoven!" he shouted to me. "We're both listening only in our head!" And he would start to conduct his frantic silent sonatas.

Our lessons went like this. He would open the book and point to different things, explaining their purpose: "Key! Treble! Bass! No sharps or flats! So this is C major! Listen now and play after me!"

And then he would play the C scale a few times, a simple chord, and then, as if inspired by an old, unreachable itch, he gradually added more notes and running trills and a pounding bass until the music was really something quite grand.

I would play after him, the simple scale, the simple chord, and then I just 40 played some nonsense that sounded like a cat running up and down on top of garbage cans. Old Chong smiled and applauded and then said, "Very good! But now you must learn to keep time!"

So that's how I discovered that Old Chong's eyes were too slow to keep up with the wrong notes I was playing. He went through the motions in half-time. To help me keep rhythm, he stood behind me, pushing down on my right shoulder for every beat. He balanced pennies on top of my wrists so I would keep them still as I slowly played scales and arpeggios. He had me curve my hand around an apple and keep that shape when playing chords. He marched stiffly to show me how to make each finger dance up and down, staccato like an obedient little soldier.

He taught me all these things, and that was how I also learned I could be lazy and get away with mistakes, lots of mistakes. If I hit the wrong notes because I hadn't practiced enough, I never corrected myself. I just kept playing in rhythm. And Old Chong kept conducting his own private reverie.

So maybe I never really gave myself a fair chance. I did pick up the basics pretty quickly, and I might have become a good pianist at that young age. But I was so determined not to try, not to be anybody different that I learned to play only the most ear-splitting preludes, the most discordant hymns.

Over the next year, I practiced like this, dutifully in my own way. And then one day I heard my mother and her friend Lindo Jong both talking in a loud bragging tone of voice so others could hear. It was after church, and I was leaning against the brick wall wearing a dress with stiff white petticoats. Auntie Lindo's daughter, Waverly, who was about my age, was standing farther down the wall about five feet away. We had grown up together and shared all the closeness of two sisters squabbling over crayons and dolls. In other words, for the most part, we hated each other. I thought she was snotty. Waverly Jong had gained a certain amount of fame as "Chinatown's Littlest Chinese Chess Champion."

"She bring home too many trophy," lamented Auntie Lindo that Sunday. 45 "All day she play chess. All day I have no time do nothing but dust off her winnings." She threw a scolding look at Waverly, who pretended not to see her.

"You lucky you don't have this problem," said Auntie Lindo with a sigh to my mother.

And my mother squared her shoulders and bragged: "Our problem worser than yours. If we ask Jing-Mei wash dish, she hear nothing but music. It's like you can't stop this natural talent."

And right then, I was determined to put a stop to her foolish pride.

A few weeks later, Old Chong and my mother conspired to have me play in a talent show which would be held in the church hall. By then, my parents had saved up enough to buy me a secondhand piano, a black Wurlitzer spinet with a scarred bench. It was the showpiece of our living room.

50   For the talent show, I was to play a piece called "Pleading Child" from Schumann's *Scenes from Childhood*. It was a simple, moody piece that sounded more difficult than it was. I was supposed to memorize the whole thing, playing the repeat parts twice to make the piece sound longer. But I dawdled over it, playing a few bars and then cheating, looking up to see what notes followed. I never really listened to what I was playing. I daydreamed about being somewhere else, about being someone else.

The part I liked to practice best was the fancy curtsy: right foot out, touch the rose on the carpet with a pointed foot, sweep to the side, left leg bends, look up and smile.

My parents invited all the couples from the Joy Luck Club to witness my debut. Auntie Lindo and Uncle Tin were there. Waverly and her two older brothers had also come. The first two rows were filled with children both younger and older than I was. The littlest ones got to go first. They recited simple nursery rhymes, squawked out tunes on miniature violins, twirled Hula Hoops, pranced in pink ballet tutus, and when they bowed or curtsied, the audience would sigh in unison, "Awww," and then clap enthusiastically.

When my turn came, I was very confident. I remember my childish excitement. It was as if I knew, without a doubt, that the prodigy side of me really did exist. I had no fear whatsoever, no nervousness. I remember thinking to myself, This is it! This is it! I looked out over the audience, at my mother's blank face, my father's yawn. Auntie Lindo's stiff-lipped smile, Waverly's sulky expression. I had on a white dress layered with sheets of lace, and a pink bow in my Peter Pan haircut. As I sat down I envisioned people jumping to their feet and Ed Sullivan rushing up to introduce me to everyone on TV.

And I started to play. It was so beautiful. I was so caught up in how lovely I looked that at first I didn't worry how I would sound. So it was a surprise to me when I hit the first wrong note and I realized something didn't sound quite right. And then I hit another and another followed that. A chill started at the top of my head and began to trickle down. Yet I couldn't stop playing, as though my hands were bewitched. I kept thinking my fingers would adjust themselves back, like a train switching to the right track. I played this strange jumble through two repeats, the sour notes staying with me all the way to the end.

55   When I stood up, I discovered my legs were shaking. Maybe I had just been nervous and the audience, like Old Chong, had seen me go through the right motions and had not heard anything wrong at all. I swept my right foot out, went down on my knee, looked up and smiled. The room was quiet, except for Old Chong, who was beaming and shouting, "Bravo! Bravo! Well done!" But then I saw my mother's face, her stricken face. The audience clapped weakly, and as I walked back to my chair, with my whole face quivering as I tried not to

cry, I heard a little-boy whisper loudly to his mother, "That was awful," and the mother whispered back, "Well, she certainly tried."

And now I realized how many people were in the audience, the whole world it seemed. I was aware of eyes burning into my back. I felt the shame of my mother and father as they sat-stiffly throughout the rest of the show.

We could have escaped during intermission. Pride and some strange sense of honor must have anchored my parents to their chairs. And so we watched it all: the eighteen-year-old boy with a fake mustache who did a magic show and juggled flaming hoops while riding a unicycle. The breasted girl with white makeup who sang from *Madama Butterfly* and got honorable mention. And the eleven-year-old boy who won first prize playing a tricky violin song that sounded like a busy bee."

After the show, the Hsus, the Jongs, and the St. Clairs from the Joy Luck Club came up to my mother and father.

"Lots of talented kids," Auntie Lindo said vaguely, smiling broadly.

"That was somethin' else," said my father, and I wondered if he was referring 60 to me in a humorous way, or whether he even remembered what I had done.

Waverly looked at me and shrugged her shoulders. "You aren't a genius like me," she said matter-of-factly. And if I hadn't felt so bad, I would have pulled her braids and punched her stomach.

But my mother's expression was what devastated me: a quiet, blank look that said she had lost everything. I felt the same way, and it seemed as if everybody were now coming up, like gawkers at the scene of an accident, to see what parts were actually missing. When we got on the bus to go home, my father was humming the busy-bee tune and my mother was silent. I kept thinking she wanted to wait until we got home before shouting at me. But when my father unlocked the door to our apartment, my mother walked in and then went to the back, into the bedroom. No accusations. No blame. And in a way, I felt disappointed. I had been waiting for her to start shouting, so I could shout back and cry and blame her for all my misery.

I assumed my talent-show fiasco meant I never had to play the piano again. But two days later, after school, my mother came out of the kitchen and saw me watching TV.

"Four clock," she reminded me as if it were any other day. I was stunned, as though she were asking me to go through the talent-show torture again. I wedged myself more tightly in front of the TV.

"Turn off TV," she called from the kitchen five minutes later.   65

I didn't budge. And then I decided. I didn't have to do what my mother said anymore. I wasn't her slave. This wasn't China. I had listened to her before and look what happened. She was the stupid one.

She came out from the kitchen and stood in the arched entryway of the living room. "Four clock," she said once again, louder.

"I'm not going to play anymore," I said nonchalantly. "Why should I? I'm not a genius."

She walked over and stood in front of the TV. I saw her chest was heaving up and down in an angry way.

70   "No!" I said, and I now felt stronger, as if my true self had finally emerged. So this was what had been inside me all along.

    "No! I won't!" I screamed.

    She yanked me by the arm, pulled me off the floor, snapped off the TV. She was frighteningly strong, half pulling, half carrying me toward the piano as I kicked the throw rugs under my feet. She lifted me up and onto the hard bench. I was sobbing by now, looking at her bitterly. Her chest was heaving even more and her mouth was open, smiling crazily as if she were pleased I was crying.

    "You want me to be someone that I'm not!" I sobbed. "I'll never be the kind of daughter you want me to be!"

    "Only two kinds of daughters," she shouted in Chinese. "Those who are obedient and those who follow their own mind! Only one kind of daughter can live in this house. Obedient daughter!"

75   "Then I wish I wasn't your daughter. I wish you weren't my mother," I shouted. As I said these things I got scared. It felt like worms and toads and slimy things crawling out of my chest, but it also felt good, as if this awful side of me had surfaced, at last.

    "Too late change this," said my mother shrilly.

    And I could sense her anger rising to its breaking point. I wanted to see it spill over. And that's when I remembered the babies she had lost in China, the ones we never talked about. "Then I wish I'd never been born!" I shouted. "I wish I were dead! Like them."

    It was as if I had said the magic words. Alakazam!—and her face went blank, her mouth closed, her arms went slack, and she backed out of the room, stunned, as if she were blowing away like a small brown leaf, thin, brittle, lifeless.

    It was not the only disappointment my mother felt in me. In the years that followed, I failed her so many times, each time asserting my own will, my right to fall short of expectations. I didn't get straight As. I didn't become class president. I didn't get into Stanford. I dropped out of college.

80   For unlike my mother, I did not believe I could be anything I wanted to be. I could only be me.

    And for all those years, we never talked about the disaster at the recital or my terrible accusations afterward at the piano bench. All that remained unchecked, like a betrayal that was now unspeakable. So I never found a way to ask her why she had hoped for something so large that failure was inevitable.

    And even worse, I never asked her what frightened me the most: Why had she given up hope?

    For after our struggle at the piano, she never mentioned my playing again. The lessons stopped. The lid to the piano was closed, shutting out the dust, my misery, and her dreams.

    So she surprised me. A few years ago, she offered to give me the piano, for my thirtieth birthday. I had not played in all those years. I saw the offer as a sign of forgiveness, a tremendous burden removed.

85   "Are you sure?" I asked shyly. "I mean, won't you and Dad miss it?"

"No, this your piano," she said firmly. "Always your piano. You only one can play."

"Well, I probably can't play anymore," I said. "It's been years."

"You pick up fast," said my mother, as if she knew this was certain. "You have natural talent. You could been genius if you want to."

"No I couldn't."

"You just not trying," said my mother. And she was neither angry nor 90 sad. She said it as if to announce a fact that could never be disproved. "Take it," she said.

But I didn't at first. It was enough that she had offered it to me. And after that, every time I saw it in my parents' living room, standing in front of the bay windows, it made me feel proud, as if it were a shiny trophy I had won back.

Last week I sent a tuner over to my parents' apartment and had the piano reconditioned, for purely sentimental reasons. My mother had died a few months before and I had been getting things in order for my father, a little bit at a time. I put the jewelry in special silk pouches. The sweaters she had knitted in yellow, pink, bright orange—all the colors I hated—I put those in moth-proof boxes. I found some old Chinese silk dresses, the kind with little slits up the sides. I rubbed the old silk against my skin, then wrapped them in tissue and decided to take them home with me.

After I had the piano tuned, I opened the lid and touched the keys. It sounded even richer than I remembered. Really, it was a very good piano. Inside the bench were the same exercise notes with handwritten scales, the same sec-ondhand music books with their covers held together with yellow tape.

I opened up the Schumann book to the dark little piece I had played at the recital. It was on the left-hand side of the page, "Pleading Child." It looked more difficult than I remembered. I played a few bars, surprised at how easily the notes came back to me.

And for the first time, or so it seemed, I noticed the piece on the right- 95 hand side. It was called "Perfectly Contented." I tried to play this one as well. It had a lighter melody but the same flowing rhythm and turned out to be quite easy. "Pleading Child" was shorter but slower; "Perfectly Contented" was longer, but faster. And after I played them both a few times, I realized they were two halves of the same song.

Questions

1. In this story, the mother firmly embraces the idea "that you could be any-thing you wanted to be in America." As a result, she tries to mold her daughter into a musical prodigy. The mother wants to compete with a friend whose daughter is a chess prodigy. What insights does the mother's obsession reveal about her spiritual state?

2. What role does the media (e.g., television, movies, popular magazines) and fantasy play in the mother's quest to make her daughter a piano prodigy? As you look at life today, does the media promote the gaining of spiritual insight and depth, or does it distract us from this task? In other words, is the media helping or hurting us spiritually?

3. In what sense do people have natural talents? In what sense do people create themselves through self-discipline and the setting of lofty goals? Do the various religious traditions help us sort out these questions?

4. In this story, the mother–daughter relationship progresses through hope, disappointment, fractures, guilt, and forgiveness. In this context, the piano is used as a motif to trace this progress. What ironies do you see in this progression?

LESLIE MARMON SILKO

Leslie Marmon Silko (b. 1948) is a Native American writer whose background includes Laguna Pueblo, Mexican, and Caucasian ancestry. She has lived much of her life in New Mexico. While growing up, Silko had a grandmother and an aunt who taught her both storytelling techniques and stories from a Native American perspective. She also studied Western literature and literary techniques as an English major at the University of New Mexico. She has published novels, short stories, and poems. Silko has also taught creative writing.

Her poem, "Where Mountain Lion Lay Down with Deer," exposes the reader to a short, but complex experience of spiritual and physical insights. The title of this poem seems like an echo from the Bible where the prophet Isaiah wrote about a future time of peace and cooperation:

> *A shoot will come up from the stump of Jesse [. . .]*
> *The Spirit of the LORD will rest on him [. . .]*
> *He will not judge by what he sees with his eyes [. . .]*
> *but with [. . .] justice he will give decisions for the poor of the earth [. . .]*
> *The wolf will live with the lamb,*
> > *the leopard will lie down with the goat,*
> > *the calf and the lion and the yearling together;*
> > *and a little child will lead them [. . .]*
> *They will neither harm nor destroy*
> *on all my holy mountain,*
> > *for the earth will be full of the knowledge of the LORD (Isaiah 11:1–9).*

Both Isaiah and Silko pointed us toward times of harmony that we do not experience today. Both poets connected their visions of peace to a mountain. However, Isaiah's vision was into the future and rooted in the Hebrew view of God and his righteous planning, and Silko's vision was rooted in the past and her ancestors.

WHERE MOUNTAIN LION LAY DOWN WITH DEER

> *I climb the black rock mountain*
> > *stepping from day to day*
> > > *silently.*
> *I smell the wind for my ancestors*

pale blue leaves   5
crushed wild mountain smell.
Returning
up the gray stone cliff
where I descended
        a thousand years ago.   10

Returning to faded black stone
where mountain lion lay down with deer.
It is better to stay up here
        watching wind's reflection
        in tall yellow flowers.   15
The old ones who remember me are gone
    the old songs are all forgotten
and the story of my birth.
How I danced in snow-frost moonlight
    distant stars to the end of the Earth,   20
How I swam away
    in freezing mountain water
    narrow mossy canyon tumbling down
        out of the mountain
        out of the deep canyon stone   25
  down
    the memory
      spilling out
      into the world.

Questions

1. Does the poem describe a literal setting? If not, what is the setting? What ideas are commonly associated with mountains, timelessness, and exploration? How do all of these factors create an environment for the reader to consider?
2. Notice how verbs are used in this poem. Some verbs are active present tense, some are present continuous tense, and some are past tense (e.g., "I climb . . ." (line 1), "I smell . . ." (line 4), "Returning" (lines 8, 11), "I danced . . ." (line 20), "I swam . . ." (line 22)). Why are these shifts in verb tense important?
3. Is it possible to read an historical, cultural, spiritual, and even political interpretation into the poem?
4. Is the poem a celebration or lamentation? Support your answer with textual evidence.

N. SCOTT MOMADAY

N. Scott Momaday (b. 1934) was born in Lawton, Oklahoma, and is a member of the Kiowa Nation. Both of his parents were teachers, who moved several times in the southwestern United States to teach at schools on Indian reservations. As a result, Momaday had a wide exposure to various Native American cultures. He also gained a rich education in the mainstream Anglo culture. He earned a B.A. from the University of New Mexico and an M.A. and Ph.D. from Stanford University. In 1969, he was awarded the Pulitzer Prize for Fiction. Momaday has taught at Stanford University, the University of Arizona at Tucson, and the University of California at Berkeley.

On a literal level, this poem is about an old, maimed bear. Momaday describes it as a "ruse of vision." It appears and disappears mysteriously. Yet, Momaday is doing more than merely presenting a bear. There is a great deal of symbolism to be considered as the poet develops our understanding of the bear.

THE BEAR

What ruse of vision,
escarping the wall of leaves,
*   rending incision*
into countless surfaces,

5 *   would cull and color*
his somnolence, whose old age
*   has outworn valor,*
all but the fact of courage?

*   Seen, he does not come,*
10 *move, but seems forever there,*
*   dimensionless, dumb*
in the windless noon's hot glare.

*   More scarred than others*
these years since the trap maimed him,
15 *   pain slants his withers,*
drawing up the crooked limb.

*   Then he is gone, whole,*
without urgency, from sight,
*   as buzzards control,*
20 *imperceptibly, their flight.*

Questions

1. Each stanza of this poem presents an image of the bear. How does each image enrich the speaker's perception of the bear? What effect does this incremental revelation have on your reading of the poem?
2. What themes do you find in this poem? What details develop those themes?
3. In line 8, the speaker asks the bear a question. What is the significance and implication of this question?

4. Explain the tone and attitude of the speaker, especially in the last stanza. What is happening to the speaker as he or she observes and comments on the physical and spiritual aspects of the bear? How would you describe such an experience?

MOVIE GUIDE FOR *A MAN FOR ALL SEASONS* (1966)

Directed by Fred Zinnemann

Screenplay by Robert Bolt

The Tensions in This Movie

The movie, *A Man for All Seasons,* was originally performed on stage in Great Britain and the United States in the early 1960s. On the surface, the story is merely an account of a man in a high political position who refuses to submit to his king's wishes. What makes this story interesting is the character of Sir Thomas More (1478–1535). His refusal is not rooted in pride, ignorance, self-promotion, rebellion, disloyalty, or any other vice. More is imprisoned and killed for being an extremely good man. Everyone—his friends, his enemies, his family, and his king—knows that More is honest and that he is faithful to the king. To make More even more interesting, he is very gracious to everyone he meets. Although he is very exacting about his own moral behavior, More is quick to forgive others their moral failures. He is a model Christian; he trusts God, obeys the church, loves his friends and enemies, is merciful to everyone, and is sincere in his heart. Yet, he is made into an enemy of the state.

More is also the model Renaissance humanist. He was richly educated, and he wrote about history and theology. Although More was politically and socially conservative in many ways, he wrote *Utopia* as an exploration of how an imaginary society might be shaped. Henry VIII, King of England, was also a humanist. He loved music, poetry, and sports. He was trained in theology. And as the movie points out, King Henry wrote a book that attacked the ideas of Martin Luther and supported the authority and traditions of the Roman Catholic Church. Both More and King Henry were men of energy and intelligence, and for a time, they worked together as a team in ruling England. But More was a man of high principles, and the king was a "practical" man who did not let moral principles hinder his desires.

The Historical Context

History is very helpful in understanding this movie. The father of Henry VIII (Henry VII) became king in 1485 after a long period of civil war. Various nobles (with the armies in their service) claimed or supported others who claimed the right to rule England. In time, Henry VII won the crown on a battlefield and consolidated his power. The next year, a son, Arthur, was born to King Henry. Arthur would have been king, but he died at the age of fifteen. As a result, the next son

(Henry VIII) became king when his father died in 1509. It is important to remember the fragile nature of social order in the past. When Henry VIII later demands a male heir, his demands have some justification. His father had fought to gain power and establish peace. Various nobles might still be willing to overthrow the Tudor dynasty started by Henry VII. Later, when Henry VIII demands a male heir, he is merely following the logic of his situation. It was assumed that a female heir (such as his daughters Mary and Elizabeth) would not be able to ensure social and political order. Such are the internal politics of England at that time.

Foreign affairs also have a role in understanding this movie. To the south of England, there is France, which sometimes wars against England. To the north is Scotland, another enemy. Further away, Spain has recently been united under King Ferdinand and Queen Isabella. (They are supporting explorations by Christopher Columbus, who discovered the Americas.) Spain is expanding its power, and Henry VII wanted to develop a cooperative relationship with this new superpower. To cultivate that cooperation, King Henry arranged a marriage between his son Arthur and a daughter of Ferdinand and Isabella, Catherine of Aragon. This arrangement was set up when Arthur and Catherine were small children. Later, when Arthur died, Henry wanted to continue the relationship with Spain and asked the pope for permission to arrange a marriage between his next son (Henry VIII) and Catherine. Years later, when all of the male babies born to Catherine died, Henry VIII wanted the pope to annul his marriage to Catherine, so that he could seek a wife who would produce a male heir. (Catherine gave birth to Mary, who later ruled England for a short time.) To get the annulment (a simple divorce was not possible under Roman Catholic canon law), King Henry needed pressure to be applied to the pope. That job was given to Cardinal Thomas Wolsey, who was serving as the king's top administrator. However, the King and Queen of Spain, who wanted to protect the honor and position of their daughter, were able to persuade the pope to forbid the annulment. Eventually, Henry VIII assumed supreme authority over the church in England, demanded the submission of the British clergy, and arranged the annulment within the context of the Church of England. Thus, the king simply ignored the pope and hundreds of years of tradition. All of these events are part of the background of this movie.

More's Character

In the middle of this swirl of politics, there is an honest, intelligent, and truly Christian person. The inner strength of Thomas More guides him through every situation. More has confidence, but he is not arrogant. He is tender, but he never cowers. He clearly understands the twists and turns of politics, but he does not compromise his integrity. He gives respect and obedience to the king, but More is always in possession of himself and his life.

Tips for Watching This Movie

Viewing this movie more than once is essential. Before you view the movie a second time, it would be helpful to study the history of England from 1450 to 1570. Some people might enjoy studying events before Henry VIII became king in order to look for ways in which those events influenced the king's decisions. Some people might be interested in studying Henry VIII's political and romantic relationships while serving as king. Others might find it intriguing to study the aftermath of Henry VIII by looking at Edward VI's reign from 1547 to 1553, Lady Jane Grey's reign of nine days in 1553, Mary I's reign from 1553 to 1558, and Elizabeth I's reign from 1558 to 1603.

Another area of study is the Reformation. What exactly did Martin Luther say and do? Why did those things lead to fragmentation in the Roman Catholic Church? Why did Henry VIII reject Luther, but later break from Rome? Luther was forced out of the Roman Catholic Church as an individual, but Henry VIII willfully separated his nation from Rome. A study of this period in history reveals a great deal of drama.

Key Characters and Their Relationships

Sir Thomas More, a lawyer, humanist scholar, and trusted servant of King Henry VIII

Alice More, More's wife

Margaret More (Meg), More's daughter, who is highly educated and who loves and marries William Roper

William Roper (the Younger), a young man who supports Martin Luther's criticisms of the Roman Catholic Church (this criticism led to Rome condemning and excommunicating Luther and the creation of the Lutheran Church)

Henry VIII, the King of England and Wales

Catherine of Aragon, a daughter of King Ferdinand and Queen Isabella of Spain; the first wife of Henry VIII

Cardinal Thomas Wolsey, a high church official, who at this time is serving as the top administrator for Henry VIII; later, Wolsey dies in prison because he did not convince the pope to grant the annulment that the king wanted

Thomas Cromwell, an administrator who supports the king's break with Rome

Richard Rich, a young man who is looking for a "position" that will give him power and wealth, but More recommends that Rich would make a great teacher

Duke of Norfolk, a friend of More, who later is forced by the king to help prosecute More

Matthew, the head servant in More's household, who gives information to More's enemies

Anne Boleyn, the second wife of Henry VIII; she is educated, attractive, and strong (later, she will be killed for treason)

Archbishop Thomas Cranmer, a leader in the Church in England and a supporter of Henry VIII's separation from Rome

Questions

1. In what ways are the life and character of Thomas More similar to and different from the lives and characters of Job, Esther, and Daniel in the Bible?
2. In literary discussions, a "foil" is a person or thing that highlights (draws attention to) someone or something else. Richard Rich is a foil to Thomas More. Make a list of More's strengths, and then make a list of Rich's weaknesses. What connections do you see between the two lists?
3. The characters in this movie give various references to faith, prayer, and one's relationship with God. Make a list of four or five characters and consider the role that spirituality plays in their lives. What can be learned from those characters?
4. What lessons did you learn from this movie? Does this movie encourage you to live and to think in new ways?

Chapter 4

Challenges of Spirituality: Faith, Dilemma, Duplicity, and Doubt

Nathaniel Hawthorne (1804–1864) was born in Salem, Massachusetts, and lived most of his life in New England. His life and works were guided by New England Puritanism, but after two hundred years, that tradition seemed to be worn and lifeless. However, Hawthorne's works are hardly lifeless; he used the moral concerns and symbolism found in his spiritual and cultural heritage to create rich examinations of human experience. Hawthorne presented characters who struggle with their passions, with feelings of guilt, or with private gloom. He created an intriguing complexity in his characters and in their cultural experiences.

Personally, Hawthorne did not embrace his Christian heritage. Like Ralph Waldo Emerson and Henry David Thoreau, Hawthorne was a transcendentalist who valued the intuitive search for spirituality. They did not seek the Christian God or seek spirituality through formal institutions or creeds.

It is interesting that Hawthorne had a habit of being at the right place at the right time. During his lifetime of limited travels, he had personal contact with Louisa May Alcott, Henry David Thoreau, Ralph Waldo Emerson, Franklin Pierce, Abraham Lincoln, Henry Wadsworth Longfellow, Elizabeth Barrett Browning, and Robert Browning.

"Young Goodman Brown" is both an entertaining and a thought-provoking tale. Like many writers of his time, Hawthorne wanted his writings to instruct his readers. He wanted his readers to consider deep questions about reality, morality, and their inner selves.

YOUNG GOODMAN BROWN

Young Goodman Brown came forth at sunset, into the street of Salem village, but put his head back, after crossing the threshold, to exchange a parting kiss with his young wife. And Faith, as the wife was aptly named, thrust her own pretty head into the street, letting the wind play with the pink ribbons of her cap, while she called to Goodman Brown.

"Dearest heart," whispered she, softly and rather sadly, when her lips were close to his ear, "prithee, put off your journey until sunrise, and sleep in your own bed tonight. A lone woman is troubled with such dreams and such thoughts, that she's afeared of herself, sometimes. Pray, tarry with me this night, dear husband, of all nights in the year!"

"My love and my Faith," replied young Goodman Brown, "of all nights in the year, this one night must I tarry away from thee. My journey, as thou callest it, forth and back again, must needs be done 'twixt now and sunrise. What, my sweet, pretty wife, dost thou doubt me already, and we but three months married!"

5 "Then God bless you!" said Faith with the pink ribbons, "and may you find all well, when you come back."

"Amen!" cried Goodman Brown. "Say thy prayers, dear Faith, and go to bed at dusk, and no harm will come to thee."

So they parted; and the young man pursued his way, until, being about to turn the corner by the meeting-house, he looked back and saw the head of Faith still peeping after him, with a melancholy air, in spite of her pink ribbons.

"Poor little Faith!" thought he, for his heart smote him. "What a wretch am I, to leave her on such an errand! She talks of dreams, too. Methought, as she spoke, there was trouble in her face, as if a dream had warned her what work is to be done tonight. But no, no! 't would kill her to think it. Well; she's a blessed angel on earth; and after this one night, I'll cling to her skirts and follow her to Heaven."

With this excellent resolve for the future, Goodman Brown felt himself justified in making more haste on his present evil purpose. He had taken a dreary road, darkened by all the gloomiest trees of the forest, which barely stood aside to let the narrow path creep through, and closed immediately behind. It was all as lonely as could be; and there is this peculiarity in such a solitude, that the traveller knows not who may be concealed by the innumerable trunks and the thick boughs overhead; so that, with lonely footsteps, he may yet be passing through an unseen multitude.

"There may be a devilish Indian behind every tree," said Goodman Brown 10 to himself; and he glanced fearfully behind him, as he added, "What if the devil himself should be at my very elbow!"

His head being turned back, he passed a crook of the road, and looking forward again, beheld the figure of a man, in grave and decent attire, seated at the foot of an old tree. He arose at Goodman Brown's approach, and walked onward, side by side with him.

"You are late, Goodman Brown," said he. "The clock of the Old South was striking, as I came through Boston; and that is full fifteen minutes agone."

"Faith kept me back awhile," replied the young man, with a tremor in his voice, caused by the sudden appearance of his companion, though not wholly unexpected.

It was now deep dusk in the forest, and deepest in that part of it where these two were journeying. As nearly as could be discerned, the second traveller was about fifty years old, apparently in the same rank of life as Goodman

Brown, and bearing a considerable resemblance to him, though perhaps more in expression than features. Still, they might have been taken for father and son. And yet, though the elder person was as simply clad as the younger, and as simple in manner too, he had an indescribable air of one who knew the world, and would not have felt abashed at the governor's dinner-table, or in King William's court, were it possible that his affairs should call him thither. But the only thing about him that could be fixed upon as remarkable, was his staff, which bore the likeness of a great black snake, so curiously wrought, that it might almost be seen to twist and wriggle itself like a living serpent. This, of course, must have been an ocular deception, assisted by the uncertain light.

"Come, Goodman Brown!" cried his fellow-traveller, "this is a dull pace for the beginning of a journey. Take my staff, if you are so soon weary."   15

"Friend," said the other, exchanging his slow pace for a full stop, "having kept covenant by meeting thee here, it is my purpose now to return whence I came. I have scruples, touching the matter thou wot'st of.

"Sayest thou so?" replied he of the serpent, smiling apart. "Let us walk on, nevertheless, reasoning as we go, and if I convince thee not, thou shalt turn back. We are but a little way in the forest, yet."

"Too far, too far!" exclaimed the goodman, unconsciously resuming his walk. "My father never went into the woods on such an errand, nor his father before him. We have been a race of honest men and good Christians, since the days of the martyrs. And shall I be the first of the name of Brown that ever took this path and kept—"

"Such company, thou wouldst say," observed the elder person, interrupting his pause. "Well said, Goodman Brown! I have been as well acquainted with your family as ever a one among the Puritans; and that's no trifle to say. I helped your grandfather, the constable, when he lashed the Quaker woman so smartly through the streets of Salem. And it was I that brought your father a pitch-pine knot, kindled at my own hearth, to set fire to an Indian village, in King Philip's war. They were my good friends, both; and many a pleasant walk have we had along this path, and returned merrily after midnight. I would fain be friends with you, for their sake."

"If it be as thou sayest," replied Goodman Brown, "I marvel they never spoke of these matters. Or, verily, I marvel not, seeing that the least rumor of the sort would have driven them from New England. We are a people of prayer, and good works to boot, and abide no such wickedness."

"Wickedness or not," said the traveller with twisted staff, "I have a very 20 general acquaintance here in New England. The deacons of many a church have drunk the communion wine with me; the selectmen, of divers towns, make me their chairman; and a majority of the Great and General Court are firm supporters of my interest. The governor and I, too—but these are state secrets."

"Can this be so!" cried Goodman Brown, with a stare of amazement at his undisturbed companion. "Howbeit, I have nothing to do with the governor and council; they have their own ways, and are no rule for a simple husbandman like me. But, were I to go on with thee, how should I meet the eye of that good old man, our minister, at Salem village? Oh, his voice would make me tremble, both Sabbath-day and lecture-day!"

Thus far, the elder traveller had listened with due gravity, but now burst into a fit of irrepressible mirth, shaking himself so violently, that his snakelike staff actually seemed to wriggle in sympathy.

"Ha! ha! ha!" shouted he, again and again; then composing himself, "Well, go on, Goodman Brown, go on; but, prithee, don't kill me with laughing!"

"Well, then, to end the matter at once," said Goodman Brown, considerably nettled, "there is my wife, Faith. It would break her dear little heart; and I'd rather break my own!"

25   "Nay, if that be the case," answered the other, "e'en go thy ways, Goodman Brown. I would not, for twenty old women like the one hobbling before us, that Faith should come to any harm."

As he spoke, he pointed his staff at a female figure on the path, in whom Goodman Brown recognized a very pious and exemplary dame, who had taught him his catechism in youth, and was still his moral and spiritual adviser, jointly with the minister and Deacon Gookin.

"A marvel, truly, that Goody Cloyse should be so far in the wilderness, at nightfall!" said he. "But, with your leave, friend, I shall take a cut through the woods, until we have left this Christian woman behind. Being a stranger to you, she might ask whom I was consorting with, and whither I was going."

"Be it so," said his fellow-traveller. "Betake you to the woods, and let me keep the path."

Accordingly, the young man turned aside, but took care to watch his companion, who advanced softly along the road, until he had come within a staff's length of the old dame. She, meanwhile, was making the best of her way, with singular speed for so aged a woman, and mumbling some indistinct words, a prayer, doubtless, as she went. The traveller put forth his staff, and touched her withered neck with what seemed the serpent's tail.

30   "The devil!" screamed the pious old lady.

"Then Goody Cloyse knows her old friend?" observed the traveller, confronting her, and leaning on his writhing stick.

"Ah, forsooth, and is it your worship, indeed?" cried the good dame. "Yea, truly is it, and in the very image of my old gossip, Goodman Brown, the grandfather of the silly fellow that now is. But, would your worship believe it? My broomstick hath strangely disappeared, stolen, as I suspect, by that unhanged witch, Goody Cory, and that, too, when I was all anointed with the juice of smallage and cinquefoil and wolf's-bane—"

"Mingled with fine wheat and the fat of a new-born babe," said the shape of old Goodman Brown.

"Ah, your worship knows the recipe," cried the old lady, cackling aloud. "So, as I was saying, being all ready for the meeting, and no horse to ride on, I made up my mind to foot it; for they tell me there is a nice young man to be taken into communion tonight. But now your good worship will lend me your arm, and we shall be there in a twinkling."

35   "That can hardly be," answered her friend. "I will not spare you my arm, Goody Cloyse, but here is my staff, if you will."

So saying, he threw it down at her feet, where, perhaps, it assumed life, being one of the rods which its owner had formerly lent to the Egyptian Magi. Of this fact, however, Goodman Brown could not take cognizance. He had cast up his eyes in astonishment, and looking down again, beheld neither Goody Cloyse nor the serpentine staff, but his fellow-traveller alone, who waited for him as calmly as if nothing had happened.

"That old woman taught me my catechism!" said the young man; and there was a world of meaning in this simple comment.

They continued to walk onward, while the elder traveller exhorted his companion to make good speed and persevere in the path, discoursing so aptly, that his arguments seemed rather to spring up in the bosom of his auditor, than to be suggested by himself. As they went he plucked a branch of maple, to serve for a walking-stick, and began to strip it of the twigs and little boughs, which were wet with evening dew. The moment his fingers touched them, they became strangely withered and dried up, as with a week's sunshine. Thus the pair proceeded, at a good free pace, until suddenly, in a gloomy hollow of the road, Goodman Brown sat himself down on the stump of a tree, and refused to go any farther.

"Friend," said he, stubbornly, "my mind is made up. Not another step will I budge on this errand. What if a wretched old woman do choose to go to the devil, when I thought she was going to Heaven! Is that any reason why I should quit my dear Faith, and go after her?"

"You will think better of this by and by," said his acquaintance, composedly. "Sit here and rest yourself a while; and when you feel like moving again, there is my staff to help you along." 40

Without more words, he threw his companion the maple stick, and was as speedily out of sight as if he had vanished into the deepening gloom. The young man sat a few moments by the roadside, applauding himself greatly, and thinking with how clear a conscience he should meet the minister, in his morning walk, nor shrink from the eye of good old Deacon Gookin. And what calm sleep would be his, that very night, which was to have been spent so wickedly, but purely and sweetly now, in the arms of Faith! Amidst these pleasant and praiseworthy meditations, Goodman Brown heard the tramp of horses along the road, and deemed it advisable to conceal himself within the verge of the forest, conscious of the guilty purpose that had brought him thither, though now so happily turned from it.

On came the hoof-tramps and the voices of the riders, two grave old voices, conversing soberly as they drew near. These mingled sounds appeared to pass along the road, within a few yards of the young man's hiding-place; but owing, doubtless, to the depth of the gloom, at that particular spot, neither the travellers nor their steeds were visible. Though their figures brushed the small boughs by the wayside, it could not be seen that they intercepted, even for a moment, the faint gleam from the strip of bright sky, athwart which they must have passed. Goodman Brown alternately crouched and stood on tiptoe, pulling aside the branches, and thrusting forth his head as far as he durst, without discerning so much as a shadow. It vexed him the more, because he could have sworn, were such a thing possible, that he recognized the voices of the minister and Deacon Gookin, jogging along quietly, as they were wont to do, when bound to some ordination or ecclesiastical council. While yet within hearing, one of the riders stopped to pluck a switch.

"Of the two, reverend Sir," said the voice like the deacon's, "I had rather miss an ordination dinner than to-night's meeting. They tell me that some of our community are to be here from Falmouth and beyond, and others from Connecticut and Rhode Island; besides several of the Indian powwows, who, after their fashion, know almost as much deviltry as the best of us. Moreover, there is a goodly young woman to be taken into communion."

"Mighty well, Deacon Gookin!" replied the solemn old tones of the minister. "Spur up, or we shall be late. Nothing can be done, you know, until I get on the ground."

45   The hoofs clattered again, and the voices, talking so strangely in the empty air, passed on through the forest, where no church had ever been gathered, nor solitary Christian prayed. Whither, then, could these holy men be journeying, so deep into the heathen wilderness? Young Goodman Brown caught hold of a tree, for support, being ready to sink down on the ground, faint and over-burthened with the heavy sickness of his heart. He looked up to the sky, doubting whether there really was a Heaven above him. Yet, there was the blue arch, and the stars brightening in it.

"With Heaven above, and Faith below, I will yet stand firm against the devil!" cried Goodman Brown.

While he still gazed upward, into the deep arch of the firmament, and had lifted his hands to pray, a cloud, though no wind was stirring, hurried across the zenith, and hid the brightening stars. The blue sky was still visible, except directly overhead, where this black mass of cloud was sweeping swiftly northward. Aloft in the air, as if from the depths of the cloud, came a confused and doubtful sound of voices. Once, the listener fancied that he could distinguish the accents of town's people of his own, men and women, both pious and ungodly, many of whom he had met at the communion-table, and had seen others rioting at the tavern. The next moment, so indistinct were the sounds, he doubted whether he had heard aught but the murmur of the old forest, whispering without a wind. Then came a stronger swell of those familiar tones, heard daily in the sunshine, at Salem village, but never, until now, from a cloud at night. There was one voice, of a young woman, uttering lamentations, yet with an uncertain sorrow, and entreating for some favor, which, perhaps, it would grieve her to obtain. And all the unseen multitude, both saints and sinners, seemed to encourage her onward.

"Faith!" shouted Goodman Brown, in a voice of agony and desperation; and the echoes of the forest mocked him, crying—"Faith! Faith!" as if bewildered wretches were seeking her, all through the wilderness.

The cry of grief, rage, and terror was yet piercing the night, when the unhappy husband held his breath for a response. There was a scream, drowned immediately in a louder murmur of voices fading into far-off laughter, as the dark cloud swept away, leaving the clear and silent sky above Goodman

Brown. But something fluttered lightly down through the air, and caught on the branch of a tree. The young man seized it and beheld a pink ribbon.

"My Faith is gone!" cried he, after one stupefied moment. "There is no 50 good on earth, and sin is but a name. Come, devil! for to thee is this world given."

And maddened with despair, so that he laughed loud and long, did Goodman Brown grasp his staff and set forth again, at such a rate, that he seemed to fly along the forest path, rather than to walk or run. The road grew wilder and drearier, and more faintly traced, and vanished at length, leaving him in the heart of the dark wilderness, still rushing onward, with the instinct that guides mortal man to evil. The whole forest was peopled with frightful sounds; the creaking of the trees, the howling of wild beasts, and the yell of Indians; while, sometimes, the wind tolled like a distant church bell, and sometimes gave a broad roar around the traveller, as if all Nature were laughing him to scorn. But he was himself the chief horror of the scene, and shrank not from its other horrors.

"Ha! ha! ha!" roared Goodman Brown, when the wind laughed at him. "Let us hear which will laugh loudest! Think not to frighten me with your deviltry! Come witch, come wizard, come Indian powwow, come devil himself! and here comes Goodman Brown. You may as well fear him as he fear you!"

In truth, all through the haunted forest, there could be nothing more frightful than the figure of Goodman Brown. On he flew, among the black pines, brandishing his staff with frenzied gestures, now giving vent to an inspiration of horrid blasphemy, and now shouting forth such laughter, as set all the echoes of the forest laughing like demons around him. The fiend in his own shape is less hideous than when he rages in the breast of man. Thus sped the demoniac on his course, until, quivering among the trees, he saw a red light before him, as when the felled trunks and branches of a clearing have been set on fire, and throw up their lurid blaze against the sky, at the hour of midnight. He paused, in a lull of the tempest that had driven him onward, and heard the swell of what seemed a hymn, rolling solemnly from a distance, with the weight of many voices. He knew the tune. It was a familiar one in the choir of the village meeting-house. The verse died heavily away, and was lengthened by a chorus, not of human voices, but of all the sounds of the benighted wilderness, pealing in awful harmony together. Goodman Brown cried out; and his cry was lost to his own ear, by its unison with the cry of the desert.

In the interval of silence, he stole forward, until the light glared full upon his eyes. At one extremity of an open space, hemmed in by the dark wall of the forest, arose a rock, bearing some rude, natural resemblance either to an altar or a pulpit, and surrounded by four blazing pines, their tops aflame, their stems untouched, like candles at an evening meeting. The mass of foliage, that had overgrown the summit of the rock, was all on fire, blazing high into the night, and fitfully illuminating the whole field. Each pendent twig and leafy festoon was in a blaze. As the red light arose and fell, a numerous congregation alternately shone forth, then disappeared in shadow, and again grew, as it were, out of the darkness, peopling the heart of the solitary woods at once.

55   "A grave and dark-clad company!" quoth Goodman Brown.

In truth, they were such. Among them, quivering to-and-fro, between gloom and splendor, appeared faces that would be seen, next day, at the council-board of the province, and others which, Sabbath after Sabbath, looked devoutly heavenward, and benignantly over the crowded pews, from the holiest pulpits in the land. Some affirm that the lady of the governor was there. At least, there were high dames well known to her, and wives of honored husbands, and widows a great multitude, and ancient maidens, all of excellent repute, and fair young girls, who trembled lest their mothers should espy them. Either the sudden gleams of light, flashing over the obscure field, bedazzled Goodman Brown, or he recognized a score of the church members of Salem village, famous for their especial sanctity. Good old Deacon Gookin had arrived, and waited at the skirts of that venerable saint, his reverend pastor. But, irreverently consorting with these grave, reputable, and pious people, these elders of the church, these chaste dames and dewy virgins, there were men of dissolute lives and women of spotted fame, wretches given over to all mean and filthy vice, and suspected even of horrid crimes. It was strange to see, that the good shrank not from the wicked, nor were the sinners abashed by the saints. Scattered, also, among their pale-faced enemies, were the Indian priests, or powwows, who had often scared their native forest with more hideous incantations than any known to English witchcraft.

"But, where is Faith?" thought Goodman Brown; and, as hope came into his heart, he trembled.

Another verse of the hymn arose, a slow and mournful strain, such as the pious love, but joined to words which expressed all that our nature can conceive of sin, and darkly hinted at far more. Unfathomable to mere mortals is the lore of fiends. Verse after verse was sung, and still the chorus of the desert swelled between, like the deepest tone of a mighty organ. And, with the final peal of that dreadful anthem, there came a sound, as if the roaring wind, the rushing streams, the howling beasts, and every other voice of the unconverted wilderness were mingling and according with the voice of guilty man, in homage to the prince of all. The four blazing pines threw up a loftier flame, and obscurely discovered shapes and visages of horror on the smoke-wreaths, above the impious assembly. At the same moment, the fire on the rock shot redly forth, and formed a glowing arch above its base, where now appeared a figure. With reverence be it spoken, the apparition bore no slight similitude, both in garb and manner, to some grave divine of the New England churches.

"Bring forth the converts!" cried a voice, that echoed through the field and rolled into the forest.

60   At the word, Goodman Brown stepped forth from the shadow of the trees, and approached the congregation, with whom he felt a loathful brotherhood, by the sympathy of all that was wicked in his heart. He could have well-nigh sworn, that the shape of his own dead father beckoned him to advance, looking downward from a smoke-wreath, while a woman, with dim features of despair, threw out her hand to warn him back. Was it his mother? But he had no power to retreat one step, nor to resist, even in thought, when the minister and good old Deacon Gookin seized his arms, and led him to the blazing rock. Thither came also the slender form of a veiled female, led between Goody

Cloyse, that pious teacher of the catechism, and Martha Carrier, who had received the devil's promise to be queen of hell. A rampant hag was she! And there stood the proselytes, beneath the canopy of fire.

"Welcome, my children," said the dark figure, "to the communion of your race! Ye have found, thus young, your nature and your destiny. My children, look behind you!"

They turned; and flashing forth, as it were, in a sheet of flame, the fiend-worshippers were seen; the smile of welcome gleamed darkly on every visage.

"There," resumed the sable form, "are all whom ye have reverenced from youth. Ye deemed them holier than yourselves, and shrank from your own sin, contrasting it with their lives of righteousness and prayerful aspirations heavenward. Yet, here are they all, in my worshipping assembly! This night it shall be granted you to know their secret deeds; how hoary-bearded elders of the church have whispered wanton words to the young maids of their households; how many a woman, eager for widow's weeds, has given her husband a drink at bedtime, and let him sleep his last sleep in her bosom; how beardless youths have made haste to inherit their father's wealth; and how fair damsels—blush not, sweet ones!—have dug little graves in the garden, and bidden me, the sole guest, to an infant's funeral. By the sympathy of your human hearts for sin, ye shall scent out all the places—whether in church, bed-chamber, street, field, or forest—where crime has been committed, and shall exult to behold the whole earth one stain of guilt, one mighty blood-spot. Far more than this! It shall be yours to penetrate, in every bosom, the deep mystery of sin, the fountain of all wicked arts, and which inexhaustibly supplies more evil impulses than human power—than my power, at its utmost!—can make manifest in deeds. And now, my children, look upon each other."

They did so; and, by the blaze of the hell-kindled torches, the wretched man beheld his Faith, and the wife her husband, trembling before that unhallowed altar.

"Lo! there ye stand, my children," said the figure, in a deep and solemn 65 tone, almost sad, with its despairing awfulness, as if his once angelic nature could yet mourn for our miserable race. "Depending upon one another's hearts, ye had still hoped that virtue were not all a dream! Now are ye undeceived!— Evil is the nature of mankind. Evil must be your only happiness. Welcome, again, my children, to the communion of your race!"

"Welcome!" repeated the fiend-worshippers, in one cry of despair and triumph.

And there they stood, the only pair, as it seemed, who were yet hesitating on the verge of wickedness, in this dark world. A basin was hollowed, naturally, in the rock. Did it contain water, reddened by the lurid light? or was it blood? or, perchance, a liquid flame? Herein did the Shape of Evil dip his hand, and prepare to lay the mark of baptism upon their foreheads, that they might be partakers of the mystery of sin, more conscious of the secret guilt of others, both in deed and thought, than they could now be of their own. The husband cast one look at his pale wife, and Faith at him. What polluted wretches would the next glance show them to each other, shuddering alike at what they disclosed and what they saw!

"Faith! Faith!" cried the husband. "Look up to Heaven, and resist the Wicked One!"

Whether Faith obeyed, he knew not. Hardly had he spoken, when he found himself amid calm night and solitude, listening to a roar of the wind, which died heavily away through the forest. He staggered against the rock, and felt it chill and damp, while a hanging twig, that had been all on fire, besprinkled his cheek with the coldest dew.

70   The next morning, young Goodman Brown came slowly into the street of Salem village staring around him like a bewildered man. The good old minister was taking a walk along the grave-yard, to get an appetite for breakfast and meditate his sermon, and bestowed a blessing, as he passed, on Goodman Brown. He shrank from the venerable saint, as if to avoid an anathema. Old Deacon Gookin was at domestic worship, and the holy words of his prayer were heard through the open window. "What God doth the wizard pray to?" quoth Goodman Brown. Goody Cloyse, that excellent old Christian, stood in the early sunshine, at her own lattice, catechising a little girl, who had brought her a pint of morning's milk. Goodman Brown snatched away the child, as from the grasp of the fiend himself. Turning the corner by the meetinghouse, he spied the head of Faith, with the pink ribbons, gazing anxiously forth, and bursting into such joy at the sight of him that she skipt along the street, and almost kissed her husband before the whole village. But Goodman Brown looked sternly and sadly into her face, and passed on without a greeting.

Had Goodman Brown fallen asleep in the forest, and only dreamed a wild dream of a witch-meeting?

Be it so, if you will. But, alas! it was a dream of evil omen for young Goodman Brown. A stern, a sad, a darkly meditative, a distrustful, if not a desperate man did he become, from the night of that fearful dream. On the Sabbath day, when the congregation were singing a holy psalm, he could not listen, because an anthem of sin rushed loudly upon his ear, and drowned all the blessed strain. When the minister spoke from the pulpit, with power and fervid eloquence, and with his hand on the open Bible, of the sacred truths of our religion, and of saint-like lives and triumphant deaths, and of future bliss or misery unutterable, then did Goodman Brown turn pale, dreading lest the roof should thunder down upon the gray blasphemer and his hearers. Often, awaking suddenly at midnight, he shrank from the bosom of Faith, and at morning or eventide, when the family knelt down in prayer, he scowled, and muttered to himself, and gazed sternly at his wife, and turned away. And when he had lived long, and was borne to his grave, a hoary corpse, followed by Faith, an aged woman, and children and grandchildren, a goodly procession, besides neighbors not a few, they carved no hopeful verse upon his tombstone; for his dying hour was gloom.

Questions

1. Some of the characters and places (e.g., Deacon Gookin, Goody Cloyse, Goody Cory, Boston, Salem, and South Church) in this story are historical. Where does reality end and fiction begin in this story? What was Hawthorne attempting to communicate with this tension?

2. Is this story a dream? Is it a nightmare or a hallucination? Is the story caused by an evil entity, by a character's own psychosis, or by the pressures of society? In this story, what is natural, and what is supernatural?
3. Is this story an allegory, like *Everyman* and John Bunyan's *Pilgrim's Progress?* If it is an allegory, what significance comes from the name "Goodman Brown"? Brown is a common name in American culture, such as Smith. Perhaps it symbolizes every man or any ordinary person. The name "Goodman" seems odd, because Jesus spoke against calling anyone "good" (see Matthew 19:17, Mark 10:18, and Luke 18:19). What do you think?
4. As Goodman Brown ventures into the unknown, dark forest for a spiritual encounter, he is described as young. Thus, he is viewed as inexperienced and untried. He is also leaving the security of home and facing danger and risks. What role does good and evil play in this journey? What was Hawthorne communicating about this character.

WILLIAM BUTLER YEATS

William Butler Yeats (1865–1939) was born in Ireland to a Protestant family. He lived in England and in Ireland. In 1923, he received the Nobel Prize in Literature. Along with his fame in poetry, he was involved in writing and producing plays. From time to time, he explored spirituality through the occult, the Theosophical Society, and mystical experiences. He also served as an Irish Senator and helped run a publishing company for poets.

The poem, "The Second Coming," was written in 1920 after the shocking and futile "war to end all wars" (World War I). Before 1914, it was common to impose Darwin's evolutionary model onto the history of European civilization. Many people assumed that Europe's power, education, science, culture, and morals were the evolutionary pinnacle of human success. In this context, some viewed liberal Christianity as the highest form of religion yet to evolve. Then World War I demonstrated that indeed, "Things fall apart; the centre cannot hold." The senseless nature of the war, along with its use of the latest technology, seemed to prove that Europeans had deceived themselves—they had not evolved higher than the savages.

Yeats is an interesting and lively poet. His works invite multiple interpretations and feelings. "The Second Coming" is particularly rich with images (many are connected to the Apocalypse in the biblical Book of Revelation).

THE SECOND COMING

Turning and turning in the widening gyre
The falcon cannot hear the falconer;
Things fall apart; the center cannot hold;
Mere anarchy is loosed upon the world,

5 *The blood-dimmed tide is loosed, and everywhere*
 The ceremony of innocence is drowned;
 The best lack all conviction, while the worst
 Are full of passionate intensity.
 Surely some revelation is at hand;
10 *Surely the Second Coming is at hand.*
 The Second Coming! Hardly are those words out
 When a vast image out of Spiritus Mundi
 Troubles my sight; somewhere in sands of the desert
 A shape with lion body and the head of a man,
15 *A gaze blank and pitiless as the sun,*
 Is moving its slow thighs, while all about it
 Reel shadows of the indignant desert birds.
 The darkness drops again; but now I know
 That twenty centuries of stony sleep
20 *Were vexed to nightmare by a rocking cradle,*
 And what rough beast, its hour come round at last,
 Slouches towards Bethlehem to be born?

Questions

1. What meanings can be found in Yeats' phrase, "The best lack all conviction, while the worst / Are full of passionate intensity"?
2. Yeats introduced "[a] shape with lion body and the head of a man," which seems to move slowly in the shadows, and then retreats into darkness again. What images and feelings are created by Yeats at this point in the poem?
3. The poem ends by referring to "twenty centuries of stony sleep / Were vexed to nightmare by a rocking cradle, / And what rough beast, its hour come round at last, / Slouches towards Bethlehem to be born?" Yeats used "twenty centuries," "rocking cradle," and "Bethlehem" to lead the reader to think about the birth of Jesus. What seems to be Yeats' intent by using this ending?
4. In what ways are you attracted to this poem? Is there anything in this poem that is repulsive to you? If so, why?

EMILY DICKINSON

Emily Dickinson (1830–1886) lived a very reclusive life in Massachusetts. In spite of, or because of, her isolation, Dickinson filled her life with writing letters and writing poetry. However, only a few people knew about her poetry during her lifetime. After her death, Dickinson's family members began to publish her reservoir of almost 1,800 poems. Today, Dickinson is recognized as one of the best poets that the United States has produced.

The poetry of Dickinson is short, filled with powerful images, and often mysterious in its messages. For example, "The Lightning is a yellow Fork" is a single sentence, a single extended thought. It challenges the reader to ponder the relationship that God has with humanity, and humanity's relationship with God. Dickinson's "Some keep the Sabbath going to church" is suggestive of her life in seclusion. Rather than meeting with other people in a place of worship, the poet meets with God alone.

When reading this selection, it is helpful to know that a "bobolink" is a song bird, a "chorister" is a member of a group of singers, a "surplice" was the special clothing worn by the clergy, and a "sexton" was a worker at a church who was sometimes associated with ringing bells and/or digging graves.

SOME KEEP THE SABBATH GOING TO CHURCH

Some keep the Sabbath going to Church—
I keep it, staying at Home—
With a Bobolink for a Chorister—
And an Orchard, for a Dome—

Some keep the Sabbath in Surplice—   5
I, just wear my Wings—
And instead of tolling the Bell, for Church,
Our little Sexton–sings.

God preaches, a noted Clergyman—
And the sermon is never long.   10
So instead of getting to Heaven, at last—
I'm going, all along.

THE LIGHTNING IS A YELLOW FORK

The Lightning is a yellow Fork
From Tables in the sky
By inadvertent fingers dropt
The awful Cutlery

Of mansions never quite disclosed   5
And never quite concealed
The Apparatus of the Dark
To ignorance revealed.

Questions

1. In "Some keep the Sabbath going to church," why did Dickinson end with "I'm going all along"?
2. What was Dickinson's overall message in "Some keep the Sabbath going to church"? Was she saying that large churches and rituals are wrong, or was she merely saying that she personally prefers a quieter form of worship?
3. A person's experiences of God can vary over his or her lifetime. How did Dickinson experience God while writing "The Lightning is a yellow Fork"?

What do the words *inadvertent, apparatus,* and *Dark* suggest about that relationship?

4. In "The Lightning is a yellow Fork," what did Dickinson mean by "never quite disclosed / And never quite concealed"? Does God reveal himself to humanity? If so, in what ways is that revelation clear and unclear?

GWENDOLYN ELIZABETH BROOKS

Gwendolyn Elizabeth Brooks (1917–2000) was an African American poet who lived most of her life on the South Side of Chicago. In spite of their modest resources, her loving parents made sure that she received the best education possible. In time, their efforts bore fruit; she became a much respected poet. She was awarded the Pulitzer Prize in 1950, and she was given an invitation in 1962 by President John F. Kennedy to participate in a government-sponsored poetry festival. She taught poetry courses at various universities, and she was appointed Poet Laureate of Illinois in 1968.

In "the preacher: ruminates behind the sermon," Brooks asked the reader to consider the feelings and experiences of God. Is God lonely or bored? Is God proud and removed from normal people? Would God prefer to be a human with friends? Too often when people think about God, they view him as a distant, old grandfather figure, who is old and out of touch with our experiences and needs. Or, sometimes, people view God as a vending machine; we send up a few prayers, like coins put into a candy machine, and we hope that he automatically sends down some answers, like candy from a machine. Although people would not admit to viewing God in such ways, Brooks helps us see both God and our expectations of God from a new, more honest perspective.

THE PREACHER: RUMINATES BEHIND THE SERMON

I think it must be lonely to be God.
Nobody loves a master. No. Despite
The bright hosannas, bright dear-Lords, and bright
Determined reverence of Sunday eyes.

5   *Picture Jehovah striding through the hall*
Of His importance, creatures running out
From servant-corners to acclaim, to shout
Appreciation of His merit's glare.

But who walks with Him?—dares to take His arm,
10 *To slap Him on the shoulder, tweak His ear,*
Buy Him a Coca-Cola or a beer,
Pooh-pooh His politics, call Him a fool?

Perhaps—who knows?—He tires of looking down.
Those eyes are never lifted. Never straight.
Perhaps sometimes He tires of being great   15
In solitude. Without a hand to hold.

Questions

1. Brooks asked important questions about God, but the poem also leads the reader to certain conclusions. Do you agree with those conclusions?
2. Does this poem help you define God's character more carefully? Explain your answer.
3. This poem seems to assume that God does not have friendships or other relationships. What do you think? Does the God of the Bible have relationships? If so, what are they like? You might consider Abraham, in Genesis, who is called a friend of God (see 2 Chronicles 20:7 and James 2:33).
4. What sections of this poem do you agree with? What sections do you disagree with?

PAUL LAURENCE DUNBAR

Paul Laurence Dunbar (1872–1906) was born in Dayton, Ohio, to parents who were former slaves. Interestingly, his father had escaped from slavery and served as a Union soldier in the Civil War. Although he was very poor, Dunbar was a dynamic personality who held leadership positions in his essentially all-white high school. At his high school, he began a life-long friendship with Orville and Wilber Wright, the inventors of the first successful airplane. Dunbar's life also intersected with two other very famous people; he had opportunities to meet Frederick Douglass (the most famous African American leader of the first half of the nineteenth century) and Booker T. Washington (the most famous African American leader of the second half of the nineteenth century). Dunbar published many poems, novels, and short stories. He also edited a newspaper for the black community in Dayton.

WE WEAR THE MASK

We wear the mask that grins and lies,
It hides our cheeks and shades our eyes,—
This debt we pay to human guile;
With torn and bleeding hearts we smile,
And mouth with myriad subtleties.   5
Why should the world be over-wise,
In counting all our tears and sighs?
Nay, let them only see us, while
        We wear the mask.

10   *We smile, but, O great Christ, our cries*
    To thee from tortured souls arise.
    We sing, but oh the clay is vile
    Beneath our feet, and long the mile;
    But let the world dream otherwise,
15   *We wear the mask!*

Questions

1. What was Dunbar talking about when he used the word *mask*?
2. Notice how Dunbar shifted the last word in this line: "Why should the world be overwise." It is natural to read the sentence as "Why should the world be *otherwise?*" But the poet surprised us with an unexpected, but similar word—*overwise*. What was he doing here?
3. Obviously, this poem speaks about the experiences of African Americans in a white-dominated culture. In what ways do we all wear masks and smiles? What might be the spiritual significance of wearing masks and smiles?
4. In what ways do you feel an affinity with Dunbar's feelings and experiences?

LANGSTON HUGHES

Langston Hughes (1902–1967), during his youth, moved a great deal. He lived in Kansas, Illinois, Ohio, and briefly in Mexico. Later, he moved to New York City and attended Columbia University for a year. While in New York, Hughes was drawn into the Harlem Renaissance. This was a very special time and place; African American artists cultivated poetry, fiction, and music within their own environment and won the respect of both black and white Americans. Hughes also worked as a crewman on a merchant ship for a time and traveled to Africa. He spent some time in Paris, and he finished college in Pennsylvania. In addition to writing poetry, he wrote essays, newspaper articles, an autobiography, novels, and plays.

At the age of twelve, Hughes experienced a religious encounter that probably influenced his religious perception for the rest of his life. While attending a Christian revival service with a family friend, Hughes faked a conversion experience because he felt pressured to do so. Hughes was also disappointed that Jesus did not respond to his prayers. This retelling of Hughes' youthful religious experience is part of his autobiography, *The Big Sea*. The account, more of a confession, reveals the mounting pressure he felt to be "saved," and it expresses his regret at his hypocrisy.

SALVATION

1   I was saved from sin when I was going on thirteen. But not really saved. It happened like this. There was a big revival at my Auntie Reed's church. Every night for weeks there had been much preaching, singing, praying, and shouting,

and some very hardened sinners had been brought to Christ, and the membership of the church had grown by leaps and bounds. Then just before the revival ended, they held a special meeting for children, "to bring the young lambs to the fold." My aunt spoke of it for days ahead. That night I was escorted to the front row and placed on the mourners' bench with all the other young sinners, who had not yet been brought to Jesus.

My aunt told me that when you were saved you saw a light, and some- 2 thing happened to you inside! And Jesus came into your life! And God was with you from then on! She said you could see and hear and feel Jesus in your soul. I believed her. I had heard a great many old people say the same thing and it seemed to me they ought to know. So I sat there calmly in the hot, crowded church, waiting for Jesus to come to me.

The preacher preached a wonderful rhythmical sermon, all moans and 3 shouts and lonely cries and dire pictures of hell, and then he sang a song about the ninety and nine safe in the fold, but one little lamb was left out in the cold. Then he said: "Won't you come? Won't you come to Jesus? Young lambs, won't you come?" And he held out his arms to all us young sinners there on the mourners' bench. And the little girls cried. And some of them jumped up and went to Jesus right away. But most of us just sat there.

A great many old people came and knelt around us and prayed, old 4 women with jet-black faces and braided hair, old men with work-gnarled hands. And the church sang a song about the lower lights are burning, some poor sinners to be saved. And the whole building rocked with prayer and song.

Still I kept waiting to *see* Jesus. 5

Finally all the young people had gone to the altar and were saved, but 6 one boy and me. He was a rounder's son named Westley. Westley and I were surrounded by sisters and deacons praying. It was very hot in the church, and getting late now. Finally Westley said to me in a whisper: "God damn! I'm tired o' sitting here. Let's get up and be saved." So he got up and was saved.

Then I was left all alone on the mourners' bench. My aunt came and knelt 7 at my knees and cried, while prayers and songs swirled all around me in the little church. The whole congregation prayed for me alone, in a mighty wail of moans and voices. And I kept waiting serenely for Jesus, waiting, waiting—but he didn't come. I wanted to see him, but nothing happened to me. Nothing! I wanted something to happen to me, but nothing happened.

I heard the songs and the minister saying: "Why don't you come? My dear 8 child, why don't you come to Jesus? Jesus is waiting for you. He wants you. Why don't you come? Sister Reed, what is this child's name?"

"Langston," my aunt sobbed. 9

"Langston, why don't you come? Why don't you come and be saved? Oh, 10 Lamb of God! Why don't you come?"

Now it was really getting late. I began to be ashamed of myself, holding 11 everything up so long. I began to wonder what God thought about Westley, who certainly hadn't seen Jesus either, but who was now sitting proudly on the platform, swinging his knickerbockered legs and grinning down at me, surrounded by deacons and old women on their knees praying. God had not struck Westley dead for taking his name in vain or for lying in the temple. So I decided that maybe to save further trouble, I'd better lie, too, and say that Jesus had come, and get up and be saved.

12   So I got up.

13   Suddenly the whole room broke into a sea of shouting, as they saw me rise. Waves of rejoicing swept the place. Women leaped into the air. My aunt threw her arms around me. The minister took me by the hand and led me to the platform.

14   When things quieted down, in a hushed silence, punctuated by a few ec-static "Amens," all the new young lambs were blessed in the name of God. Then joyous singing filled the room.

15   That night, for the last time in my life but one—for I was a big boy twelve years old—I cried. I cried, in bed alone, and couldn't stop. I buried my head under the quilts, but my aunt heard me. She woke up and told my uncle I was crying because the Holy Ghost had come into my life, and because I had seen Jesus. But I was really crying because I couldn't bear to tell her that I had lied, that I had deceived everybody in the church, that I hadn't seen Jesus, and that now I didn't believe there was a Jesus any more, since he didn't come to help me.

Questions

1. Who or what is most to blame for how the twelve-year-old boy felt during and after his religious encounter?

2. Although the story uses a first person point of view, the narrator is able to create an interesting complexity. Hughes offered numerous perspectives, each of which had a duality (a double viewpoint). For example, (a) there is the vision of the twelve-year-old boy and the vision of the adult narrator who is writing about his childhood experience; (b) there is the private, personal self of the child and the public narrator's self of the adult writer; and (c) there is a self that writes, as opposed to the self that is written about. What are the effects of this duality? And how does it create irony, satire, and even humor?

3. At the end of the story, the twelve-year-old boy cries about two disap-pointments: He "couldn't bear to tell [his aunt] that [he] lied" about his "salvation," and that "Jesus . . . didn't come to help" him. When writing as an adult, was Hughes still experiencing disappointment and sadness? Did the adult author arrive at a conclusion about spirituality?

4. Using this selection as a starting point, what thoughts and experiences guided your youthful understanding of salvation and spirituality?

RICHARD EBERHART

Richard Eberhart (1904–2005) grew up in Minnesota. He studied at the University of Minnesota, Dartmouth College, St. John's College at Cambridge, and Harvard University. In addition to writing numerous books of poetry, his career included tutoring a prince in Siam (now Thailand), military service in World War II, and teaching at various colleges.

His poem, "The Fury of Aerial Bombardment," is a reminder about the harsh realities of warfare. In such a context, humans often ask why: Why do humans kill each other? Why does God allow it? Why is warfare a constant feature of human history? Are we learning anything from that history?

This poem contains the phrases, "belt feed lever" and "belt feed pawl." Both are actual parts of the Browning machine gun used in World War II when Eberhart served in the U.S. Navy. The use of the word *pawl* might also be a pun. *Pawl* sounds like an animal's paw. Perhaps Eberhart is pointing out two struggles: On one level, the humans in the poem are struggling to distinguish between two metal parts of a gun in order to properly use it. On another level, perhaps the humans are struggling to distinguish between using the human and subhuman parts of themselves.

An interesting line is "Was man made stupid to see his own stupidity?" Eberhart gave a rich complexity in this simple line. The term *man-made* was commonly used at this time; it distinguished natural materials (e.g., wood, leather, and stone) from plastics and other unnatural materials that were being introduced. But the poem uses the term *man-made* to refer to the nature of humanity. Thus, the question is indirectly raised: Is humanity's stupidity man-made (the fault of humanity), or were humans (man) made (by God) to be stupid? Furthermore, what is the relationship between stupidity and violence? Some violence, such as the Nazi violence against the Jews, is carefully planned by very rational and intelligent people. On one level, the Holocaust was not an example of stupidity. Eberhart challenged us to explore many important issues in this short poem.

THE FURY OF AERIAL BOMBARDMENT

You would think the fury of aerial bombardment
Would rouse God to relent; the infinite spaces
Are still silent. He looks on shock-pried faces.
History, even, does not know what is meant.

You would feel that after so many centuries   5
God would give man to repent; yet he can kill
As Cain could, but with multitudinous will,
No farther advanced than in his ancient furies.

Was man made stupid to see his own stupidity?
Is God by definition indifferent, beyond us all?   10
Is the eternal truth man's fighting soul
Wherein the Beast ravens in its own avidity?

Of Van Wettering I speak, and Averill,
Names on a list, whose faces I do not recall
But they are gone to early death, who late in school   15
Distinguished the belt feed lever from the belt holding pawl.

Questions

1. After reading this poem, who or what do you think bears the responsibility for humanity's tendency to go to war: God, all humanity, specific individuals, political groups, economic forces, or another source?

2. How does this poem help you think about stupidity and intelligence, and their role in warfare? What other factors cause warfare: pride, selfishness, shortsighted thinking, sin (the violation of God's plan for humanity), or another source?

3. In contrast to the causes of war, what factors and attitudes contribute to cooperation among humans? Peace is assumed to be a good goal in this poem, but when is peace too high a price to pay?

4. Why does the poet choose the names "Van Wettering" and "Averill"? Why does he put Van Wettering before Averill? What is the importance of "the list"?

SANDRA CISNEROS

Sandra Cisneros (b. 1954) was born in Chicago to a family with strong roots in Mexico. During her childhood, her family often moved back and forth from Mexico to Chicago. Thus, Cisneros was torn between two cultures. She was also the only daughter surrounded by six brothers, adding another dynamic to her life. Cisneros is both comfortable and uncomfortable as she uses both English and Spanish to express herself.

After attending many schools (because of the family's many moves), she received a B.A. from Loyola University in 1976 and an M.F.A. from the University of Iowa's Writers' Workshop in 1978. Her first novel, *The House on Mango Street*, reflects some of her Hispanic family's struggles. Later, she wrote numerous novels and collections of short stories. Esperanza, the protagonist in *The House on Mango Street*, is a poor, Latina adolescent who longs for a house of her own. She is torn between wanting to break away from her past and wanting to identify with her Chicana, Mexican, and American heritages.

FROM THE HOUSE ON MANGO STREET

We didn't always live on Mango Street. Before that we lived on Loomis on the third floor, and before that we lived on Keeler. Before Keeler it was Paulina, and before that I can't remember. But what I remember most is moving a lot. Each time it seemed there'd be one more of us. By the time we got to Mango Street we were six—Mama, Papa, Carlos, Kiki, my sister Nenny and me.

The house on Mango Street is ours and we don't have to pay rent to anybody or share the yard with the people downstairs or be careful not to make too much noise and there isn't a landlord banging on the ceiling with a broom. But even so, it's not the house we'd thought we'd get.

We had to leave the flat on Loomis quick. The water pipes broke and the landlord wouldn't fix them because the house was too old. We had to leave fast. We were using the washroom next door and carrying water over in empty milk gallons. That's why Mama and Papa looked for a house, and that's why we moved into the house on Mango Street, far away, on the other side of town.

They always told us that one day we would move into a house, a real house that would be ours for always so we wouldn't have to move each year. And our house would have running water and pipes that worked. And inside it would have real stairs, not hallway stairs, but stairs inside like the houses on T.V. And we'd have a basement and at least three washrooms so when we took a bath we didn't have to tell everybody. Our house would be white with trees around it, a great big yard and grass growing without a fence. This was the house Papa talked about when he held a lottery ticket and this was the house Mama dreamed up in the stories she told us before we went to bed.

But the house on Mango Street is not the way they told it at all. It's small 5 and red with tight little steps in front and windows so small you'd think they were holding their breath. Bricks are crumbling in places, and the front door is so swollen you have to push hard to get in. There is no front yard, only four little elms the city planted by the curb. Out back is a small garage for the car we don't own yet and a small yard that looks smaller between the two buildings on either side. There are stairs in our house, but they're ordinary hallway stairs, and the house has only one washroom, very small. Everybody has to share a bedroom—Mama and Papa, Carlos and Kiki, me and Nenny.

Once when we were living on Loomis, a nun from my school passed by and saw me playing out front. The laundromat downstairs had been boarded up because it had been robbed two days before and the owner had painted on the wood YES WE'RE OPEN so as not to lose business.

Where do you live? she asked.

There, I said pointing up to the third floor.

You live *there?*

There. I had to look to where she pointed—the third floor, the paint peel- 10 ing, wooden bars Papa had nailed on the windows so we wouldn't fall out. You live *there?* The way she said it made me feel like nothing. *There.* I lived *there.* I nodded.

I knew then I had to have a house. A real house. One I could point to. But this isn't it. The house on Mango Street isn't it. For the time being, Mama says. Temporary, says Papa. But I know how those things go.

Questions

1. Setting (place, circumstances, and time) are often vitally important in literature and in our daily lives. How does the setting play a role in this selection?
2. How does the setting, as well as the conversation with the nun, affect Esperanza's sense of self (her identity)?
3. How does this story help you answer the following questions? When does a house become a home? What is the so-called "American dream," and

how does one achieve it? What spiritual issues lie behind the dream of owning a home?

4. What are your reactions after reading this selection? Do you feel close to Esperanza? Do you have empathy toward her? Why or why not?

BICH MINH NGUYEN

Bich Minh Nguyen (b. 1974) was born in Vietnam. As a baby, she and her family narrowly escaped from the country when the Communists took over the southern capital of Saigon. In time, her family settled in Grand Rapids, Michigan. She earned an M.F.A. in creative writing from the University of Michigan and she now teaches at Purdue University. She has published a successful novel, *Short Girls* (2009), edited anthologies of short stories and essays, and written a memoir, *Stealing Buddha's Dinner* (2007).

Her memoir focuses on her childhood experiences in Grand Rapids. Her writing style is simple, yet enticing as she shares her innocent perceptions of herself and her American experience. Added dimensions of her story include the economic and cultural struggles of her family; her hard-drinking, hardworking Vietnamese father who marries and eventually divorces a Latina woman; her haphazard training in Buddhism from her grandmother; her exposure to evangelical Christianity from the little girl next door; and her attempts to find an American identity by eating American food, listening to pop music, and watching television. The book's title, *Stealing Buddha's Dinner*, is based on a brief moment in this selection when Nguyen steals a plum from the family's altar to Buddha.

Nguyen's struggles are unique, yet they are also very common. She wonders about moral and religious issues, but lacks guidance. She feels guilt, thankfulness, envy, and loneliness. She is honestly human as she searches for a unifying vision of herself, her family, her social experiences, and the universe.

When reading this selection, it is helpful to know the following details about the names and relationships:

Noi is Nguyen's Buddhist grandmother.

Anh is Nguyen's sister.

Rosa is Nguyen's Hispanic stepmother. Rosa has rejected her Roman Catholic heritage and works hard managing the family, helping others in need, and studying sociology.

Jennifer Vander Wal is the girl next door. Nguyen and Jennifer often play and talk together. During the summer described in this section, Jennifer is practicing for a part in a play at her church.

The program, "Agapaopolis," is a vacation Bible school program sponsored by the evangelical church. (*Agape* is the Greek word for the highest kind of love and *polis* means city. Thus, the program is about a city of godly love, but young Nguyen seems to be clueless about the deeper meaning of the church's program.)

FROM STEALING BUDDHA'S DINNER

My sister Anh and I attended Catholic School for four days in the fall of 1982. St. Joseph's Elementary had old stone halls that arched into echoes when I and the other third-graders followed Sister Wendy down to the library. Much to my disappointment, the younger nuns wore regular clothes. I only saw black-clad figures and wimples, the fabric stirring slightly, on the older nuns, the administrator nuns. My frame of reference for them was *The Sound of Music,* and I kept hoping that these nuns would break into song. But there were no wayward Marias in this lot. . .

Like many immigrant parents, mine believed in education as a ticket, a necessity, and the only way forward. Rosa believed in it more than anyone; she'd devoted her whole career to it. But therein lay one of her many contradictions. She worked in public schools, and had thrown off the mantle of her Catholic upbringing years ago, but she also believed that St. Joseph's would provide us with better learning and discipline, the latter of which Anh and I both needed, being prone to temper tantrums.

On that first day of school, before we got our uniforms, Anh wore her favorite dress. It was my favorite, too: a beautiful emerald-green polyester that I called silk, with covered buttons and a sash. At recess—she never had a problem making friends—I watched her from my solitary spot on a wooden jungle gym. She and a group of girls were playing basketball. Her skirt swished as she dribbled the ball, the fabric shining in the sunlight. The next day we had stiff, pleated navy jumpers, plaid blouses, white knee socks. Even though the uniform was scratchy and uncomfortable, I liked that having it meant one less thing to worry about. If everyone dressed the same, I reasoned, everyone would fit in the same. But when I walked into the classroom and all of the students swiveled their heads to stare at me, I remembered that a uniform could not hide my skin or my face. I didn't know then that many Vietnamese were actually Catholics and that some of the refugees in Grand Rapids had been sponsored by local Catholic churches. I didn't know there was any tension between Catholics and Reformed Christians. All such subtleties escaped me; I was still trying to figure out who God was supposed to be.

At lunchtime, everyone ate right at their desks. There was no cafeteria at St. Joseph's and no talking among the students. All morning my gaze had returned to the crucifix pinned above the chalkboard in the center of the room. Sister-Wendy informed us that we would take turns saying the lunchtime prayer, and she called on a wispy girl named Lindsay to go first. Lindsay stood up and launched an effortless speech having something to do with gratefulness and Mary, holy mother of God. I copied the other students by lowering my head and pretending to keep my eyes closed, but I was wondering how Mary could be the mother of God. Plus, wasn't she supposed to be a virgin? I knew well the images of Mary with her tranquil expression and blue robe. I pictured her gently chastising God, whom I pictured as Zeuslike, sporting a great flowing beard.

When everyone said "Amen" I repeated it softly. I spent the rest of the lunch hour realizing that I, too, would be called on at some point to say the prayer. There were a little over a dozen of us in the class, which meant that everyone would be praying out loud many times over the course of the year. I wondered if people would simply repeat themselves, and if they did, if they would get in trouble. Were there points for originality? Creativity? Expression? This was public speaking of a terrifying kind, and I knew I could not surmount it. How could I utter words that I' had dismissed to Jennifer Vander Wal? I could not give thanks, or bow. my head legitimately, or declare *Amen.*

At home I told Rosa about the prayers. She sat down at once to write notes for me and Anh, informing our teachers that we were Buddhist and not Catholic, and therefore not allowed to lead the prayer, ever. The next day Sister Wendy read the note with a somber face. I could see the disapproval in her eyes, and when she put the paper away she glanced at me as if I were some strange, unsightly specimen that she did not know how to treat.

Because St. Joseph's started a full week ahead of public school, I finally got to celebrate my end-of-August birthday during the school year. Birthdays, everyone knew, could only be celebrated appropriately if the birthday kid brought candy for the whole class. Rosa surprised me by buying exactly the kind I wanted: Hershey's miniatures, the variety pack with mini Mr. Goodbars, Krackles, regular Hershey's, and my beloved Special Dark. My classmates regarded me with frank assessment as I handed out the candy. Word had gotten around that I was excused from prayer, which maybe explained why I hadn't yet made any friends. Possibly I was aligned with Satan, someone come to test their faith. Or I was someone to be approached with care, the way missionaries' subjects have to be won over and then broken down. But perhaps they also felt pity, a kind of danger as they unwrapped the chocolates and pressed them into their mouths.

Two days later Rosa pulled Anh and me out of St. Joseph's. She chalked it up to the reality of tuition fees, the chore of keeping our uniforms clean, and having to drive us to and from school every day. The fact was that Ken-O-Sha was an easy three blocks from our house, walkable in any weather. Rosa didn't mention religion, but I knew that was one of the reasons. She had abandoned Catholicism—though a few years later she would reconsider it—and she preferred to keep our household that way, too. Each December my siblings and I would help Rosa unfold the trusty artificial Christmas tree and trim it with the ornaments we had made out of metallic ribbons and Styrofoam balls, thinking only of the gifts we might get to unwrap. In school, we sang "O Come All Ye Faithful" and "Joy to the World" and failed to connect the words to the religion. "Oh, it's just Christmas," my stepmother said. "Nobody has to think about religion until they're grown up."

But of course I did think about it, especially when I moved into my grandmother's room to get away from my sisters. Noi couldn't read my diary, and she didn't mind if I used her closet as my own hideaway. For a while we shared her double bed until Rosa bought me a convertible chair that unfolded into a single bed.

Every evening Noi meditated, sitting on her bedroom floor in front of the family altar and Buddha statue, her back perfectly straight. She didn't stir at all, not even when I barged in, forgetting the hour. When we settled into bed we always slept with our heads facing Buddha as a sign of respect. It wouldn't do to stick our feet out to him. With such a figure looming above me, I thought a lot about reincarnation. I had always vaguely accepted it as the answer to the question of what would happen after death. It made sense to me that one could return and live again. "You get better and better lives," Rosa explained to me, "depending on what kind of person you are in your life now." She talked about reincarnation as something positive, and didn't mention nirvana at all. My father never said anything to correct her.

I took this view of reincarnation on literal terms. I began to guess at the lives I had had. I became convinced that I had once been a sad and lonely blond girl who lived in a cold mansion isolated on a moor in England. I saw myself sitting close to the fireplace in my bedroom, looking out the window at a bleak, gray landscape. No visitors. I had died young there. Then I began to worry about my next life. In terms of being a good person, I had to admit that I wasn't much of one. I often wished Jennifer Vander Wal might fall in mud and spoil her clothes or that Anh and Crissy might receive electric shocks when they tried to read my diary. I harbored hateful feelings toward Rosa and my father— for not letting me join the class trip to Kellogg's cereal factory, for not getting me the backpack I wanted, for yelling at me when they thought I looked at them askance. With such vengeance churning in my mind, I worried I was already doomed to a much worse life the next time around. I began imagining horrible possibilities that lay in wait for me: I could be a street urchin, a burglar, a starving farmer. I pictured myself imprisoned and a chill went through me as if to confirm the truth of the premonition. I was a criminal in the making. Next life's lifer.

. . .

In the early years in Grand Rapids, my grandmother attended Buddhist temple in a rented house on the south side of town. She was one of the leaders of this makeshift community, and when she stepped out of my father's car on Sunday mornings, wearing her dark *ao dai* and jade pearls, everyone nodded at her with deference. Slowly, she and her friends gathered donations to purchase a vacant church. It sat on a barren plot of land in a section of town that in twenty years would be overrun with strip malls and nail salons. My father helped renovate the church, removing all of the pews to create one open room, refinishing the wood floors to a high gleam, carting in a Buddha statue for the altar. The Buddha stood ten feet tall, a golden presence among masses of flowers and candles.

On Sundays, monks in mustard-colored robes led the prayers and I remember watching Noi join the rows of people already prostrating themselves, all chanting the same chant. I wanted to join, too, but my old shyness kept me hesitating at the door. I worried that I would slip in my socks and fall, causing a scene. In this environment Noi seemed almost unknown to me. She wasn't my grandmother then, but a spiritual being. I backed away and headed to the basement, where women were setting up *cha gio* and sweet bean pastries. My father, who mostly came to temple to socialize with his friends, was already laughing with them in a circle. I felt so out of place—too American, not truly Buddhist—that I never did muster the nerve to enter the prayer room, let alone approach the imposing statue of Buddha.

I decided to practice at home. Here, Buddha was a lot smaller and more familiar to me. He sat on his old shelf, cross-legged, his robe draping in his lap as he held his hands together, palms up. He wore a finely pebbled cap. He had closed eyes and droopy earlobes, which my father said signified his princely origins. It amused Noi to see me taking notes on when to light the candles and incense. She clasped her hands at her chest, rocking them to a repeated singsong chant, every so often stepping forward to tap the little copper bell that lay on the altar. When she bowed and prostrated herself I did the same, trying to pick up the meaning of the movements. Once, when I asked, my father tried to explain the nature of Buddhist prayer to me. "It's not like when the people in church pray to God," he said.

My father said that when Noi meditated she emptied her mind of all thoughts. He claimed that once, in Vietnam, she did it so completely that she began to levitate, her body becoming as weightless as her mind.

As I meditated, I kept my back straight. Noi was strict about that; if she came across one of us kids slouching in front of the TV or at the table she'd give our backs a good hard poke with her finger. After a while, the posture did become habitual, but it didn't help keep my mind from wandering. I thought about ways to empty my mind of all thoughts. *Empty empty empty,* I thought, then chastised myself for thinking it. The more I tried to clear my head, the more cluttered it became. I thought about how Blair Warner on *The Facts of Life* kept her hair so beautifully wavy. I thought about the Rick Springfield record I wanted for my birthday, remembering the tension of the "Jessie's Girl" video—Rick staring at himself in the bathroom mirror, then smashing it with his guitar. *I wanna tell her that I love her but the point is probably moot.* I thought about Noi's room: the blue comforter, the little TV that gave us *Days of Our Lives* and *Silver Spoons;* the stereo system and stack of Vietnamese opera and folk song cassettes. Over the two windows, one looking out on Florence Street and the other facing the Harrisons' house, vinyl shades hung beneath gauzy white curtains. Behind me, Noi's cultivated plants grew and grew.

After a while I couldn't help opening my eyes. Even before I adjusted to the dark I focused on the solid wood credenza that served as the altar. Among the candles, incense, trays of fruit, and vases of gladioli stood black-and-white portraits of my grandfather and uncle—both of them so young and handsome when they died—and Noi's mother. She looked stern and regal, the opaqueness of her *ao dai* matched by her round velvet hat. It had taken my father three years of letters, with American dollars hidden carefully between the pages, to get my grandfather's and uncle's ashes dug up from the burial ground in Saigon and sent to us in Michigan. Noi couldn't bear the thought of abandoning them in Vietnam. At least her parents' ashes were safe in Hanoi with her sisters.

It didn't scare me to think of them resting in the ceramic, floral-patterned urns. My father had always said that their spirits were with us and it seemed a comfort. Not a ghost, but something like memory, a respect for the past. It made sense, too, to offer fruit to the spirits and Buddha. At each mealtime Noi also set aside a plate for the ancestors; she would never let anyone go hungry. Buddha, of course, had more abstemious tastes and didn't need so much. Whatever Noi set on the altar took on a glow of greater resonance, turning an ordinary orange into a radiant globe. In the fall and winter there were apples, pears, tangerines, oranges, and grapefruit. Summer meant plums, peaches, nectarines, and cantaloupe. Bananas were year-round, if they were smooth and unspotted, and sometimes grapes if Noi could get them past Rosa's boycott. The most treasured fruits were mangoes, pomegranates, kiwis, and pineapples. Then, after a period of days that only Noi determined, she would take a piece of fruit from its wrought-iron tray and it would be transformed into human food again.

On Tet, Buddha's birthday, and the anniversary of her husband's and son's deaths, Noi added to the altar an expensive assortment of dried papaya, persimmon, and coconut, tins of cashews and pistachios, and plates heaped with *banh chung* rice cakes, red bean cake pastries, *cha gio,* noodle dishes, and fried shrimp chips. I would imagine my ancestors and relatives descending into the room. They would be more invisible than Wonder Woman's plane outlined in white. They would pick at the fruit, perhaps wishing for the kinds my father talked about having in Vietnam, like the one my father used to hack open on a tree stump with a cleaver. *Stinkyfruit,* he called it, sighing with remembered satisfaction.

. . .

The summer after my third-grade year, I helped Jennifer Vander Wal practice songs for her Sunday school musical. She was only in the chorus, and fiercely resented the girl who had gotten the lead female role of Susie, a vain character who had to learn her lesson that pride goeth before a fall. Still, Jennifer and I practiced every line of *Agapaopolis.* According to the songs, it was a wonderful place—part Candyland, part Disneyland, part heaven. Jennifer had tapes of the musical from Zondervan, a big Christian bookstore based in Grand Rapids, and we listened to the cheerful melodies for hours. "Agapaopo*lisss,*" we sang together. "A place you're wishing that you are!" The star of the show was a gentle young boy who spent the musical leading his friends toward the gates of Agapaopolis. Susie, on the other hand, tossed her hair about and pranced onstage. Jennifer sang Susie's lines with bitterness: "Looking out for good ol' number one, always looking out for good ol' number one. Think you're gonna make it into high society, but you've got a lot to learn about humility!"

One day Jennifer invited her best friends from school, Amy and Rachel, to play with us. They were also in the *Agapaopolis* chorus, and after a practice session—Jennifer loved to be the stand-in for Susie—we played four square in the Vander Wals' driveway. As we bounced a basketball back and forth to each other we compared notes on Clearbrook Christian versus Ken-O-Sha Elementary. At Clearbrook, the girls informed me, everyone liked Dandy Bars and only Jell-O brand pudding cups would do. "We like Swiss Miss," I lied, citing the cheaper brand that my stepmother sometimes bought. Rachel, a tall girl with a close crop of brassy curls, said, "What's your favorite song? *We* like 'There's Always Something There to Remind Me.'"

"I have the *Thriller* record," I bragged, though really it was Anh's, paid for with some of her birthday money. Jennifer had disobeyed her parents when she listened to it, admiring the glow of Michael Jackson's white cuffs on the album cover. Her parents screened every element of media for possible dirtiness; they were suspicious of videos, music with good beats, and anything that might be associated with break dancing. Though my parents had their own worries about dirty music, they couldn't help liking Michael Jackson and his excellent dance moves.

"Wanna go listen to it?" I asked. "We can watch videos, too."

"Can we?" Amy asked, looking to her friends for guidance.

"*I* have records we can listen to," Jennifer said. I knew she meant the Christian ballads her parents collected for her. She always upped the moral ante around her Clearbrook friends. "Anyway, I want to practice *Agapaopolis* again."

"You should see the 'Billie Jean' video," I said to Amy and Rachel. "It's totally awesome."

"We're not supposed to listen to that song," Rachel said primly, sending the basketball in my direction. "It goes against the Lord."

I bounced it back. "How do you know?"

"You just know, just like you know the power of the Lord."

"Not *everybody* knows," Jennifer burst out contemptuously. "*Some* people aren't even baptized and they're going to hell."

I threw the ball with greater force, sending Amy scrambling after it. When she tossed it back I held the ball, pausing the game. I couldn't stop myself from speaking. "If there's a God he can strike me down right now," I said. The girls shrank back and exchanged looks. They waited, perhaps for God to indeed strike me down. For just a moment I waited, too. The cloud puffs in the blue sky shifted a little. A breeze rippled the leaves of the Vander Wals' birch tree, whose bark Jennifer and I had often peeled off to use as paper for our notes. I knew I would have to go home after this, leave Jennifer and her friends to their Kool-Aid and cookies, their dolls and their gossip, their *Agapaopolis*. Later, after Jennifer had had time to think the day over, she would tell me that God is forgiving. That He would give me so many chances to reach out to Him if only I just would.

When the premiere of *Agapaopolis* arrived, I declined Jennifer's invitation to come along to the church and watch. In spite of my curiosity to see the hated girl who played Susie, and to see the production whose songs I had practiced for weeks, I didn't want to sit in the audience with the rest of the Vander Wal family, surrounded by other Christians. I would be too outnumbered, the obvious outsider, nonbeliever, the black-haired possible devil.

Maybe because I was surrounded by so much Christianity, I often regarded Buddha as a stand-in for God. I prayed to him many times for things I wanted: Top 40 albums, new shoes, chocolate cake. I prayed for miracles, too: twenty-twenty vision, a pretty face, big bank accounts for my parents. Whenever God was cited—in the Pledge of Allegiance or on coins—in my mind I substituted the word *Buddha*.

I prayed often during that *Agapaopolis* summer. As I ate ice cream sandwiches from Gas City or filched my favorite blue-hued Otter Pops from the freezer, I would pray for Rosa to realize she should buy me as many sweets as I liked. I prayed for prettier clothes, more money, my own bedroom filled with books and records and tapes. It was a summer of Laura Branigan's "Solitaire," the Police warning us about every breath we took, and David Bowie murmuring "shhhh" to his little China Girl. Crissy was off with her forbidden friends while Anh and I roamed, restless, turning up the radio whenever WGRD played Culture Club and Duran Duran. We played four square, Life, and pickle with Jennifer and our brothers. We watched MTV, wishing we could be as cool as Martha Quinn. All the while I prayed, yet none of my prayers were answered. I woke up with the same blurry vision, the same flat face punctured by the two dimples I hated, the same shortness that made tall people's elbows a constant danger.

So I decided to take it one step further. It was time to tempt Buddha's wrath and see what happened.

One late afternoon when Noi was out watering the garden, I slipped into her room. For once, I was practically alone in the house.

As I studied the altar, I realized that fruit was all that Buddha had to eat. Except for holidays it was the same thing day in and day out—lunch was dinner, dinner was breakfast. My father had tried to explain that Buddha believed in simplicity and having as few things as possible. So I guessed that he was okay with just fruit—maybe he even preferred it. I couldn't comprehend that. Looking up at Buddha I wanted to ask, *That's all?* I didn't know what it was not to want.

For I could hardly name all the different meals I wished to have. Dinners of sirloin tips and Shake 'n Bake. Beef Stroganoff and shepherd's pie. Jeno's pizzas and thermoses of SpaghettiOs. Great squares of Jell-O bouncing through the air as they did in the commercials; Bundt cakes; chocolate parfaits; rounds of crusty lattice-topped pies.

In Noi's room the shades were closed against the sun. The air smelled of her favorite sandalwood incense. I sat on the bed for a moment, listening to the quiet of the house. The heat pressed in on me and I shut my eyes, trying to meditate. But I could think of nothing but the altar. The burnished statue of Buddha rose above me. His always closed eyes, his gown of glimmering folds. He was nothing like the fat, happy Buddha Statue we had in the basement. That Buddha, dyed a festive red, had an open mouth and eyes squished up in laughter. He sat with one knee raised, showing off his potbelly, not at all resembling this smooth Buddha with his face of radiant calm.

With one fingertip I touched the stem of a plum, whose violet skin always looked dusty. For just a moment, I hovered over it. Then the fruit was lying in the flat of my hand. I looked up at Buddha. His eyes were still closed. Sometimes, when we wanted to scare each other, Anh and I talked about how one day Buddha's eyes would fly open, shooting out beams of light. I waited a minute longer, until I heard the sound of the basement door opening and sliding shut. Then I ran out of the room, pushing the plum into my shorts pocket as I hurried out the front door.

I crossed our yard to the Vander Wals'—Jennifer must have been at vacation Bible school—and shimmied up their plum tree. How many times had Jennifer and I sat up here among the leaves, dreaming up one of our clubs? In the full bloom of summer the leaf-thick limbs took us in and kept us hidden. I settled into my usual spot, where two sturdy branches seemed to create a lounge chair just right for my size. I pulled Buddha's plum from my pocket and examined it as I had when my sister and I were little, marveling at the mystery of fruit. I looked for some answer in its skin but found nothing. The guilt I felt was the same as shame. I knew that this was where the test would end—me in the tree with the stolen plum. My father had said that Buddha had given up all possessions of his royal birth and become enlightened. Buddha never claimed to be a god. He could not be tested. He had no wrath. He granted no miracles or wishes. He asked me to prove nothing.

As I sat in the Vander Wals' tree, Christianity seemed about as real as Agapaopolis. It seemed as distant from my person as blond hair and blue eyes. It also seemed manipulative, what with all that fire and hell. When Jennifer talked about the Lord it was with equal parts love and fear. Noi didn't fear, or even really love, Buddha. She didn't worship him; she gave him her respect. That showed in the way we slept with our heads facing him and in the fruit, incense, and candles set forth each day. When she bowed and chanted she wasn't praying out of fear, or to save herself, or to ask for something good to happen for her. The Christians were God's minions, but Noi was not Buddha's.

I bit into the plum. I was struck, as always, by the contrast of the yellow flesh, limned with the scarlet underside of the skin. I took small bites so as not to waste a drop of juice. Too soon, the fruit was gone and the pit lay in my palm. It was an eye, I realized. A wrinkled, wizened eye. I thought about how the spirits were always watching out for us. They were never too far away. I set the eye on a branch where I could face it, and it me. I sat there for a long time. I heard the sound of Linda Vander Wal's car leaving and then returning, bringing Jennifer back from Bible school. I listened to the car doors slam and the murmur of their voices, the screen door shutting them into their house. The daylight began to glow—that quiescent hour before the beginning of sunset—and I knew it was time to go home. I left the plum's eye in the plum tree. It was gone the next time I climbed up there. I imagined it carried off by the wind, or by my ancestors' spirits, coming to collect the meager offering I had left behind.

Questions

1. Can you empathize with Nguyen's feelings of guilt (about her unkind thoughts toward other people) and her challenging spirit (she asks God to "strike her down" and she steals from Buddha)? Explain your answer.

2. Nguyen is trying to define herself in a very confusing environment. Did you have similar or different experiences in your childhood? What were some of the key experiences or insights that helped you to define yourself?

3. Nguyen is also trying to understand the nature of morality and religion. Did you have similar or different experiences that influenced your early understanding of morality and religion?
4. Are children universally curious about spiritual issues? Should religion be kept away from children, as the stepmother suggests in this selection? What is religion, and why are people interested in it?

MOVIE GUIDE FOR *SERGEANT YORK* (1941)

Directed by Howard Hawks

Screenplay by Harry Chandlee, Abem Finkel, John Huston, and Howard Koch

Sergeant York gives a fairly accurate account of a poor, young man from Tennessee named Alvin York. The context of the movie is World War I. During the first two years of the war in Europe, Americans are living peacefully. York and his community are particularly cut off from world events. But York's life quickly changes when the United States enters the war.

Underlying Themes

Because of the producers' commitment to accuracy, this movie creates a great deal of complexity for the viewer (because real life is normally more complex than we care to believe or see in a film). For example, this movie brings up many thought-provoking questions: (a) Is it right to kill another human being? (b) What exactly does the Bible say about war and killing? (c) Should the government force someone to disobey his or her conscience? (d) What relationship should exist between the government and religious groups?

Another underlying theme in this production is the inability of people (particularly York) to find the words needed to express their thoughts and feelings. On several occasions, York struggles to make his feelings understood by his sweetheart and others. When he leaves home to go to war, York does not know what to say to his loving mother, and she does not know what to say to him. Later, when he returns from the war and York has an opportunity to talk to his mother by telephone, they again struggle to know what to say. In a humorous, but sweet contrast, York's girlfriend, Gracie Williams, seems comfortable and confident in expressing her thoughts and feelings throughout the movie. This film also touches on the different dialects of English used in the United States, and the social tensions created by such dialects.

Furthermore, this film exposes the many social issues that are present in early twentieth-century American culture: (a) the poverty and ignorance that plagued many rural areas of the United States at this time, (b) the sharp divisions between folk cultures and city life, (c) the prejudices against "conscientious objectors" (and the general issue of prejudice, in all of its forms), and

(d) the temptations of fame and money in contrast to the commitment that one should have to family and to others.

In contrast to these indirect themes, the clearly dominant theme in this film is the constant presence of religion and God's providence. In scene after scene, the audience is reminded that God, church, providence, the Bible, and the devil are normal parts of York's daily life. In spite of all of these serious concerns, the movie is very humorous.

An Overview of the Movie

The movie begins by introducing young Alvin York, who enjoys wild living, fighting, and hard-drinking. His mother does not approve of York's behavior, but she understands the frustrations of her son, who is trying to farm worthless soil in order to support his poverty-stricken mother, brother, and sister. York's fighting and drinking are irresponsible, yet there is a depth to York's character. He is deeply committed to his family. In these introductory scenes, York is not interested in spiritual things, but the local pastor urges York to wait and listen for God in his life. The pastor reminds York that everyone needs spiritual "roots" to make them strong.

In time, York's attention turns to Gracie Williams, an attractive neighbor. She gives York new hope and direction in his life. Rather than drinking and fighting, York is now committed to buying some quality "bottom land" so that he can have his own farm, and then marry Gracie. Struggling against the odds, York works day and night to make the final payment on a plot of land. A crisis comes about when York runs out of time and does not have enough money to get the land. In addition to losing the chance to buy the land, York loses all of the money held on deposit for the land. This crisis pushes York back to drinking, and his anger leads to thoughts of revenge against those who have cheated him. During an electrical storm, York finally becomes aware of God's presence in his life, and he experiences a conversion to Christianity. The details of this experience are left painfully vague in the movie, but it is clear that his life has been changed. York learns to love and forgive his enemies. He also learns to trust the Bible as God's truth to guide all of his actions.

This commitment to the Bible leads to the next conflict in the story. The United States enters World War I, and York is about to be drafted into the armed forces. The problem is York's understanding of the commandment "Thou shalt not kill." York is absolutely convinced that all killing is wrong, and he is ready to rebel against the government in order to obey God. Through a long series of events, York comes to accept his service in the U.S. Army, and he eventually kills a large number of enemy soldiers in order to save the lives of others. When presenting this crisis of conscience, the moviemakers do something very unusual—they show a character quietly meditating. York struggles with the meaning of various Bible passages and with his conscience. Eventually, he comes to a conclusion while his dog waits. Normally, the media is focused on quick decisions and quick actions, so these scenes of meditation are surprising.

In time, York returns from the war as a great hero. But even the final scenes of the movie offer a complexity to the audience. The welcoming crowds and the news media view York as a hero because he has killed and captured so many enemy soldiers. Yet, the movie leads us to view York as a hero because he rejects fame and fortune to return to his simple way of life, to his family, to his community, and to his down-home sweetheart. He is also a hero because he does not want to profit from a war that has cost so many lives.

York's final words in the movie are as follows: "The Lord sure does move in mysterious ways." In the context, this comment confirms York's continuing sense that God is guiding and loving him.

Tips for Watching This Movie

As with any quality movie, viewing this film more than once is very helpful. With each viewing, consider one or two of the issues mentioned above: (a) people's struggles to express themselves, (b) the role of dialects and education in creating cultural divisions, (c) the presence of God in daily life, (d) the Christian commandment to forgive and love one's enemies, (e) the role of the Bible in life, (f) the struggle to correctly interpret the Bible, (g) the blindness caused by prejudice, and so forth.

Questions

1. In one scene, York leaves home to begin his service in the U.S. Army. The women of the family (his mother and sister) stand at the gate and ask, "What are they fighting fer?" What interpretations can be given to this scene?
2. At one point, the Army officer gives York a sermon about the importance of freedom and how it has guided American culture. Do you agree with his understanding of freedom and its role in American history? Explain your answer.
3. How does York change from the beginning of the movie until the end? In what ways does he remain the same?
4. York struggles to obey God's word and to obey the government. Eventually, he comes to a resolution. How would you resolve the questions of killing, warfare, obedience to God, obedience to the government, and obedience to one's conscience? What logic (what line of thinking) would you use to find a solution?

Chapter 5

Life, Redemption, Death, and Afterlife in Context of Spirituality

Spirituals are religious songs developed and used by African Americans during the period of slavery. At first, these songs were handed down orally. Later, they were recorded by people like Richard Allen, an influential black church leader in Philadelphia, who wanted to preserve the songs for future generations to enjoy.

Most, if not all, spirituals have religious content and express a hope that the burdens of slavery will come to an end. They express faith in the God of the Bible, refer to biblical stories, and convey a devotion to Judeo-Christian principles. A common theme is the Exodus, which is the story of the Jews' enslavement in Egypt, their passing through the Red Sea, and their eventual deliverance into God's Promised Land. Spirituals helped slaves to anticipate their own freedom, both literally and spiritually. Spirituals also helped slaves to delineate their self-worth as children of God. Such self-concepts subverted the dominant, dehumanizing perception of slaves as chattel and as inferior human beings.

Spirituals demonstrate African Americans' trust in and submission to God, yet spirituals are also subversive. The slaves used spirituals as a means for creating their religious, cultural, and personal independence. Spirituals, such as "Swing Low, Sweet Chariot," "Steal Away to Jesus," and "God's Going to Trouble the Water," express the common concerns and longings of the slaves: (a) the quest for personal and group identity; (b) a sequential hope that today's struggles will be followed by flight, migration, emancipation, and righteous judgment; and (c) a search for joy and peace that transcends the sufferings of daily life.

The two spirituals below, "Go Down Moses" and "I Know Moon-Rise," are representative of the many spirituals handed down from generation to generation. The form and style of spirituals have some similarities to Hebrew poetry and other oral poetry. Some of the form and style have roots in African oral traditions. Stylistic features include catalog, parallelism, performance, repetition, and the antiphonal call-and-response modes of language use. The tendency toward long, seemingly irrelevant repetition of names, phrases, words, and acts serves two important functions: It aids audience participation and memory. This repetition immortalizes hope and solidifies the beliefs of the community.

GO DOWN, MOSES

Go down, Moses,
Way down in Egyptland
Tell old Pharaoh
To let my people go.

When Israel was in Egyptland   5
Let my people go
Oppressed so hard they could not stand
Let my people go.

Go down, Moses,
Way down in Egyptland   10
Tell old Pharaoh
"Let my people go."

"Thus saith the Lord," bold Moses said,
"Let my people go;
If not I'll smite your first-born dead   15
Let my people go.

"No more shall they in bondage toil,
Let my people go;
Let them come out with Egypt's spoil,
Let my people go."   20

The Lord told Moses what to do
Let my people go;
To lead the children of Israel through,
Let my people go.

Go down, Moses,   25
Way down in Egyptland,
Tell old Pharaoh,
"Let my people go!"

I KNOW MOON-RISE

"I know moon-rise, I know star-rise,
*   Lay dis body down.*
I walk in de moonlight, I walk in de starlight,
*   To lay dis body down.*
I'll walk in de graveyard, I'll walk through de graveyard,   5
*   To lay dis body down.*

I'll lie in de grave and stretch out my arms;
   Lay dis body down.
I go to de judgment in de evenin' of de day,
10   *When I lay dis body down;*
And my soul and your soul will meet in de day
   When I lay dis body down."

Questions

1. Discuss the ways in which a sense of new identity or new self-concept, even pride, resonates in these two spirituals.
2. Compare the themes and formal features of the two spirituals. In what ways do they address or envisage spiritual, physical, and psychological triumph over slavery? What moral and spiritual codes do they generally assert?
3. First read "Go Down Moses" to yourself silently. Then, read the poem aloud to yourself or, even better, to a friend. What differences did you notice between the silent and the aloud readings? What effect did the repetition have when the poem was read silently? What effect did the repetition have when the poem was read aloud?
4. Read Psalm 136 in the Bible and compare it with "Go Down Moses." Now imagine a large group of people, who are divided into two subgroups, alternating the singing of stanzas from Psalm 136 and "Go Down Moses." Or, imagine a "caller," or leader, singing those stanzas, which change, and a group repeating the constant chorus or refrain. How would such group dynamics change both the intellectual and emotional experience of these two works?

WILLIAM CULLEN BRYANT

William Cullen Bryant (1794–1878) was born in Massachusetts and spent much of his adult life in New York City. From an early age, he wrote and published poetry. He also practiced law and worked as the editor and manager of a New York newspaper. In contrast to his Puritan ancestors, Bryant followed the Unitarian Church's more general affirmation of the goodness of humanity and the equality of all paths to the divine. His personal philosophy and his poetry were guided by the Romantic movement's emphasis on (a) the individual's private feelings and creativity, and (b) the morally and spiritually uplifting qualities of nature on the individual's soul.

Bryant's most famous poem, "Thanatopsis," was written when he was seventeen years of age. In this work, Bryant opens with both the beauty and harshness of nature. Then, he settles into submission to the cycle of life and death, which is very similar to Eastern religious thought. Questions surrounding death and how one should face death have long haunted humans. For example, what level of consciousness do people have after death? Bryant suggests that our individual consciousness will disappear. In the biblical Book of

Job, these same issues are mixed with Job's moral struggles. At one point in that work, Job concludes,

> *I know that my Redeemer lives,*
> *and that in the end he will stand upon the earth.*
> *And after my skin has been destroyed,*
> *yet in my flesh I will see God;*
>
> *I myself will see him*
> *with my own eyes—I, and not another.*
> *How my heart yearns within me! (Job 19:25–27 NIV)*

It is interesting to contrast the reflections found in Bryant's poem with those of the biblical character of Job.

THANATOPSIS

To him who in the love of Nature holds
Communion with her visible forms, she speaks
A various language; for his gayer hours
She has a voice of gladness, and a smile
And eloquence of beauty, and she glides   5
Into his darker musings, with a mild
And healing sympathy, that steals away
Their sharpness, ere he is aware. When thoughts
Of the last bitter hour come like a blight
Over thy spirit, and sad images   10
Of the stern agony, and shroud, and pall,
And breathless darkness, and the narrow house,
Make thee to shudder, and grow sick at heart;—
Go forth, under the open sky, and list
To Nature's teachings, while from all around—   15
Earth and her waters, and the depths of air—
Comes a still voice.—

                Yet a few days, and thee
The all-beholding sun shall see no more
In all his course; nor yet in the cold ground,   20
Where thy pale form was laid, with many tears,
Nor in the embrace of ocean, shall exist
Thy image. Earth, that nourished thee, shall claim
Thy growth, to be resolved to earth again,
And, lost each human trace, surrendering up   25
Thine individual being, shalt thou go
To mix for ever with the elements,
To be a brother to the insensible rock
And to the sluggish clod, which the rude swain

30 *Turns with his share, and treads upon. The oak*
    Shall send his roots abroad, and pierce thy mould.

        Yet not to thine eternal resting-place
    Shalt thou retire alone, nor couldst thou wish
    Couch more magnificent. Thou shalt lie down
35 *With patriarchs of the infant world—with kings,*
    The powerful of the earth—the wise, the good,
    Fair forms, and hoary seers of ages past,
    All in one mighty sepulchre. The hills
    Rock-ribbed and ancient as the sun,—the vales
40 *Stretching in pensive quietness between;*
    The venerable woods—rivers that move
    In majesty, and the complaining brooks
    That make the meadows green; and, poured round all,
    Old Ocean's gray and melancholy waste,—
45 *Are but the solemn decorations all*
    Of the great tomb of man. The golden sun,
    The planets, all the infinite host of heaven,
    Are shining on the sad abodes of death,
    Through the still lapse of ages. All that tread
50 *The globe are but a handful to the tribes*
    That slumber in its bosom.—Take the wings
    Of morning, pierce the Barcan wilderness,
    Or lose thyself in the continuous woods
    Where rolls the Oregon, and hears no sound,
55 *Save his own dashings—yet the dead are there:*
    And millions in those solitudes, since first
    The flight of years began, have laid them down
    In their last sleep—the dead reign there alone.
    So shalt thou rest, and what if thou withdraw
60 *In silence from the living, and no friend*
    Take note of thy departure? All that breathe
    Will share thy destiny. The gay will laugh
    When thou art gone, the solemn brood of care
    Plod on, and each one as before will chase
65 *His favorite phantom; yet all these shall leave*
    Their mirth and their employments, and shall come
    And make their bed as thee. As the long train
    Of ages glides away, the sons of men,
    The youth in life's fresh spring, and he who goes
70 *In the full strength of years, matron and maid,*
    The speechless babe, and the gray-headed man—
    Shall one by one be gathered to thy side,
    By those, who in their turn shall follow them.

        So live, that when thy summons comes to join
75 *The innumerable caravan, which moves*

To that mysterious realm, where each shall take
His chamber in the silent halls of death,   80
Thou go not, like the quarry-slave at night,
Scourged to his dungeon, but, sustained and soothed
By an unfaltering trust, approach thy grave,
Like one who wraps the drapery of his couch
About him, and lies down to pleasant dreams.

Questions

1. How did Bryant define "death" in this poem? What assumptions about reality are guiding that definition?
2. What did Bryant mean when he wrote, "Nature [. . .] speaks / A various language"? What types of messages do people find in nature?
3. When considering life and death, what advice did the poet give to the reader?
4. Bryant did not give a specific definition of the terms *God* or the *human spirit* in this poem. What did Bryant seem to mean by these terms? What evidence do you have for your conclusions?

BENJAMIN FRANKLIN

Benjamin Franklin (1706–1790) was very much a "Founding Father" of the United States. His career, his values, and his personal goals helped to shape the direction and personality of the thirteen colonies and the country that developed from them. Although he was not a deeply religious man, Franklin's parents and his religious culture trained him to focus on moral introspection, individualism, hard work, creativity, and social service. As a result, Franklin taught Americans, through his writings and through his energetic lifestyle, to follow his Puritan heritage. The extremely popular *Poor Richard's Almanack,* published each year from 1733 to 1758, was a printed expression of Franklin's personality. His career as an inventor, scientist, diplomat, and public servant also expressed ideals that many Americans adopted. It seems that Franklin believed that God created the world and gently guided human affairs; he also believed that each individual needs to carefully and consciously guide his or her life by following strict moral principles. Thus, his life and his writings implied that hard work is one's own salvation.

THE EPHEMERA: AN EMBLEM OF HUMAN LIFE

You may remember, my dear friend, that when we lately spent that happy day in the delightful garden and sweet society of the Moulin Joly, I stopped a little in one of our walks and stayed some time behind the company. We had been shown numberless skeletons of a kind of little fly, called an ephemera, whose successive generations, we were told, were bred and expired within the day. I

happened to see a living company of them on a leaf, who appeared to be engaged in conversation. You know I understand all the inferior animal tongues.
My too great application to the study of them is the best excuse I can give for
the little progress I have made in your charming language. I listened through
curiosity to the discourse of these little creatures; but as they, in their national
vivacity, spoke three or four together, I could make but little of their conversation. I found, however, by some broken expressions that I heard now and
then, they were disputing warmly on the merit of two foreign musicians, one a
cousin, the other a *moscheto;* in which dispute they spent their time, seemingly as regardless of the shortness of life as if they had been sure of living a
month. Happy people! thought I, you are certainly under a wise, just, and
mild government, since you have no public grievances to complain of, nor
any subject of contention but the perfections and imperfections of foreign
music! I turned my head from them to an old gray-headed one, who was single on another leaf, and talking to himself. Being amused with his soliloquy,
I put it down in writing, in hopes it will likewise amuse her to whom I am so
much indebted for the most pleasing of all amusements, her delicious company and heavenly harmony.

　　"It was," said he, "the opinion of learned philosophers of our race, who
lived and flourished long before my time, that this vast world, the Moulin Joly,
could not itself subsist more than eighteen hours; and I think there was some
foundation for that opinion, since, by the apparent motion of the great luminary
that gives life to all nature, and which in my time has evidently declined considerably toward the ocean at the end of our earth, it must then finish its course,
be extinguished in the waters that surround us, and leave the world in cold and
darkness, necessarily producing universal death and destruction. I have lived
seven of those hours, a great age, being no less than four hundred and twenty
minutes of time. How very few of us continue so long! I have seen generations
born, flourish, and expire. My present friends are the children and grandchildren of the friends of my youth, who are now, alas, no more! And I must soon
follow them; for, by the course of nature, though still in health, I cannot expect
to live above seven or eight minutes longer. What now avails all my toil and
labor in amassing honeydew on this leaf, which I cannot live to enjoy! What the
political struggles I have been engaged in for the good of my compatriot inhabitants of this bush, or my philosophical studies for the benefit of our race in
general! for in politics, what can laws do without morals? Our present race of
ephemerae will in a course of minutes become corrupt, like those of other and
older bushes, and consequently as wretched. And in philosophy how small our
progress! Alas! art is long, and life is short! My friends would comfort me with
the idea of a name they say I shall leave behind me; and they tell me I have
lived long enough to nature and to glory. But what will fame be to an
ephemera who no longer exists? And what will become of all history in the
eighteenth hour, when the world itself, even the whole Moulin Joly, shall come
to its end, and be buried in universal ruin?"

　　To me, after all my eager pursuits, no solid pleasures now remain but the
reflection of a long life spent in meaning well, the sensible conversation of a

few good lady ephemerae, and now and then a kind smile and a tune from the ever amiable *Brillante*.

B. Franklin

Questions

1. From the context of the essay, what does Franklin mean by the term *Moulin Joly?*
2. From this short piece, what seems to be Franklin's conclusions about the meaning and purpose of life? What role does the spiritual have in this meaning and purpose?
3. What types of relationships are most important to Franklin?
4. In what ways do you agree with Franklin? In what ways do you disagree with Franklin and his society?

HENRY JAMES

Henry James (1843–1916) was born into a family of American intellectuals. Because his family had some wealth, he was able to get much of his early education from tutors across Europe. Later, James spent much of his adult life in England. James was a very creative writer who carefully explored the relationships and personal perspectives of his characters. As a result, he has been called a psychological novelist. It is interesting that his famous brother, William James, also explored human thoughts, emotions, and relationships in his chosen fields of philosophy and psychology. Henry James wrote twenty-two novels and many short stories.

Henry James's story, "The Middle Years," invites us to consider the calling of the artist and the nature of art. In her article, "The Madness of Art: Henry James's 'The Middle Years'," Joyce Carol Oates says that "clearly, 'The Middle Years' is a confession of the artist's anxiety over the worth of his art and the terrifying aloneness to which the demands of his art have brought him." There is an interesting contrast between this summary of James's story and the account of Adam and Eve in Genesis 2 and 3. In Genesis, the humans are first given community and meaningful work in the Garden of Eden. Later, after the humans rebel against God's plan and authority, their sense of community is lost and their work is unsatisfying. Behind this theme of community and meaningful work seems to be a universal search for personal significance and spiritual meaning. James's story helps us to consider these concerns.

THE MIDDLE YEARS

The April day was soft and bright, and poor Dencombe, happy in the conceit of reasserted strength, stood in the garden of the hotel, comparing, with a deliberation, in which, however, there was still something of languor, the attractions of easy strolls. Ho liked the feeling of the south, so far as yon could have it in the north, he liked the sandy cliffs and the clustered pines, he liked even the colorless sea. "Bournemouth as a health-resort" had always sounded second-rate to him, but now he was reconciled to the moderate. The sociable country postman, passing through the garden, had just given him a small parcel, which he took out with him, leaving the hotel to the right and creeping to a convenient bench that he knew of, a safe recess in the cliff. It looked to the south, to the tinted walls of the island, and was protected behind by the sloping shoulder of the down. Ho was sufficiently tired when ho reached it, and for a moment he was disappointed; he was better, of course, but better, after all, than what? He should never again, as at one or two great moments of the past, be better than himself. The infinite of life had gone, and what was left of the dose was a small glass engraved like a thermometer by the apothecary. He sat and stared at the sea, which appeared all surface and twinkle, far shallower than the spirit of man. It was the abyss of human illusion that was the real, the tideless deep, He held his packet, which had come by book-post, unopened on his knee, liking, in the lapse of so many joys (his illness had made him feel his age), to know that it was there, but taking for granted there could be no complete renewal. of the pleasure, dear to young experience, of seeing one's self "just out." Dencombe, who had a reputation, had come out too often and knew too well in advance how he should look.

His postponement associated itself vaguely, after a little, with a group of three persons, two ladies and a young man, whom, beneath him, straggling and seemingly silent, he could see move slowly together along the sands. The gentleman had his head bent over a book and was occasionally brought to a stop by the charm of this volume, which, as Dencombe could perceive even at a distance, had a cover intensely red. Then his companions, going a little farther, waited for him to come up, poking their parasols into the beach, looking around them at the sea and sky, and clearly sensible of the beauty of the day. To these things the young man with the book was still more clearly indifferent; lingering, credulous, absorbed, he was an object, of envy to an observer from whose connection with literature all such artlessness had faded. One of the ladies was large and mature; the other had the spareness of comparative youth and of a social situation possibly inferior. The large lady carried back Dencombe's imagination to the age of crinoline; she wore a hat of the shape of a mushroom, decorated with a blue veil, and had the air, in her aggressive amplitude, of clinging to a vanished fashion or even a lost cause. Presently her companion produced from under the folds of a mantle a limp, portable chair which she stiffened out and of which the large lady took possession. This act, and something in the movement of either party, instantly characterised the performers—they performed for Dencombe's recreation—as opulent matron and humble dependant. What, moreover, was the use of being an approved novelist if one couldn't establish a relation between such figures; as, for instance, that the young man was the son of the opulent matron, and that the humble dependant, the daughter of a clergyman or an officer, nourished a secret passion for him? Was that not visible from the way she stole behind her protectress to look back at him?—back to where he had let himself come to a full stop when his mother sat down to rest. His book was a novel; it had the catch-penny cover, and while the romance of life stood neglected at his aide he lost himself in that of the circulating library. He moved mechanically to where the sand was softer, and ended by plumping down in it to finish his chapter at his ease. The humble dependant, discouraged by his remoteness, wandered, with a sensitive droop of the head, in another direction, and the exorbitant lady, watching the waves, offered a confused resemblance to a flying-machine that had broken down.

When his drama began to drop Dencombe remembered that he had, after all, another pastime. Though such promptitude on the part of the publisher was rare, he was already able to draw from its wrapper his "latest," perhaps his last The cover of "The Middle Years" was properly meretricious, the smell of the fresh pages was sweet; but for the moment he went no farther—he had become conscious of a strange alienation. He had forgotten what his book was about. Had the assault of his old ailment, which he had so fallaciously come to Bournemouth to ward off, interposed utter blankness as to what had preceded it? He had finished the revision of proof before quitting London, but his subsequent fortnight in bed had passed the sponge over color. He couldn't have chanted to himself a single sentence, couldn't have turned with curiosity or confidence to any particular page. His subject had already gone from him, leaving scarcely a superstition behind He uttered a low moan as he took the measure of this anomaly, so definitely it seemed to represent the progressive decay of his faculties. The tears filled his mild eyes; something precious had passed away. This was the pang that had been sharpest during the last few years—the sense of ebbing time, of shrinking opportunity; and now he felt not so much that his last chance was going as that it was gone indeed. He had done all that he should ever do, and yet he had not done what he wanted. This was the laceration—that practically his career was over: it was as violent as a rough hand at his throat. He rose from his seat nervously, like a creature haunted by a dread, then he fell back in his weakness and nervously opened his book. It was a single volume; he preferred single volumes and aimed at a rare compression. He began to read, and little by little, in this occupation, he was pacified and reassured. Everything came "back to him, but came back with a strangeness, came back, above all, with a high and magnificent beauty. He read his own prose, he turned his own leaves, and had, as he sat there with the spring sunshine on the page, an emotion peculiar and intense. His career was over, no doubt, but it was over, after all, with *that*.

He had forgotten during his illness the work of the previous year; but what he had chiefly forgotten was that it was extraordinarily good. He lived once more into his story and was drawn down, as by a siren's band, to where, in the dim underworld of fiction, great silent subjects loom. He recognized his motive and surrendered to his talent. Never, probably, had that talent, such as it was, been so great. His difficulties were still there, but what was also there, to his perception, though probably, alas! to nobody else's, was the art that in most cases had surmounted them. In his surprised enjoyment of this ability he had a glimpse of a possible reprieve. Surely its force was not spent—there was life and service in it yet. It had not come to him easily, it had been backward and roundabout. It was the child of time, the nursling of delay; he had struggled and suffered for it, making sacrifices not to be counted, and now that it was really mature was it to cease to yield, to confess itself brutally beaten? There was an infinite charm for Dencombe in feeling as he had never felt before that diligence *vincit omnia*. The result produced in his little book was somehow a result beyond his conscious intention; it was as if he had planted his genius, had trusted his method, and they had grown, up and flowered with this sweetness. If the achievement had been real, however, the process had been manful enough. What he saw so intensely to-day, what he felt as a nail driven in, was that only now, at the very last, had he come into possession. His development had been abnormally slow, almost grotesquely gradual. He had been hindered and retarded by experience, and for long periods had only groped his way. It had taken too much of his life to produce too little of his art. The art had come, but it had come after everything else. At such a rate a first existence was too short—long enough only to collect material; so that to fructify, to use the material, one must have a second age, an extension. This extension was what poor Dencombe sighed for. As he turned the last leaves of his volume he murmured, "Ah for another go!—ah for a better chance!"

The three persons he had observed on the sands had vanished and then reappeared; they had now wandered up a path, an artificial and easy ascent, which led to the top of the cliff. Dencombe's bench, was half-way down, on a sheltered ledge, and the large lady, a massive, heterogeneous person, with a bold "black eye and a kind red face, now took a few moments to rest. She wore dirty gauntlets and immense diamond ear-rings; at first she looked vulgar, but she contradicted this announcement in an agreeable off-hand voice. While her companions stood waiting for her the plumped herself on the end of Dencombe's seat. The young man had gold spectacles, through which, with his finger still in his red-covered book, he glanced at the volume, bound in the same shade of the same color, lying on the lap of the original occupant of the bench. After an instant Dencombe understood that he was struck with a resemblance, had recognized the gilt stamp on the crimson cloth, was reading "The Middle Years," and now perceived that somebody else had kept pace with him. The stranger was startled, possibly even a little ruffled, to find that he was not the only person who had been favored with an early copy. The eyes of the two proprietors met for a moment, and Dencombe derived amusement from the expression of those of his competitor, those, it might even be inferred, of his admirer. They confessed to some resentment—they seemed to say: "Hang it, has he got it *already?*— Of course he's a "brute of a reviewer!" Dencombe shuffled his copy out of eight while the opulent matron, rising from her repose, broke out: "I feel already the good of this air!"

"I can't say I do," said the scantier lady; "I find myself quite let down."

"I find myself horribly hungry. At what time did you order lunch?" her protectress pursued.

The young person put the question by. "Doctor Hugh always orders it."

"I ordered nothing to-day—I'm going to make you diet," said their comrade.

"Then I shall go home and sleep. *Qui dort dine!*"

"Can I trust you to Miss Vernham?" asked Doctor Hugh of his elder companion.

"Don't I trust *you?*" she archly inquired.

"Not too much!" Miss Vernham, with her eyes on the ground, permitted herself to declare, "You must come with us at least to the house," she went on, while the personage on whom they appeared to be in attendance began to mount higher. She had got a little out of ear-shot; nevertheless Miss Vernham became, so far as Dencombe was concerned, less distinctly audible to murmur to the young man : "I don't think you realize all you *owe* the Countess!"

Absently, a moment, Doctor Hugh caused his gold-rimmed spectacles to shine at her.

"Is that the way I strike you? I see—I see!"

"She's awfully good to us," continued Miss Vernham, compelled by her interlocutor's immovability to stand there in spite of this discussion of private matters. Of what use would it have been that Dencombe should be sensitive to shades had he not detected in that immovability a strange influence from the quiet old convalescent in the great tweed cape? Miss Vernham appeared suddenly to become aware of some such connection, for she added, in a moment: "If you want to sun yourself here you can come back after you've seen us home."

Doctor Hugh, at this, hesitated, and Dencombe, in spite of a desire to pass for unconscious, risked a covert glance at him. What his eyes met this time, as it happened, was on the part of the young lady a queer stare, naturally vitreous, which made her aspect remind him of some figure (he couldn't name it), in a play or a novel, some sinister governess or tragic old maid. She seemed to scrutinize him, to challenge him, to say with a glazed impertinence: "What have *you* got to do with us?" At the same instant the rich humor of the Countess reached them from above: "Come, come, my little lambs, you should follow your old *bergère!*" Miss Vernham turned away at this, pursuing the ascent, and Doctor Hugh, after another mute appeal to Dencombe and a moment's evident demur, deposited his book on the bench, as if to keep his place or even as a sign that he would return, and bounded without difficulty up the rougher part of the cliff.

Equally innocent and infinite are the pleasures of observation and the resources engendered by the habit of analyzing life. It amused poor Dencombe, as he dawdled in his tepid air-bath, to think that he was waiting for a revelation of something at the back of a fine young mind. He looked hard at the book on the end of the bench, but he wouldn't have touched it for the world. It served his purpose to have a theory which should not be exposed to refutation. He already felt better of his melancholy; he had, according to his old formula, put his head at the window. A passing "Countess" could draw off the fancy when, like the elder of the ladies who had just retreated, she was as obvious as the giantess of a caravan. It was indeed general views that were terrible; short ones, contrary to an opinion sometimes expressed, were the refuge, were the remedy. Doctor Hugh couldn't possibly be anything but a reviewer who had understandings for early copies with publishers or with newspapers. He reappeared in a quarter of an hour, with visible relief at finding Dencombe on the spot, and the gleam of white teeth in an embarrassed but generous smile. He was perceptibly disappointed at the eclipse of the other copy of the book; it was a pretext the less for speaking to the stranger. But he spoke, notwithstanding; he held up his own copy and broke out pleadingly:

"*Do* say, if you have occasion to speak of it, that it's the best thing he has done yet!"

Dencombe responded with a laugh: "Done yet" was so amusing to him, made such a grand avenue of the future. Better still, the young man took *him* for a reviewer! He pulled out "The Middle Years" from under his cape, but instinctively concealed any tell-tale look of paternity. This was partly because a man was always a fool for calling attention to his work. "Is that what *you're* going to say?" he inquired of his visitor.

"I'm not quite sure I shall write anything. I don't, as a regular thing—I enjoy in peace. But it's awfully fine."

Dencombe debated a moment. If his interlocutor bad begun to abuse him he would have instantly confessed to his identity, but there was no harm in drawing him on a little to praise. He drew him on with such success that in a few moments his new acquaintance was seated by his side, confessing candidly that Dencombe's novels were the only ones he could read a second time. He had come the day before from London, where a friend of his, a journalist, had lent him his copy of the last—the copy sent to the office of the journal and already the subject of a "notice" which, as was pretended there (but one had to allow for "swagger") it had taken a full quarter of an hour to prepare. He intimated that he was ashamed for his friend, and in the case of a work demanding and repaying study, of such summary practices; and with his fresh appreciation and inexplicable wish to express it, he speedily became for poor Dencombe a remarkable, a delightful apparition. Chance had brought the weary man of letters face to face with the greatest admirer in the new generation whom it was supposable he possessed. The admirer, in truth, was mystifying, so rare a case was it to find a bristling young doctor—he looked like a German physiologist—enamoured of literary form. It was an accident, but happier than most accidents, so that Dencombe, exhilarated as well as confounded, spent half an hour in making his visitor talk while he kept himself quiet. He explained his premature possession of "The Middle Years" by an allusion to the friendship of the publisher, who, knowing he was at Bournemouth for his health, had paid him this graceful attention. He admitted that he had been ill, for Doctor Hugh would infallibly have guessed it; he even went so far as to wonder whether he mightn't look for some hygienic "tip" from a personage combining so bright an enthusiasm with the latest medical lore. It would shake his faith a little perhaps to have to take a doctor seriously who could take *him* so seriously, but he enjoyed this gushing modern youth and he felt, with an acute pang, that there would still be work to do in a world in which such odd combinations were presented. It was not true, what he had tried for renunciation's sake to believe, that all the combinations were exhausted. They were not, they were not—they were infinite; the exhaustion was in the miserable artist.

Doctor Hugh was an ardent physiologist, saturated with the spirit of the age—in other words he had just taken his degree; but he was independent and various, he talked like a man who would have liked to love literature best. He would fain have made fine phrases, but nature had denied him the gift. Some of the finest in "The Middle Years" had struck him inordinately, and he took the liberty of reading them to Dencombe in support of his plea. He grew vivid, in the balmy air, to his companion, for whose deep refreshment he seemed to have been sent; and was particularly ingenuous in describing how recently he had become acquainted, and how instantly infatuated, with the only man who had put flesh between the ribs of an art that was starving on superstitions. He had not yet written to him—he was deterred by a sentiment of respect Dencombe at this moment felicitated himself more than ever on having consistently dodged the photographers. His visitor's attitude promised him a luxury of intercourse, but he surmised that a certain security in it, for Doctor Hugh, would depend not a little on the Countess. He learned without delay with what variety of Countess they were concerned, as well as the nature of the tie that united the curious trio. The large lady, an Englishwoman by birth and the daughter of a celebrated barytone, whose taste, without his talent, she had inherited, was the widow of a French nobleman and mistress of all that remained of the handsome fortune, the fruit of her father's earnings, that had constituted her dower. Miss Vernham, an odd creature but an accomplished pianist, was attached to her person at a salary. The Countess was generous, independent, eccentric; she travelled with her minstrel and her medical man. Ignorant and passionate, she had nevertheless moments in which she was almost irresistible. Dencombe saw her sit for her portrait in Doctor Hugh's free sketch, and felt the picture of his young friend's relation to her frame itself in his mind. This young friend, for a representative of the new psychology, was himself easily hypnotized, and if he became abnormally communicative it was only a sign of his real subjection. Dencombe did accordingly what he wanted with him, even without being known as Dencombe.

Taken ill on a journey in Switzerland, the Countess had picked him up at an hotel, and the accident of his happening to please her had made her offer him, with her imperious liberality, terms that couldn't fail to dazzle a practitioner without patients and whose resources had been drained dry by his studies. It was not the way he would have elected to spend his time, but it was time that would pass quickly, and meanwhile she was wonderfully kind. She exacted perpetual attention, but it was impossible not to like her. He gave details about his queer patient, a "type" if there ever was one, who had in connection with her flushed obesity and in addition to the morbid strain of a violent and aimless will, a grave organic disorder; but he came back to his loved novelist, whom he was so good as to pronounce more essentially a poet than many of those who went in for verse, with a zeal excited, as all his indiscretion had been excited, by the happy chance of Dencombe's sympathy and the coincidence of their occupation. Dencombe bad confessed to a slight personal acquaintance with the author of "The Middle Years," but had not felt himself as ready as he could have wished when his companion, who had never yet encountered a being so privileged, began to be eager for particulars. He even thought that Doctor Hugh's eye at that moment emitted a glimmer of suspicion. But the young man was too inflamed to be shrewd, and repeatedly caught up the book to exclaim: "Did you notice this?" or "Weren't you immensely struck with that?" "There's a beautiful passage toward the end," he broke out; and again he laid his hand upon the volume. As he turned the pages he came upon something else, while Dencombe saw him suddenly change color. He bad taken up, as it lay on the bench, Dencombe's copy instead of his own, and his neighbor immediately guessed the reason of his start. Doctor Hugh looked grave an instant; then he said: "I see you've been altering the text!" Dencombe was a passionate corrector, a fingerer of style; the last thing he ever arrived at was a form final for himself. His ideal would have been to publish secretly, and then, on the published text, treat himself to the terrified revise, sacrificing always a first edition and beginning for the world with the second. This morning, in "The Middle Years," his pencil had pricked a dozen lights. He was amused at the effect of the young man's reproach; for an instant it made him change color. He stammered, at any rate, ambiguously; then, through a blur of ebbing consciousness, saw Doctor Hugh's mystified eyes. He only had time to feel he was about to be ill again—that emotion, excitement, fatigue, the heat of the sun, the solicitation of the air, had combined to play him a trick, before, stretching out a hand to his visitor with a plaintive cry, he lost his senses altogether.

Later he knew that he had fainted and that Doctor Hugh had got him home in a bath-chair, the conductor of which, prowling within hail for custom, had happened to remember seeing him in the garden of the hotel. He had recovered his perception in the transit, and had, in bed, that afternoon, a vague recollection of Doctor Hugh's young face, as they went together, bent over him in a comforting laugh and expressive of something more than a suspicion of his identity. That identity was ineffaceable now, and all the more that he was disappointed, disgusted. He had been rash, been stupid, had gone out too soon, stayed out too long. He oughtn't to have exposed himself to strangers, he ought to have taken his servant. He felt as if he had fallen into a hole too deep to descry any little patch of heaven. He was confused about the time that had elapsed—he pieced the fragments together. He had seen his doctor, the real one, the one who had treated him from the first and who had again been very kind. His servant was in and out on tiptoe, looking very wise after the fact. He said more than once something about the sharp young gentleman. The rest was vagueness, in so far as it wasn't despair. The vagueness, however, justified itself by dreams, dozing anxieties from which he finally emerged to the consciousness of a dark room and a shaded candle.

"You'll be all right again—I know all about you now," said a voice near him that he knew to be young. Then his meeting with Doctor Hugh came back. He was too discouraged to joke about it yet, but he was able to perceive, after a little, that the interest of it was intense for his visitor. "Of course I can't attend you professionally—you've got your own man, with whom I've talked and who's excellent," Doctor Hugh went on. "But you must let me come to see you as a good friend. I've just looked in before going to bed. You're doing beautifully, but it's a good job I was with you on the cliff. I shall come in early to-morrow. I want to do something for you. I want to do *everything*. You've done a tremendous lot for *me*." The young man held his hand, bending over him, and poor Dencombe, weakly aware of this living pressure, simply lay there and accepted his devotion. He couldn't do anything less—he needed help too much.

The idea of the help he needed was very present to him that night, which he spent in a lucid stillness, an intensity of thought that constituted a reaction from his hours of stupor. He was lost, he was lost—he was lost if he couldn't be saved. He was not afraid of suffering, of death; he was not even in love with life; but he had had a deep demonstration of desire. It came over him in the long, quiet hours that only with "The Middle Years" had he taken his flight; only on that day, visited by soundless processions, had he recognized his kingdom. He had had a revelation of his range. What he dreaded was the idea that his reputation should stand on the unfinished. It was not with his past but with his future that it should properly he concerned. Illness and age rose before him like spectres with pitiless eyes: how was he to bribe such fates to give him the second chance? He had had the one chance that all men have—he had had the chance of life. He went to sleep again very late, and when he awoke Doctor Hugh was sitting by his head. There was already, by this time, something beautifully familiar in him.

"Don't think I've turned out your physician," he said; "I'm acting with his consent. He has been here and seen you. Somehow he seems to trust me. I told him how we happened to come together yesterday, and he recognizes that I've a peculiar right."

Dencombe looked at him with a calculating earnestness. "How have you squared the Countess?"

The young man blushed a little, but he laughed. "Oh, never mind the Countess!"

"You told me she was very exacting."

Doctor Hugh was silent a moment. "So she is."

"And Miss Vernham's an *intrigante*."

"How do you know that?"

"I know everything. One *has* to, to write decently!"

"I think she's mad," said limpid Doctor Hugh.

"Well, don't quarrel with the Countess—she's a present help to you."

"I *don't* quarrel," Doctor Hugh replied. "But I don't get on with silly women." Then he added to Dencombe: "You seem very much alone."

"That often happens at my age. I've outlived, I've lost by the way."

Doctor Hugh hesitated; then surmounting a soft scruple: "Whom have you lost?"

"Every one."

"Ah, no," the young man murmured, laying a hand on his arm.

"I once had a wife—I once had a son. My wife died when my child was born, and my boy, at school, was carried off by typhoid."

"I wish *I'd* been there!" said Doctor Hugh, simply.

"Well—if you're *here!*" Dencombe answered, with a smile that, in spite of dimness, showed how much he liked to be sure of his companion's whereabouts.

"You talk strangely of your age. You're not old."

"Hypocrite—so early!"

"I speak physiologically."

"That's the way I've been speaking for the last five years, and it's exactly what I've been saying to myself. It isn't till we *are* old that we begin to tell ourselves we're not!"

"Yet I know *I'm* young," Doctor Hugh declared.

"Not so well as I!" laughed his patient, whose visitor indeed would have established the truth in question by the honesty with which he changed the point of view, remarking that it must be one of the charms of ago—at any rate in the case of high distinction—to feel that one has" labored and achieved. Doctor Hugh employed the common phrase about earning one's rest, and it made poor Dencombe, for an instant, almost angry. He recovered himself, however, to explain, lucidly enough, that if he, ungraciously, knew nothing of such a balm, it was doubtless because he had wasted inestimable years. He had followed literature from the first, but he had taken a lifetime to get alongside of her. Only to-day, at last, had he begun to *see,* so that what he had hitherto done was a movement without a direction. He had ripened too late, and was so clumsily constituted that he had had to teach himself by mistakes.

"I prefer your flowers, then, to other people's fruit, and your mistakes to other people's successes," said gallant Doctor Hugh. "It's for your mistakes I admire you."

"You're happy—you don't *know,*" Dencombe answered.

Looking at his watch the young man had got up; he named the hour of the afternoon at which he would return. Dencombe warned him against committing himself too deeply, and expressed again all his dread of making him neglect the Countess—perhaps incur her displeasure.

"I want to be like *you*—I want to learn by mistakes!" Doctor Hugh laughed.

"Take care you don't make too grave a one! But do come back," Dencombe added, with the glimmer of a new idea.

"You should have had more vanity!" Doctor Hugh spoke as if he knew the exact amount required to make a man of letters normal.

"No, no—I only should have had more time. I want another go."

"Another go?"

"I want an extension."

"An extension?" Again Doctor Hugh repeated Dencombe's words, with which he seemed to have been struck.

"Don't you know?—I want to *live*."

The young man, for good-by, had taken his hand, which closed with a certain force. They looked at each other hard a moment. "You *will* live," said Doctor Hugh.

"Don't be superficial. It's too serious!"

"You *shall* live!" Dencombe's visitor declared, turning pale.

"Ah, that's better!" And as he retired the invalid, with a nervous laugh, sank gratefully back.

All that day and all the following night he wondered if it mightn't be managed. His doctor came again, his servant was attentive, but it was to his confident young friend that he found himself mentally appealing. His collapse on the cliff was plausibly explained, and his liberation, on a better basis, promised for the morrow; meanwhile, however, the intensity of his meditations kept him tranquil and made him indifferent. The idea that occupied him was none the less absorbing because it was a morbid fancy. Here was a clever son of the age, ingenious and ardent, who happened to have set him up for connoisseurs to worship. This servant of his altar had all the new learning in science and all the old reverence in faith; wouldn't he therefore put his knowledge at the disposal of his sympathy, his craft at the disposal of his love? Couldn't he be trusted to invent a remedy for a poor artist to whose art he had paid a tribute? If he couldn't, the alternative was hard: Dencombe would have to surrender to silence, unvindicated and undivided. The rest of the day and all the next he toyed in secret with this sweet futility. Who would work the miracle for him but the young man who could combine such lucidity with such passion? He thought of the fairy-tales of science and charmed himself into forgetting that he looked for a magic that was not of this world. Doctor Hugh was an apparition, and that placed him above the law. He came and went while his patient, who sat up, followed him with supplicating eyes. The interest of knowing the great author had made the young man begin "The Middle Years" afresh, and would help him to find a deeper meaning in its pages, Dencombe had told him what he "tried for;" with all his intelligence, on a first perusal. Doctor Hugh had failed to guess it. The baffled celebrity wondered then who in the world *would* guess it: he was amused once more at the thoroughness with which an intention could be missed. Yet he wouldn't rail at the general mind to-day—consoling as that ever had been; the revelation of his own slowness had seemed to make all stupidity sacred.

Doctor Hugh, after a little, was visibly worried, confessing, on inquiry, to a source of embarrassment at home. "Stick to the Countess—don't mind *me*," Dencombe said, repeatedly; for his companion was frank enough about the large lady's attitude. She was so jealous that she had fallen ill—she resented such a breach of allegiance. She paid so much for his fidelity that she must have it all; she refused him the right to other sympathies, charged him with scheming to make her die alone, for it was needless to point out how little Miss Vernham was a resource in trouble. When Doctor Hugh mentioned that the Countess would already have left Bournemonth if he hadn't kept her in bed, poor Dencombe held his arm tighter and said with decision: "Take her straight away." They had gone out together, walking back to the sheltered nook in which, the other day, they had met. The young man, who had given his companion a personal support, declared with emphasis that his conscience was clear—he could carry on two patients together. Didn't he dream, for his future, of a time when he should have to look after live hundred? Longing equally for virtue Dencombe replied that in this golden age no individual would pretend to have contracted with him for *all* his attention. On the part of the Countess was not such an avidity lawful? Doctor Hugh denied it, said there was no contract, but only a free understanding, and that a sordid servitude was impossible to a generous spirit; he liked, moreover, to talk about art, and that was the subject on which, this time, as they sat again together on the sunny bench, he tried most to engage the author of "The Middle Years." Dencombe, soaring again a little on the weak wings of convalescence, and still haunted by that happy notion of an organised rescue, found another strain of eloquence to plead the cause of a certain splendid "last manner," the very citadel, as it would prove, of his reputation, the stronghold into which his real treasure would be gathered. While his listener gave up the morning and the great still sea appeared to wait, he had a wonderful explanatory hour. Even for himself he was inspired as he told of what his treasure would consist—the precious metals he would dig from the mine, the jewels rare, festoons of rubies, he would hang between the columns of his temple. He was wonderful for himself, so thick his convictions crowded; but he was still more wonderful for Doctor Hugh, who assured him, none the less, that the very pages he had just published were already encrusted with gems. The young man, however, panted for the combinations to come, and, before the face of the beautiful day, renewed to Dencombe his guarantee that his profession would hold itself responsible for such a life. Then he suddenly clapped his hand upon his watch-pocket and asked leave to absent himself for half an hour. Dencombe waited there for his return, but was at last recalled to the actual by the fall of a shadow across the ground. The shadow darkened into that of Miss Vernham, the young lady in attendance on the Countess; whom Dencombe, recognizing her, perceived so clearly to have come to speak to him, that he rose from his bench to acknowledge the civility. Miss Vernham, however, proved not particularly civil; she looked strangely agitated, and her type was now unmistakable.

"Excuse me if I inquire," she said, "whether it's too much to hope that you may be induced to leave Doctor Hugh alone." Then, before Dencombe, greatly disconcerted, could protest: "You ought to be informed that you stand in his light; that you may do him a terrible injury."

"Do you mean by causing the Countess to dispense with his services?"

"By causing her to disinherit him." Dencombe stared at this, and Miss Vernham pursued, in the gratification of seeing she could produce an impression:

"It has depended on himself to come into something very handsome. He has had a magnificent prospect, but I think you've succeeded in spoiling it."

"Not intentionally, I assure you. Is there no hope the accident may be repaired?" Dencombe asked.

"She was ready to do anything for him. She takes great fancies, she lets herself go—it's her way. She has no relations, she's free to dispose of her money, and she's very ill."

"I'm very sorry to hear it," Dencombe stammered.

"Wouldn't it be possible for you to leave Bournemouth? *That's* what I've come to ask of you."

Poor Dencombe sank down on his bench. "I'm very ill myself, but I'll try!"

Miss Vernham still stood there with her colorless eyes and the brutality of her good conscience. "Before it's too late, please!" she said; and with this she turned her back, in order, quickly, as if it had been a business to which she could spare but a precious moment, to pass out of his sight.

Oh, yes, after this Dencombe was certainly very ill. Miss Vernham had upset him with her rough, fierce news; it was the sharpest shock to him to discover what was at stake for a penniless young man of fine parts. He sat trembling on his bench, staring at the waste of waters, feeling sick with the directness of the blow. He was indeed too weak, too unsteady, too alarmed; but he would make the effort to get away, for he couldn't accept the guilt of interference, and his honor was really involved. He would hobble home, at any rate, and then he would think what was to be done. He made his way back to the hotel and, as he went, had a characteristic vision of Miss Vernham's great motive. The Countess hated women, of course, Dencombe was lucid about that; so the hungry pianist had no personal hopes and could only console herself with the bold conception of helping Doctor Hugh in order either to marry him after he had got his money or to induce him to recognize her title to compensation and buy her off. If she had befriended him at a fruitful crisis he would really, as a man of delicacy, and she knew what to think of that point, have to reckon with her.

At the hotel Dencombe's servant insisted on his going back to bed. The invalid had talked about catching a train and had begun with orders to pack; after which his shaken nerves had yielded to a queer head and a rising temperature. He consented to see his physician, who immediately was sent for, but he wished it to be understood that his door was irrevocably closed to Doctor Hugh. He had his plan, which was so fine that he rejoiced in it after getting back to bed. Doctor Hugh, suddenly finding himself snubbed without mercy, would, in natural disgust and to the joy of Miss Vernham, renew his allegiance to the Countess. When his physician arrived Dencombe learned that he was feverish and that this was very wrong ; he was to cultivate calmness and try, if possible, not to think. For the rest of the day he wooed stupidity; but there was an ache that kept him sentient, the probable sacrifice of his "extension," the limit of his course. His medical adviser was anything but pleased; his successive relapses were ominous. He charged this personage to put out a strong hand and take Doctor Hugh off his mind—it would contribute, so much to his being quiet. The agitating name, in his room, was not mentioned again, but his security was a smothered fear, and it was not confirmed by the receipt, at ten o'clock that evening, of a telegram which his servant opened and read for him and to which, with an address in London, the signature of Miss Vernham was attached. "Beseech you to use all influence to make our friend join us here in the morning. Countess much the worse for dreadful journey, but everything may still be saved." The two ladies had gathered themselves up and had been capable in the afternoon of a spiteful revolution. They had started for the capital, and if the elder one, as Miss Vernham had announced, was very ill, she had wished to make it clear that she was proportionately reckless. Poor Dencombe, who was not reckless, and who only desired that everything should indeed be "saved," sent this missive straight off to the young man's lodging, and had on the morrow the pleasure of knowing that he had quitted Bournemouth by an early train.

Two days later he pressed in with a copy of a literary journal in his hand. He had returned because he was nervous, and for the pleasure of flourishing the great review of "The Middle Years." Here at least was something adequate—it rose to the occasion; it was an acclamation, a reparation, a critical attempt to place the author in the niche he had fairly won. Dencombe accepted and submitted; he made neither objection nor inquiry, for old complications had returned, and he had had two atrocious days. He was convinced not only that he should never again leave his bed, so that his young friend might pardonably remain, but that the demand he should make on the patience of beholders would be very moderate indeed. Doctor Hugh had been to town, and he tried to find in his eyes some confession that the Countess was pacified and his legacy clinched; but all he could see there was the light of his juvenile joy in two or three of the phrases of the newspaper. Dencombe couldn't read them, but when his visitor had insisted on repeating them more than once he was able to shake an unintoxicated head, "Ah, no, they would have been true of what I *could* have done!"

"What people 'could have done' is mainly what they *have* done," Doctor Hugh contended.

"Mainly, yes; but I've been an idiot!" said Dencombe.

Doctor Hugh did remain; the end was coming fast. Two days later Dencombe observed to him, by way of the feeblest of jokes, that there would now be no question whatever of a second chance. At this the young man stared; then he exclaimed: "Why, it has come to pass—it has come to pass! The second chance has been the public's—the chance to find the point of view, to pick up the pearl!"

"Oh, the pearl!" poor Dencombe uneasily sighed. A smile as cold as a winter sunset flickered on his drawn lips as he added: "The pearl is the unwritten—the pearl is the unalloyed, the *rest,* the lost!"

From that moment he was less and less present, heedless, to all appearance, of what went on around him. His disease was definitely mortal, of an action as relentless, after the short arrest that had enabled him to fall in with Doctor Hugh, as a leak in a great ship. Sinking steadily, though this visitor, a man of rare resources, now cordially approved by his physician, showed endless art in guarding him from pain, poor Dencombe kept no reckoning of favor or neglect, betrayed no symptom of regret or speculation. Yet toward the last he gave a sign of having noticed that for two days Doctor Hugh had not been in his room, a sign that consisted of his suddenly opening his eyes to ask of him if he had spent the interval with the Countess.

"The Countess is dead," said Doctor Hugh. "I knew that in a particular contingency she wouldn't resist. I went to her grave."

Dencombe's eyes opened wider, "She left you 'something handsome?'"

The young man gave a laugh almost too light for a chamber of woe. "Never a penny. She roundly cursed me."

"Cursed you?" Dencombe murmured.

"For giving her up. I gave her up for *you*. I had to choose," his companion explained.

"You chose to let a fortune go?"

"I chose to accept, whatever they might be, the consequences of my infatuation," smiled Doctor Hugh. Then, to jest more soothingly: "A fortune be hanged! It's *your* fault if I can't get your things out of my head."

The immediate tribute to his jest was a long, bewildered moan; after which, for many hours, for many days, Dencombe lay motionless and absent. A response so absolute, such a glimpse of a definite result and such a proof of honor worked together in his mind and, producing a strange commotion, slowly altered and transfigured his despair. The sense of cold submersion left him—he seemed to float without an effort. The incident was extraordinary as evidence, and it shed an intenser light. At the last he signed to Doctor Hugh to listen, and, when he was down on his knees by the pillow, brought him very near.

"You've made me think that it's all a delusion."

"Not your glory, my dear friend," stammered the young man.

"Not my glory—what there is of it! It *is* glory—to have been tested, to have had our little quality and cast our little spell. The thing is to have made somebody care. *You're* crazy, of course, but that doesn't affect the law."

"You're a great success!" said Doctor Hugh, putting into his voice the ring of all young cheer.

Dencombe lay taking this in; then he gathered strength to speak once more. "A second chance—*that's* the delusion. There never was to be but one. We work in the dark—we do what we can—we give what we have. Our doubt is our passion and our passion is our task. The rest is the madness of art."

"If you've doubted, if you've despaired you've always *done* it," his visitor subtly argued.

"We've done *something*," Dencombe conceded.

"Something is all. It's the feasible. It's *you!*"

"Comforter!" poor Dencombe ironically sighed.

"But it's true," insisted his friend.

"It's true. It's frustration that doesn't count."

"Frustration's only life," said Doctor Hugh.

"Yes, it's what passes." Poor Dencombe was barely audible, but he had marked with the words the virtual end of his first and only chance.

Questions

1. The dying novelist says at the end of the story that "a second chance [at life is a] . . . delusion. There never was to be but one. We work in the dark—we do what we can—we give what we have. Our doubt is our passion and our passion is our task. The rest is the madness of art." What, in your opinion, is the novelist's perception of life, work, and death? Do you agree? Why or why not?
2. The story of Dencombe is full of ironies and paradoxes. He perceives himself to be doomed yet triumphant, tragic yet victorious; he is sad that he will never have "another go" at life, yet he feels that he will "possess his kingdom" because of his life's work. Does he die a happy or an unhappy man? Is his sense of achievement genuine?
3. Dencombe is lonely, but he is also depressed, exhausted, and mysteriously ill. He perceives himself to be (at least initially) a failure. Doctor Hugh, on the other hand, admires and adores Dencombe. The doctor perceives him as being successful. Why would two educated people, a doctor and an artist, perceive the same thing so differently?
4. What does this story seem to assume about spirituality and values?

STEPHEN CRANE

Stephen Crane (1871–1900) was born in Newark, New Jersey. He was the last of fourteen children born to a Methodist preacher and to a mother who was a social activist. (She was involved in the Temperance Movement, which was the fight to stop the abuse of alcohol and its harmful effects on families.) Crane's parents saw God's loving and merciful hand guiding human affairs, and they believed that each person was free to either embrace God or reject him. In time, Crane rejected this heritage and saw humans as living without God's support or love in a cruel world. Furthermore, Crane saw little freedom in the human experience; we lack the necessary power to deal with the overwhelming social and economic forces surrounding us. The harsh images and the misery found in Crane's novels mark him as a staunch determinist and champion of the American naturalist movement that flourished from 1900 to 1914.

Crane worked as a journalist, and his novels and short stories have a harsh, journalistic approach also. His first novel, *Maggie, A Girl of the Street,* presents the decline of a young girl into prostitution and death because of the social and economic pressures of slum life. His second and most successful novel, *The Red Badge of Courage,* portrays a young farm boy's exposure to horror and death during the Civil War. His most famous short story, "The Open Boat," presents people struggling in a small boat in a storm. In the story, the world, and presumably God, is indifferent to the plight of humans. Chance, not God, determines the outcome of events. Crane concluded that individuals are powerless to choose their own destiny.

A MYSTERY OF HEROISM

The dark uniforms of the men were so coated with dust from the incessant wrestling of the two armies that the regiment almost seemed a part of the clay bank which shielded them from the shells. On the top of the hill a battery was arguing in tremendous roars with some other guns, and to the eye of the infantry the artillerymen, the guns, the caissons, the horses, were distinctly outlined upon the blue sky. When a piece was fired, a red streak as round as a log flashed low in the heavens, like a monstrous bolt of lightning. The men of the battery wore white duck trousers, which somehow emphasized their legs; and when they ran and crowded in little groups at the bidding of the shouting officers, it was more impressive than usual to the infantry.

Fred Collins, of A Company, was saying: "Thunder! I wisht I had a drink. Ain't there any water round here?"

Then somebody yelled, "There goes th' bugler!"

As the eyes of half the regiment swept in one machinelike movement, there was an instant's picture of a horse in a great convulsive leap of a death wound and a rider leaning back with a crooked arm and spread fingers before his face. On the ground was the crimson terror of an exploding shell, with fibers of flame that seemed like lances. A glittering bugle swung clear of the rider's back as fell headlong the horse and the man. In the air was an odor as from a conflagration.

Sometimes they of the infantry looked down at a fair little meadow which spread at their feet. Its long green grass was rippling gently in a breeze. Beyond it was the gray form of a house half torn to pieces by shells and by the busy axes of soldiers who had pursued firewood. The line of an old fence was now dimly marked by long weeds and by an occasional post. A shell had blown the well-house to fragments. Little lines of gray smoke ribboning upward from some embers indicated the place where had stood the barn.

From beyond a curtain of green woods there came the sound of some stupendous scuffle, as if two animals of the size of islands were fighting. At a distance there were occasional appearances of swift-moving men, horses, batteries, flags, and with the crashing of infantry volleys were heard, often, wild and frenzied cheers. In the midst of it all Smith and Ferguson, two privates of A Company, were engaged in a heated discussion which involved the greatest questions of the national existence.

The battery on the hill presently engaged in a frightful duel. The white legs of the gunners scampered this way and that way, and the officers redoubled their shouts. The guns, with their demeanors of stolidity and courage, were typical of something infinitely self-possessed in this clamor of death that swirled around the hill.

One of a "swing" team was suddenly smitten quivering to the ground, and his maddened brethren dragged his torn body in their struggle to escape from this turmoil and danger. A young soldier astride one of the leaders swore and fumed in his saddle and furiously jerked at the bridle. An officer screamed out an order so violently that his voice broke and ended the sentence in a falsetto shriek.

The leading company of the infantry regiment was somewhat exposed, and the colonel ordered it moved more fully under the shelter of the hill. There was the clank of steel against steel.

A lieutenant of the battery rode down and passed them, holding his right arm carefully in his left hand. And it was as if this arm was not at all a part of him, but belonged to another man. His sober and reflective charger went slowly. The officer's face was grimy and perspiring, and his uniform was tousled as if he had been in direct grapple with an enemy. He smiled grimly when the men stared at him. He turned his horse toward the meadow.

Collins, of A Company, said: "I wisht I had a drink. I bet there's water in that there ol' well yonder!"

"Yes; but how you goin' to git it?"

For the little meadow which intervened was now suffering a terrible onslaught of shells. Its green and beautiful calm had vanished utterly. Brown earth was being flung in monstrous handfuls. And there was a massacre of the young blades of grass. They were being torn, burned, obliterated. Some curious fortune of the battle had made this gentle little meadow the object of the red hate of the shells, and each one as it exploded seemed like an imprecation in the face of a maiden.

The wounded officer who was riding across this expanse said to himself: "Why, they couldn't shoot any harder if the whole army was massed here!"

A shell struck the gray ruins of the house, and as, after the roar, the shattered wall fell in fragments, there was a noise which resembled the flapping of shutters during a wild gale of winter. Indeed, the infantry paused in the shelter of the bank appeared as men standing upon a shore contemplating a madness of the sea. The angel of calamity had under its glance the battery upon the hill. Fewer white-legged men labored about the guns. A shell had smitten one of the pieces, and after the flare, the smoke, the dust, the wrath of this blow were gone, it was possible to see white legs stretched horizontally upon the ground. And at that interval to the rear, where it is the business of battery horses to stand with their noses to the fight awaiting the command to drag their guns out of the destruction, or into it, or wheresoever these incomprehensible humans demanded with whip and spur—in this line of passive and dumb spectators, whose fluttering hearts yet would not let them forget the iron laws of man's control of them—in this rank of brute-soldiers there had been relentless and hideous carnage. From the ruck of bleeding and prostrate horses, the men of the infantry could see one animal raising its stricken body with its forelegs and turning its nose with mystic and profound eloquence toward the sky.

Some comrades joked Collins about his thirst. "Well, if yeh want a drink so bad, why don't yeh go git it?"

"Well, I will in a minnet, if yeh don't shut up!"

A lieutenant of artillery floundered his horse straight down the hill with as little concern as if it were level ground. As he galloped past the colonel of the infantry, he threw up his hand in swift salute. "We've got to get out of that," he roared angrily. He was a black-bearded officer, and his eyes, which resembled beads, sparkled like those of an insane man. His jumping horse sped along the column of infantry.

The fat major, standing carelessly with his sword held horizontally behind him and with his legs far apart, looked after the receding horseman and laughed. "He wants to get back with orders pretty quick, or there'll be no batt'ry left," he observed.

The wise young captain of the second company hazarded to the lieutenant-colonel that the enemy's infantry would probably soon attack the hill, and the lieutenant-colonel snubbed him.

A private in one of the rear companies looked out over the meadow, and then turned to a companion and said, "Look there, Jim!" It was the wounded officer from the battery, who some time before had started to ride across the meadow, supporting his right arm carefully with his left hand. This man had encountered a shell, apparently, at a time when no one perceived him, and he could now be seen lying face downward with a stirruped foot stretched across the body of his dead horse. A leg of the charger extended slantingly upward, precisely as stiff as a stake. Around this motionless pair the shells still howled.

There was a quarrel in A Company. Collins was shaking his fist in the faces of some laughing comrades. "Dern yeh! I ain't afraid t' go. If yeh say much, I will go!"

"Of course, yeh will! You'll run through that there medder, won't yeh?"

Collins said, in a terrible voice: "You see now!"

At this ominous threat his comrades broke into renewed jeers.

Collins gave them a dark scowl, and went to find his captain. The latter was conversing with the colonel of the regiment.

"Captain," said Collins, saluting and standing at attention—in those days all trousers bagged at the knees—"Captain, I want t' get permission to go git some water from that there well over yonder!"

The colonel and the captain swung about simultaneously and stared across the meadow. The captain laughed. "You must be pretty thirsty, Collins?"

"Yes, sir, I am."

"Well—ah," said the captain. After a moment, he asked, "Can't you wait?"

"No, sir."

The colonel was watching Collins' face. "Look here, my lad," he said, in a pious sort of voice—"Look here, my lad"—Collins was not a lad—"don't you think that's taking pretty big risks for a little drink of water?"

"I dunno," said Collins uncomfortably. Some of the resentment toward his companions, which perhaps had forced him into this affair, was beginning to fade. "I dunno w'ether 'tis."

The colonel and the captain contemplated him for a time.

"Well," said the captain finally.

"Well," said the colonel, "if you want to go, why, go."

Collins saluted. "Much obliged t' yeh."

As he moved away the colonel called after him. "Take some of the other boys' canteens with you an' hurry back now."

"Yes, sir, I will."

The colonel and the captain looked at each other then, for it had suddenly occurred that they could not for the life of them tell whether Collins wanted to go or whether he did not.

They turned to regard Collins, and as they perceived him surrounded by gesticulating comrades, the colonel said: "Well, by thunder! I guess he's going."

Collins appeared as a man dreaming. In the midst of the questions, the advice, the warnings, all the excited talk of his company mates, he maintained a curious silence.

They were very busy in preparing him for his ordeal. When they inspected him carefully, it was somewhat like the examination that grooms give a horse before a race; and they were amazed, staggered, by the whole affair. Their astonishment found vent in strange repetitions.

"Are yeh sure a-goin'?" they demanded again and again.

"Certainly I am," cried Collins at last, furiously.

He strode sullenly away from them. He was swinging five or six canteens by their cords. It seemed that his cap would not remain firmly on his head, and often he reached and pulled it down over his brow.

There was a general movement in the compact column. The long animal-like thing moved slightly. Its four hundred eyes were turned upon the figure of Collins.

"Well, sir, if that ain't th' derndest thing! I never thought Fred Collins had the blood in him for that kind of business."

"What's he goin' to do, anyhow?"

"He's goin' to that well there after water."

"We ain't dyin' of thirst, are we? That's foolishness."

"Well, somebody put him up to it, an' he's doin' it."

"Say, he must be a desperate cuss."

When Collins faced the meadow and walked away from the regiment, he was vaguely conscious that a chasm, the deep valley of all prides, was suddenly between him and his comrades. It was provisional, but the provision was that he return as a victor. He had blindly been led by quaint emotions, and laid himself under an obligation to walk squarely up to the face of death.

But he was not sure that he wished to make a retraction, even if he could do so without shame. As a matter of truth, he was sure of very little. He was mainly surprised.

It seemed to him supernaturally strange that he had allowed his mind to maneuver his body into such a situation. He understood that it might be called dramatically great.

However, he had no full appreciation of anything, excepting that he was actually conscious of being dazed. He could feel his dulled mind groping after the form and color of this incident. He wondered why he did not feel some keen agony of fear cutting his sense like a knife. He wondered at this, because human expression had said loudly for centuries that men should feel afraid of certain things, and that all men who did not feel this fear were phenomena—heroes.

He was, then, a hero. He suffered that disappointment which we would all have if we discovered that we were ourselves capable of those deeds which we most admire in history and legend. This, then, was a hero. After all, heroes were not much.

No, it could not be true. He was not a hero. Heroes had no shames in their lives, and, as for him, he remembered borrowing fifteen dollars from a friend and promising to pay it back the next day, and then avoiding that friend for ten months. When at home his mother had aroused him for the early labor of his life on the farm, it had often been his fashion to be irritable, childish, diabolical; and his mother had died since he had come to the war.

He saw that, in this matter of the well, the canteens, the shells, he was an intruder in the land of fine deeds.

He was now about thirty paces from his comrades. The regiment had just turned its many faces toward him.

From the forest of terrific noises there suddenly emerged a little uneven line of men. They fired fiercely and rapidly at distant foliage on which appeared little puffs of white smoke. The spatter of skirmish firing was added to the thunder of the guns on the hill. The little line of men ran forward. A color-sergeant fell flat with his flag as if he had slipped on ice. There was hoarse cheering from this distant field.

Collins suddenly felt that two demon fingers were pressed into his ears. He could see nothing but flying arrows, flaming red. He lurched from the shock of this explosion, but he made a mad rush for the house, which he viewed as a man submerged to the neck in a boiling surf might view the shore. In the air, little pieces of shell howled and the earthquake explosions drove him insane with the menace of their roar. As he ran, the canteens knocked together with a rhythmical tinkling.

As he neared the house, each detail of the scene became vivid to him. He was aware of some bricks of the vanished chimney lying on the sod. There was a door which hung by one hinge.

Rifle bullets called forth by the insistent skirmishers came from the far-off bank of foliage. They mingled with the shells and the pieces of shells until the air was torn in all directions by hootings, yells, howls. The sky was full of fiends who directed all their wild rage at his head.

When he came to the well, he flung himself face downward and peered into its darkness. There were furtive silver glintings some feet from the surface.

He grabbed one of the canteens and, unfastening its cap, swung it down by the cord. The water flowed slowly in with an indolent gurgle.

And now as he lay with his face turned away he was suddenly smitten with the terror. It came upon his heart like the grasp of claws. All the power faded from his muscles. For an instant he was no more than a dead man.

The canteen filled with a maddening slowness, in the manner of all bottles. Presently he recovered his strength and addressed a screaming oath to it. He leaned over until it seemed as if he intended to try to push water into it with his hands. His eyes as he gazed down into the well shone like two pieces of metal, and in their expression was a great appeal and a great curse. The stupid water derided him.

There was the blaring thunder of a shell. Crimson light shone through the swift-boiling smoke and made a pink reflection on part of the wall of the well. Collins jerked out his arm and canteen with the same motion that a man would use in withdrawing his head from a furnace.

He scrambled erect and glared and hesitated. On the ground near him lay the old well bucket, with a length of rusty chain. He lowered it swiftly into the well. The bucket struck the water and then, turning lazily over, sank. When, with hand reaching tremblingly over hand, he hauled it out, it knocked often against the walls of the well and spilled some of its contents.

In running with a filled bucket, a man can adopt but one kind of gait. So, through this terrible field over which screamed practical angels of death, Collins ran in the manner of a farmer chased out of a dairy by a bull.

His face went staring white with anticipation—anticipation of a blow that would whirl him around and down. He would fall as he had seen other men fall, the life knocked out of them so suddenly that their knees were no more quick to touch the ground than their heads. He saw the long blue line of the regiment, but his comrades were standing looking at him from the edge of an impossible star. He was aware of some deep wheel ruts and hoof-prints in the sod beneath his feet.

The artillery officer who had fallen in this meadow had been making groans in the teeth of the tempest of sound. These futile cries, wrenched from him by his agony, were heard only by shells, bullets. When wild-eyed Collins came running, this officer raised himself. His face contorted and blanched from pain, he was about to utter some great beseeching cry. But suddenly his face straightened and he called: "Say, young man, give me a drink of water, will you?"

Collins had no room amid his emotions for surprise. He was mad from the threats of destruction.

"I can't!" he screamed, and in his reply was a full description of his quaking apprehension. His cap was gone and his hair was riotous. His clothes made it appear that he had been dragged over the ground by the heels. He ran on.

The officer's head sank down and one elbow crooked. His foot in its brassbound stirrup still stretched over the body of his horse and the other leg was under the steed.

But Collins turned. He came dashing back. His face had now turned gray and in his eyes was all terror. "Here it is! here it is!"

The officer was as a man gone in drink. His arm bent like a twig. His head drooped as if his neck were of willow. He was sinking to the ground, to lie face downward.

Collins grabbed him by the shoulder. "Here it is. Here's your drink. Turn over. Turn over, man, for God's sake!"

With Collins hauling at his shoulder, the officer twisted his body and fell with his face turned toward that region where lived the unspeakable noises of the swirling missiles. There was the faintest shadow of a smile on his lips as he looked at Collins. He gave a sigh, a little primitive breath like that from a child.

Collins tried to hold the bucket steadily, but his shaking hands caused the water to splash all over the face of the dying man. Then he jerked it away and ran on.

The regiment gave him a welcoming roar. The grimed faces were wrinkled in laughter.

His captain waved the bucket away. "Give it to the men!"

The two genial, skylarking young lieutenants were the first to gain possession of it. They played over it in their fashion.

When one tried to drink, the other teasingly knocked his elbow. "Don't, Billie! You'll make me spill it," said the one. The other laughed.

Suddenly there was an oath, the thud of wood on the ground, and a swift murmur of astonishment among the ranks. The two lieutenants glared at each other. The bucket lay on the ground, empty.

Questions

1. Why does Collins make this dangerous journey? Is he guided by his own character or by outside forces? What factors are beyond his control?
2. A typical Crane story shows a character gripped by a strong emotion. Select and discuss one or two passages in the story, such as Collins' trip to and his return from the well, where we watch a character controlled by some emotion.
3. Describe the reactions of Collins' company to his dash for water. Is Collins a hero? Explain why you agree or disagree.
4. Discuss the use of irony in the story, especially verbal and situational ironies in both the title and the ending of the story.

SYLVIA PLATH

Sylvia Plath (1932–1963) was an American poet, who lived much of her life in the Boston area. After finishing college, Plath attended Cambridge University in England and met Ted Hughes, a successful English poet. They married and lived in the London area during the last years of her life. After earlier attempts, Plath killed herself at the age of 30. During her short life, Plath published numerous works in poetry and prose. In this poem Plath views her death as a future event, as a past event, and as a moment experienced in the present.

LAST WORDS

I do not want a plain box, I want a sarcophagus
With tigery stripes, and a face on it
Round as the moon, to stare up.
I want to be looking at them when they come
5   *Picking among the dumb minerals, the roots*
I see them already—the pale, star-distance faces.
Now they are nothing, they are not even babies.
Imagine them without fathers or mothers, like the first gods.
They will wonder if I was important.
10   *I should sugar and preserve my days like fruit!*
My mirror is clouding over –
A few more breaths, and it will reflect nothing at all.
The flowers and the faces whiten to a sheet.

I do not trust the spirit. It escapes like steam
15   *In dreams, through mouth-hole or eye-hole. I can't stop it.*
One day it won't come back. Things aren't like that.
They stay, their little particular lusters
Warmed by much handling. They almost purr.
When the soles of my feet grow cold,
20   *The blue eye of my turquoise will comfort me.*
Let me have my copper cooking pots, let my rouge pots
Bloom about me like night flowers, with a good smell.
They will roll me up in bandages, they will store my heart
Under my feet in a neat parcel.
25   *I shall hardly know myself. It will be dark,*
And the shine of these small things sweeter than the face of Ishtar.

21 October, 1961

Questions

1. Why does Plath imagine future gravediggers (or just explorers), who do not yet exist, discovering her dead body?
2. Not long ago in the field of medicine, before today's electronic instruments to test for brainwaves and heartbeat, medical personnel would hold a mirror or a glass to the nose of a person to test for any faint breathing. If the mirror did not cloud over, the person might be declared dead. Given this context, how do you understand Platt's references to "My mirror is clouding over"?

3. What does Plath mean by the phrase, "I do not trust the spirit"? How do the surrounding lines help you understand this line?

4. Is it healthy or unhealthy for one to meditate on his or her coming death? Can such meditations add to and enrich our lives? Will they detract from our lives?

YUSEF KOMUNYAKAA

Yusef Komunyakaa (b. 1947) was originally from Louisiana. He earned degrees from the University of Colorado Springs, Colorado State University, and the University of California, Irvine. During his service in the U.S. Army, he had a tour of duty in Vietnam, and he gained experience writing and editing for a U.S. Army newspaper. Since then, he has published numerous books of poetry and won many awards. He has also helped students in public schools and universities learn to express themselves through poetry.

To understand the poem, "Facing It," one must have some knowledge of the Vietnam Veterans Memorial in Washington, D.C. The memorial is simply a wall, almost 82 yards (75 meters) long, that is bent in the middle to form an angle. The wall is made of highly polished, black granite that starts low in the grass and rises to a height of about 10 feet (3 meters). On the wall is a simple list of names of all of the American soldiers, airmen, and sailors who died or were declared missing during the Vietnam War. The stone is so highly polished that it acts like a black mirror for the visitors who walk along it. Often visitors will place a piece of paper over a name on the wall and use a crayon or marker to rub a copy of the name onto the paper. (Photographs of the monument can be found on many Web sites.) These details of the physical wall are very important for understanding the spiritual, emotional, and relational features of Komunyakaa's poem.

FACING IT

My black face fades,
hiding inside the black granite.
I said I wouldn't,
dammit: No tears.
I'm stone. I'm flesh. 5
My clouded reflection eyes me
like a bird of prey, the profile of night
slanted against morning. I turn
this way—the stone lets me go.
I turn that way—I'm inside 10
the Vietnam Veterans Memorial

> *again, depending on the light*
> *to make a difference.*
> *I go down the 58,022 names,*
> 15 *half-expecting to find*
> *my own in letters like smoke.*
> *I touch the name Andrew Johnson;*
> *I see the booby trap's white flash.*
> *Names shimmer on a woman's blouse*
> 20 *but when she walks away*
> *the names stay on the wall.*
> *Brushstrokes flash, a red bird's*
> *wings cutting across my stare.*
> *The sky. A plane in the sky.*
> 25 *A white vet's image floats*
> *closer to me, then his pale eyes*
> *look through mine. I'm a window.*
> *He's lost his right arm*
> *inside the stone. In the black mirror*
> 30 *a woman's trying to erase names:*
> *No, she's brushing a boy's hair.*

Questions

1. What are some of the multiple meanings in Komunyakaa's words and images? For example, the poet starts with "My black face fades." On one level, the poet's face is literally dark, because he is an African American. On another level, everyone's face (regardless of its original coloring) is reflected back to them as black when they look into the black granite. What other multiple meanings do you find in this poem?

2. Why does the poet write, "I'm stone. I'm flesh"? An essential part of all religions is the quest to define who we are. In this poem, what relationships exist among our physical, emotional, social, and spiritual selves?

3. Why does the poem end with the mundane action of a woman brushing a boy's hair? With what is this action contrasted?

4. Although this poem is not overtly religious, it captures what many people feel when they visit the Vietnam Veterans Memorial or other war memorials for those who were killed or were declared to be missing. Often such visits become deeply religious moments of thought. Why is this so?

(MARY) FLANNERY O'CONNOR

(Mary) Flannery O'Connor (1925–1964) lived most of her short life in Georgia. She received an M.F.A. from the University of Iowa's Writers' Workshop. O'Connor was a Southern writer, whose style has been called "Southern Gothic" or grotesque. In other words, she wrote about the "hard" realities of human wickedness and the feebleness of our efforts to cope with life. Personally, she was very committed to Roman Catholicism, but her novels and stories focus on more general moral concerns that appeal to a broad range of audiences. Her works often have a strong element of foreshadowing and often point to the human need for redemption.

A GOOD MAN IS HARD TO FIND

The grandmother didn't want to go to Florida. She wanted to visit some of her connections in east Tennessee and she was seizing every chance to change Bailey's mind. Bailey was the son she lived with, her only boy. He was sitting on the edge of his chair at the table, bent over the orange sports section of the *Journal.* "Now look here, Bailey," she said, "see here, read this," and she stood with one hand on her thin hip and the other rattling the newspaper at his bald head. "Here this fellow that calls himself The Misfit is aloose from the Federal Pen and headed toward Florida and you read here what it says he did to these people. Just you read it. I wouldn't take my children in any direction with a criminal like that aloose in it. I couldn't answer to my conscience if I did."

Bailey didn't look up from his reading so she wheeled around then and faced the children's mother, a young woman in slacks, whose face was as broad and innocent as a cabbage and was tied around with a green head-kerchief that had two points on the top like rabbit's ears. She was sitting on the sofa, feeding the baby his apricots out of a jar. "The children have been to Florida before," the old lady said. "You all ought to take them somewhere else for a change so they would see different parts of the world and be broad. They never have been to east Tennessee."

The children's mother didn't seem to hear her, but the eight-year-old boy, John Wesley, a stocky child with glasses, said. "If you don't want to go to Florida, why dontcha stay at home?" He and the little girl, June Star, were reading the funny papers on the floor.

"She wouldn't stay at home to be queen for a day," June Star said without raising her yellow head.

"Yes, and what would you do if this fellow, The Misfit, caught you?" the 5 grandmother said.

"I'd smack his face," John Wesley said.

"She wouldn't stay at home for a million bucks," June Star said. "Afraid she'd miss something. She has to go everywhere we go."

"All right, Miss," the grandmother said. "Just remember that the next time you want me to curl your hair."

June Star said her hair was naturally curly.

The next morning the grandmother was the first one in the car, ready to 10 go. She had her big black valise that looked like the head of a hippopotamus in one corner, and underneath it she was hiding a basket with Pitty Sing, the cat, in it. She didn't intend for the cat to be left alone in the house for three days because he would miss her too much and she was afraid he might brush against one of the gas burners and accidentally asphyxiate himself. Her son, Bailey, didn't like to arrive at a motel with a cat.

She sat in the middle of the back seat with John Wesley and June Star on either side of her. Bailey and the children's mother and the baby sat in front and they left Atlanta at eight forty-five with the mileage on the car at 55890. The grandmother wrote this down because she thought it would be interesting to say how many miles they had been when they got back. It took them twenty minutes to reach the outskirts of the city.

The old lady settled herself comfortably, removing her white cotton gloves and putting them up with her purse on the shelf in front of the back window. The children's mother still had on slacks and still had her head tied up in a green kerchief, but the grandmother had on a navy blue straw sailor hat with a bunch of white violets on the brim and a navy blue dress with a small white dot in the print. Her collars and cuffs were white organdy trimmed with lace and at her neckline she had pinned a purple spray of cloth violets containing a sachet. In case of an accident, anyone seeing her dead on the highway would know at once that she was a lady.

She said she thought it was going to be a good day for driving, neither too hot nor too cold, and she cautioned Bailey that the speed limit was fifty-five miles an hour and that the patrolmen hid themselves behind billboards and small clumps of trees and sped out after you before you had a chance to slow down. She pointed out interesting details of the scenery: Stone Mountain; the blue granite that in some places came up to both sides of the highway; the brilliant red clay banks slightly streaked with purple; and the various crops that made rows of green lacework on the ground. The trees were full of silver-white sunlight and the meanest of them sparkled. The children were reading comic magazines and their mother had gone back to sleep.

"Let's go through Georgia fast so we won't have to look at it much," John Wesley said.

15   "If I were a little boy," said the grandmother, "I wouldn't talk about my native state that way. Tennessee has the mountains and Georgia has the hills."

"Tennessee is just a hillbilly dumping ground," John Wesley said, "and Georgia is a lousy state too."

"You said it," June Star said.

"In my time," said the grandmother, folding her thin veined fingers, "children were more respectful of their native states and their parents and everything else. People did right then. Oh look at the cute little pickaninny!" she said and pointed to a Negro child standing in the door of a shack. "Wouldn't that make a picture, now?" she asked and they all turned and looked at the little Negro out of the back window. He waved.

"He didn't have any britches on," June said.

20   "He probably didn't have any," the grandmother explained. "Little niggers in the country don't have things like we do. If I could paint, I'd paint that picture," she said.

The children exchanged comic books.

The grandmother offered to hold the baby and the children's mother passed him over the front seat to her. She set him on her knee and bounced him and told him about the things they were passing. She rolled her eyes and screwed up her mouth and stuck her leathery thin face into his smooth bland one. Occasionally he gave her a faraway smile. They passed a large cotton field with five or six graves fenced in the middle of it, like a small island. "Look at the graveyard!" the grandmother said, pointing it out. "That was the old family burying ground. That belonged to the plantation."

"Where's the plantation?" John Wesley asked.

"Gone With the Wind," said the grandmother. "Ha. Ha."

When the children finished all the comic books they had brought, they 25 opened the lunch and ate it. The grandmother ate a peanut butter sandwich and an olive and would not let the children throw the box and the paper napkins out the window. When there was nothing else to do they played a game by choosing a cloud and making the other two guess what shape it suggested. John Wesley took one the shape of a cow and June Star guessed a cow and John Wesley said, no, an automobile, and June Star said he didn't play fair, and they began to slap each other over the grandmother.

The grandmother said she would tell them a story if they would keep quiet. When she told a story, she rolled her eyes and waved her head and was very dramatic. She said once when she was a maiden lady she had been courted by a Mr. Edgar Atkins Teagarden from Jasper, Georgia. She said he was a very good-looking man and a gentleman and that he brought her a water melon every Saturday afternoon with his initials cut in it, E. A. T. Well, one Saturday, she said, Mr. Teagarden brought the watermelon and there was nobody at home and he left it on the front porch and returned in his buggy to Jasper, but she never got the watermelon, she said, because a nigger boy ate it when he saw the initials, E. A. T.! This story tickled John Wesley's funny bone and he giggled and giggled but June Star didn't think it was any good. She said she wouldn't marry a man that just brought her a watermelon on Saturday. The grandmother said she would have done well to marry Mr. Teagarden because he was a gentleman and had bought Coca-Cola stock when it first came out and that he had died only a few years ago, a very wealthy man.

They stopped at The Tower for barbecued sandwiches. The Tower was a part stucco and part wood filling station and dance hall set in a clearing outside of Timothy. A fat man named Red Sammy Butts ran it and there were signs stuck here and there on the building and for miles up and down the highway saying, TRY RED SAMMY'S FAMOUS BARBECUE. NONE LIKE FAMOUS RED SAMMY'S! RED SAM! THE FAT BOY WITH THE HAPPY LAUGH. A VETERAN! RED SAMMY'S YOUR MAN!

Red Sammy was lying on the bare ground outside The Tower with his head under a truck while a gray monkey about a foot high, chained to a small chinaberry tree, chattered nearby. The monkey sprang back into the tree and got on the highest limb as soon as he saw the children jump out of the car and run toward him.

Inside, The Tower was a long dark room with a counter at one end and tables at the other and dancing space in the middle. They all sat down at a broad table next to the nickelodeon and Red Sam's wife, a tall burnt-brown woman with hair and eyes lighter than her skin, came and took their order. The children's mother put a dime in the machine and played "The Tennessee Waltz," and the grandmother said that tune always made her want to dance. She asked Bailey if he would like to dance but he only glared at her. He didn't have a naturally sunny disposition like she did and trips made him nervous. The grandmother's brown eyes were very bright. She swayed her head from side to side and pretended she was dancing in her chair. June Star said play something she could tap to so the children's mother put in another dime and played a fast number and June Star stepped out onto the dance floor and did her tap routine.

30   "Ain't she cute?" Red Sam's wife said, leaning over the counter. "Would you like to come be my little girl?"

"No, I certainly wouldn't," June Star said. "I wouldn't live in a broken-down place like this for a million bucks!" and she ran back to the table.

"Ain't she cute?" the woman repeated, stretching her mouth politely.

"Aren't you ashamed?" hissed the grandmother.

Red Sam came in and told his wife to quit lounging on the counter and hurry with these people's order. His khaki trousers reached just to his hip bones and his stomach hung over them like a sack of meal swaying under his shirt. He came over and sat down at a table nearby and let out a combination sigh and yodel. "You can't win," he said. "You can't win," and he wiped his sweating red face off with a gray handkerchief. "These days you don't know who to trust," he said. "Ain't that the truth?"

35   "People are certainly not nice like they used to be," said the grandmother.

"Two fellers come in here last week," Red Sammy said, "driving a Chrysler. It was an old beat-up car but it was a good one and these boys looked all right to me. Said they worked at the mill and you know I let them fellers charge the gas they bought? Now why did I do that?"

"Because you're a good man!" the grandmother said at once.

"Yes'm, I suppose so," Red Sam said as if he were struck with the answer.

His wife brought the orders, carrying the five plates all at once without a tray, two in each hand and one balanced on her arm. "It isn't a soul in this green world of God's that you can trust," she said. "And I don't count nobody out of that, not nobody," she repeated, looking at Red Sammy.

40   "Did you read about that criminal, The Misfit, that's escaped?" asked the grandmother.

"I wouldn't be a bit surprised if he didn't attack this place right here," said the woman. "If he hears about it being here, I wouldn't be none surprised to see him. If he hears it's two cent in the cash register, I wouldn't be a tall surprised if he . . ."

"That'll do," Red Sam said. "Go bring these people their Co'Colas," and the woman went off to get the rest of the order.

"A good man is hard to find," Red Sammy said. "Everything is getting terrible. I remember the day you could go off and leave your screen door unlatched. Not no more."

He and the grandmother discussed better times. The old lady said that in her opinion Europe was entirely to blame for the way things were now. She said the way Europe acted you would think we were made of money and Red Sam said it was no use talking about it, she was exactly right. The children ran outside into the white sunlight and looked at the monkey in the lacy chinaberry tree. He was busy catching fleas on himself and biting each one carefully between his teeth as if it were a delicacy.

They drove off again into the hot afternoon. The grandmother took cat 45 naps and woke up every five minutes with her own snoring. Outside of Toombsboro she woke up and recalled an old plantation that she had visited in this neighborhood once when she was a young lady. She said the house had six white columns across the front and that there was an avenue of oaks leading up to it and two little wooden trellis arbors on either side in front where you sat down with your suitor after a stroll in the garden. She recalled exactly which road to turn off to get to it. She knew that Bailey would not be willing to lose any time looking at an old house, but the more she talked about it, the more she wanted to see it once again and find out if the little twin arbors were still standing. "There was a secret panel in this house," she said craftily, not telling the truth but wishing that she were, "and the story went that all the family silver was hidden in it when Sherman came through but it was never found . . ."

"Hey!" John Wesley said. "Let's go see it! We'll find it! We'll poke all the woodwork and find it! Who lives there? Where do you turn off at? Hey, Pop, can't we turn off there?"

"We never have seen a house with a secret panel!" June Star shrieked. "Let's go to the house with the secret panel! Hey, Pop, can't we go see the house with the secret panel!"

"It's not far from here, I know," the grandmother said. "It wouldn't take over twenty minutes."

Bailey was looking straight ahead. His jaw was as rigid as a horseshoe. "No," he said.

The children began to yell and scream that they wanted to see the 50 house with the secret panel. John Wesley kicked the back of the front seat and June Star hung over her mother's shoulder and whined desperately into her ear that they never had any fun even on their vacation, and that they could never do what THEY wanted to do. The baby began to scream and John Wesley kicked the back of the seat so hard that his father could feel the blows in his kidney.

"All right!" he shouted and drew the car to a stop at the side of the road. "Will you all shut up? Will you all just shut up for one second? If you don't shut up, we won't go anywhere."

"It would be very educational for them," the grandmother murmured.

"All right," Bailey said, "but get this: this is the only time we're going to stop for anything like this. This is the one and only time."

"The dirt road that you have to turn down is about a mile back," the grandmother directed. "I marked it when we passed."

50   "A dirt road," Bailey groaned.

After they had turned around and were headed toward the dirt road, the grandmother recalled other points about the house, the beautiful glass over the front doorway and the candle-lamp in the hall. John Wesley said that the secret panel was probably in the fireplace.

"You can't go inside this house," Bailey said. "You don't know who lives there."

"While you all talk to the people in front, I'll run around behind and get in a window," John Wesley suggested.

"We'll all stay in the car," his mother said.

60   They turned onto the dirt road and the car raced roughly along in a swirl of pink dust. The grandmother recalled the times when there were no paved roads and thirty miles was a day's journey. The dirt road was hilly and there were sudden washes in it and sharp curves on dangerous embankments. All at once they would be on a hill, looking down over the blue tops of trees for miles around, then the next minute, they would be in a red depression with the dust-coated trees looking down on them.

"This place had better turn up in a minute," Bailey said, "or I'm going to turn around."

The road looked as if no one had traveled on it in months.

"It's not much farther," the grandmother said and just as she said it, a horrible thought came to her. The thought was so embarrassing that she turned red in the face and her eyes dilated and her feet jumped up, upsetting her valise in the corner. The instant the valise moved, the newspaper top she had over the basket under it rose with a smart and Pitty Sing, the cat, sprang onto Bailey's shoulder.

The children were thrown to the floor and their mother, clutching the baby, was thrown out the door onto the ground; the old lady was thrown into the front seat. The car turned over once and landed right-side-up in a gulch on the side of the road. Bailey remained in the driver's seat with the cat—gray-striped with a broad white face and an orange nose—clinging to his neck like a caterpillar.

65   As soon as the children saw they could move their arms and legs, they scrambled out of the car, shouting, "We've had an ACCIDENT!" The grandmother was curled up under the dashboard, hoping she was injured so that Bailey's wrath would not come down on her all at once. The horrible thought she had had before the accident was that the house she had remembered so vividly was not in Georgia but in Tennessee.

Bailey removed the cat from his neck with both hands and flung it out the window against the side of a pine tree. Then he got out of the car and started looking for the children's mother. She was sitting against the side of the red gutted ditch, holding the screaming baby, but she only had a cut down her face and a broken shoulder. "We've had an ACCIDENT!" the children screamed in a frenzy of delight.

"But nobody's killed," June Star said with disappointment as the grandmother limped out of the car, her hat still pinned to her head but the broken front brim standing up at a jaunty angle and the violet spray hanging off the side. They all sat down in the ditch, except the children, to recover from the shock. They were all shaking.

"Maybe a car will come along," said the children's mother hoarsely.

"I believe I have injured an organ," said the grandmother, pressing her side, but no one answered her. Bailey's teeth were clattering. He had on a yellow sport shirt with bright blue parrots designed in it and his face was as yellow as the shirt. The grandmother decided that she would not mention that the house was in Tennessee.

The road was about ten feet above and they could see only the tops of 70 the trees on the other side of it. Behind the ditch they were sitting in there were more woods, tall and dark and deep. In a few minutes they saw a car some distance away on top of a hill, coming slowly as if the occupants were watching them. The grandmother stood up and waved both arms dramatically to attract their attention. The car continued to come on slowly, disappeared around a bend and appeared again, moving even slower on top of the hill they had gone over. It was a big black battered hearse-like automobile. There were three men in it.

It came to a stop just over them and for some minutes, the driver looked down with a steady expressionless gaze to where they were sitting, and didn't speak. Then he turned his head and muttered something to the other two and they got out. One was a fat boy in black trousers and a red sweat shirt with a silver stallion embossed on the front of it. He moved around on the right side of them and stood staring, his mouth partly open in a kind of loose grin. The other had on khaki pants and a blue striped coat and a gray hat pulled down very low, hiding most of his face. He came around slowly on the left side. Neither spoke.

The driver got out of the car and stood by the side of it, looking down at them. He was an older man than the other two. His hair was just beginning to gray and he wore silver-rimmed spectacles that gave him a scholarly look. He had a long creased face and didn't have on any shirt or undershirt. He had on blue jeans that were too tight for him and was holding a black hat and a gun. The two boys also had guns.

"We've had an ACCIDENT!" the children screamed.

The grandmother had the peculiar feeling that the bespectacled man was someone she knew. His face was as familiar to her as if she had known him all her life but she could not recall who he was. He moved away from the car and began to come down the embankment, placing his feet carefully so that he wouldn't slip. He had on tan and white shoes and no socks, and his ankles were red and thin. "Good afternoon," he said. "I see you all had a little spill."

"We turned over twice!" said the grandmother.

75

"Oncet," he corrected. "We seen it happen. Try their car and see will it run, Hiram," he said quietly to the boy with the gray hat.

"What you got that gun for?" John Wesley asked. "Whatcha gonna do with that gun?"

"Lady," the man said to the children's mother, "would you mind calling them children to sit down by you? Children make me nervous. I want all you to sit down right together there where you're at."

"What are you telling us what to do for?" June Star asked.

80   Behind them the line of woods gaped like a dark open mouth. "Come here," said their mother.

"Look here now," Bailey began suddenly, "we're in a predicament! We're in . . ."

The grandmother shrieked. She scrambled to her feet and stood staring. "You're The Misfit!" she said. "I recognized you at once!"

"Yes'm," the man said, smiling slightly as if he were pleased in spite of himself to be known, "but it would have been better for all of you, lady, if you hadn't of reckernized me."

Bailey turned his head sharply and said something to his mother that shocked even the children. The old lady began to cry and The Misfit reddened.

85   "Lady," he said, "don't you get upset. Sometimes a man says things he don't mean. I don't reckon he meant to talk to you thataway."

"You wouldn't shoot a lady, would you?" the grandmother said and removed a clean handkerchief from her cuff and began to slap at her eyes with it.

The Misfit pointed the toe of his shoe into the ground and made a little hole and then covered it up again. "I would hate to have to," he said.

"Listen," the grandmother almost screamed, "I know you're a good man. You don't look a bit like you have common blood. I know you must come from nice people!"

"Yes mam," he said, "finest people in the world." When he smiled he showed a row of strong white teeth. "God never made a finer woman than my mother and my daddy's heart was pure gold," he said. The boy with the red sweat shirt had come around behind them and was standing with his gun at his hip. The Misfit squatted down on the ground. "Watch them children, Bobby Lee," he said. "You know they make me nervous." He looked at the six of them huddled together in front of him and he seemed to be embarrassed as if he couldn't think of anything to say. "Ain't a cloud in the sky," he remarked, looking up at it. "Don't see no sun but don't see no cloud neither."

90   "Yes, it's a beautiful day," said the grandmother. "Listen," she said, "you shouldn't call yourself The Misfit because I know you're a good man at heart. I can just look at you and tell."

"Hush!" Bailey yelled, "Hush! Everybody shut up and let me handle this!" He was squatting in the position of a runner about to sprint forward but he didn't move.

"I pre-chate that, lady," The Misfit said and drew a little circle in the ground with the butt of his gun.

"It'll take a half a hour to fix this here car," Hiram called, looking over the raised hood of it.

"Well, first you and Bobby Lee get him and that little boy to step over yonder with you," The Misfit said, pointing to Bailey and John Wesley. "The boys want to ask you something," he said to Bailey. "Would you mind stepping back in them woods there with them?"

"Listen," Bailey began, "we're in a terrible predicament! Nobody realizes 95 what this is," and his voice cracked. His eyes were as blue and intense as the parrots in his shirt and he remained perfectly still.

The grandmother reached up to adjust her hat brim as if she were going to the woods with him but it came off in her hand. She stood staring at it and after a second she let it fall on the ground. Hiram pulled Bailey up by the arm as if he were assisting an old man. John Wesley caught hold of his father's hand and Bobby Lee followed. They went off toward the woods and just as they reached the dark edge. Bailey turned and supporting himself against a gray naked pine trunk, he shouted, "I'll be back in a minute, Mamma, wait on me!"

"Come back this instant!" his mother shrilled but they all disappeared into the woods.

"Bailey Boy!" the grandmother called in a tragic voice but she found she was looking at The Misfit squatting on the ground in front of her. "I just know you're a good man," she said desperately. "You're not a bit common!"

"Nome, I ain't a good man," The Misfit said after a second as if he had considered her statement carefully, "but I ain't the worst in the world neither. My daddy said I was a different breed of dog from my brothers and sisters. 'You know,' Daddy said, 'It's some that can live their whole life without asking about it and it's others has to know why it is, and this boy is one of the latters. He's going to be into everything!'" He put on his black hat and looked up suddenly and then away deep into the woods as if he were embarrassed again. "I'm sorry I don't have on a shirt before you ladies," he said, hunching his shoulders slightly. "We buried our clothes that we had on when we escaped and we're just making do until we can get better. We borrowed these from some folks we met," he explained.

"That's perfectly all right," the grandmother said. "Maybe Bailey has an 100 extra shirt in his suitcase."

"I'll look and see terrectly," The Misfit said.

"Where are they taking him?" the children's mother screamed.

"Daddy was a card himself," The Misfit said. "You couldn't put anything over on him. He never got in trouble with the Authorities though. Just had the knack of handling them."

"You could be honest too if you'd only try," said the grandmother. "Think how wonderful it would be to settle down and live a comfortable life and not have to think about somebody chasing you all the time."

105   The Misfit kept scratching in the ground with the butt of his gun as if he were thinking about it. "Yes'm, somebody is always after you," he murmured.

The grandmother noticed how thin his shoulder blades were just behind his hat because she was standing up looking down on him. "Do you ever pray?" she asked.

He shook his head. All she saw was the black hat wiggle between his shoulder blades. "Nome," he said.

There was a pistol shot from the woods, followed closely by another. Then silence. The old lady's head jerked around. She could hear the wind move through the tree tops like a long satisfied insuck of breath. "Bailey Boy!" she called.

"I was a gospel singer for a while," The Misfit said. "I been most everything. Been in the arm service, both land and sea, at home and abroad, been twicet married, been an undertaker, been with the railroads, plowed Mother Earth, been in a tornado, seen a man burnt alive oncet," and he looked up at the children's mother and the little girl who were sitting close together, their faces white and their eyes glassy; "I even seen a woman flogged," he said.

110   "Pray, pray," the grandmother began, "pray, pray. . . ."

"I never was a bad boy that I remember of," The Misfit said in an almost dreamy voice, "but somewheres along the line I done something wrong and got sent to the penitentiary. I was buried alive," and he looked up and held her attention to him by a steady stare.

"That's when you should have started to pray," she said. "What did you do to get sent to the penitentiary that first time?"

"Turn to the right, it was a wall," The Misfit said, looking up again at the cloudless sky. "Turn to the left, it was a wall. Look up it was a ceiling, look down it was a floor. I forget what I done, lady. I set there and set there, trying to remember what it was I done and I ain't recalled it to this day. Oncet in a while, I would think it was coming to me, but it never come."

"Maybe they put you in by mistake," the old lady said vaguely.

115   "Nome," he said. "It wasn't no mistake. They had the papers on me."

"You must have stolen something," she said.

The Misfit sneered slightly. "Nobody had nothing I wanted," he said. "It was a head-doctor at the penitentiary said what I had done was kill my daddy but I known that for a lie. My daddy died in nineteen ought nineteen of the epidemic flu and I never had a thing to do with it. He was buried in the Mount Hopewell Baptist churchyard and you can go there and see for yourself."

"If you would pray," the old lady said, "Jesus would help you."

"That's right," The Misfit said.

120   "Well then, why don't you pray?" she asked trembling with delight suddenly.

"I don't want no hep," he said. "I'm doing all right by myself."

Bobby Lee and Hiram came ambling back from the woods. Bobby Lee was dragging a yellow shirt with bright blue parrots in it.

"Throw me that shirt, Bobby Lee," The Misfit said. The shirt came flying at him and landed on his shoulder and he put it on. The grandmother couldn't name what the shirt reminded her of. "No, lady," The Misfit said while he was buttoning it up, "I found out the crime don't matter. You can do one thing or you can do another, kill a man or take a tire off his car, because sooner or later you're going to forget what it was you done and just be punished for it."

The children's mother had begun to make heaving noises as if she couldn't get her breath. "Lady," he asked, "would you and that little girl like to step off yonder with Bobby Lee and Hiram and join your husband?"

"Yes, thank you," the mother said faintly. Her left arm dangled helplessly 125 and she was holding the baby, who had gone to sleep, in the other. "Hep that lady up, Hiram," The Misfit said as she struggled to climb out of the ditch, "and Bobby Lee, you hold onto that little girl's hand."

"I don't want to hold hands with him," June Star said. "He reminds me of a pig."

The fat boy blushed and laughed and caught her by the arm and pulled her off into the woods after Hiram and her mother.

Alone with The Misfit, the grandmother found that she had lost her voice. There was not a cloud in the sky nor any sun. There was nothing around her but woods. She wanted to tell him that he must pray. She opened and closed her mouth several times before anything came out. Finally she found herself saying, "Jesus, Jesus," meaning, Jesus will help you, but the way she was saying it, it sounded as if she might be cursing.

"Yes'm," The Misfit said as if he agreed. "Jesus thown everything off balance. It was the same case with Him as with me except He hadn't committed any crime and they could prove I had committed one because they had the papers on me. Of course," he said, "they never shown me my papers. That's why I sign myself now. I said long ago, you get you a signature and sign everything you do and keep a copy of it. Then you'll know what you done and you can hold up the crime to the punishment and see do they match and in the end you'll have something to prove you ain't been treated right. I call myself The Misfit," he said, "because I can't make what all I done wrong fit what all I gone through in punishment."

There was a piercing scream from the woods, followed closely by a pistol 130 report. "Does it seem right to you, lady, that one is punished a heap and another ain't punished at all?"

"Jesus!" the old lady cried. "You've got good blood! I know you wouldn't shoot a lady! I know you come from nice people! Pray! Jesus, you ought not to shoot a lady. I'll give you all the money I've got!"

"Lady," The Misfit said, looking beyond her far into the woods, "there never was a body that give the undertaker a tip."

There were two more pistol reports and the grandmother raised her head like a parched old turkey hen crying for water and called, "Bailey Boy, Bailey Boy!" as if her heart would break.

"Jesus was the only One that ever raised the dead," The Misfit continued, "and He shouldn't have done it. He thown everything off balance. If He did what He said then it's nothing for you to do but thow away everything and follow Him, and if He didn't, then it's nothing for you to do but enjoy the few minutes you got left the best way you can—by killing somebody or burning down his house or doing some other meanness to him. No pleasure but meanness," he said and his voice had become almost a snarl.

135   "Maybe He didn't raise the dead," the old lady mumbled, not knowing what she was saying and feeling so dizzy that she sank down in the ditch with her legs twisted under her.

    "I wasn't there so I can't say He didn't." The Misfit said, "I wisht I had of been there," he said, hitting the ground with his fist. "It ain't right I wasn't there because if I had of been there I would of known. Listen lady," he said in a high voice, I had of been there I would of known and I wouldn't be like I am now." His voice seemed about to crack and the grandmother's head cleared for an instant. She saw the man's face twisted close to her own as if he were going to cry and she murmured, "Why you're one of my babies. You're one of my own children!" She reached out and touched him on the shoulder. The Misfit sprang back as if a snake had bitten him and shot her three times through the chest. Then he put his gun down on the ground and took off his glasses and began to clean them.

    Hiram and Bobby Lee returned from the woods and stood over the ditch, looking down at the grandmother who half sat and half lay in a puddle of blood with her legs crossed under her like a child's and her face smiling up at the cloudless sky.

    Without his glasses, The Misfit's eyes were red-rimmed and pale and defenseless-looking. "Take her off and thow her where you thown the others," he said, picking up the cat that was rubbing itself against his leg.

    "She was a talker, wasn't she?" Bobby Lee said, sliding down the ditch with a yodel.

140   "She would of been a good woman," The Misfit said, "if it had been somebody there to shoot her every minute of her life."

    "Some fun!" Bobby Lee said.

    "Shut up, Bobby Lee," The Misfit said. "It's no real pleasure in life."

Questions

1. Often in literature and in life, people place special meanings on journeys. For example, we often think of life as a journey. Could the journey in this story symbolize a moral and/or spiritual pilgrimage?

2. The grandmother and Red Sammy discuss the difficulty of finding a "good man" in the modern world. How does this conversation advance the plot and dramatize the theme of good and evil in the story?

3. The second part of the story departs from standard morality, logical reason, and normal syntax to a landscape that is surrealistic (strange and bizarre), bleak, and bloodstained. In this harsh context, can you find any grace? What is "grace"?

4. At the end of the story, what does the Misfit mean when he says of the grandmother, "She would of been a good woman . . . if it had been somebody there to shoot her every minute of her life"?

EVERYMAN

Everyman is a late fifteenth-century morality play. It was written in English by an unknown author. Like other morality plays from the late Medieval period, it is meant to communicate a simple moral lesson to both educated and illiterate audiences.

This play has been compared to John Bunyan's famous novel *Pilgrim's Progress*. While both works are religious allegories and both have a protagonist who represents all of humanity, this comparison is very superficial. *Everyman* focuses on doing good works as the only avenue into heaven. *Pilgrim's Progress* focuses on the inadequacy of human works in finding salvation. For Bunyan, one's relationship with God is solely based on the grace and forgiveness that Jesus provided through his death. The author of *Everyman* wanted to challenge the audience to do good works in order to win God's love and acceptance. Another point of comparison is with Augustine's *Confessions*. Augustine (in agreement with John Bunyan) presented himself as being absolutely empty. It is only God's grace and mercy that gave Augustine a relationship with God. Compared to Augustine's intimate prayers to God, Everyman's relationship with God seems to be more distant.

These two conceptions of spirituality are crucial in understanding the history of Christianity. Some Christians follow the teachings of Augustine, Luther, Calvin, and Bunyan and believe that each person's relationship with God is based on the individual coming to the humble realization that he or she is powerless and is overwhelmed by sin and spiritual corruption. Only the death of Jesus can wash away one's sins and give a person a healthy spiritual relationship with God. On the other hand, some Christians follow the teachings represented in *Everyman*. They conclude that each person needs to do good works in order to have a relationship with God. They view the death of Jesus as a means for gaining grace from God or as a powerful example of self-sacrifice, yet each person must still struggle to gain salvation or deliverance from the corruption of sin.

EVERYMAN

Characters
God

Messenger	Knowledge
Death	confession
Everyman	Beauty
Fellowship	Strength
Kindred	Discretion
Cousin	Five Wits
Goods	Angel
Good Deeds	Doctor

HERE BEGINNETH A TREATISE HOW THE HIGH FATHER OF HEAVEN SENDETH DEATH TO SUM-
MON EVERY CREATURE TO COME AND GIVE ACCOUNT OF THEIR LIVES IN THIS WORLD, AND IS
IN MANNER OF A MORAL PLAY.

	MESSENGER. I pray you all give your audience,	
	And hear this matter with reverence,	
	By figure* a moral play:	content
	The Summoning of Everyman *called it is,*	
5	*That of our lives and ending* shows*	death
	How transitory we be all day.*	life
	This matter is wondrous precious,	
	But the intent of it is more gracious,	
	And sweet to bear away.	
10	*The story saith: Man, in the beginning*	
	Look well, and take good heed to the ending,	
	Be you never so gay!	
	Ye think sin in the beginning full sweet,	
	Which in the end causeth the soul to weep,	
15	*When the body lieth in clay.**	death
	Here shall you see how Fellowship and Jollity,	
	Both Strength, Pleasure, and Beauty,	
	Will fade from thee as flower in May;	
	For ye shall hear how our Heaven King	
20	*Calleth Everyman to a general reckoning:**	judgment
	Give audience, and hear what he doth say.	[Exit.]

God speaketh:

	GOD. I perceive, here in my majesty,	
	How that all creatures be to me unkind,*	sinners
	Living without dread* in worldly prosperity:	fear
25	*Of ghostly sight the people be so blind,*	
	Drowned in sin, they know me not for their God;	
	In worldly riches is all their mind,	
	They fear not my righteousness,* the sharp rod.	judgment
	My law* that I showed, when I for them died,	salvation
30	*They forget clean,* and shedding of my blood red;*	completely
	I hanged between two,* it cannot be denied;	the crucifixion
	To get them life I suffered to be dead;*	death on cross
	I healed their feet, with thorns hurt was my head.	
	I could do no more than I did, truly;	
35	*And now I see the people do clean* forsake me:*	completely
	They use the seven deadly sins* damnable,	reference to pride, envy, gluttony, lust, anger, greed, and sloth
	As pride, covetise, wrath, and lechery	
	Now in the world be made commendable;	

And thus they leave of angels the heavenly company.
Every man liveth so after his own pleasure,   40
And yet of their life they be nothing sure:
I see the more that I them forbear
The worse they be from year to year.
All that liveth appaireth* fast;   retrogress
Therefore I will, in all the haste,   45
Have a reckoning of every man's person;
For, and* I leave the people thus alone   if
In their life and wicked tempests,*   ways
Verily they will become much worse than beasts;
For now one would by envy another up eat;*   devour   50
Charity* they do all clean forget.   love
I hoped well that every man
In my glory should make his mansion,
And thereto I had them all elect;*   saved
But now I see, like traitors deject,*   devout secularists   55
They thank me not for the pleasure that I to them meant,
Nor yet for their being* that I them have lent.   life
I proffered the people great multitude of mercy,
And few there be that asketh it heartily.*   sincerely
They be so cumbered* with wordly riches   encumbered   60
That needs on them I must do justice,
On every man living without fear.
Where art thou, Death, thou mighty messenger?

   [Enter Death]

DEATH. *Almighty God, I am here at your will,*
   Your commandment to fulfil.   65
GOD. *Go thou to Everyman,*
   And show him, in my name,
   A pilgrimage he must on him* take,   alone
   Which he in no wise* may escape;   way
   And that he bring with him a sure reckoning   70
   Without delay or any tarrying.   [God withdraws]
DEATH. *Lord, I will in the world go run overall,**   all over
   And cruelly outsearch both great and small;
   Every man will I beset that liveth beastly
   Out of God's laws, and dreadeth not folly.   75
   He that loveth riches I will strike with my dart,
   His sight to blind, and from heaven to depart*—   cast out
   Except that alms be his good friend—
   In hell for to dwell, world without end.
   Lo, yonder I see Everyman walking.   80
   Full little he thinketh on my coming;
   His mind is on fleshly lusts and his treasure,

And great pain it shall cause him to endure
Before the Lord, Heaven King.

[Enter Everyman]

85   *Everyman, stand still! Whither art thou going*
Thus gaily? Hast thou thy Maker forget?
EVERYMAN. *Why askest thou?*
*Wouldest thou wit?**   *Don't you know?*
DEATH. *Yea, sir; I will show you:*
90   *In great haste I am sent to thee*
From God out of his majesty.
EVERYMAN. *What, sent to me?*
DEATH. *Yea, certainly.*
*Though thou have forget** him here,   forgotten*
95   *He thinketh on thee in the heavenly sphere,*
*As, ere** we depart, thou shalt know.   soon as*
EVERYMAN. *What desireth God of me?*
DEATH. *That shall I show thee:*
A reckoning he will needs have
100   *Without any longer respite.**   delay*
EVERYMAN. *To give a reckoning longer leisure** I crave;   more time*
*This blind** matter troubleth my wit.   overlooked or disregarded*
DEATH. *On thee thou must take a long journey;*
*Therefore thy book of count** with thee thou bring,   records*
105   *For turn again** thou cannot by no way.   second chance or more time*
And look thou be sure of thy reckoning,
For before God thou shalt answer, and show
Thy many bad deeds, and good but a few;
How thou hast spent thy life, and in what wise,
110   *Before the chief Lord of paradise.*
Have ado that we were in that way,
*For, wit** thou well, thou shalt make** none attorney.   note;   have*
EVERYMAN. *Full** unready I am such reckoning to give.   completely*
I know thee not. What messenger art thou?
115   DEATH. *I am Death, that no man dreadeth,**   is afraid of no man*
*For every man I rest,** and no man spareth;   seize*
For it is God's commandment
That all to me should be obedient.
EVERYMAN. *O Death, thou comest when I had thee least in mind!*
120   *In thy power it lieth me to save;*
*Yet of my good will** I give thee, if thou will be kind—   possessions*
Yea, a thousand pound shalt thou have—
*And defer** this matter till another day.   postpone*
DEATH. *Everyman, it may not be, by no way.*
125   *I set** not by gold, silver, nor riches,   live*
*Ne** by pope, emperor, king, duke, ne princes;   nor*

For, and* I would receive gifts great,   *if*
All the world I might get;
But my custom* is clean contrary.   *belief*
I give thee no respite. Come hence, and not tarry.   130
EVERYMAN. Alas, shall I have no longer respite?
 I may say Death giveth no warning!
 To think on thee, it maketh my heart sick,
 For all unready is my book of reckoning.
 But twelve year and I might have abiding,   135
 My counting-book* I would make so clear *accounting book*
 That my reckoning I should not need to fear.
 Wherefore, Death, I pray thee, for God's mercy,
 Spare me till I be provided of remedy.* *when I am ready*
DEATH. Thee availeth not to cry, weep, and pray;   140
 But haste thee lightly that thou were gone that journey,
 And prove* thy friends if thou can;   *test*
 For, wit thou well, the tide abideth* no man, *time awaits*
 And in the world each living creature
 For Adam's sin must die of nature.*   *of course* 145
EVERYMAN. Death, if I should this pilgrimage take,
 And my reckoning surely make,
 Show me, for saint charity,
 Should I not come* again shortly?*   *be born*
DEATH. No, Everyman; and thou be once there,* *dead* 150
 Thou mayst never more come here,
 Trust me verily.
EVERYMAN. O gracious God in the high seat celestial,
 Have mercy on me in this most need!
 Shall I have no company from this vale terrestrial 155
 Of mine acquaintance, that way me to lead?* *accompany*
DEATH. Yea, if any be so hardy*   *daring*
 That would go with thee and bear thee company.
 Hie thee that thou were gone to God's magnificence,
 Thy reckoning to give before his presence.   160
 What, weenest* thou thy life is given thee, *understand*
 And thy worldly goods also?
EVERYMAN. I had wend* so, verily.   *assumed*
DEATH. Nay, nay; it was but lent thee;
 For as soon as thou art go,*   *dead* 165
 Another a while shall have it, and then go therefro,* *Another shall have*
 Even as thou hast done.   *your worldly*
 Everyman, thou art mad! Thou hast thy wits five, *possessions and*
 And here on earth will not amend thy life;   *use them*
 For suddenly I do come.   170
EVERYMAN. O wretched caitiff,* whither shall I flee, *coward*
 That I might scape* this endless sorrow?   *escape*

> *Now, gentle Death, spare me till to-morrow,*
175   *That I may amend* me*   *seek advice*
> *With good advisement.*
> DEATH. *Nay, thereto I will not consent,*
> *Nor no man will I respite;**   *give*
> *But to the heart suddenly I shall smite*
180   *Without any advisement.*
> *And now out of thy sight I will me hie;*
> *See thou make thee ready shortly,*
> *For thou mayst say this is the day*
> *That no man living may scape* away.*   *escape*

[Exit Death]

185 EVERYMAN. *Alas, I may well weep with sighs deep!*
> *Now have I no manner of company*
> *To help me in my journey, and me to keep;**   *protect*
> *And also my writing* is full unready.*   *account*
> *How shall I do now for to excuse me?*
190   *I would to God I had never be get!**   *been born*
> *To my soul a full great profit it had* be;*   *would*
> *For now I fear pains huge and great.*
> *The time passeth. Lord, help, that all wrought!*
> *For though I mourn it availeth nought.*
195   *The day passeth, and is almost ago;**   *ended*
> *I wot not well* what for to do.*   *I do not know*
> *To whom were I best my complaint to make?*
> *What and* I to Fellowship thereof spake,*   *if*
> *And showed him of this sudden chance?*
200   *For in him is all mine affiance;**   *hope*
> *We have in the world so many a day**   *often*
> *Be good friends in sport and play.*
> *I see him yonder, certainly.*
> *I trust that he will bear me company;*
205   *Therefore to him will I speak to ease my sorrow.*
> *Well met, good Fellowship, and good morrow!*

Fellowship speaketh:

> FELLOWSHIP. *Everyman, good morrow, by this day!*
> *Sir, why lookest thou so piteously?*
> *If any thing be amiss, I pray thee me say,*
210   *That I may help to remedy.*
> EVERYMAN. *Yea, good Fellowship, yea;*
> *I am in great jeopardy.**   *danger*
> FELLOWSHIP. *My true friend, show to* me your mind;*   *tell me*
> *I will not forsake thee to my life's end,*
215   *In the way of good company.*

EVERYMAN. *That was well spoken, and lovingly.*

FELLOWSHIP. *Sir, I must needs know your heaviness;**   agony
   I have pity to see you in any distress.
   If any have you wronged, ye shall revenged be,
   Though I on the ground be slain for thee —
   Though that I know before that I should die.   220

EVERYMAN. *Verily, Fellowship, gramercy.**   thank you

FELLOWSHIP. *Tush! by thy thanks I set not a straw.*
   Show me your grief, and say no more.

EVERYMAN. *If I my heart should to you break,**   reveal
   And then you to turn your mind from me,   225
   And would not me comfort when ye hear me speak,
   Then should I ten times sorrier be.

FELLOWSHIP. *Sir, I say as I will do indeed.*

EVERYMAN. *Then be you a good friend at need:**   indeed
   I have found you true herebefore.   230

FELLOWSHIP. *And so ye shall evermore;*
   For, in faith, and thou go to hell,
   I will not forsake thee by the way.

EVERYMAN. *Ye speak like a good friend; I believe you well.*
   I shall deserve* it, and I may.   reciprocate 235

FELLOWSHIP. *I speak of no deserving, by this day!*
   For he that will say, and nothing do,
   Is not worthy with good company to go;
   Therefore show me the grief of your mind,
   As to your friend most loving and kind.   240

EVERYMAN. *I shall show you how it is:*
   Commanded I am to go a journey,
   A long way, hard and dangerous,
   And give a strait count,* without delay,   honest, accurate account
Before the high Judge, Adonai.*   God   245
   Wherefore, I pray you, bear me company,
   As ye have promised, in this journey.

FELLOWSHIP. *That is matter* indeed. Promise is duty;*   serious
   But, and* I should take such a voyage on me,   if
I know it well, it should be to my pain;*   detriment   250
   Also it maketh me afeard,* certain.   afraid
   But let us take counsel here as well as we can,
   For your words would fear* a strong man.   frighten

EVERYMAN. *Why, ye said if I had need*
   Ye would me never forsake, quick ne dead,*   alive or dead 255
   Though it were to hell, truly.

FELLOWSHIP. *So I said, certainly,*
   But such pleasures be set aside, the sooth to say;
   And also, if we took such a journey,
   When should we come again?   260

EVERYMAN. *Nay, never again, till the day of doom.*

FELLOWSHIP. *In faith,* then will not I come there!* truth
Who hath you these tidings brought?

EVERYMAN. *Indeed, Death was with me here.*

265 FELLOWSHIP. *Now, by God that all hath bought,*
If Death were the messenger,
For no man that is living to-day
I will not go that loath* journey — dreadful
Not for the father that begat me!

270 EVERYMAN. *Ye promised otherwise, pardie.** verily, by God

FELLOWSHIP. *I wot well I said so, truly;*
And yet if thou wilt eat, and drink, and make good cheer,
Or haunt to women the lusty company,
I would not forsake you while the day is clear,

275 *Trust me verily.*

EVERYMAN. *Yea, thereto ye would be ready!*
To go to mirth, solace, and play,
Your mind will sooner apply,
Than to bear me company in my long journey.

280 FELLOWSHIP. *Now, in good faith, I will not that way.*
But and* thou will murder, or any man kill, if
In that I will help thee with a good will.

EVERYMAN. *O, that is a simple advice indeed.*
Gentle fellow, help me in my necessity!

285 *We have loved long, and now I need;*
And now, gentle Fellowship, remember me.

FELLOWSHIP. *Whether ye have loved me or no,*
By Saint John, I will not with thee go.

EVERYMAN. *Yet, I pray thee, take the labour, and do so much for me*

290 *To bring me forward,* for saint charity,* to
And comfort me till I come without* the town. leave

FELLOWSHIP. *Nay, and thou would give me a new gown,*
I will not a foot with thee go;
But, and thou had tarried, I would not have left thee so.

295 *And as now God speed thee in thy journey,*
For from thee I will depart as fast as I may.

EVERYMAN. *Whither away, Fellowship? Will thou forsake me?*

FELLOWSHIP. *Yea, by my fay!* To God I betake* thee.* faith; commit

EVERYMAN. *Farewell, good Fellowship; for thee my heart is sore.*

300 *Adieu for ever! I shall see thee no more.*

FELLOWSHIP. *In faith, Everyman, farewell now at the ending;*
For you I will remember that parting is mourning.

[Exit Fellowship]

EVERYMAN. *Alack! shall we thus depart* indeed —* part
Ah, Lady,* help! — without any more comfort? Virgin Mary

Lo, Fellowship forsaketh me in my most need.   305
For help in this world whither shall I resort?
Fellowship herebefore with me would merry make,
And now little sorrow for me doth he take.
It is said, 'In prosperity men friends may find,
Which in adversity be full unkind.'   310
Now whither for succour shall I flee,
Sith* that Fellowship hath forsaken me?   seeing or knowing
To my kinsmen I will, truly,
Praying them to help me in my necessity;
I believe that they will do so,   315
For kind will creep where it may not go.
I will go say,* for yonder I see them.   try
Where be ye now, my friends and kinsmen?

[Enter Kindred and Cousin]

KINDRED. *Here be we now at your commandment.*
   Cousin, I pray you show us your intent   320
   In any wise, and do not spare.
COUSIN. *Yea, Everyman, and to us declare*
   If ye be disposed to go anywhither;*   anywhere
   For, wit you well, we will live and die together.
KINDRED. *In wealth and woe we will with you hold,**   be with you   325
   For over his kin a man may be bold.
EVERYMAN. *Gramercy, my friends and kinsmen kind.*
   Now shall I show you the grief of my mind:
   I was commanded by a messenger,
   That is a high king's chief officer;   330
   He bade me go a pilgrimage, to my pain,
   And I know well I shall never come again;
   Also I must give a reckoning strait,
   For I have a great enemy that hath me in wait,*   besieged me
   Which intendeth me for to hinder.   335
KINDRED. *What account is that which ye must render?*
   That would I know.
EVERYMAN. *Of all my works I must show*
   How I have lived and my days spent;
   Also of ill deeds that I have used*   done   340
   In my time, sith* life was me lent;   since
   And all virtues that I have refused.
   Therefore, I pray you, go thither with me
   To help to make mine account, for saint charity.
COUSIN. *What, to go thither? Is that the matter?*   345
   Nay, Everyman, I had liefer* fast bread and water   beloved
   All this five year and more.
EVERYMAN. *Alas, that ever I was bore!**   born

> *For now shall I never be merry,*
> *If that you forsake me.*

350

KINDRED. *Ah, sir, what ye be a merry man!*
> *Take good heart to you, and make no moan.*
> *But one thing I warn you, by Saint Anne —*
> *As for me, ye shall go alone.*

355 EVERYMAN. *My Cousin, will you not with me go?*

COUSIN. *No, by our Lady! I have the cramp in my toe.*
> *Trust not to me, for, so God me speed,*
> *I will deceive you in your most need.*

KINDRED. *It availeth not us to tice.**   *entice*

360

> *Ye shall have my maid with all my heart;*
> *She loveth to go to feasts, there to be nice,*
> *And to dance, and abroad to start:*
> *I will give her leave to help you in that journey,*
> *If that you and she may agree.*

365 EVERYMAN. *Now show me the very effect* of your mind;*   *drift*
> *Will you go with me, or abide behind?*

KINDRED. *Abide behind? Yea, that will I, and I may!*
> *Therefore farewell till another day.*   [Exit Kindred]

EVERYMAN. *How should I be merry or glad?*

370

> *For fair promises men to me make,*
> *But when I have most need they me forsake.*
> *I am deceived; that maketh me sad.*

COUSIN. *Cousin Everyman, farewell now,*
> *For verily I will not go with you.*

375

> *Also of mine own an unready reckoning*
> *I have to account; therefore I make tarrying.*
> *Now God keep thee, for now I go.*   [Exit Cousin]

EVERYMAN. *Ah, Jesus, is all come hereto?**   *to this*
> *Lo, fair words maketh fools fain;**   *happy*

380

> *They promise, and nothing will do, certain.*
> *My kinsmen promised me faithfully*
> *For to abide with me steadfastly,*
> *And now fast away* do they flee:*   *quickly*
> *Even so Fellowship promised me.*

385

> *What friend were best me of to provide?*
> *I lose my time here longer to abide.*
> *Yet in my mind a thing there is:*
> *All my life I have loved riches;*
> *If that my Good* now help me might,*   *Goods*

390

> *He would make my heart full light.*
> *I will speak to him in this distress —*
> *Where art thou, my Goods and riches?*

[Goods speaks from a corner]

GOODS. *Who calleth me? Everyman? What! hast thou haste?*
    I lie here in corners, trussed and piled so high,
    And in chests I am locked so fast,   395
    Also sacked* in bags. Thou mayst see with thine eye   *packed*
    I cannot stir; in packs low I lie.
    What would ye have? Lightly* me say.   *on a whim*
EVERYMAN. *Come hither, Good, in all the haste thou may,*
    For of counsel I must desire thee.   400
GOODS. *Sir, and ye in the world have sorrow or adversity,*
    That can I help you to remedy shortly.
EVERYMAN. *It is another disease that grieveth me;*
    In this world it is not, I tell thee so.
    I am sent for, another way to go,   `'` 405
    To give a strait count general
    Before the highest Jupiter of all;
    And all my life I have had joy and pleasure in thee,
    Therefore, I pray thee, go with me;
    For, peradventure, thou mayst before God Almighty   410
    My reckoning help to clean and purify;
    For it is said ever among*   *by all*
    That money maketh all right that is wrong.
GOODS. *Nay, Everyman, I sing another song.*
    I follow no man in such voyages;   415
    For, and* I went with thee,   *if*
    Thou shouldst fare much the worse for me;
    For because on me thou did set thy mind,
    Thy reckoning I have made blotted and blind,*   *heedless*
    That thine account thou cannot make truly;   420
    And that hast thou for* the love of me.   *because of*
EVERYMAN. *That would grieve me full sore.**   *very much*
    When I should come to that fearful answer.
    Up, let us go thither together.
GOODS. *Nay, not so! I am too brittle, I may not endure;*   425
    I will follow no man one foot, be ye sure.
EVERYMAN. *Alas, I have thee loved, and had great pleasure*
    All my life-days on good and treasure.
GOODS. *That is to thy damnation, without leasing,*
    For my love is contrary to the love everlasting;   430
    But if thou had me loved moderately during,
    As to the poor to give part of me,
    Then shouldst thou not in this dolour* be,   *calamity*
    Nor in this great sorrow and care.
EVERYMAN. *Lo, now was I deceived ere* I was ware,**   *before;*   *aware* 435
    And all I may wite* my spending of time.   *blame*
GOODS. *What, weenest thou* that I am thine?*   *you think*
EVERYMAN. *I had wend* so.*   *thought*

GOODS. *Nay, Everyman, I say no.*

440   *As for a while I was lent thee;*
         A season thou hast had me in prosperity.
         My condition* is man's soul to kill;   function or job
         If I save one, a thousand I do spill.*   destroy
         Weenest thou that I will follow thee?

445   *Nay, not from this world, verily.*

EVERYMAN. *I had wend otherwise.*

GOODS. *Therefore to thy soul Good is a thief;*
         For when thou art dead, this is my guise*—   deceitful nature
         Another to deceive in this same wise

450   *As I have done thee, and all to his soul's reprief.**   condemnation

EVERYMAN. *O false Good, cursed may thou be,*
         Thou traitor to God, that hast deceived me
         And caught me in thy snare!

GOODS. *Marry, thou brought thyself in care,**   trouble or danger

455   *Whereof I am glad;*
         I must needs laugh, I cannot be sad.

EVERYMAN. *Ah, Good, thou hast had long my heartly* love;*   deepest or
         I gave thee that which should be the Lord's above.   wholehearted
         But wilt thou not go with me indeed?

460   *I pray thee truth to say.*

GOODS. *No, so God me speed!*
         Therefore farewell, and have good day.

                              [Exit Goods]

EVERYMAN. *O, to whom shall I make my moan*
         For to go with me in* that heavy journey?   on

465   *First Fellowship said he would with me gone;**   he would go with me
         His words were very pleasant and gay,
         But afterward he left me alone.
         Then spake I to my kinsmen, all in despair,
         And also they gave me words fair;

470   *They lacked no fair speaking,*
         But all forsook me in the ending.
         Then went I to my Goods, that I loved best,
         In hope to have comfort, but there had I least;
         For my Goods sharply did me tell

475   *That he bringeth many into hell.*
         Then of myself I was ashamed,
         And so I am worthy to be blamed;
         Thus may I well myself hate.
         Of whom shall I now counsel take?

480   *I think that I shall never speed**   have success
         Till that I go to my Good Deed.
         But, alas, she is so weak

> That she can neither go nor speak;*
> Yet will I venture on* her now.
> My Good Deeds, where be* you?

move
risk asking
are 485

[Good Deeds speaks from the ground]

GOOD DEEDS. *Here I lie, cold in the ground;*
   Thy sins hath me sore bound,
   That I cannot stir.
EVERYMAN. *O Good Deeds, I stand in fear!*
   I must you pray of counsel,
   For help now should come right well.
GOOD DEEDS. *Everyman, I have understanding*
   That ye be summoned account to make
   Before Messias, of Jerusalem King;
   And you do by me, that journey with you will I take.
EVERYMAN. *Therefore I come to you, my moan* to make;*
   I pray you that ye will go with me.
GOOD DEEDS. *I would full fain,* but I cannot stand, verily.*
EVERYMAN. *Why, is there anything on you fall?**
GOOD DEEDS. *Yea, sir, I may thank you of* all;*
   If ye had perfectly cheered me,
   Your book of count full ready had* be.*
   Look, the books of your works and deeds eke!
   Behold how they lie under the feet,
   *To your soul's heaviness.**
EVERYMAN. *Our Lord Jesus help me!*
   For one letter here I cannot see.*
GOOD DEEDS. *There is a blind* reckoning in time of distress.*
EVERYMAN. *Good Deeds, I pray you help me in this need,*
   Or else I am for ever damned indeed;
   Therefore help me to make reckoning
   *Before the Redeemer of all thing,**
   *That King is, and was, and ever shall.**
GOOD DEEDS. *Everyman, I am sorry of your fall,*
   And fain would I help you, and* I were able.*
   EVERYMAN. *Good Deeds, your counsel I pray you give me.*
GOOD DEEDS. *That shall I do verily;*
   Though that on my feet I may not go,
   I have a sister that shall with you also,
   Called Knowledge, which shall with you abide,
   To help you to make that dreadful reckoning.

plea

very gladly
has anything fallen on you?
for 500

account; would as well

detriment 505

credit
lack of

510

things
shall be

. *gladly; if* 515

520

[Enter Knowledge]

KNOWLEDGE. *Everyman, I will go with thee, and be thy guide,*
   In thy most need to go by thy side.
EVERYMAN. *In good condition I am now in every thing,*

525   *And am wholly content with this good thing,*
      Thanked* be God my creator.   *Thanks*
    GOOD DEEDS. *And when she hath brought you there*
       Where thou shalt heal thee of thy smart,*   *severe penalty*
      Then go you with your reckoning and your Good Deeds together,
530   *For to make you joyful at heart*
      Before the blessed Trinity.
    EVERYMAN. *My Good Deeds, gramercy!*
      I am well content, certainly,
      With your words sweet.
535   KNOWLEDGE. *Now go we together lovingly*
      To Confession, that cleansing river.
    EVERYMAN. *For joy I weep; I would we were there!*
      But, I pray you, give me cognition*   *direction to*
      Where dwelleth that holy man, Confession.
540   KNOWLEDGE. *In the house of salvation:*
      We shall find him in that place,
      That shall us comfort, by God's grace.

    [Knowledge takes Everyman to Confession]

      Lo, this is Confession. Kneel down and ask mercy,
      For he is in good conceit* with God Almighty.   *favor*
545   EVERYMAN. *O glorious fountain, that all uncleanness doth clarify,**   *cleanse*
      Wash from me the spots of vice unclean,
      That on me no sin may be seen.
      I come with Knowledge for my redemption,
      Redempt* with heart and full contrition;   *redemptive*
550   *For I am commanded a pilgrimage to take,*
      And great accounts before God to make.
      Now I pray you, Shrift,* mother of salvation,   *absolution or forgiveness*
      Help my Good Deeds for my piteous exclamation.*   *outcry*
    CONFESSION. *I know your sorrow well, Everyman.*
555   *Because with Knowledge ye come to me,*
      I will you comfort as well as I can,
      And a precious jewel I will give thee,
      Called penance, voider* of adversity;   *expeller*
      Therewith shall your body chastised be,
560   *With abstinence and perseverance in God's service.*
      Here shall you receive that scourge of me,
      Which is penance strong that ye must endure,
      To remember thy Saviour was scourged for thee
      With sharp* scourges, and suffered it patiently;   *severe*
565   *So must thou, ere thou scape* that painful pilgrimage.*   *escape*
      Knowledge, keep him in this voyage,
      And by that time Good Deeds will be with thee.
      But in any wise be siker* of mercy,   *seeker*

For your time draweth fast; and ye will saved be,
Ask God mercy, and he will grant truly. 570
When with the scourge of penance man doth him bind,*himself afflict
The oil of forgiveness then shall he find.
EVERYMAN. Thanked* be God for his gracious work! *Thanks*
For now I will my penance begin;
This hath rejoiced and lighted* my heart, *relieved* 575
Though the knots be painful and hard within.
KNOWLEDGE. Everyman, look your penance that ye fulfil,
What pain that ever it to you be;
And Knowledge shall give you counsel at will
How your account ye shall make clearly. 580
EVERYMAN. O eternal God, O heavenly figure,
O way of righteousness, O goodly vision,
Which descended down in a virgin pure
Because* he would every man redeem, *so*
Which Adam forfeited by his disobedience: 585
O blessed Godhead, elect and high divine,* *God*
Forgive my grievous offence;
Here I cry thee mercy in this presence.
O ghostly* treasure, O ransomer and redeemer, *Holy*
Of all the world hope and conductor, 590
Mirror of joy, and founder of mercy,
Which enlumineth heaven and earth thereby,
Hear my clamorous complaint,* though it late be; *plea*
Receive my prayers, of thy benignity;
Though I be a sinner most abominable, 595
Yet let my name be written in Moses' table.
O Mary, pray to the Maker of all thing,* *things*
Me for to help at my ending;* *death*
And save me from the power of my enemy,
For Death assaileth me strongly. 600
And, Lady, that I may be mean* of thy prayer *beneficiary*
Of your Son's glory to be partner,
By the means of his passion, I it crave;
I beseech you help my soul to save.
Knowledge, give me the scourge of penance; 605
My flesh therewith shall give acquittance:* *submit*
I will now begin, if God give me grace.
KNOWLEDGE. Everyman, God give you time and Space!* *grace*
Thus I bequeath you in the hands of our Saviour;
Now may you make your reckoning sure. 610
EVERYMAN. In the name of the Holy Trinity,
My body sore punished shall be:
Take this, body, for the sin of the flesh!

[Scourges himself]

	*Also thou delightest to go gay and fresh,**	*gayly arrayed*
615	*And in the way of damnation thou did me bring,*	
	Therefore suffer now strokes of punishing.	
	*Now of penance I will wade the water clear,**	*wash clean*
	To save me from purgatory, that sharp fire.	

[Good Deeds rises from the ground]

	GOOD DEEDS. *I thank God, now I can walk and go,*	
620	*And am delivered of my sickness and woe.*	
	*Therefore with Everyman I will go, and not spare;**	*abandon*
	His good works I will help him to declare.	
	KNOWLEDGE. *Now, Everyman, be merry and glad!*	
	Your Good Deeds cometh now; ye may not be sad.	
625	*Now is your Good Deeds whole and sound,*	
	Going upright upon the ground.	
	EVERYMAN. *My heart is light, and shall be evermore;*	
	Now will I smite faster than I did before.	
	GOOD DEEDS. *Everyman, pilgrim, my special friend,*	
630	*Blessed be thou without end;**	*forever*
	For thee is preparate the eternal glory.*	*prepared for*
	Ye have me made whole and sound,	
	Therefore I will bide by thee in every stound.**	*abide; tribulation*
	EVERYMAN. *Welcome, my Good Deeds; now I hear thy voice,*	
635	*I weep for very sweetness of love.*	
	KNOWLEDGE. *Be no more sad, but ever rejoice;*	
	God seeth thy living in his throne above.	
	*Put on this garment to thy behoof,**	*benefit*
	Which is wet with your tears,	
640	*Or else before God you may it miss,*	
	When ye to your journey's end come shall.	
	EVERYMAN. *Gentle Knowledge, what do ye it call?*	
	KNOWLEDGE. *It is a garment of sorrow:*	
	*From pain it will you borrow;**	*relieve*
645	*Contrition it is,*	
	That geteth forgiveness;	
	It pleaseth God passing well.*	*extremely*
	GOOD DEEDS. *Everyman, will you wear it for your heal?**	*salvation; redemption*
	EVERYMAN. *Now blessed be Jesu,* Mary's Son,*	*Jesus*
650	*For now have I on true contrition.*	
	And let us go now without tarrying;	
	Good Deeds, have we clear our reckoning?	
	GOOD DEEDS. *Yea, indeed, I have it here.*	
	EVERYMAN. *Then I trust we need not fear;*	
655	*Now, friends, let us not part in twain.**	*two*
	KNOWLEDGE. *Nay, Everyman, that will we not, certain.*	

GOOD DEEDS. *Yet must thou lead with thee*
   Three persons of great might.
EVERYMAN. *Who should they be?*
GOOD DEEDS. *Discretion and Strength they hight,* are called*   named 660
   And thy Beauty may not abide* behind.   stay
KNOWLEDGE. *Also, ye must call to mind*
   Your Five Wits* as for your counsellors.*   senses;   advocates
GOOD DEEDS. *You must have them ready at all hours.*
EVERYMAN. *How shall I get them hither?*   665
KNOWLEDGE. *You must call them all together,*
   And they will hear you incontinent.*   immediately
EVERYMAN. *My friends, come hither and be present,*
   Discretion, Strength, my Five Wits, and Beauty.

[Enter Beauty, Strength, Discretion, and Five Wits]

BEAUTY. *Here at your will we be all ready.*   670
   What will ye that we should do?
GOOD DEEDS. *That ye would with Everyman go,*
   And help him in his pilgrimage.
   Advise* you, will ye with him or not in that voyage?   deliberate
STRENGTH. *We will bring him all thither,*   675
   To his help and comfort, ye may believe me.
DISCRETION. *So will we go with him all together.*
EVERYMAN. *Almighty God, lofed* may thou be!*   blessed
   I give thee laud* that I have hither brought   praise
   Strength, Discretion, Beauty, and Five Wits.   680
     Lack I nought.
   And my Good Deeds, with Knowledge clear,
   All be in my company at my will here;
   I desire no more to my business.*   for my journey
STRENGTH. *And I, Strength, will by you stand in distress,*
   Though thou would in battle fight on the ground.   685
FIVE WITS. *And though it were through the world round,*
   We will not depart for sweet ne sour.*   for better or worse
BEAUTY. *No more will I unto death's hour,**   until the end
   Whatsoever thereof befall.
DISCRETION. *Everyman, advise you first of all;*   690
   Go with a good advisement* and deliberation.   consultation
   We all give you virtuous monition*   good admonition
   That all shall be well.
EVERYMAN. *My friends, harken* what I will tell:*   listen to
   I pray God reward you in his heavenly sphere.   695
   Now harken, all that be here,
   For I will make my testament
   Here before you all present:

> *In alms half my good I will give with my hands twain**   two hands*
700 *In the way of charity, with good intent,*
> *And the other half still shall remain*
> *In queth,* to be returned there* it ought to be.*   *bequest; where*
> *This I do in despite* of the fiend of hell,*   *spite*
> *To go quit out* of his peril*   *free*
705 *Ever after and this day.*
> *KNOWLEDGE. Everyman, harken what I say:*
> *Go to priesthood, I you advise,*
> *And receive of him in any wise**   *the specified way*
> *The holy sacrament and ointment together.*
710 *Then shortly see ye turn* again hither;*   *return*
> *We will all abide* you here.*   *wait for*
> *FIVE WITS. Yea, Everyman, hie you that ye ready were.*
> *There is no emperor, king, duke, ne baron,*
> *That of God hath commission**   *power*
715 *As hath the least priest in the world being;**   *of the living*
> *For of the blessed sacraments pure and benign*
> *He beareth the keys,* and thereof hath the cure*   *authority*
> *For man's redemption — it is ever sure —*
> *Which God for our soul's medicine*
720 *Gave us out of his heart with great pine.**   *agony*
> *Here in this transitory life, for thee and me,*
> *The blessed sacraments seven there be:*
> *Baptism, confirmation, with priesthood good,*
> *And the sacrament of God's precious flesh and blood,*
725 *Marriage, the holy extreme unction, and penance;*
> *These seven be good to have in remembrance,*
> *Gracious sacraments of high divinity.*
> *EVERYMAN. Fain would I receive that holy body,*
> *And meekly to my ghostly* father I will go.*   *Holy*
730 *FIVE WITS. Everyman, that is the best that ye can do.*
> *God will you to salvation bring,*
> *For priesthood exceedeth all other thing:*
> *To us Holy Scripture they do teach,*
> *And converteth man from sin heaven to reach;**   *to salvation*
735 *God hath to them more power given*
> *Than to any angel that is in heaven.*
> *With five words he may consecrate,*
> *God's body in flesh and blood to make,*
> *And handleth his Maker between his hands.*
740 *The priest bindeth and unbindeth all bands,**   *bonds*
> *Both in earth and in heaven.*
> *Thou ministers all the sacraments seven;*
> *Though we kissed thy feet, thou were worthy;*
> *Thou art surgeon that cureth sin deadly:*

No remedy we find under God   745
But all only priesthood.
Everyman, God gave priests that dignity,
And setteth them in his stead among us to be;
Thus be they above angels in degree.*   status or rank

[Everyman goes to the priest to receive the last sacraments]

KNOWLEDGE. *If priests be good, it is so, surely.*   750
  But when Jesus hanged on the cross with great smart,*   pain
  There he gave out of his blessed heart
  The same sacrament in great torment:
  He sold them not to us, that Lord omnipotent.
  Therefore Saint Peter the apostle doth say   755
  That Jesu's curse hath all they
  Which God their Saviour do buy or sell,
  Or they for any money do take or tell.*   ask
  Sinful priests giveth the sinners example bad;
  Their children sitteth by other men's fires, I have heard;   760
  And some haunteth women's company
  With unclean life, as lusts of lechery:
  These be with sin made blind.
FIVE WITS. *I trust to God no such may we find;*
  Therefore let us priesthood honour,   765
  And follow their doctrine for our souls' succour.
  We be their sheep, and they shepherds be
  By whom we all be kept in surety.
  Peace, for yonder I see Everyman come,
  Which hath made true satisfaction.   770
GOOD DEEDS. *Methink it is he indeed.*

  [Re-enter Everyman]

EVERYMAN. *Now Jesu be your alder speed!**   good fortune
  I have received the sacrament for my redemption,
  And then mine extreme unction:
  Blessed be all they that counselled me to take it!   775
  And now, friends, let us go without longer respite;*   delay
  I thank God that ye have tarried so long.
  Now set each of you on this rood* your hand,   crucifix
  And shortly follow me:
  I go before there* I would be; God be our guide!   where   780
STRENGTH. *Everyman, we will not from you go**   leave you
  Till ye have done this voyage long.
DISCRETION. *I, Discretion, will bide by* you also.*   be with
KNOWLEDGE. *And though this pilgrimage be never so strong,**   healthy
  I will never part you fro.*   from you   785
STRENGTH. *Everyman, I will be as sure by thee*

As ever I did by Judas Maccabee.

[Everyman comes to his grave]

EVERYMAN. *Alas, I am so faint I may not stand;*
    My limbs under me doth fold.
790   *Friends, let us not turn again to this land,**   earth*
    Not for all the world's gold;
    *For into this cave** must I creep   grave*
    And turn to earth, and there to sleep.
BEAUTY. *What, into this grave? Alas!*
795   EVERYMAN. *Yea, there shall ye consume,** more and less.   decay*
   BEAUTY. *And what, should I smother here?*
   EVERYMAN. *Yea, by my faith, and never more appear.*
    In this world live no more we shall,
    But in heaven before the highest Lord of all.
800   BEAUTY. *I cross out all this; adieu, by Saint John!*
    I take my tap in my lap, and am gone.
   EVERYMAN. *What, Beauty, whither will ye?*
   BEAUTY. *Peace, I am deaf; I look not behind me,*
    Not and thou wouldest give me all the gold in thy chest   [Exit Beauty]
805   EVERYMAN. *Alas, whereto may I trust?*
    Beauty goeth fast away from me;
    She promised with me to live and die.
   STRENGTH. *Everyman, I will thee also forsake and deny;*
    *Thy game liketh** me not at all.**   is not pleasing me; completely*
810   EVERYMAN. *Why, then, ye will forsake me all?**   completely*
    *Sweet Strength, tarry a little space.**   a little more*
   STRENGTH. *Nay, sir, by the rood** of grace!   cross*
    I will hie me from thee fast,
    *Though thou weep till thy heart to-brast.**   breaks*
815   EVERYMAN. *Ye would ever bide by me, ye said.*
   STRENGTH. *Yea, I have you far enough conveyed.*
    Ye be old enough, I understand,
    *Your pilgrimage to take on hand;**   your own*
    I repent me that I hither came.
820   EVERYMAN. *Strength, you to displease I am to blame;*
    *Yet promise is debt, this ye well wot.**   know*
   STRENGTH. *In faith, I care not.*
    Thou art but a fool to complain;
    You spend your speech and waste your brain.
825   *Go thrust thee into the ground!*   [Exit Strength]
   EVERYMAN. *I had wend surer I should you have found.*
    He that trusteth in his Strength
    *She him deceiveth at the length.**   in the long run*
    Both Strength and Beauty forsaketh me;
830   *Yet they promised me fair and lovingly.*

DISCRETION. *Everyman, I will after Strength be gone;*
As for me, I will leave you alone.
EVERYMAN. *Why, Discretion, will ye forsake me?*
DISCRETION. *Yea, in faith,* I will go from thee,* truth
For when Strength goeth before 835
I follow after evermore.
EVERYMAN. *Yet, I pray thee, for the love of the Trinity,*
Look in my grave once piteously.
DISCRETION. *Nay, so nigh will I not come;*
Farewell, every one! [Exit Discretion] 840
EVERYMAN. *O, all thing faileth, save God alone —*
Beauty, Strength, and Discretion;
For when Death bloweth his blast,* trumpet
They all run from me full fast.
FIVE WITS. *Everyman, my leave now of thee I take;* 845
I will follow the other, for here I thee forsake.
EVERYMAN. *Alas, then may I wail and weep,*
For I took you for my best friend.
FIVE WITS. *I will no longer thee keep;*
Now farewell, and there an end. [Exit Five Wits] 850
EVERYMAN. *O Jesu, help! All hath forsaken me.*
GOOD DEEDS. *Nay, Everyman; I will bide with thee.*
I will not forsake thee indeed;
Thou shalt find me a good friend at* need. in
EVERYMAN. *Gramercy, Good Deeds! Now may I true friends see.* 855
They have forsaken me, every one;
I loved them better than my Good Deeds alone.
Knowledge, will ye forsake me also?
KNOWLEDGE. *Yea, Everyman, when ye to Death shall go;*
But not yet, for no manner of danger. 860
EVERYMAN. *Gramercy, Knowledge, with all my heart.*
KNOWLEDGE. *Nay, yet I will not from hence depart*
Till I see where ye shall become.* end
EVERYMAN. *Methink, alas, that I must be gone*
To make my reckoning and my debts pay, 865
For I see my time is nigh spent away.
Take example,* all ye that this do hear or see, heed
How they that I loved best do forsake me,
Except my Good Deeds that bideth truly.
GOOD DEEDS. *All earthly things is but vanity:* 870
Beauty, Strength, and Discretion do man forsake,
Foolish friends, and kinsmen, that fair spake —
All fleeth save Good Deeds, and that am I.
EVERYMAN. *Have mercy on me, God most mighty;*
And stand by me, thou mother and maid, holy Mary. 875
GOOD DEEDS. *Fear not; I will speak for thee.*

880   EVERYMAN. *Here I cry God mercy.*
        GOOD DEEDS. *Short our end, and minish* our pain;*   lessen
        Let us go and never come again.
        EVERYMAN. *Into thy hands, Lord, my soul I commend;*
        Receive it, Lord, that it be not lost.
885   *As thou me boughtest,* so me defend,*   redeemed
        And save me from the fiend's boast,
        That I may appear with that blessed host
        That shall be saved at* the day of doom.   on
        In manus tuas, of mights most
        For ever, commendo spiritum meum.

890   [He sinks into his grave]

        KNOWLEDGE. *Now hath he suffered that we all shall endure;*
        The Good Deeds shall make all sure.
        Now hath he made ending;
        Methinketh that I hear angels sing,
895   *And make great joy and melody*
        Where Everyman's soul received shall be.
        ANGEL. *Come, excellent elect spouse, to Jesu!*
        Hereabove thou shalt go
        Because of thy singular virtue.
900   *Now the soul is taken the body fro,**   from the body
        Thy reckoning is crystal-clear.
        Now shalt thou into the heavenly sphere,
        Unto the which all ye shall come
        That liveth well before the day of doom.

        [Enter Doctor]

905   DOCTOR. *This moral men may have in mind.*
        Ye hearers, take it of worth,* old and young,   to heart
        And forsake Pride, for he deceiveth you in the end;
        And remember Beauty, Five Wits, Strength, and Discretion,
        They all at the last do every man forsake,
910   *Save* his Good Deeds there doth he take.*   Except
        But beware, for and* they be small   if
        Before God, he hath no help at all;
        None excuse may be there for every man.
        Alas, how shall he do then?
915   *For after death amends may no man make,*
        For then mercy and pity doth him forsake.*   are not available
        If his reckoning be not clear when he doth come,
        God will say: 'Ite, maledicti, in ignem eternum.'*   In Latin, Matthew
        And he that hath his account whole and sound,   25:41, 'Depart from
920   *High in heaven he shall be crowned;*   me, ye cursed, into
        Unto which place God bring us all thither,   everlasting fire.'
        That we may live body and soul together.

Thereto help the Trinity!
Amen, say ye, for saint charity.

THUS ENDETH THIS MORAL PLAY OF EVERYMAN

Questions

1. As you read *Everyman,* notice how each character (Beauty, Kindred, Five Wits, Worldly Goods, etc.) has a simple, allegorical meaning. What can we learn by studying the characters, their names, and their qualities?
2. Death says that he will do God's will. What is the relationship between God and Death? How are God and Death represented at the beginning, middle, and end of the play?
3. Goods and riches will not go with Everyman; they were lent to Everyman for a brief time. They tell Everyman that they "will deceive others, too." How do they deceive Everyman? How would you describe Everyman's relationship with Goods and riches?
4. Note how the audience is drawn into relating to Everyman's struggles and eventual success. How does this connection between Everyman and the audience contribute to the overall message or goal of the play?

CREDITS

INDEX